An Echo in the Mountains

An Echo in the Mountains

Al Purdy after a Century

Edited by

NICHOLAS BRADLEY

McGill-Queen's University Press
Montreal & Kingston • London • Chicago

© McGill-Queen's University Press 2020

ISBN 978-0-2280-0336-6 (cloth)
ISBN 978-0-2280-0337-3 (paper)
ISBN 978-0-2280-0429-5 (ePDF)
ISBN 978-0-2280-0430-1 (ePUB)

Legal deposit third quarter 2020
Bibliothèque nationale du Québec

Printed in Canada on acid-free paper that is 100% ancient forest free (100% post-consumer recycled), processed chlorine free

This book has been published with the help of a grant from the Canadian Federation for the Humanities and Social Sciences, through the Awards to Scholarly Publications Program, using funds provided by the Social Sciences and Humanities Research Council of Canada.

Funded by the Government of Canada / Financé par le gouvernement du Canada Canada Council for the Arts / Conseil des arts du Canada

We acknowledge the support of the Canada Council for the Arts.

Nous remercions le Conseil des arts du Canada de son soutien.

Library and Archives Canada Cataloguing in Publication

Title: An echo in the mountains : Al Purdy after a century / edited by Nicholas Bradley.

Names: Bradley, Nicholas, 1978- editor.

Description: Includes bibliographical references and index.

Identifiers: Canadiana (print) 20200246313 | Canadiana (ebook) 20200246364 | ISBN 9780228003373 (softcover) | ISBN 9780228003366 (hardcover) | ISBN 9780228004295 (PDF) | ISBN 9780228004301 (ePUB)

Subjects: LCSH: Purdy, Al, 1918-2000–Criticism and interpretation. | CSH: Canadian poetry (English)–20th century–History and criticism. | CSH: Poets, Canadian (English)–20th century.

Classification: LCC PS8531.U8 Z592 2020 | DDC C811/.54–dc23

This book was designed and typeset by Peggy & Co. Design in 10.5/13 Sabon.

For my teachers –
"Travailler, toujours travailler"
And for Eurithe Purdy

Contents

Acknowledgments   ix
Abbreviations   xi

Introduction: Al Purdy's Century:
A Programmatic Beginning   3
Nicholas Bradley

PART ONE
Transcendence, Love, and the Persistent Legend:
In Search of Al Purdy

1   The Man Who Lived beyond Himself: Transcendental Al   45
    Doug Beardsley

2   His Muses, *a mensa et toro*   56
    Linda Rogers

3   Purdy's Mock Love Poetry:
    Misogyny, Nation, and Progress   63
    Shane Neilson

PART TWO
Land Claims: Al Purdy and the Unpeaceable Kingdom

4   The Too Easily Kept Illusions:
    Myth-making, Private Canons, and Patterns of Exclusion   77
    J.A. Weingarten

5   Unsettling the North: Shame in *North of Summer*   106
    Misao Dean

6   Rune and Riddle in "The Runners"   126
    Ian Rae

7   The Poet and the Ethnographer:
    Purdy, Marius Barbeau, and the Poetry of Myth   147
    Nicholas Bradley

PART THREE
Myths, Masks, and Texts:
Al Purdy's Entangled Lives and Works

8   Scholarly Editing: A Way to Read "House Guest"   173
    Eli MacLaren

9   Six Ways of Looking at "Elegy for a Grandfather"   197
    Jamie Dopp

10 "One of us": Purdy, Elite Culture, and the Visual Arts   218
    Ernestine Lahey

11 "Concerning Ms. Atwood": Purdy, Margaret Atwood,
    and the *Malahat Review*   240
    Natalie Boldt

12 Purdy's Poetics: Intuitive Formalism
    in *A Splinter in the Heart*   263
    Carl Watts

Appendix: Purdy's Self-Repetitions   285

Contributors   289

Index   291

Acknowledgments

More often than not, Al Purdy's books were dedicated to Eurithe Purdy. I have followed suit, in admiration and gratitude for her hospitality and help. The dedication also hints at my perpetual debt to those who first taught me how to read Purdy's poetry.

I am obliged to the authors in this volume, whose willingness to contribute essays I take as a sign of continuing interest in Purdy's words, and of the belief in their importance. I hope that readers share my enthusiasm for the contributors' enriching commentary. I am also thankful to the anonymous reviewers for the press, whose insights register throughout these pages. And to Mark Abley, Kathleen Fraser, and everyone at McGill-Queen's University Press, my thanks for shepherding the book into existence. Patricia Kennedy provided meticulous editing. *An Echo in the Mountains* has benefited immensely from the research assistance of Laura Dosky, Hayley Evans, and especially Jonathan Johnson, whose labours on *We Go Far Back in Time: The Letters of Earle Birney and Al Purdy, 1947–1987* continue to prove useful years later. I have also relied on support from Jean Baird and The Al Purdy A-frame Association, and on the assistance of librarians and archivists at Queen's University and the Universities of British Columbia, Saskatchewan, Toronto, and Victoria. The research for this book was conducted using funds from the University of Victoria and the Social Sciences and Humanities Research Council of Canada.

Preparing this volume has allowed me to revisit some of my own writing on Purdy and his works, and I hope that the clarification of certain ideas serves his readers. I have enjoyed the opportunity to test my ideas about Purdy's poetry and his place in Canadian letters on several classes at the University of Victoria. Students have listened to me think out loud about the strange man who lived up the highway, half an hour from our campus, and I am thankful for their patience, perceptive responses, and laughter at Al's rambunctiousness.

I am deeply grateful to Bruce Arthur and Jen Cavanagh for their hospitality in Toronto and Prince Edward County, and for their sustaining friendship. Finally, thank you to young Adam Ross, who mowed the lawn while I was away in Ameliasburgh, and to his dad, who may have helped.

A version of Chapter 3 was published in *Constructive Negativity: Prize Culture, Evaluation, and Dis/ability in Canadian Poetry*, by Shane Neilson, 135–47 (Windsor, ON: Palimpsest Press, 2019).

A version of Chapter 7 was published as "Al Purdy, Marius Barbeau, and the Poetry of Myth: A Note on a Forgotten Manuscript." *Papers of the Bibliographical Society of Canada/Cahiers de la Société bibliographique du Canada* 55, no. 1 (Spring 2017): 91–106.

In Chapter 4, the excerpt of "Letter to Sir John A. Macdonald" is used with the permission of Marilyn Dumont. Personal communications are included with the permission of Louise Bernice Halfe.

In Chapter 8, "Visiting Poet" is reprinted, with the kind permission of Gordon Johnston, from: Gordon Johnston, *But for Now* (Montreal & Kingston: McGill-Queen's University Press, 2013).

Permission to quote unpublished correspondence in Chapter 11 was generously granted by Margaret Atwood.

The copyright to Al Purdy's published and unpublished writing is held by the Estate of Al Purdy, and administered by Harbour Publishing.

Abbreviations

The following abbreviations are used throughout the book when page numbers are provided in parenthetical references. Apart from certain simplifications, the abbreviations for works by Al Purdy are in essence those used in *The Last Canadian Poet* (1999), by Sam Solecki, and *The Ivory Thought* (2008), edited by Gerald Lynch, Shoshannah Ganz, and Josephene T.M. Kealey.

WORKS BY AL PURDY

Poetry

BA	*Being Alive: Poems, 1958–78* (1978)
BB	*The Blur in Between: Poems, 1960–61* (1962)
BR	*Beyond Remembering: The Collected Poems of Al Purdy* (2000)
CH	*The Cariboo Horses* (1965)
CP	*The Collected Poems of Al Purdy* (1986)
CSL	*The Crafte So Longe to Lerne* (1959)
ER	*Emu, Remember!* (1956)
IS	*In Search of Owen Roblin* (1974)
LB	*Love in a Burning Building* (1970)
NS	*North of Summer: Poems from Baffin Island* (1967)
NSM	*Naked with Summer in Your Mouth* (1994)
PA	*Poems for All the Annettes*, first edition (1962)
PA68	*Poems for All the Annettes*, revised edition (1968)
PB	*Piling Blood* (1984)
RR	*Rooms for Rent in the Outer Planets: Selected Poems,*

	1962–1996 (1996)
SB	*The Stone Bird* (1981)
SD	*Sex and Death* (1973)
Sun.	*Sundance at Dusk* (1976)
TP	*To Paris Never Again* (1997)
WG	*Wild Grape Wine* (1968)
WS	*The Woman on the Shore* (1990)

Prose

MS	*Morning and It's Summer: A Memoir* (1983)
RBS	*Reaching for the Beaufort Sea: An Autobiography* (1993)
SA	*Starting from Ameliasburgh: The Collected Prose of Al Purdy* (1995)
SH	*A Splinter in the Heart: A Novel* (1990)

Correspondence

YA	*Yours, Al: The Collected Letters of Al Purdy* (2004)

CRITICISM

LCP	*The Last Canadian Poet: An Essay on Al Purdy* (1999), by Sam Solecki

An Echo in the Mountains

– say the names say the names
and listen to yourself
an echo in the mountains

Al Purdy, "Say the Names"

INTRODUCTION

Al Purdy's Century: A Programmatic Beginning

Nicholas Bradley

A few years ago, I found myself at a dinner party with several distinguished scholars when the subject of literary anniversaries arose. After explaining to the international group that Al Purdy had been a significant Canadian poet, I noted that the hundredth anniversary of his birth in 1918 would soon be upon us.[1] I suggested that the time was right to reassess his body of work, which despite its prominent place in Canadian literature was in want of trenchant criticism. The guest of honour sniffed. "When an author is read a century after his *death*," he said, "*then* he has made his mark." Chastened, and feeling suitably parochial, I returned to my salad.

But my esteemed colleague was not wrong. Although twenty years have passed since Purdy died in 2000, his heyday, which lasted roughly from 1965, the year of *The Cariboo Horses*, to 1986, the year of his first *Collected Poems*, is not an utterly distant period of literary history.[2] Purdy has not been forgotten, yet it is too early to say with genuine certainty whether his poems will be appreciated, let alone revered, when another century has elapsed. The Canadian poets who died one hundred years ago – at the time of the Great War, or in the 1920s – are for the most part not read today so much as studied, and, even then, perhaps not intensively. Their names – William Wilfred Campbell (c. 1860–1918), Marjorie Pickthall (1883–1922), Charles Mair (1838–1927), and so on – are familiar to specialists but not, so far as it is possible to tell, to any reading public. John McCrae (1872–1918) is an obvious exception; "In Flanders Fields" is possibly the single best-known Canadian poem, but it marks the beginning and the end of McCrae's popular legacy. Some long-lived poets, who obscure any neat chronological distinction between "early" and "modern" Canadian literature, are safely canonical – Charles

G.D. Roberts (1860–1943), for instance – while others, such as Robert Service (1874–1958) have popular currency. E. Pauline Johnson (1861–1913) has undergone a critical revival; mounting attention to Indigenous writers and orators, whether contemporary or historical, as in the case of Johnson, complicates Purdy's standing as the national poet.[3] But, as a general rule, readers in this country are quick to forget the past, and there is little precedent in Canadian literary history for a truly lasting reputation. International figures such as Georg Trakl (d. 1914), Rupert Brooke (d. 1915), Edward Thomas (d. 1917), Wilfred Owen (d. 1918), Isaac Rosenberg (d. 1918), and Henry Lawson (d. 1922) have greater claims on posterity than their Canadian contemporaries.

We may still be surprised, however, by Purdy – the "sensitive man" in the tavern ("At the Quinte Hotel," *PA68* 95; *BR* 130), the "foolish old man with brain on fire" ("Listening to Myself," *TP* 32; *BR* 334). In my experience as a teacher, no Canadian authors consistently arouse as much interest among students as Purdy and Margaret Atwood, although it is increasingly her reputation as a writer of speculative fiction that precedes Atwood, and not her distinction as a poet. Accustomed to associating poetry with propriety, students are astounded even today by the frankness and vulgarity of Purdy's writing. Scandalized and impressed, they express curiosity about his life and times, and about his works, especially poems that name places they recognize. No teacher wishes to extinguish excitement, or to suggest that poetry is the preserve of metaphysicians, but the immediate, bibulous appeal of Purdy's writing often overshadows its intelligence and complexity, "the cusswords and bitter anger" and drunken buffoonery distracting from his tendency to allude and elude ("Song of the Impermanent Husband," *CH* 27; *BR* 61). Purdy was a clown, but not only a clown, and his enduring reputation as an accidental poet conceals essential aspects of his gargantuan oeuvre, including its philosophical inclinations. Before and after his death, Purdy's readers have faced an overwhelming amount of writing and an equally formidable legend – the myth and mystique of Al.

An Echo in the Mountains aims not only, or necessarily, to challenge the legend, but instead to illuminate the persistent complexities of Purdy's life and works, particularly in view of the changing nature of Canadian literary studies. The scale and editorial state of his writing present interpretative obstacles, while Purdy's association with Canadian nationalism threatens to make his work seem passé, if not retrograde, at a time when Canadian criticism is preoccupied with the colonial underpinnings of the country and the field; these problems are linked, for an emphasis on certain thematic aspects of his writing has left other dimensions relatively unexamined. The major commentary to date on Purdy's poetry, Sam Solecki's *The Last Canadian Poet: An Essay on Al Purdy*, was published in 1999, and the most recent significant collection of studies, *The Ivory Thought: Essays on Al Purdy*, was published in 2008.[4] Each book is indispensable, and Solecki's extended *Essay* will remain the critical point of departure for the foreseeable future. But in the two decades since *The Last Canadian Poet*, a considerable quantity of archival documents has been published, and new biographical and textual information about Purdy has come to light.[5] The ordinary passage of time also prompts shifts in perspective: like all authors whose works compel revisitation, Purdy looks different now from in decades gone by, and a single, stable, or definitive idea of the author and his importance is, in all probability, a thing of the past (if it ever existed). The disciplinary concerns of Canadian literary studies have shifted enormously since 2000, and the historical and cultural context of Purdy's works has undergone intense reappraisal. His anniversary was fittingly marked by the publication of a book of tribute, *Beyond Forgetting: Celebrating 100 Years of Al Purdy* (2018), an anthology of poems by Canadian authors, but his centenary additionally presents an occasion to reflect critically on his works and days, his epoch and contemporaries.[6] If Purdy deserves commemoration, he also merits criticism that moves beyond hagiography and *idées reçues*.[7]

The timeliness of a new reckoning was also suggested by the national sesquicentennial in 2017. The perception of Purdy as the quintessential Canadian poet is not without justification. He lived through most of the twentieth century, his adulthood spanning the period after the Second World War, an era in which Canada established its modern identity. The anniversary year, 1967, was marked by the International and Universal Exposition in Montreal, by Charles de Gaulle's undiplomatic speech (*"Vive le Québec libre!"*), and by Chief Dan George's "Lament for Confederation." (But traces of the past always linger. The sitting prime minister, Lester B. Pearson, was born at the close of the nineteenth century.) Purdy was then in full stride. In 1967 he published *North of Summer: Poems from Baffin Island*, a volume based on his Arctic travels, which had been no small undertaking in 1965: he appeared to be an intrepid explorer of Canadian places and themes. *North of Summer* was illustrated by A.Y. Jackson, the august Canadian painter, and the book has understandably been mistaken for a celebration of the Great White North.[8]

Purdy was also writing and revising poems that were gathered the following year in *Wild Grape Wine*, a boozy collection that partook of the bacchanalian spirit of the Age of Aquarius – a suitable book for the year of Trudeaumania, although in truth neither Purdy nor the bachelor Trudeau, who was born in 1919, was young. The titles of the poems in *Wild Grape Wine* registered Purdy's national subjects: "Canadian," "Lament for the Dorsets," "The North West Passage," "Mackenzie King's Ruins," "John Diefenbaker," "A Ghost in the House of Commons," "A Walk on Wellington Street," "Dominion Day," "William Lyon Mackenzie," "Liberal Leadership Convention," and so on. In "Over the Pacific," Purdy even dared to discern "the essence of Canada" in the call of "the northern loon" (WG 35). In the late 1960s, the intrinsic connection of Purdy's literary project to his country's landscapes, people, history, and politics seemed self-evident. What Purdy would have thought of Canada at one hundred and fifty – of the country and its discontents – can only be imagined, but how he is read at this point in Canadian history, and in the wake of over fifty years of critical commentary, is the subject of *An Echo in the Mountains*.

The argument of this introductory essay, and by extension the book as a whole, is that scholars of Canadian literature have not come to terms with the many versions of the poet that emerge from his intimidatingly vast body of work. I do not propose to displace the persuasive account of Solecki, whose Purdy is bound to Canada as other major poets are tied to their nations and national histories. "Purdy," he writes, "is the Canadian poet with the strongest sense of a 'national patrimony,' in Whitman's words the one best 'fit to cope with our occasions,' terms that will be less startling to Canadian readers and critics if they keep in mind not only Whitman and Purdy but also W.B. Yeats, Seamus Heaney, Czesław Miłosz, and Derek Walcott" (LCP xii).[9] Instead I suggest that Purdy's writing in all genres – at once a coherent, Whitmanian song of himself and a dizzyingly miscellaneous collection of statements on innumerable subjects – remains to be charted in detail, and that manifold interpretations may arise from revisionary studies. Purdy's pronounced Canadian themes have been duly noted for decades, but less appreciated, for instance, is the influence of modern European poetry; Miłosz, Anna Akhmatova, Osip Mandelstam, Rainer Maria Rilke, Andrei Voznesensky, and Yevgeny Yevtushenko offered Purdy exemplary literary modes that differed from prevailing styles in Canadian letters. Purdy was a frequent traveller and a voracious reader with eclectic tastes, and although it would be perverse to isolate his poetry from its national context, the obviously and ostentatiously Canadian content coexists with other obsessions, such as a profound interest in ancient Greece and Rome.[10] Purdy was notorious for wearing loud shirts, but his true poet's costume was motley: he wore a patchwork of literary passions, influences, and modes.

For comprehensible biographical, cultural, and literary-historical reasons, the Purdy of the 1960s and early 1970s has been emphasized at the expense of the Purdy of the late 1970s and 1980s, his middle period standing in for his entire career. The Purdy of the 1990s, moreover, is virtually unknown to criticism and scholarship. Although it touches on the 1950s, 1980s, and 1990s, *An Echo in the Mountains* nonetheless focuses on the works of the 1960s and 1970s to show how what seems most familiar about Purdy, including his nationalism, requires rethinking, and to suggest why reading Purdy in the new millennium is inherently difficult: the terms according to which Purdy has been understood were largely set in the 1960s, or in relation to that decade, but literary and critical attitudes have changed dramatically since then. The chapters in this book draw various and sometimes conflicting portraits of the poet. That variety will, I hope, enliven the study of Purdy and of Canadian poetry more generally, for Purdy is not the only author facing critical lassitude or indifference. Other writers of his time – such as Louis Dudek (1918–2001), almost his exact contemporary – likewise deserve to be re-examined. In "Say the Names," one of his final poems, Purdy evoked both the power and the impermanence of a voice in the wilderness: "say the names say the names / and listen to yourself / an echo in the mountains" (BR 579). Purdy echoes in the pages ahead, alternately booming and fading, hovering between sound and silence.

RECOVERING THE RECENT PAST

Like all literary-historical studies, a retrospective account of Purdy's works must attend to the unfolding of time. Fewer and fewer of his contemporaries survive. Leonard Cohen and D.G. Jones both died in 2016, for example, one more conspicuously than the other, and Peter Trower died in 2017. David W. McFadden died in 2018; although he was much younger than Purdy, their careers overlapped. Patrick Lane followed in 2019. These poets were preceded by P.K. Page (d. 2010), Robert Kroetsch (d. 2011), and Jay Macpherson (d. 2012). Canada itself, and the idea of Canada, changed irrevocably between 1967 and 2017. The very map has been altered; Purdy's Baffin Island is now part of Nunavut, not the Northwest Territories. After the Constitution Act of 1982, the Multiculturalism Act of 1988, and the Truth and Reconciliation Commission, which concluded in 2015 – to name only three indications of a country in transformation – the sense of nationhood reflected in Canadian literature of the mid-twentieth century may seem antiquated, irrelevant, or undesired. Yet the near-coincidence of anniversaries – Canada's in 2017 and Purdy's in 2018 – affords an opportunity to reconsider a poet's legacy and fundamental assumptions about what is known both affectionately and derisively as "CanLit."[11]

The circumstances of Purdy's early success illustrate the ease with which details of Canadian literary history can be overlooked. His rise to pre-eminence in the early and middle 1960s coincided with great public and institutional anticipation of the Centennial, but at the beginning of the decade, Purdy still laboured in virtual anonymity. His disastrous debut, *The Enchanted Echo* (1944), was long forgotten, and his chapbooks of the 1950s had developed his modest reputation only incrementally. By 1967, however, Purdy was a celebrity of sorts. Like Dr Burt Parks in Mordecai Richler's *The Incomparable Atuk* (1963), he was "'world-famous … all over Canada'" (40). Although he was not wholly unknown outside the country, his remarkable success at home was tied to his markedly Canadian themes and sensibilities. He was, after all, "the world's most Canadian poet," in George Bowering's devilish phrase (1). In the accepted narrative of Purdy's development, *Poems for All the Annettes* (1962) was the turning point in his career; *The Cariboo Horses*, his first major success; and *North of Summer*, the confirmation of his brilliance and constitutive nationalism.[12] It was impossible thereafter to imagine Canadian literature without Purdy, or Purdy without Canada. He was the poet of the arch-Canadian experience, the embodiment of the national imagination. When Atwood wrote in *Survival: A Thematic Guide to Canadian Literature* (1972) that "[y]ou could make a whole anthology of Canadian poems about tumbled-down houses and deserted farms" (124), she chose Purdy's "The Country North of Belleville" to illustrate the paradigm of colonial settlement and "the abandonment of the farm … and the takeover of Nature once again" (123).

Yet as Atwood knew, Purdy's nationalism was never uncomplicated. In the second poem in *North of Summer*, the prospective adventurer makes an ironic, anticlimactic discovery. "The North West Passage," Purdy wrote,

>   is found
>
> needs no more searching
> and for lack of anything better to do
> waiting the plane's departure north from Frobisher
> I lounge on the bed poring over place-names
> on maps
>   and baby it's cold outside[.] (NS 20; BR 97)

Redolent of belatedness and boredom, the ambivalent lines express a world-weariness that runs through Purdy's poetry. The only romance left lies in the "place-names / on maps" that the poem reiterates – "Frobisher," "Baffin," "Ungava," "Thule," "Ellesmereland" (*NS* 20–1; *BR* 97–8) – and the speaker must borrow Frank Loesser's wintry words when his own fail him.[13]

The gulf between literary-historical narratives of convenience and the ironies and contradictions of literary works, their polysemy and unruliness, is difficult to bridge. Purdy and his contemporaries were transitional figures located between high modernism and the eclecticism of contemporary writing, and closely associated with the rise of Canadian literature as a quasi-official phenomenon sustained by public institutions, the Canada Council foremost among them. The creation of a national cultural infrastructure in the period preceding the centenary, driven by rare political enthusiasm for public support of the arts, resulted in a boom in cultural activities, including the creation and dissemination of literary works. The ascendance of Purdy, Atwood, Cohen, Kroetsch, Margaret Laurence, Alice Munro, Michael Ondaatje, and other luminaries was accompanied by the emergence of Canadian literary studies as a distinct field of scholarship and teaching. As W.J. Keith observes, the world of Canadian letters was in flux: "The era of cheap paperback reprints had just begun; the proliferation of universities meant that there were more students enrolled in studies at an advanced level; the celebration of Canada's centennial aroused a national optimism that included an interest in the country's literary heritage. And, above all, a number of unusually talented writers found that they had a wide range of untapped national subject matter" (71). Purdy was hailed as a pivotal figure in the new Canadian literary sphere, but the notion of a coherent national literature fell out of critical favour almost immediately after he and other writers of the time had fashioned substantial bodies of work. Since the early 1980s at least, Canadian critics have been engaged in the long project of dismantling the sudden canon and of questioning the grounds on which "CanLit" was (and is) premised. One unintended consequence of the field's fragmentation has been a calcification of ideas about the literature of the postwar period, and neglect of the literature itself.

Despite the arresting title of Solecki's study, Purdy was not the final Canadian to write poems – "It was a mistake of terminology," as Purdy might have put it ("At the Quinte Hotel," *PA68* 96; *BR* 131). Solecki contended that the vision of Canada promulgated by Purdy's poetry, and on which its reception depended, had by the end of the century been rendered untenable. Canada's foundational myths and the supposition of a common experience had been abandoned, and with them the assumption that authors could speak to and for the country, or at least one of the two distinct polities. Instead of two solitudes, there were now many.[14] Canadian literature as it is understood today is unquestionably more diverse, in all senses, cultural and aesthetic, than it was once taken to be. Scholars have ever more Canadian literature to study, but, perhaps as a result, the essential work of exhuming unpublished documents, preparing editions and commentaries, and writing biographies and sustained studies has languished in the cases of various authors once considered major.[15] If the importance of these authors is still normally granted, their letters, journals, drafts, and other papers remain insufficiently studied, and pose distinct editorial and interpretative challenges.[16] A critical paradox may thus be observed: relatively little is fully grasped about certain writers who occupy prominent places in what survives of a national canon. My semi-polemical contention is that those of us who study and teach Canadian literature have an incomplete sense of our subject. (To put it less cantankerously, "our subject" is no longer singular, and a plethora of topics demands critical attention and expertise.)

As Atwood remembers it, with a trace of nostalgia, Canada was another country as the 1960s started. It was prim: "[t]he Canadian obscenity trial of D.H. La[w]rence's *Lady Chatterley's Lover* was yet to take place: that would happen in 1962, argued before the Supreme Court by poet-lawyer F.R. Scott" (*Burgess* 12–13). And it was unsupportive of its authors:

> At the beginning of the decade – in 1960 – there was only a handful of publishers in English Canada who published books by Canadians. Of these, most were "branch plants" – their head offices were elsewhere, in cultural capitals such as London, New York, and Paris (for francophones). Oxford University Press and Macmillan were among these branch plants. Some publishers, such as The Ryerson Press and McClelland and Stewart and the notoriously teetotalling Clarke Irwin, which served grape juice at book launches, were Canadian-owned. (*Burgess* 17, 19)

Such obstacles to literary culture were not inconsequential, and if the postwar period was characterized by provincialism, as Atwood suggests, then little wonder that the iconoclastic Purdy made a vivid impression. Atwood recalls that "[i]n 1960, Hugh MacLennan and Morley

Callaghan were the big names in Canadian fiction, insofar as there were some" (13). Today the names may generate little excitement, connoting, albeit unfairly, clumsy allegory and turgid realism.[17] But ferment was in the air: "Irving Layton was cutting a swath in poetry, with Leonard Cohen coming on strong" (13). By 1960, Cohen had published only *Let Us Compare Mythologies* (1956), but *The Spice-Box of Earth* was issued in 1961; Atwood implies that a new era was foretokened. And by the mid-sixties, everything had changed. Purdy, who was "always ... going somewhere" ("The Madwoman on the Train," CH 13; BR 67), who greeted the day "stumbling yawning nude" ("Late Rising at Roblin Lake," CH 101; BR 88), had finally arrived, the times having caught up to his attitudes and interests.[18] They would not serve grape juice at *his* book launches.

Enticing they may be, but such narratives, whether they concern particular authors or entire periods, simplify and distort the literary past. For Philip Larkin, "[s]exual intercourse began / In nineteen sixty-three ... Between the end of the *Chatterley* ban / and the Beatles' first LP" (34). It is tempting to suggest that something comparably stimulating began at this juncture in Canadian literature, but a split from the past is less apparent than continuities and developments. Atwood's memoir requires no special defence, but triumphalist accounts of Canadian literature's miraculous advent betray the halting, haphazard nature of cultural change. Basic scholarship promises to unsettle literary-historical truisms, as do studies of cultural milieux in all their complexity and inconsistency. The late 1950s and early 1960s in fact encompassed competing modes and moods. MacLennan and Callaghan may have been "the big names," but *The Watch That Ends the Night* was not the only notable novel of the late 1950s. In 1959, Sheila Watson published *The Double Hook*, Marie-Claire Blais *La belle bête*, and Richler *The Apprenticeship of Duddy Kravitz* (cf. Mount 6–7, 44). The first issues of the scholarly journal *Canadian Literature* and the literary magazine *Prism* appeared in 1959; both quarterlies were published at the University of British Columbia, where the mimeographed poetry newsletter *Tish* would soon be a *succès de scandale*. *Poems for All the Annettes* was published in 1962, but so were other noteworthy volumes of poetry, including Earle Birney's *Ice Cod Bell or Stone*, John Newlove's *Grave Sirs*, and Phyllis Webb's *The Sea Is Also a Garden*: Purdy was one poet among many. And if *Poems for All the Annettes* was something original, it was also recognizably the work of the author of *Emu, Remember!* (1956) and *The Crafte So Longe to Lerne* (1959). As Peter Stevens noted in 1966, it "shows a major break with the method, even though the themes remain basically the same" as those of earlier volumes ("In" 25). The success of *Poems for All the Annettes* came not *ex nihilo*, but as a result of Purdy's semi-public apprenticeship, as Solecki asserts: the chapbooks of the 1950s "show Purdy trying out voices and styles, going to school in modern poetry from Hopkins to Layton" (*LCP* 221).[19]

Nor did *Poems for All the Annettes* appear in an intellectual void. The Canadian cultural world may have been relatively small – the country's population was approximately eighteen million in 1960 – but it was vibrant. In 1962, Robert Finch won the Governor General's Award for poetry in English for *Acis in Oxford* (1961), and Malcolm Lowry won (posthumously) the prize for fiction for *Hear Us O Lord from Heaven Thy Dwelling Place* (1961); Northrop Frye was chairman of the English Sub-Committee for the awards. Marius Barbeau, Lawren Harris, A.Y. Jackson, E.J. Pratt, and Ethel Wilson were among the Canada Council Medallists for 1961; the new award was intended to recognize "contributions in the arts, humanities and social sciences that represent major achievements in the cultural development of Canada." Atwood and Roch Carrier were awarded Canada Council fellowships to study literature in 1962–63. Miriam Waddington won a Senior Arts Fellowship for poetry. The Barbadian writer George Lamming received a Senior Non-Resident Fellowship "to write a novel in Canada." Birney received funding for the study of "contemporary Canadian prose and poetry in Commonwealth countries," as did George Clutesi of Victoria for "Canadian-Indian folklore in B.C." The previous year (1961–62), the Canada Council gave $4,500 to Barbeau "[t]o prepare for publication a glossary and grammar of the Huron-Wyandot language"; and the *Canadian Forum* received $2,800 "[t]o assist publication in 1962" (*Canada Council* 66, 67, 75, 76, 88, 99, 102, 107, 120).

Purdy's connections to such figures are well established. He had met Lowry in Vancouver, for instance, and written about him in *The Crafte So Longe to Lerne*. Frye was an early supporter. Birney was a mentor of crucial importance. Atwood became a friend. Barbeau's books fuelled Purdy's anthropological interests. At the beginning of the 1960s, Purdy did not belong to the Canadian literary establishment, but neither was he altogether removed from the intelligentsia. As A.W. Purdy, or Alfred W. Purdy, he published poems in the *Forum* in the late 1950s and early 1960s, including "Rain Poem?" "Olympic Room," "After the Rats," "From the Chin P'ing Mei," "Driftwood Logs," "Waiting for an Old Woman to Die," "Collecting the Square Root of Minus One," "For Norma in Lieu of an Orgasm," "Poem for One of the Annettes," "The Widower," "Biography," "The Machines," "Critique," and "My Grandfather Talking – 30 Years Ago."[20] The *Forum*, its front page proclaimed, was "an independent journal of opinion and the arts," and its contributors were prominent or rising names in Canadian letters, as this incomplete, but not unrepresentative, list suggests: Birney, Bowering, Layton, Milton Acorn, Fred Cogswell, John Robert Colombo, Ramsay Cook, Robert Fulford, Ralph Gustafson, Daryl Hine, Robin Mathews, Anne Marriott, Gwendolyn MacEwen, William McConnell, W.L. Morton, Alden Nowlan, Desmond Pacey, Peter Dale Scott, Anne Wilkinson, Milton Wilson, George Woodcock. (That the authors were virtually all men scarcely needs to be mentioned.) Purdy's poetry was legitimated by publication in the *Forum*, which was a venue for the cultural elite and those who sought to join it. And Purdy would have noticed in the *Forum* writing by peers and by figures he admired. In the September 1959 issue, for instance, were two poems by Birney – "Wind-Chimes in a Ruin" and "Five Poor Men Speak Up c. 1931," an adaptation "from the Hungarian" of Attila József – and "Fruition," a delicate lyric of eight lines by Atwood (cf. Mount 7, 299).

The fourteen poems that Purdy placed in the *Forum* between 1959 and 1962 suggest a poet of notable variety, or one uncertain of his preferred mode and style, and one less concerned with conventionally beautiful images or eloquent turns of phrase than with the sundry uses of bombast ("For Norma in Lieu of an Orgasm") and deliberate inelegance ("The Machines"). The poems include satires ("Olympic Room," "Critique," "Biography") and portraits ("The Widower," "The Machines"), an affected meditation on poetry ("Rain Poem?"), autobiographical depictions of impoverishment ("After the Rats," "Collecting the Square Root of Minus One"), and the bawdy, roistering addresses to Norma and Annette. "From the Chin P'ing Mei" is "poetic chinoiserie," as Frye wrote, in the manner of Ezra Pound (224).[21] Minor aspects of Purdy's stylistic development may be observed, such as his abandonment of capital letters at the beginning of each line, and some echoes sound clearly, as in the first line of "Waiting for an Old Woman to Die," which mimics Donne's "The Canonization." If Purdy's writerly progress and the literary culture of the day are to be understood precisely, with historical accuracy, then it is to such venues as the *Forum* that literary historians must return: revisiting old poems and critical statements alike may prove edifying in unanticipated ways.

REREADING PURDY: THE PARTS AND THE WHOLE

In the *Forum* of March 1963, Eli Mandel reviewed four new volumes of Canadian poetry: James Reaney's *Twelve Letters to a Small Town*, D.G. Jones's *The Sun Is Axeman*, Alden Nowlan's *The Things Which Are*, and *Poems for All the Annettes*, which received exceedingly high praise:[22]

> I have been expecting an explosion of language from Alfred Purdy for some time now, and his *Poems for All the Annettes* sounds to me like the big bang. There is no still centre here and certainly no unifying pattern within which multifarious experience can take on meaning.[23] Purdy's is a book in which intelligence wars with the senses, desire and restraint clash with ear-splitting force, and syntax threatens at any moment to tear itself to pieces simply out of spite at its own difficulties. (279)[24]

In Mandel's estimation, Purdy, Reaney, Jones, and Nowlan had escaped the limitations of regional coteries, such as the "particularly limp group writing as though Vancouver's damp had somehow soaked their diction" – the *Tish* poets (278). Unlike those ostensible trivialists, Purdy had seized upon a vital means of expressing existential dread:

> Indeed, much of the best work in *Poems for All the Annettes* involves Purdy's terrifying sense of the elusiveness of experience, his feeling for the transient form ("Archeology of Snow" [*sic*] may be the central poem from this point of view), his sense of the lost metaphor, the unfinished drama, the patterns that never succeeded; hence, all the fragments: of speech, of personality, of civilizations long gone; and hence too his lust for something permanent, even a fossil or even the agonies of all the Annettes he has known. (280)

A few years after, Peter Stevens noted that "[t]he theme of permanence and art's relation to it ... is a main theme" in the earlier *Pressed on Sand* (1955) – "and it is a theme Purdy returns to time and again in his poetry" ("In" 23). Still later, Mike Doyle wrote that "Archaeology of Snow" is "frequently seen as [the] centre-piece of *Poems for All the Annettes*" (13), its theme, "that man leaves traces though almost everything melts away," characteristic of Purdy's shuttling from the personal to the public and even professedly universal (14).

These statements indicate what was an emerging interpretative consensus, but naturally critics could only test their ideas against what was then available of Purdy's poetry. Doyle in 1974 could have read more poems than Mandel and Stevens in the 1960s, yet the reader of *Beyond Remembering: The Collected Poems of Al Purdy* (2000) has an altogether different basis for judgment – a larger and more varied selection of poems. Purdy's oeuvre in its totality is so vast that many words, phrases, and images recur frequently. Nonetheless, "Archaeology of Snow" contains especially meaningful terms from the poet's private lexicon, such as *illusion, immortal, permanent,* and *shadow,* which are repeated throughout his works both before and after *Poems for All the Annettes* (see Appendix).[25] "Archaeology of Snow" also contains a phrase, "being alive," on which Purdy drew repeatedly (*PA* 18; *BR* 40). It leads to "you remain alive" in "Necropsy of Love" (*CH* 23; *BR* 68), to "fumbling to stay alive" in "What It Was–" (*CH* 48; *BR* 83), to "where just to be alive is a triumph" in "Arctic River" (*NS* 22), to "the echo of being alive once" in "Shoeshine Boys on the Avenida Juarez" (*WG* 26; *BR* 142), to "a double reward for being alive" in "For Curt Lang" (*BR* 587), and above all to the title of *Being Alive,* Purdy's selected poems of 1978. That phrase stands with *Reaching for the Beaufort Sea, Starting from Ameliasburgh, Rooms for Rent in the Outer Planets,* and *Beyond Remembering* as an epitome of his imaginative endeavour. As Stan Dragland wrote, "*Being Alive* is the right title for his collected poems; too bad he'd used it before" (34). Evidently Purdy was not afraid to reuse the phrase whenever necessary, its importance greater than the artistic fault of repetition (see Appendix for further examples). His early critics, in short, could never have seen many such connections that now are almost plainly visible.

Visible – and vital to interpretation. Purdy may not have had D.H. Lawrence in mind each time he wrote "being alive," but the frequency with which the phrase appears is a reminder of Lawrence's forceful influence on Purdy's imagination. In the poem "Being Alive" (from *Pansies,* 1929), Lawrence decreed that "[t]he only reason for living is being fully alive" (*Poems* 1.453). He provided a related but more expansive statement of existential principles in *Apocalypse* (1931), the final, rhapsodic passage of which expresses ideas and impulses that reside at the centre of Purdy's literary project:

> Man wants his physical fulfilment first and foremost, since now, once and once only, he is in the flesh and potent. For man, the vast marvel is to be alive. For man, as for flower and beast and bird, the supreme triumph is to be most vividly, most perfectly alive. Whatever the unborn and the dead may know, they cannot know the beauty, the marvel of being alive in the flesh. The dead may look after the afterwards. But the magnificent here and now of life in the flesh is ours, and ours alone, and ours only for a time. We ought to dance with rapture that we should be alive and in the flesh, and part of the living, incarnate cosmos. I am part of the sun as my eye is part of me. That I am part of the earth my feet know perfectly, and my blood is part of the sea. (149)[26]

The passage was unusually important to Purdy. The evidence lies in the last fifteen lines of "Death of DHL," from *Piling Blood* (1984), in which Lawrence's prose is transformed into Purdy's verse, the quotation marks misleadingly (see Solecki, *LCP* 254) implying strict fidelity to the original:

> "For me, the vast marvel is to be
> alive. For man, or for flowers or
> beast and bird, the supreme triumph
> is to be most vividly and perfectly
> alive. Whatever the unborn and the dead
> may know, they cannot know the beauty,
> the marvel of being alive in the flesh.
> The dead may look after the afterwards.
> But the magnificent here and now of
> life in the flesh is ours, and ours alone,
> and ours only for a time.
> I am part of the sun as my eye
> is part of me. That I am part of the earth
> my feet know perfectly, and my blood
> is part of the sea –" (*PB* 94–5; *BR* 390–1)[27]

Expertly reading the whole of Purdy – a hypothetical *Complete Works* constituted by his published and unpublished writing in all genres – requires making associative leaps from early works to late, and from Purdy's works to those of other authors. His ideal reader would be as encyclopedic and ingenious as the poet himself, and able to hear in what Mandel called the "explosion of language" underlying patterns and the perpetual dialogue with the literary past (279).

Purdy demonstrated his broad knowledge of poetry in an essay on Leonard Cohen published in 1965 (see *SA* 194–204). Although his critical judgments are often expressed simplistically, he alluded in his analysis to Birney ("Leonard" 7), Layton (7), Edith Sitwell (9), Rimbaud (9), Chatterton (9), Dylan Thomas (9, 13), Yeats (9), Swinburne (9, 14), Chesterton (10), Jeffers (13), Housman (13), Laurence Hope (14), Donne (14), Waller (14), and Dowson (14). He referred to "avant-garde work south of the border" and dismissed contemporary English poetry (7). And he brushed aside his apparent erudition: "I'm not very fond of that favourite game," he wrote self-deprecatingly about detecting influence (while cleverly alluding to Cohen's novel of 1963) (14). The essay also shows Purdy to have been conscious of the shape of poets' careers, and possibly to have been self-conscious about his own slow beginnings (9); he was then in his middle forties. Although it should be no surprise that any poet is well versed in poetry, the essay confirms that the sense of Purdy as a naive poet was outdated even in the 1960s. To detect the influence or relevance of a given author, as Purdy did concerning Cohen, it is necessary to have read that author's writing, and so critical discussion of allusion or antecedence always reveals something of the critic's knowledge and tastes. Some of the poets Purdy named were especially important to him: Birney, Layton, Thomas, Yeats, Jeffers, and Housman all exerted their influence on his poetry, while Chesterton and Donne remained beloved, even if their bearing on his mature poems is harder to discern.[28] His persistent gestures outward constitute one means by which he escaped the strictly Canadian milieu. (His canon is primarily but not exclusively male. To what extent this fact is due to personal predilection and to what extent it reflects received understandings of the Great Tradition is cause for speculation.)

As I suggested, the obsessive and allusive qualities of Purdy's writing are illustrated by "Archaeology of Snow," a parodic poem of courtly love in which the speaker laments the utter disappearance of a beautiful woman: "But gone Anna / next day gone" (*PA* 15; *BR* 37). Her vanishing is absolute: she remains only in memory and, in a source of the frank poem's comedy, in the snow, which bears the imprint of "her / heavy buttocks." Anna's posterior is "printed" in the snow, as words are printed on the snow-white page, which renders her not only the object of the speaker's devotion, but also a foil for the bawdy, bodily poet, as if Purdy (or his proxy) in pursuing the absent Anna were confronting the futility of combatting time with words – or, in the terms of "The Horseman of Agawa," of "pitting fish eggs and bear grease against eternity / which is kind of ludicrous or kind of beautiful I guess" (*SD* 14; *BR* 209). Faithful paramour, the speaker visits Anna's imprint "[f]or a month's weeks" (*PA* 16; *BR* 38), but she disappears for a second time when Montreal's frozen landscape begins to thaw, the poem once again signalling its conventionally romantic theme and setting: "spring is coming and brooks / and water and earth are moving" (*PA* 17; *BR* 39). Anna inspires the love song of Alfred W. Purdy, but her evanescence leads the speaker to long for glimpses of eternity. Will declared, in Sonnet 24, "Mine eye hath played the painter and hath stelled / Thy beauty's form in table of my heart," while Al seeks "a few more moments / to hang in a private art gallery / of permanent imaginings" (*PA* 17; *BR* 39). The speaker realizes that "the snow itself WASN'T HER" (*PA* 17; *BR* 39) – that the representation is no substitute for reality – but, rather desperately, insists that the trace, like a poem, provides a kind of stability:

> She has to [be] there[29]
> Only the snow is melted
> the form is HERE
>   has to be
>   must be
> As if we were all immortal
> in some way I've not fathomed
> as if all we are
> co-exists in so many forms
> we encounter the entire race
> of men just by being
>   alive here[.] (PA 17–18; BR 40)

The speaker understands that permanence is illusory, that "being / alive" in the Heraclitean world (Bowering 58) is a temporary condition, but he wishes vainly that it were not so. Trilobites, buttocks, and even poets leave their mark, but rock erodes, snow melts, and poems are forgotten (see Bowering 58–62; cf. New 92).[30]

Decades later, Purdy observed in "For Curt Lang" that poetry usually enjoys a short life: "poor Norma poor Curt / entombed in a verse that may last / at most fifty or a hundred years" (BR 588). Therefore *carpe diem* – in the face of death, a tryst in the drifts, as in "Archaeology of Snow," or even unrequited love, such as Curt's for Norma. Purdy improbably links Horace, the Augustan poet whose lines supply the epigraph – "*O Lydia, Lydia, why are you sound asleep / while all night long I suffer in the alley?*" (BR 586)[31] – to the Vancouver of Lang's youth:

> How awful to spend the night in an alley
> trapped in a little English Prefect
> wide-awake and dreaming sexual dreams
> at age 17 in 1952
> beer-drunk and comically romantic
> forbidden to love delicious Norma
> afflicted with a permanent erection
> condemned to this dreadful fate
> by your hard-boiled friend Purdy
> thus allowing Norma a good night's sleep[.] (BR 586)

The references to Norma tie the elegy for the priapic Lang, published as a new poem in *Beyond Remembering*, to *Poems for All the Annettes* and "For Norma in Lieu of an Orgasm." Virtually from beginning to end, Purdy was a poet of fleeting time and the poignant brevity of all human life and achievement. Once he counselled insouciance, telling Norma "not to believe in / pain / sorrow / or death at all" (*PA* 21; *BR* 43), but now Norma "grows old and me older / the new millennium around the corner" (*BR* 587). Purdy's poems oscillate between celebrations of pleasure and sober contemplations of mortality. *Sex and Death*: the title was reductive but not inaccurate. As he wrote, "those are the great themes of human literature, the best literature ... For in my book, sex and death must always include love and life" (*SD* 4).

BEYOND REMEMBERING: THE REVISIONIST HISTORY OF PURDY'S MID-CAREER

The works on which Purdy's reputation is founded, those poems that have been widely anthologized and amply discussed, form a small part of an extensive corpus. Over his long career, Purdy published dozens of books and hundreds of poems. Because he revised his poetry thoroughly and frequently, many poems exist in several distinct forms. As a consequence of his tremendous productivity, critics inevitably have a distorted sense of the shape and scope of Purdy's career. Not all his poetry remains in print, and much of what was published during his lifetime has garnered relatively little critical attention. Numerous unpublished poems complement the published poetry – the exact number is uncertain – while poems that appeared only in periodicals and not in his books constitute another mass of unexamined writing. Although not every neglected poem is a masterpiece, Purdy's body of work in its entirety is of utmost interest to scholars of his life and times: the matter of how he spent his days and educated his imagination may be elucidated by previously unstudied works. In his essay on Cohen, Purdy referred to the duration of poetic careers: "If Dylan Thomas had lived longer than his 39 years he would have found it necessary to change. He was at a dead end, with exaggeration piled on exaggeration. But Jeffers, with his nihilistic view of mankind, lived long into his seventies and didn't change. Neither did A.E. Housman and his hopeless view of human life" ("Leonard" 13). Like Jeffers and Housman, Purdy lived a long life, and his literary development cannot be understood accurately without understanding the nature of his assembled works.

For many casual readers, however, *Beyond Remembering* is a book to be dipped into rather than read from cover to cover. The most impressive poems are not the first eight, which represent the 1950s – a thin selection that Purdy authorized (*BR* 599). Yet a comprehensive reading of *Beyond Remembering* reveals the variety of Purdy's writing and, conversely, the omnipresent connections that link discrete works. The omissions are telling too. As were his works of the 1950s, Purdy's poems of the early 1960s were carefully pruned for *Beyond Remembering*. Twenty-four of the thirty-seven poems in the first *Poems for All the Annettes* were omitted from *Beyond Remembering*, for example. Editors are obligated to make difficult and sometimes impossible decisions, but readers who first encounter the early Purdy in *Beyond Remembering* will unavoidably acquire a partial sense of the poet's labours. Critics too must constrain themselves, and in *The Last Canadian Poet*, Solecki discussed only some of the omitted poems. He undoubtedly knew *Poems for All the Annettes* well, and of course no critical study can be truly catholic, yet it remains the case that the standard compendium and the definitive study both give short shrift to the early 1960s.

Beyond Remembering begins with "At Evergreen Cemetery" (25), an oblique account of Purdy's mother's funeral. As Solecki notes (*LCP* 226), the poem was published in the *Canadian Forum* in December 1958: it belongs to the end of the decade, and is a trial run for "Evergreen Cemetery" in *Poems for All the Annettes*, which also concerns Purdy's mother, Eleanor (see Lalonde 177–9). Like much of Purdy's writing about his family, "At Evergreen Cemetery" is ambivalent and grudging. It establishes a contrast between the frantic activity and common sentiments of daily life, and the hush of death:

> The still grey face and withered body:
> without resistance winter enters in,
> as if she were a stone or fallen tree,
> her temperature the same as the landscape's –[.] (*BR* 25)[32]

The disparity between movement and stasis, between possibility and finality, is illustrated in the last lines, which turn away from the dead "she" to depict the speaker himself, "having the sense of something going / on without my knowledge" and "waiting to re-enter a different world." The promise of transformation is diminished by the speaker's passivity; the poem expresses a resignation that in time will exemplify one aspect of Purdy's demeanour. (On the poem's complicated textual history, see Chapter 8.)

The next poem, "From the Chin P'ing Mei," also confronts death.[33] The "funeral procession / of a dead lady" (*BR* 26) echoes the funeral procession at the end of "At Evergreen Cemetery"; the similarity casts a biographical light on the second poem. The third poem, "On the Decipherment of 'Linear B,'" announces Purdy's interest in ancient history and archaeology, and especially the ancient Mediterranean.[34] The first pages of *Beyond Remembering* move from the death of a parent to the death of a fictive noblewoman and to the difficulty of recovering the past: the introductory poems are preoccupied with disappearance, and with what the living can know of death and lost time, those undiscovered countries. The hero of "Decipherment" is Michael Ventris, the "code-breaker" who "figured it out" and brought "all the dusty Cretan sibilants" "back to life" (BR 26) – who performed a sort of resurrective miracle.[35] Pronounced correspondences link Purdy's poems, and accentuate the necessity and difficulty of reading his poetry as a whole, as an endless returning to constant themes, images, and significant words. In the comically prurient "Spring Song," the fourteenth poem in *Beyond Remembering*, the speaker's vantage is "from under an / old Pontiac" (BR 44). The same car reappears in "My '48 Pontiac," from *Wild Grape Wine*, in which it meets its demise.[36] The two poems stand on their own, yet the repetition, and others like it, suggest that Purdy's innumerable individual poems are very nearly parts of a single, lifelong work.

The first pages of *Beyond Remembering* likewise illustrate Purdy's growing emphasis on particular settings. Although "At Evergreen Cemetery" belongs to Trenton, the setting is never identified explicitly as Mount Evergreen Cemetery in Trenton, and the identities of the speaker and the deceased are only implied. Neither does "Evergreen Cemetery" name Trenton (BR 47), but the reference to "death's / ceded town" is consistent with Purdy's general impression of Trenton. "At Roblin Lake" (BR 30–1) is the first poem in *Beyond Remembering* to name a location in Purdy country, but not until "Remains of an Indian Village," one of the selections from *Poems for All the Annettes*, does Purdy place Canadian history and geography at the centre of a poem.[37] In the latter poem, a Stoic or Jeffersian encounter with material evidence of the troubling past, Purdy links his historiographical and philosophical impulses. The setting is post-apocalyptic – "after the plague, / after smallpox" (BR 51) – and the speaker seeks to comprehend "overwhelming" death by suggesting the persistence of change: "everything fades / and wavers into something else" (52). The "Indian Village" and its erstwhile inhabitants did not, of course, vanish only as part of the cyclical nature of things, or by the decree of the "tutelary gods of decay" (51): they were destroyed by the invaders and their diseases. The speaker's attempts to ponder "their absence" (52) and to "hear their broken consonants" (53) signal Purdy's awkward reckoning with his unsought place in a colonized landscape, his tendency to lament but thereby to aestheticize the atrocities of Canada's colonial history.

Decades later, the past still impinged on Purdy's imagination. His historical and literary-historical obsessions are particularly prominent in *Naked with Summer in Your Mouth* (1994), where once again the abundance of Purdy's poetry poses interpretative challenges. *Beyond Remembering* includes thirty poems from *Naked with Summer in Your Mouth*, but omits twenty-seven, many of which emphasize Purdy's bookish side.[38] The range of references in this late collection is striking. The first poem, "Grosse Isle," begins with an epigraph from Auden. "Capitalistic Attitudes" refers to Ralph Gustafson, Pasternak, Mayakovsky, Pushkin, Voznesensky, and Blok. "Pound" concerns the American poet, and "Yeats" the Irish. "On Robert Frost" names Frost, Pound, MacLeish, Hemingway, William Carlos Williams, and Karl Shapiro.[39] "Procne into Swallow" and "Procne into Robin" are Ovidian (see Solecki, LCP 261). "Archilochus in the Demotic" alludes to Yeats and, as Solecki noted, "mentions Pindar, Simonides, Homer, Pound, and 'Margaret A.'" (LCP 261). "The Crucifix across the Mountains" shows Lawrence's continuing influence; in a note, Purdy indicates that the "poem is taken from DHL's essay of the same title" (NSM 129).[40] The last lines of the poem turn from *Mitteleuropa* to southern Ontario:

> And it is a strange feeling for me
> beside Roblin Lake near Ameliasburgh
> to be talking about Jesus as the Son of God
> as if he were divine
> and I struggling to be human –[.] (NSM 75)

The last phrase is a variation of "being alive," the fundamental condition with which Purdy grapples. Closely related is the phrase "being human" – another basic premise. In "On Being Human," again from *Naked with Summer in Your Mouth*, Purdy evokes his mother's final moments and her ultimate reproach: "'I thought you'd feel terrible'" (NSM 91; BR 508). In the poem's last lines – "I am still ashamed / and I am still alive" – the speaker is reduced to simple assertions of emotional and existential fact, the repeated word "still" suggesting the persistence or endurance that marks a vain stand against "the undulating green waves of time," in a phrase from "The Country North of Belleville" (CH 75; BR 80). Purdy demonstrates a topical continuity as well: he has returned at this late stage to the subject of "At Evergreen Cemetery," the first poem in *Beyond Remembering*.

As in both "Remains of an Indian Village" and "On Being Human," and as the late poems in *Beyond Remembering* prove repeatedly, Purdy often treats death and life together, scrabbling for meaning. In "Chac Mool at Chichen Itza," for instance, he imagines a portentous warning from a limestone sculpture, "the god with a broken face": "*You who refuse to believe in gods / shall find nothing else to believe in –*" (NSM 22; BR 484).[41] In what T.S. Eliot called "the well-lighted desert of atheism"

(*Notes* 72), in the "cactus land" of "The Hollow Men" (*Collected* 90), in "the grey desert" where might be "glimpsed the flux / of what exists and does not yet exist" ("In the Desert," *NSM* 29, 30; *BR* 485), Purdy searches for "a cactus flower" (*NSM* 29; *BR* 485). His sterile earth, however, is also "the earth of Lawrence / who could not bear to leave the place" (*NSM* 89; *BR* 506). In "Pneumonia," Purdy names the English writer first – before "Yeats & García Márquez," before "Sakharov & Frank Scott & Margaret Laurence," before "all your friends" and "all your selves" (he is addressing himself) (*NSM* 89; *BR* 506, 507) – as if to rank the always-living Lawrence foremost among those whom he would miss if his fever did not break.[42] Sweating in the hospital, Purdy sees himself in the position of Lawrence in "Death of DHL," although Purdy was not, it transpires, truly *in extremis*; "Pneumonia" is a partly comical return to the earlier poem. Like Lawrence, Purdy cannot "bear to leave" the sublunary world (*NSM* 89; *BR* 506): "I don't want to leave earth / at least not until I look once more / into their eyes and reach beyond indifference" (*NSM* 88; *BR* 506). The finality of death is for Purdy an article of faith. "I believe in death," he writes in "For Eurithe," "the atoms of our bodies scattered forever / on the garbage dump of time" (*PB* 82). If, like Lawrence, he knows "how marvellous it is / to be alive" ("In Mexico," *TP* 113; *BR* 571), he also understands that human answers to existential questions are feeble consolations: "sadly there seems no answer / no real answer to anything" (*TP* 113; *BR* 571–2).[43] The universe is indifferent, and mortal existence meaningless, and yet, Purdy insists, we must find meaning in it. He was too great a sensualist to retreat from ordinary delights. His reference to "all the beer I ever drank" (*NSM* 88; *BR* 506) is not simply a joke, another manifestation of the boozer of "At the Quinte Hotel," but rather an expression of enthusiasm for the humble pleasures with which our days may be filled. Give him each day his daily beer, or book, for only life, the intellectual life included, can stave off death.

As such chains of association suggest, reading widely and deeply in Purdy's assembled poems shows, almost ad nauseam, how intensely one work illuminates another. The principle applies even to poems that for various reasons might appear banal, silly, or outdated. "Shopping at Loblaws," for instance, portrays the lecherous speaker's bumbling pursuit through the grocery store of a woman whose "little behind" "waggl[es] both syllables in unison" (*BR* 145). Published in *Wild Grape Wine* (*WG* 30–1), it was retained in the *Collected Poems* (*CP* 122–4) and *Beyond Remembering*, but the ramblings of the leering "Emasculus Promiscuous" (*BR* 146) could reasonably be accused of triviality.[44] As ribald as "Spring Song," "Shopping at Loblaws" knowingly depicts women as commodities for the consumption of the male onlooker, "Me Neanderthal me," eros embodied (*BR* 146).[45] But this whimsy also reveals darker fascinations.

The unrefined speaker pursues a hind – Thomas Wyatt provides the canonical precedent, the parodied classic – who, when she observes him, sees into the evolutionary past, Purdy punning on the *derrière*: "Her eyes look past me at some river bottom / full of unpackaged molluscs and slugs and snails" (BR 146). (What are little boys made of? Slugs and snails and puppy-dogs' tails.)

Yet if the chauvinist is a primitive creature, not fully human, so are we all, Purdy suggests, for base instinct resides within modern minds, "the sub- / conscious caged hot in white bone" (BR 146). In his comic mode, Purdy sets his lusty Neanderthal-self loose in the supermarket. In his tragic mode, however, he recognizes that his grasp on existence is tenuous. In "My Grandfather's Country," a more serious and consequential poem than "Shopping at Loblaws," Purdy contends that the fate of all things is oblivion: "failed farms sink back into earth / the clearings join and fences no longer divide" (WG 126; BR 555). But in the version of the poem in *Collected Poems* and *Beyond Remembering*, he notes a primal desire for life: "some god in ourselves buried deep in the dying flesh," he writes, "clutches at life and will not let go" (CP 148; BR 555). "Neanderthal me" is not far off and, as always, the interplay of life and death in any one poem is thrown into relief by Purdy's endless wrestling with foundational concerns.

PURDY AFTER A CENTURY

If Purdy's poems present critics with a profusion of interpretative opportunities, so his life and archives present scholars with pressing tasks, ranging from the relatively minor, such as the discovery of letters and ephemera, to the formidable, such as a comprehensive edition of his collected works. Various aspects of his career await examination, including his overlooked genres (radio plays and journalism), his institutional affiliations (to the Canada Council, the Canadian Broadcasting Corporation, the National Film Board), his influence as an occasional teacher of creative writing, and his place in the Canadian intellectual world of the mid-century, particularly in relation to such figures as Frye, Claude Bissell, Donald Creighton, George Grant, Harold Innis, and Marshall McLuhan.[46] Among his contemporaries were writers such as Austin Clarke and Harold Ladoo, who are often unfairly relegated to minor roles in Canadian literary history. Thousands of archived letters require editing and publication. Some of Purdy's contemporaries have been the subjects of impressive works of biographical scholarship, among them Elspeth Cameron's *Earle Birney: A Life* (1994), Ira Nadel's *Various Positions: A Life of Leonard Cohen* (1996), Sandra Djwa's *Journey with No*

Maps: A Life of P.K. Page (2012), and Miriam Nichols's *A Literary Biography of Robin Blaser: Mechanic of Splendor* (2019). The absence of a biography of Purdy is conspicuous, perhaps especially so after Rebecca Wigod's *He Speaks Volumes: A Biography of George Bowering* (2018), which contains numerous references to Purdy, with whom Bowering maintained an "epic," decades-long correspondence (187; see 187–8). Purdy's life was not unblemished. His personal relations with family members were flawed, and his correspondence attests to a range of vices: temper, egotism, gloominess, vulgarity. But there would be no literary criticism if only the works of faultless authors were studied, and the writing of his life is probably the most urgent task in Purdy studies.[47]

As such interpretative and editorial investigations unfold, Purdy and his works will naturally be reinterpreted and newly understood, but the expense of time and energy is only truly justified if he continues to be thought a significant writer. Purdy's place in the Canadian canon is secure on historical grounds, commentators having asserted for decades his central position in the national literature, but his poetry today is not universally loved (nor was it ever). The critic James Pollock, in a book of essays published in 2012, placed him among the "bad and mediocre but endlessly-anthologized poets" of Canada (178). In Pollock's estimation, Purdy's failings were those of his time: "The celebrated poets of earlier generations – Al Purdy, George Bowering, John Newlove, Dorothy Livesay and so on – were notably poor writers, and consequently their work has not worn well" (204).[48] Purdy's body of work can withstand exacting engagement, but the sheer volume of his writing obliges critics to sift and to assess as well as to explicate. His poetry, especially at its most prolix, can seem banal compared to the formal innovation and technical ingenuity of some of his modernist forerunners. "Piling Blood," for instance, unfolds over sixty-six lines of straightforward autobiographical description before turning in its devastating conclusion to poetry, compunction, and the still, sad music of humanity:

> there were no poems
> to exclude the screams
> which boarded the streetcar
> and travelled with me
> till I reached home
> turned on the record player
> and faintly
> in the last century
> heard Beethoven weeping[.] (*PB* 15; *BR* 355)[49]

In poems about work, labour is commonly a metaphor for poetic composition, but "Piling Blood" says little about writing. This work, real drudgery, dehumanizes the worker, and Purdy here is at his least romantic, refusing to allow that the bodily indignities involved in piling powdered blood, piling glass, and "shouldering sides of frozen beef" could be disguised by figurative language (PB 14; BR 354). Instead the poem is plainly, and thus painfully, realistic. The final lines doubt poetry's capacity to console; it is not only the poet's failure that concerns Purdy ("I wrote no poems"), but also the failure of art itself ("there were no poems"). The equivocal ending suggests that Beethoven's music drowns out the day's sorrow, the solace of the wordless art trumping poetry's impotent language, and that Beethoven's weeping amplifies the speaker's miseries, as if the composer were mourning the fate of humankind and, proleptically, the speaker's own fate. The historical Beethoven, of course, knew nothing of the degrading labour portrayed in "Piling Blood" – "and I heard the screams / of dying cattle" (PB 14; BR 355) – nor of the Canadian lives and landscapes that engrossed Purdy, so the poem's allusion is at once poignant and ironic. If the poem succeeds, if its autobiographical narrative compels and its conclusion moves, then it does so on its own terms, and not those of his predecessors.

His correspondence and published prose indicate convincingly that Purdy thought in terms of literary genius and a hierarchical view of artistic achievement, and sought to measure his poetry against that of the past. But his poems are now themselves part of the literary-historical past, and new judgments of his writing are inevitable in view of changing tastes, just as new critical opinions are inevitable as the disciplinary formations of English studies and Canadian literary studies respond to broader cultural and academic changes. The assumptions of the Massey era no longer hold; Canadian literature has been transformed, both as a field of cultural production and as an object of critical study. The chapters in *An Echo in the Mountains* suggest that, after his hundredth anniversary, we scarcely know Purdy. Although they represent a range of views and approaches, the chapters depart from received wisdom about Purdy, his writing, and its critical reception. The studies in the book are concerned with the masks that Purdy wore, and the myths that sprang up around him; if they do not debunk such myths entirely, that is because of the inseparability of his writing from the reputation that emerged in the first decades of his public and critical reception. Above all, the chapters dispute the critical status quo, especially the overwhelming influence of Solecki's *The Last Canadian Poet*, and struggle with the question of what it means to read Purdy in a Canada, and a Canadian literary sphere, that increasingly diverge from his own.

An Echo in the Mountains begins with a partly familiar Purdy. In Part I, three poet-critics pay tribute to him, at once showing that he continues to dwell in other writers' imaginations and recasting the nature of that residence. In Chapter 1, an essay on transcendence, Doug Beardsley presents Purdy as a nearly religious poet. Extending his earlier reflections on collaborating with Purdy (see Beardsley 221–6), he suggests, even as he celebrates Purdy's achievement, that elements of the sacred in his writing have been direly overlooked. In Chapter 2, Linda Rogers describes a female presence in Purdy's poetry, musing on his muses in a personal, biographically speculative essay. For Rogers, who knew Al (and knows Eurithe) well, Purdy's reputation, and whatever personal characteristics helped give rise to it, cannot be dismissed; yet the legend, the facts of his life, and the poems themselves rest uneasily. Purdy's poetry is often stereotypically masculine, and it has largely (although not exclusively) attracted the attention of male critics; Rogers explores the personal and poetic dynamics of Purdy's reactions to women. And in Chapter 3, Shane Neilson asks why Purdy could not, it seems, write a love poem without falling into parody. (Rogers, on the other hand, hears "Say the Names" as an unexpected love poem directed at a feminized landscape.) Writing in partial homage to Purdy, Neilson also challenges the habit of seeing him as the national poet. Implicit in Neilson's chapter are the open questions of for whom Purdy is thought to speak, and whom he is imagined to address.

Such questions receive more expansive treatment in Part II, which concerns Purdy's nationalism and representations of Canada. At first glance, the topic may seem hoary, but the four chapters reassess simplistic notions of Purdy as nationalist poet. From the vantage of the twenty-first century, Canada's mid-twentieth century appears foreign, and the works of writers of that period may seem increasingly inconsequential. The chapters in Part II attest to the importance and awkwardness of reading Purdy's writing long after the Centennial era. In particular, they address Purdy's relation to and responsibility for conventional nationalist narratives, and his depiction of Indigenous peoples and cultures.

In Chapter 4, J.A. Weingarten confronts unpalatable elements in Purdy's poems, namely the racist and sexist passages that occur throughout his works. Keenly aware of the ethical responsibilities of critics and teachers, Weingarten presents recuperative strategies for reading Purdy within a vastly expanded conception of Canadian literature. In Chapter 5, Misao Dean turns to *North of Summer*. If that book today appears naive or even offensive in its representation of the people and culture that Purdy encountered on his travels to Baffin Island and the

Kikastan Islands, the poems can be recovered, Dean suggests, as depictions of shameful encounters between colonial Canada and Indigenous people. The sense of shame expressed in the poems, and shame felt by contemporary readers at Purdy's representations of the Arctic, are essential, Dean proposes, to the book's meaning.[50] In Chapter 6, Ian Rae examines Purdy's "The Runners," analyzing the poem's riddling nature, and placing it in the context of critical assumptions about Purdy's nationalism. Purdy was fascinated by Newfoundland's archaeological sites, and "The Runners" is set in Vinland. As Annette Kolodny observes in another context, "L'Anse aux Meadows was a landing site and a place for repairing ships, but it was not the Vinland where grapes grew wild. Perhaps it is best, therefore, to think of Vinland as what it became for Euro-Americans in the nineteenth century, that is, a geographical site that was transfigured into an imagined landscape for the projection of dreams" (18). Rae shows that "The Runners" occupies an ambiguous place in Purdy's imagination of the distant colonial past and its bearing on Canada's present. And in Chapter 7 I provide a bibliographically oriented supplement to the critical analyses of Chapters 4, 5, and 6. I describe an unpublished manuscript, "Yehl the Raven and Other Creation Myths of the Haida," that sheds light on Purdy's persistent interest in Indigenous cultures. The manuscript permits the view that Purdy, in his way, sought intercultural understanding and a means of making his own writing distinctly Canadian through Indigenous stories, in an attempt that today seems clumsy and irresponsible.

The chapters in Part III turn to textual problems engendered by Purdy's compulsive rewriting and the sheer volume of material he produced in his lengthy career, and show how unexamined or unappreciated documents illuminate the complicated nature of his thinking about art, poetry, literary reputation, and authorial self-fashioning.

In Chapter 8, Eli MacLaren examines Purdy's "House Guest" in order to demonstrate the essential importance of scholarly editing to critical interpretation. MacLaren highlights interpretative problems created by editorial decisions and errors, and emphatically asserts the need for new editions and bibliographical treatments of Purdy's works. In Chapter 9, Jamie Dopp focuses on "Elegy for a Grandfather," which Russell Brown once called "Purdy's most frequently revised poem" (396). Dopp examines in detail Purdy's remembrance of his grandfather, Old Rid, a figure who resembles another person of historical interest to Purdy, Owen Roblin. Dopp's assiduous analysis of the six versions of Purdy's "Elegy" attests to the importance of careful engagement of the mutable and elusive poetic text. In Chapter 10, Ernestine Lahey suggests the extent to which Purdy was interested in and informed about the visual arts, despite the myth of his anti-elitism. Noting that Purdy contains multitudes, D.G. Jones once called Purdy "an anti-academic who coins such inkhorn words as 'muliebrity', and who expects his readers to know an Immelmann turn when they see one, whether or not they are *amateurs* of air combat during the first World War" (33).[51] Lahey likewise shows Purdy's contradictions in relation to aspects of high culture and the academy. Her attention to his early and unpublished poems also confirms the vital importance of archival studies. In Chapter 11, Natalie Boldt examines an issue of the *Malahat Review* from 1977 in search of what it reveals of the relationship between Purdy and Margaret Atwood, and of Purdy's understanding of literary celebrity. Purdy's negative opinion of Atwood's critical and popular reception elucidates the particular problems facing literary authors in Canada in the 1970s. Finally, in Chapter 12, Carl Watts analyzes Purdy's novel, *A Splinter in the Heart* (1990), in order to suggest that his unsystematic approach to writing poetry – his anti-theoretical theory – can be deduced from his fiction. Watts contends moreover that Purdy's intuitive approach is not entirely different from poetic principles advanced by some of his most enthusiastic detractors.

The chapters together affirm that Purdy remains a figure of interest both because of and despite his reputation. As time passes, fewer and fewer commentators will have known Purdy personally, and the biographical legend will no longer preside over the works. In his first century, Purdy commanded an enormous presence in Canadian literature. In his second century, when his place cannot be taken for granted, and when the nature and functions of a national literature are continually debated, his works demand conscientious and eloquent commentary. *An Echo in the Mountains* aims to provide points of departure, and topics for debate, for readers still coming to terms with Purdy after a century.

NOTES

1 Purdy was born 30 December 1918. The date of his death was until recently accepted as 21 April 2000. An article published in *Toronto Life* in 2016 revealed that Purdy in fact died on 20 April (Hofsess 64, 66). In the digital age, information about Purdy – who remained faithful to the typewriter – travels quickly and unpredictably. The account of his death by assisted suicide appeared first in the online edition of *Toronto Life* (29 February 2016) and only belatedly in print.
2 Purdy continued to write for nearly fifteen years after 1986; the *Collected Poems* was neither his final nor his definitive statement, but the late volumes, from *The Woman on the Shore* (1990) to *To Paris Never Again* (1997), are

comparatively neglected. The winners of the Governor General's Literary Awards for poetry in the 1990s were not always greatly younger than Purdy, but their names suggest a diversity of styles and subjects: Anne Szumigalski (1922–99), Don Coles (1927–2017), E.D. Blodgett (1935–2018), Don McKay (b. 1942), Lorna Crozier (b. 1948), Robert Hilles (b. 1951), Dionne Brand (b. 1953), Jan Zwicky (b. 1955), and Stephanie Bolster (b. 1969). Purdy's place among such poets, and his importance as an author of the late twentieth century, have yet to be fully assessed, and his last poems are still to be explicated in detail.

3 The relative obscurity of Canadian poets of the period before the Great War does not mean that there are no figures of interest, and a distinction may be drawn between scholarly activity and public attention. On Johnson, see *Paddling Her Own Canoe: The Times and Texts of E. Pauline Johnson (Tekahionwake)* (2000), by Veronica Strong-Boag and Carole Gerson, and *E. Pauline Johnson, Tekahionwake: Collected Poems and Selected Prose* (2002), edited by Gerson and Strong-Boag.

4 *Al Purdy: Essays on His Works* (2002), edited by Linda Rogers, is also noteworthy, but less substantial than *The Last Canadian Poet* and *The Ivory Thought*.

5 Solecki has been Purdy's principal scholarly editor, as well as the major interpreter of the poetry. His editions include *Starting from Ameliasburgh: The Collected Prose of Al Purdy* (1995) and *Yours, Al: The Collected Letters of Al Purdy* (2004) – the most significant addition to the Purdy library since *Beyond Remembering: The Collected Poems of Al Purdy* (2000), which Solecki edited with Purdy himself.

6 For the sake of transparency, I note that a poem of mine is included in *Beyond Forgetting*.

7 Purdy's critics might also contend more fully with early, unpublished, and therefore obscure studies of his works, such as Jean Wilson's "The Sense of Place and History in the Poetry of A.W. Purdy" (1968) and Elizabeth Douglas's "The Mechanics of Being Alive: Major Themes in the Poetry and Prose of Al Purdy" (1981), both of which are substantial MA theses (see Douglas, Wilson, "Sense"; cf. Wilson, "Jean" 59–61). Purdy and Wilson engaged in an interesting correspondence during her research.

8 *North of Summer* has been deemed, for instance, a "strategically nation-building collection" that "contains a settler-colonial topos of land and ownership rooted in the fundamentally ambivalent entanglements of the settler-invader subject position" (van der Marel 16, 23). Yet whatever its faults, *North of Summer* portrays Purdy as a foreigner in the North. In the book's "Postscript," he signals a lack of interest in proprietary views of the Arctic: "Oh sure, the north is our last frontier etc., which you can read about in other books than mine. Billions in minerals waiting for a guy with geiger

counter and geology degree. A national purpose for Canada – developing the north, that is. I think this last is probably true, and would mean a great deal to the country – but it remains outside my scope and intent" (*NS* 83). As always, attending to Purdy's tone is of paramount importance. See MacLaren 120–3.

9 Don Coles gently voices a dissenting view: "four of those names are too big for the sentence. Just four. Fitting Walcott into a Purdy-sized sentence is no problem" (561). Solecki's provocative claim suggests directions for further studies – a comparative account of Purdy's Canada in relation to Heaney's Ireland and Walcott's St Lucia, for instance, and of the poets' ambivalent roles as national interpreters and icons. Miłosz appears occasionally in Purdy's late poetry. In "On My Workroom Wall," a photograph of the Polish poet reflects Purdy himself: "Xerox of Milosz with cigar looking cynical" (*NSM* 76; *BR* 499). "Realism 2" is, in Purdy's words, "a response to [a poem, "Realism,"] by Czeslaw Milosz in *The New Yorker*; in which he enters imaginatively into the landscapes of some Dutch old masters" (*TP* 129).

10 "Voracious": If, as Peter Stevens suggests, "[i]t has been a cliché of Purdy criticism that the poet's reading, wayward and wide-ranging, provides him with a spectrum of reference," the point is no less important for its familiarity ("Road" 34).

11 The infamous term "Can. Lit." originates with Earle Birney (*One* 58).

12 Stevens, for instance, called 1962 a "crucial" year for Purdy ("Road" 33). He noted earlier the "central poetic upheaval" represented by Purdy's two volumes of 1962 – *Poems for All the Annettes* and *The Blur in Between* – and acclaimed *The Cariboo Horses* as "one of the best collections of Canadian poetry for some time" ("In" 22).

13 Another interpretation finds in the same lines evidence of a "self-satisfied tone" and Purdy's "revel[ling] in the absolute knowledge of land represented by the map" (van der Marel 28). If "Baby, It's Cold Outside" – the song – is now understood to hinge on outdated notions of sexual consent, as many commentators have maintained, then the allusion casts a peculiar light on the amorous politics of Purdy's poem.

14 "Many": as suggested by the title of *Other Solitudes: Canadian Multicultural Fictions*, edited by Linda Hutcheon and Marion Richmond (1990). The metaphor comes from Rilke via Hugh MacLennan's *Two Solitudes* (1945).

15 Other factors, such as the widespread shortage of permanent professorial positions, have also shaped contemporary Canadian literary studies. My account is brief and selective by design.

16 See Solecki, "Materials." Linda M. Morra's *Unarrested Archives: Case Studies in Twentieth-Century Canadian Women's Authorship* (2014) does not address Purdy's papers – the reason is obvious – but its investigation of the political and nationalist dimensions of literary archives bears on my subject. The

expanse of Purdy's papers is undoubtedly tied to his status as a suitably Canadian author: the national poet deserves space on the shelf. As Canadian literature has become increasingly sizable and eclectic, the tasks facing editors have grown in number and variety; a range of contemporary editorial concerns is treated in *Editing as Cultural Practice in Canada* (2016), edited by Dean Irvine and Smaro Kamboureli. There are, of course, numerous exceptions to the rule of critical inattention. For a recent example, see *Margaret Laurence and Jack McClelland, Letters* (2018), edited by Laura K. Davis and Linda M. Morra, highlights of which, for Purdy's readers, include a discussion in 1975 between Laurence and McClelland concerning Purdy's editing of *Storm Warning 2* (1976) (369–72), and a word of praise from Laurence about Purdy's *Wild Grape Wine* (207).

17 Again, exceptions to the rule of indifference can be found. Both MacLennan and Callaghan are examined sensitively by Colin Hill in *Modern Realism in English-Canadian Fiction* (2012) and Patrick Coleman in *Equivocal City: French and English Novels of Postwar Montreal* (2018). My intention is not to cavil, but simply to suggest the general invisibility of many authors. I agree with Brian Trehearne that "the Canadian public beyond the campuses has shown in the last forty years almost no interest in Canadian modernist writing. Like other periods of Canadian literature prior to the contemporary era, our modernism survives almost exclusively in the classroom" (466).

18 "The Madwoman on the Train" was retitled "Sestina on a Train" in *Collected Poems* and *Beyond Remembering*.

19 Solecki identifies Hopkins several times as an important presence in Purdy's development (LCP xv, 52, 76, 84, 221), but specific passages in which Purdy alludes to or draws upon Hopkins are relatively few. "In Mid-Atlantic" and "Invocation," from *Emu, Remember!* and "Letters of Marque," from *Love in a Burning Building*, are cited by Solecki as examples of Hopkins's influence (LCP 229, 238). Tim Heath suggests (199) a connection between "The Windhover" and Purdy's "The Stone Bird," from *The Stone Bird* (1981) and, in revised form, *To Paris Never Again* (1997).

20 "After the Rats," "From the Chin P'ing Mei," "Olympic Room," "Driftwood Logs," "Rain Poem?" and "Waiting …" were collected in *The Crafte So Longe to Lerne*. "Biography" and "The Machines" were included in *The Blur in Between*. "Collecting …," "For Norma …," "Poem for One …," and "The Widower" appeared in *Poems for All the Annettes*. "My Grandfather Talking …" was not collected until *The Cariboo Horses*. "Critique," I believe, remains uncollected. Of the fourteen *Forum* poems, only five – "From the Chin P'ing Mei," "The Machines," "For Norma …," "Poem for One …," and "My Grandfather Talking …" – were retained in *Beyond Remembering*.

21 "Pound": "'The River Merchant's Wife' is probably somewhere behind the original version of 'From the Chin P'ing Mei'" (Solecki, LCP 91).

22 On Jones, Mandel, and Purdy, see Atwood, *Second* 55–62.

23 "Still centre": see the final lines of "Winter Walking": "This is the still centre, / an involvement in silences" (*BB* 19; *BR* 57). Earlier in the poem the ending is foreshadowed: "Sometimes I stand still, / like a core at the centre / of my senses, hidden and still." Purdy's lines suggest T.S. Eliot's "Burnt Norton": "At the still point of the turning world" (*Collected* 191).
24 Mandel neglected to mention that one of Purdy's poems was "Eli Mandel's Sunday Morning Castle," which, as Solecki noted, "make[s] it obvious that Purdy has little patience with obscurity" (*LCP* 92) – despite the title's conspicuous allusion to "Mr. Eliot's Sunday Morning Service."
25 "Terms": "truth of an illusion" (*PA* 15; *BR* 37); "As if we were all immortal," "immortal as hell" (*PA* 18; *BR* 40); "permanent imaginings" (*PA* 17; *BR* 39); "in the green shadows" (*PA* 18; *BR* 40).
26 Lawrence's "flower and beast and bird" (*Apocalypse* 149) is a variation on the title of *Birds, Beasts and Flowers*, a volume of poetry (1923). Purdy's "Birds and Beasts," from *Piling Blood*, borrows the phrasing (Solecki, *LCP* 251) and contains another Lawrentian phrase, "being alive" (*PB* 39; *BR* 374). As Solecki showed, Lawrence is prominent in *Piling Blood*: "In *The Stone Bird* there is one poem, 'Bestiary,' influenced by several of Lawrence's, and one about him, 'D.H. Lawrence at Lake Chapala.' Three years later, *Piling Blood* has eight ... All subsequent collections show Lawrence's presence in some form" (*LCP* 84). Many other poems deriving from Purdy's travels in Mexico and Italy are Lawrentian in setting, even if they do not name the English writer.
27 On Purdy's quotation of Lawrence, see Solecki, *LCP* 84–5, 222; and Dragland 33–4. In *Piling Blood*, the poem ends with a laconic attribution – "DHL" (95) – that was omitted from *Beyond Remembering*.
28 The reference in "O Recruiting Sergeants!" to "a Turk at Lepanto" (*PA* 52; *BR* 47) suggests Chesterton's "Lepanto," as Solecki noted (*LCP* 232). Chesterton and "Lepanto" are named in a manuscript version of "Bestiary [II]," a much later poem (*LCP* 261, 274–5).
29 In the original *Poems for All the Annettes*, this line contains an error: "She has to there" (17). In the 1968 edition, the mistake was corrected: "She has to be there" (17). The version in *Beyond Remembering* omits the pronoun: "has to be there" (40).
30 Purdy's simile – "like a Cambrian trilobite" (*PA* 15; *BR* 37) – may have originated in Birney's "David" (1942): "ghostly trilobites, / Letters delivered to man from the Cambrian waves" (*David* 4; *One* 35). Purdy's geological reference in "Archaeology of Snow" anticipates the "precambrian intentions" in "Canso," the "pink precambrian granite" in "Listening," and the "weathered granite boulders / from the Precambrian" in "Tent Rings" – three poems from *North of Summer* (34, 50, 68) – and "the Cambrian / and Precambrian when there were no wolves" in "Bestiary," from *The Stone Bird* (*SB* 19; *BR* 328). Trilobites also appear in "Lament for the Dorsets" (*WG* 55; *BR* 161; see Jones 39). Jones characterizes Purdy as an essentially archaeological and

paleontological poet (38). On Purdy, Birney, Pratt, and prehistoric vocabulary, see Djwa 58.

31 Purdy probably used David Ferry's translation: "'O Lydia, Lydia, why are you sound asleep // While all night long I suffer in the alley?'" (Ferry 67). According to Doug Beardsley, Purdy knew Ferry's *Gilgamesh: A New Rendering in English Verse* (1992), but considered it "dry" (224).

32 Compare Auden's "In Memory of W.B. Yeats" (1939): "The mercury sank in the mouth of the dying day" (247). It must be a coincidence that in the same poem Auden uses the phrase "the evergreen forests" (247). Purdy's poem's first words – "The still grey face" – anticipate similar phrases in other early poems: "grey eyes" in "The Listeners" (*BR* 42), "her savage grey face" in "Evergreen Cemetery" (*BR* 48), and "the grey shape" in "Winter Walking" (*BR* 56). In "The Last Picture in the World," a late poem, Purdy describes a great blue heron on Roblin Lake as "A hunched grey shape" (*BR* 580). As Solecki notes (*LCP* 112–13), that poem is a revisioning of "After Rain," from *Being Alive* (collected in *BR* 317–19). The concluding description of the malevolent iceberg in E.J. Pratt's *The Titanic* (1935) comes to mind: "The grey shape with the palaeolithic face / Was still the master of the longitudes" (*Selected* 82). The resemblance could be deemed trivial had Purdy not written about his fondness for the lines (e.g., *YA* 34; see Djwa 53).

33 See Solecki, *LCP* 276, on the importance of the "South Gate" (*BR* 25) as an image of passage and death. Less obvious than the link to "At Evergreen Cemetery" are connections to two poems from *Poems for All the Annettes* omitted from *Beyond Remembering*: "Jade Stag," subtitled "Shang Dynasty – 1528–1027 B.C." (*PA* 31), and "Hokusai at Roblin Lake," both of which belong to the orientalist mode. "Jade Stag" tests a theme that emerges more clearly in "Lament for the Dorsets" and "The Sculptors." Also relevant is "Lu Yu (A.D. 1125–1209)," from *The Cariboo Horses*, which appears in *Beyond Remembering* simply as "Lu Yu," with the dates as subtitle (*BR* 64–5).

34 The image of "red dust in the guts of Mycenaean warriors" (*BR* 26) prefigures the setting of "At Mycenae," from *Piling Blood*. Daedalus (*BR* 26) reappears in "Canso," from *North of Summer* (35); "The Son of Someone Loved–," from *Piling Blood* (*PB* 127; *BR* 410); and "Bruegel's *Icarus*," from *To Paris Never Again* (*TP* 23; *BR* 530). Agamemnon also appears in "Scholarly Disagreements" and "Biography," from *The Blur in Between* (15, 17); "Menelaus and Helen," from *Piling Blood* (*PB* 20, 22; *BR* 357, 359); and "Herodotus of Halicarnassus," from *The Woman on the Shore* (*WS* 42; *BR* 456). In "On the Decipherment of 'Linear B,'" Purdy writes that "Knossos did burn" (*BR* 27); he mentions his own visit to Knossos in "I Am Definitely on the Side of Life I Said to Pausanias," in *Sex and Death* (81). Only Daedalus, and not Icarus, is named in "On the Decipherment of 'Linear B,'" but the greater significance of the story of father and son is emphasized by references to Icarus in such poems as "In the Wilderness" (*CH* 37), "St. Francis in Ameliasburg" (*WG* 103), "The Son of

Someone Loved–" (*PB* 126–7; *BR* 410), "Bruegel's *Icarus*" (*TP* 23–5; *BR* 530–2), and "House Party–1000 BC" (*TP* 60; *BR* 548). The personal dimension of Purdy's dwelling on the myth is a matter for biographers.

35 Solecki suggests (*LCP* 287) a connection between the surname *Ventris* and the "south wind blowing" in the poem's last line (*BR* 27), and proposes sources for the image in Purdy's reading (*LCP* 230).

36 In *Beyond Remembering*, "Spring Song" appears with poems from *Poems for All the Annettes* (1962). The version in that early collection, however, is markedly different from the one in *Beyond Remembering*. "Spring Song" was not included in the 1968 *Annettes*, but rewritten versions appeared in *Wild Grape Wine* (12–13), *Being Alive* (32–3), and elsewhere. The reference in the 1962 version to "dandelions ready for winemaking" (*PA* 28) suggests a thematic rationale for its inclusion in *Wild Grape Wine*, but in the poem as it appeared in that book, the dandelions had disappeared. Solecki writes that "Spring Song" was "touched up in the 1990s," and the version in *Beyond Remembering* is that of *Rooms for Rent in the Outer Planets* (*BR* 599; cf. *RR* 12–13). Dean Irvine's commentary is incisive: "The example of 'Spring Song,' first published in periodical form in 1962 and collected that same year in *Poems for All the Annettes*, which was heavily revised numerous times … makes plain the curious inaccuracy of Solecki's claim that the poem was merely 'touched up in the 1990s' … and could therefore be placed in *Beyond Remembering* with the grouping of poems from the 1962 edition of *Annettes*" (84).

37 The version of "Remains of an Indian Village" in *Beyond Remembering* is that of *Wild Grape Wine*, although the poem is grouped with others from *Poems for All the Annettes* (*BR* 8, 51–3).

38 Solecki writes, for instance, that he could not locate the source of the quotation at the beginning of "Country Living" (*LCP* 263):
> Spring with Pablo Neruda
> and I peering out the bathroom
> window at some imaginary
> female and he sez to her
> "I want to do to you what
> spring does to the cherry trees[.]" (*NSM* 106; *BR* 514)

The quotation is in fact a translation of "Quiero hacer contigo / lo que la primavera hace con los cerezos" – lines from the fourteenth of Neruda's *Veinte Poemas de Amor* (1924). It is difficult to know on which English rendition Purdy relied. In the version of W.S. Merwin – published in Neruda's *Selected Poems* (1970), edited by Nathaniel Tarn – the lines are rendered as "I want / to do with you what spring does with the cherry trees" (27). Purdy's prepositions could be quibbles with Merwin's translation, or errors of transcription. I have taken the lines in Spanish from Tarn's edition (26).

39 The recherché first lines of "On Robert Frost" contain a vignette from
American literary history:
> Frost boasting at Amherst
> about springing Pound from the loony bin:
> "Archie couldn't do it!
> Hemingway couldn't do it!
> Williams couldn't do it!"
> – especially proud of that because
> he disliked Pound and felt noble
> about going to Eisenhower's Attorney
> General Herbert Brownell
> and managing to sublimate his dislike[.] (NSM 40)

Solecki noted that he was "unable to find the source of this quotation" (LCP 260). The unlikely origin is, I believe, *New York Jew* (1978), a memoir by Alfred Kazin. Purdy evidently borrowed liberally:

> My last day at Amherst was the last time I saw Frost. It was the spring of 1958 in the president's house; he was sitting back in a large armchair, smugly telling all and sundry how *he*, Robert Frost alone, had succeeded in getting Ezra Pound out of St. Elizabeth's [sic] Hospital in Washington. He disliked Pound, he disliked him more than ever, but he had done it. "Archie couldn't do it!" he boasted. "Hemingway couldn't do it!" But he had gone straight to Eisenhower's Attorney General, Herbert Brownell, and Brownell had been impressed by his avowal that Ezra Pound was not a danger to the United States. (234).

Kazin does not mention Williams in this passage, and "[']Williams couldn't do it!'" may be Purdy's invention (or error). Purdy may also have read Frost's *Selected Letters* (1964), in which Lawrance Thompson shows that "Archie" – Archibald MacLeish – was the crucial figure in the Pound affair, not the deluded and self-aggrandizing Frost (see Frost 563, 570–1, 575–7).

40 Solecki adds that the essay appeared in Lawrence's *Twilight in Italy* (1916), and that Purdy's poem contains three quotations from it (LCP 261).

41 Whenever limestone appears in Purdy's poetry – as in "Place of Fire" (*Sun.* 90; BR 293), "A Handful of Earth" (BA 151; BR 313), "Near Tofino, Vancouver Island" (SB 59; BR 339), "Menelaus and Helen" (PB 19; BR 356), "Gondwanaland" (PB 89; BR 386), and "Chac Mool at Chichen Itza" (NSM 21; BR 483) – Auden's "In Praise of Limestone" (1948) is a relevant point of comparison. See Solecki, LCP 134–5, 245, 253.

42 Purdy made poetic use of the nominal coincidence in "Lawrence to Laurence," from *The Woman on the Shore*. The image in the first lines – "On my workroom wall an original letter / from DHL" (WS 71; BR 471) – in turn suggests "On My Workroom Wall," which mentions Purdy's two photographs of Laurence (NSM 76; BR 499) and "[t]wo original Lawrence letters" (NSM 77;

BR 500). Purdy clung to obsessions: any poem could be revised, any image, idea, or icon recycled.

43 The late reference to "the terror of the night" in "In Mexico" (TP 113; BR 572) is anticipated by earlier passages in Purdy's remarkably patterned poetry. For example, see "Remains of an Indian Village" (PA 58; WG 120; BR 53), the version of "News Reports at Ameliasburg" included in *Being Alive* (BA 84; BR 127–8), and "Glacier Spell" (NSM 115; BR 518). If fires keep darkness at bay, glaciers are typically reminders of the world's inhospitality. In "News Reports at Ameliasburg," they also evoke prehistoric times (PA68 71; BA 85; BR 128).

44 On the poem's "low-comedy" mode, see Atwood, *Second* 99. "Silly": "Purdy can be banal, silly, cute, overly-rhetorical, irrelevant and corny. What then makes him one of Canada's finest, as he is?" (Atwood, *Second* 60). "Behind": see Atwood, *Second* 102.

45 On Purdy's use of the word "Neanderthal," see Djwa 58. The poem "Neanderthal," from *Naked with Summer in Your Mouth*, is another portrait of the poet as an archaic human.

46 On Purdy and the CBC, see McLeod 263, 265. On Grant, see Jones's instructive observation: Purdy's "pursuit of the past is distinctly less political and nationalistic than that of a Dennis Lee or a George Grant. It is less the reaction of a threatened cultural minority than the spontaneous reaction of the traditional lyric and elegiac poet, his identification with all things, his perennial *Ubi sunt?*" (37).

47 *Pace* Tracy Ware: "The most urgent task for Purdy criticism is to come to terms with Solecki" (127).

48 For comparable statements, see Guriel 21–3, 27, 30; Pollock 210–12; Starnino, *Lazy* 87; Starnino, *Lover's* 37, 89, 99, 118; and Wells 278, 291–5.

49 Solecki notes that "references or allusions to classical music are rare in Purdy's work" and asks "an unanswerable question – which work did Purdy have in mind" (LCP 250). The answer may be Beethoven's String Quartet no. 13 in B-flat Major (op. 130), the fifth movement of which ("Cavatina") is said, following the account of Karl Holz, to have brought the composer to tears (Chua 194–5).

50 Weingarten and Dean follow in the line of Priscila Uppal's nuanced discussion of Purdy's elegiac strain and cultural identity (177–80, 185–6). Apart from the poems in *North of Summer*, "The Tarahumara Women," from *Piling Blood*, is perhaps Purdy's definitive statement on shame and Indigenous peoples.

51 "Muliebrity" appears in "Uncle Fred on Côte des Neiges" (PA 12; see Jones 42 n3). In the 1968 *Poems for All the Annettes*, the poem is retitled "Uncle John on Côte des Neiges," and the "inkhorn word" receives an ironic aside: "look it up" (PA68 86). "Immelmann": the reference (see Jones 42 n3) is to "Complaint Lodged with L.C.B.O. by a Citizen in Upper Rumbelow" (CH 49–50; cf. "Complaint Lodged with L.C.B.O. by a Citizen of Upper Rumbelow," BR 69).

REFERENCES

Atwood, Margaret. *The Burgess Shale: The Canadian Writing Landscape of the 1960s*. Edmonton: University of Alberta Press/Canadian Literature Centre, 2017.
– *Second Words: Selected Critical Prose*. Toronto: House of Anansi Press, 1982.
– *Survival: A Thematic Guide to Canadian Literature*. Toronto: House of Anansi Press, 1972.
Auden, W.H. *Collected Poems*. Edited by Edward Mendelson. New York: Vintage–Random House, 1991.
Beardsley, Doug. "Reflections on a Dynamic Collaboration." In Lynch, Ganz, and Kealey, *Ivory Thought*, 221–6.
Birney, Earle. *David and Other Poems*. Toronto: Ryerson Press, 1942.
– *One Muddy Hand: Selected Poems*. Edited by Sam Solecki. Madeira Park, BC: Harbour Publishing, 2006.
Bowering, George. *Al Purdy*. Toronto: Copp Clark, 1970.
Brown, Russell. "Editor's Note." In *The Collected Poems of Al Purdy*, edited by Russell Brown, 396. Toronto: McClelland & Stewart, 1986.
The Canada Council Annual Report, 1961–62. Ottawa, 1962.
Chua, Daniel K.L. *The "Galitzin" Quartets of Beethoven: Opp. 127, 132, 130*. Princeton, NJ: Princeton University Press, 1995.
Coles, Don. "Review of *The Last Canadian Poet: An Essay on Al Purdy*, by Sam Solecki." *English Studies in Canada* 28, no. 3 (September 2002): 560–3.
Djwa, Sandra. "Al Purdy: Ivory Thots and the Last Romantic." In Lynch, Ganz, and Kealey, *Ivory Thought*, 51–62.
Douglas, Elizabeth Jane. "The Mechanics of Being Alive: Major Themes in the Poetry and Prose of Al Purdy." MA thesis, McMaster University, 1981.
Doyle, Mike. "Proteus at Roblin Lake." *Canadian Literature*, no. 61 (Summer 1974): 7–23.
Dragland, Stan. "Al Purdy's Poetry: Openings." In *Al Purdy: Essays on His Works*, edited by Linda Rogers, 15–57. Toronto: Guernica Editions, 2002.
Eliot, T.S. *Collected Poems, 1909–1962*. London: Faber & Faber, 1974.
– *Notes towards the Definition of Culture*. London: Faber & Faber, 1948.
Ferry, David, trans. *The Odes of Horace*. 1997. New York: Noonday–Farrar, Straus and Giroux, 1998.
Frost, Robert. *Selected Letters of Robert Frost*. Edited by Lawrance Thompson. New York: Holt, Rinehart and Winston, 1964.
Frye, Northrop. *Northrop Frye on Canada*. Edited by Jean O'Grady and David Staines. Vol. 12 of *Collected Works of Northrop Frye*. Toronto: University of Toronto Press, 2003.
Guriel, Jason. *The Pigheaded Soul: Essays and Reviews on Poetry and Culture*. Erin, ON: The Porcupine's Quill, 2013.

Heath, Tim. "'Buried bones and ornaments and stuff': Purdy's Reliquary Poetics." In Lynch, Ganz, and Kealey, *Ivory Thought*, 191–212.
Hofsess, John. "By the Time You Read This, I'll Be Dead." *Toronto Life*, April 2016: 60–8.
Irvine, Dean. "Beyond Forgetting: Editing Purdy] Purdy Editing." In Lynch, Ganz, and Kealey, *Ivory Thought*, 71–90.
Jones, D.G. "Al Purdy's Contemporary Pastoral." *Canadian Poetry: Studies, Documents, Reviews*, no. 10 (Spring–Summer 1982): 32–43.
Kazin, Alfred. *New York Jew*. New York: Knopf, 1978.
Keith, W.J. "Blight in the Bush Garden: Twenty Years of 'CanLit.'" *Essays on Canadian Writing*, no. 71 (Fall 2000): 71–8.
Kolodny, Annette. *In Search of First Contact: The Vikings of Vinland, the Peoples of the Dawnland, and the Anglo-American Anxiety of Discovery*. Durham, NC: Duke University Press, 2012.
Lalonde, Jeremy. "Song and Silence in Al Purdy's Family Elegies." In Lynch, Ganz, and Kealey, *Ivory Thought*, 173–90.
Larkin, Philip. *High Windows*. London: Faber & Faber, 1974.
Laurence, Margaret, and Jack McClelland. *Margaret Laurence and Jack McClelland, Letters*. Edited by Laura K. Davis and Linda M. Morra. Edmonton: University of Alberta Press, 2018.
Lawrence, D.H. *Apocalypse and the Writings on Revelation*. Edited by Mara Kalnis. Cambridge: Cambridge University Press, 1980.
– *The Poems*. Edited by Christopher Pollnitz. 3 vols. Cambridge: Cambridge University Press, 2013–18.
Lee, Dennis. "The Poetry of Al Purdy: An Afterword." In *The Collected Poems of Al Purdy*, edited by Russell Brown, 371–91. Toronto: McClelland & Stewart, 1986.
Lynch, Gerald, Shoshannah Ganz, and Josephene T.M. Kealey, eds. *The Ivory Thought: Essays on Al Purdy*. Ottawa: University of Ottawa Press, 2008.
MacLaren, I.S. "Arctic Al: Purdy's Humanist Vision of the North." In Lynch, Ganz, and Kealey, *Ivory Thought*, 119–36.
Mandel, E.W. "Turning New Leaves (1)." *Canadian Forum*, March 1963: 278–80.
McLeod, Katherine. "Radio Poetics: Publishing and Poetry on CBC's *Anthology*." In *Public Poetics: Critical Issues in Canadian Poetry and Poetics*, edited by Bart Vautour, Erin Wunker, Travis V. Mason, and Christl Verduyn, 253–69. Waterloo, ON: Wilfrid Laurier University Press, 2015.
Mount, Nick. *Arrival: The Story of CanLit*. Toronto: House of Anansi Press, 2017.
Neruda, Pablo. *Selected Poems*. Edited by Nathaniel Tarn. London: Jonathan Cape, 1970.
New, William H. "Poet and Person." Review of *Al Purdy*, by George Bowering, and *Margaret Avison*, by Ernest Redekop. *Canadian Literature*, no. 54 (Autumn 1972): 90–2.

Pollock, James. *You Are Here: Essays on the Art of Poetry in Canada*. Erin, ON: The Porcupine's Quill, 2012.

Pratt, E.J. *Selected Poems*. Edited by Sandra Djwa, W.J. Keith, and Zailig Pollock. Toronto: University of Toronto Press, 2000.

Purdy, Al. "After the Rats." *Canadian Forum*, June 1959: 60.

– *Beyond Remembering: The Collected Poems of Al Purdy*. Edited by Al Purdy and Sam Solecki. Madeira Park, BC: Harbour Publishing, 2000.

– "Biography *(To Leo Szilard)*." *Canadian Forum*, April 1962: 16.

– *The Blur in Between: Poems, 1960–61*. Toronto: Emblem Books, 1962.

– *The Cariboo Horses*. Toronto: McClelland & Stewart, 1965.

– "Collecting the Square Root of Minus One (or: Stone Blood Makes Thirsty Vampires)." *Canadian Forum*, February 1962: 255.

– *The Crafte So Longe to Lerne*. Toronto: Ryerson Press, 1959.

– "Critique." *Canadian Forum*, January 1963: 240.

– "Driftwood Logs." *Canadian Forum*, November 1959: 192.

– *The Enchanted Echo*. Vancouver: Clarke and Stuart, 1944.

– "For Norma in Lieu of an Orgasm." *Canadian Forum*, February 1962: 254.

– "From the Chin P'ing Mei." *Canadian Forum*, October 1959: 155.

– "Leonard Cohen: A Personal Look." *Canadian Literature*, no. 23 (Winter 1965): 7–16.

– *Love in a Burning Building*. Toronto: McClelland & Stewart, 1970.

– "The Machines." *Canadian Forum*, July 1962: 91.

– "My Grandfather Talking – 30 Years Ago." *Canadian Forum*, January 1963: 240.

– *Naked with Summer in Your Mouth*. Toronto: McClelland & Stewart, 1994.

– *North of Summer: Poems from Baffin Island*. Toronto: McClelland & Stewart, 1967.

– "Olympic Room." *Canadian Forum*, May 1959: 41.

– *Piling Blood*. Toronto: McClelland & Stewart, 1984.

– "Poem for One of the Annettes." *Canadian Forum*, February 1962: 254.

– *Poems for All the Annettes*. Toronto: Contact Press, 1962.

– *The Poems of Al Purdy*. Toronto: McClelland & Stewart, 1976.

– *Pressed on Sand*. Toronto: Ryerson Press, 1955.

– "Rain Poem?" *Canadian Forum*, April 1959: 10.

– *Reaching for the Beaufort Sea: An Autobiography*. Edited by Alex Widen. Madeira Park, BC: Harbour Publishing, 1993.

– *Rooms for Rent in the Outer Planets: Selected Poems, 1962–1996*. Edited by Al Purdy and Sam Solecki. Madeira Park, BC: Harbour Publishing, 1996.

– *Selected Poems*. Toronto: McClelland & Stewart, 1972.

– *Sex and Death*. Toronto: McClelland & Stewart, 1973.

– *Starting from Ameliasburgh: The Collected Prose of Al Purdy*. Edited by Sam Solecki. Madeira Park, BC: Harbour Publishing, 1995.

- *To Paris Never Again*. Madeira Park, BC: Harbour Publishing, 1997.
- "Waiting for an Old Woman to Die." *Canadian Forum*, November 1959: 182.
- "The Widower." *Canadian Forum*, February 1962: 254.
- *Wild Grape Wine*. Toronto: McClelland & Stewart, 1968.
- *The Woman on the Shore*. Toronto: McClelland & Stewart, 1990.
- *Yours, Al: The Collected Letters of Al Purdy*. Edited by Sam Solecki. Madeira Park, BC: Harbour Publishing, 2004.

Richler, Mordecai. *The Incomparable Atuk*. London: André Deutsch, 1963.

Silverberg, Mark. "The Can(adi)onization of Al Purdy." *Essays on Canadian Writing*, no. 70 (Spring 2000): 226–51.

Solecki, Sam. *The Last Canadian Poet: An Essay on Al Purdy*. Toronto: University of Toronto Press, 1999.

- "Materials for a Biography of Al Purdy." In Lynch, Ganz, and Kealey, *Ivory Thought*, 13–30.

Starnino, Carmine. *Lazy Bastardism: Essays and Reviews on Contemporary Poetry*. Kentville, NS: Gaspereau, 2012.

- *A Lover's Quarrel: Essays and Reviews*. Erin, ON: The Porcupine's Quill, 2004.

Stevens, Peter. "In the Raw: The Poetry of A.W. Purdy." *Canadian Literature*, no. 28 (Spring 1966): 22–30.

- "The Road to the Cariboo Horses." *Essays on Canadian Writing*, no. 49 (Summer 1993): 32–41.

Trehearne, Brian. "Canadian Modernism at the Present Time." *Modernist Cultures* 13, no. 4 (Winter 2018): 465–95.

Uppal, Priscila. *We Are What We Mourn: The Contemporary English-Canadian Elegy*. Montreal and Kingston: McGill-Queen's University Press, 2009.

van der Marel, L. Camille. "Unsettling *North of Summer*: Anxieties of Ownership in the Politics and Poetics of the Canadian North." *ARIEL: A Review of International English Literature* 44, no. 4 (October 2013): 13–47.

Ware, Tracy. "Sincerely Al Purdy." Review of *Yours, Al: The Collected Letters of Al Purdy*, edited by Sam Solecki. *Canadian Poetry: Studies, Documents, Reviews*, no. 58 (Spring–Summer 2006): 123–7.

Wells, Zachariah. *Career Limiting Moves: Interviews, Rejoinders, Essays, Reviews*. Windsor, ON: Biblioasis, 2013.

White, Howard, and Emma Skagen, eds. *Beyond Forgetting: Celebrating 100 Years of Al Purdy*. Madeira Park, BC: Harbour Publishing, 2018.

Wigod, Rebecca. *He Speaks Volumes: A Biography of George Bowering*. Vancouver: Talonbooks, 2018.

Wilson, Jean. "Jean and Al's Sense of Place and History." *BC Studies*, no. 131 (Autumn 2001): 59–62.

- "The Sense of Place and History in the Poetry of A.W. Purdy." MA thesis, University of Saskatchewan, 1968.

PART ONE

Transcendence, Love, and the Persistent Legend: In Search of Al Purdy

1

The Man Who Lived beyond Himself: Transcendental Al

Doug Beardsley

Al Purdy disliked words like *love* and *inspiration*. I tremble to think of how he would feel about the word *transcendence*.

He was a spokesman for his country and for the common man in Canada, though there was not one thing common about him. Al wrote in a colloquial tone with long unfolding lines that ran on like the Canadian prairies. He sought to embody the country he was born into and to give voice to what it meant to be Canadian. And he succeeded; oh, how he succeeded. On the surface he seemed a simple man – in the best sense. Internally, however, he was a complex cauldron of unrelieved energy, living a deep inner life that constantly sought the one right word from among the zillion possibilities that presented themselves in his incredible computer-mind.

As we grew together over a quarter century, from first meeting, through a prolonged, guarded acquaintanceship, to "cordial feeling" (a favourite phrase of Al's), to friend, dear friend, and, finally, confidant, Al revealed more and more of his early youth, what he called his "shadowy days on both sides of now." It turned out we had much in common.

Al's father was United Empire Loyalist, his mother an observant Christian. Over a half-century later, Al still hadn't forgotten the framed plaque near the front door: "Christ is the Master of this house, the unseen Listener of every conversation." It made Al forever fearful of God, because "He could see what I was doing under the quilts." Both Al and I turned away from such a strict upbringing, but we both knew some semblance of that religious heritage never left you. You were shaped by it, even as you rejected it. Eurithe, Al's wife, used the word *spiritual*: "Yes," she said, "Al was spiritual – he wouldn't have liked it said of himself, but he was." Born in 1918, Al was a modern poet who had grown out of the romantic tradition: Wordsworth's "Tintern Abbey" and Coleridge's "Dejection: An Ode" echoed in his shadowed mind. He was well aware of the transfiguring power of the imagination. And of the romantics' pursuit of transcendence. He was also cognizant of the fact that the religious imagination is poetic. Intuitively, he recognized the power of the symbolic imagination and the value of "looking up in order to be safe in looking down" (Blackmur 320).

Five months after Al died, Howie White published *Beyond Remembering*, a collection edited by Sam Solecki that contained all the poems that Al wanted to be remembered by. Harbour Publishing held a book launch in Victoria and invited poets to read what they felt were Al's best poems. I read "The Darkness" (BR 346–8), but in selecting that poem I read through the entire six-hundred-plus pages. It was and is a valuable collection, not least because it grouped the poems by decade, and in chronological order.

I had long considered "The Darkness," in its various versions, to be one of Al's most contemplative poems, with "Orchestra," "The Dead Poet," "Home Thoughts," the sadly neglected "Untitled" from *To Paris Never Again* (1997), and the well-anthologized "The Country North of Belleville" following closely behind. Irving Layton often commented that if a poet wrote half a dozen excellent poems, posterity would judge him or her to be a major poet. Al felt that Irving was being far too strict and exclaimed that one or two great poems would qualify the poet for the highest status. In fact, he held to a personal standard of five or six great poems per Immortal Bard.

There are days when I return to these half-dozen poems of Al's and a few others and am amazed at the effect they continue to have on me. At the end of a quarter-hour rereading, I feel altered, my senses heightened. I am more aware of my immediate surroundings. The world around me has changed; I have become something more than I was before. Is it possible that a reader, viewer, or listener takes on some of the attributes of great art after experiencing it? Each time I read Al, I feel more fully human, more alive. He was full of wonder at the world.

In May 2006, the University of Ottawa held a symposium on Al's work entitled "The Ivory Thought" and published a selection of essays from that conference two years later. Eurithe was the honoured guest, and I was one of the presenters (see Beardsley 221–6). After the symposium, she urged me to follow her down to Belleville and stay at the A-frame for a night or two "in order to complete the decade-long circle of friendship" that Al and I experienced.

What I could see of the A-frame was as I had pictured it, but the entrance was barely discernible amid the overgrown firs and occasional spruce that shrouded the front deck. Here, everything went straight up. In contrast, the backyard grass was cut like a lawn, with Roblin Lake only a few hundred yards beyond. This horizontal landscape unfolded like a Whitmanesque long line. I often sat in Al's plastic white chair beneath the occasional maple and spruce, contemplating the juxtaposition of the towering church spire with the flat landscape – the spire across the water that Al had immortalized in "Wilderness Gothic." The front of the cottage seemed to suggest the dark inner side of Al, while the back seemed designed to bring forth his more meditative, pastoral sensibility. Just before dusk I entered Al's study. It was a tiny, untidy room, with a cot at one end and a single chair and desk at the other. It was only when I went to pull the blinds to ensure a good night's sleep that it came to me.

There were no windows. I could not close "the dark velvet curtains" ("The Darkness," *BR* 348): there were none. The small bed faced a brown wooden bookcase half-filled with *National Geographic* and suspense novels. Above the simple cot there was a magazine photograph of Margaret Laurence, a New Canadian Library poster advertising "the best of Canadian reading," one small part of which included a cover photo of Al's novel, *A Splinter in the Heart* (1990), and an out-of-date calendar depicting a fishing vessel, lighthouse, and harbour to remind Al of his West Coast home.

Had there once been a window over the desk that had been boarded up with this white-grained panelling? I found no evidence. The panelling above the large, rectangular, heavily battered aluminum desk served as a giant bulletin board, pincushioned with cut-outs that harboured a pantheon of gods and goddesses, including Gabrielle Roy, the aforementioned Ms Laurence, Harold Ballard, Al's sister-in-law, Don Coles, Margaret Atwood, Tiff Findley, Gary Snyder, Czesław Miłosz, William Everson, Archibald MacLeish, D.H. Lawrence, Rudyard Kipling (whose verse Al would recite without asking), and, of course, Eurithe. Well, I was certain of what had brought me to this place. But where was I?

In the middle of the night I awoke on Al's damp cot, convinced I had gone mad. I was in Al's mind. Inside his brain. In that spacious internal place of absolute isolation where all the words in the world were safely stowed. Al had – consciously or unconsciously – designed his study to mirror the interior of his brain. I was in the place where he went to write.

Al had a theory that "when you write a line, there are hundreds or thousands of thoughts in your mind, they form like lightning in your head, and you must choose one out of all these. And you do. But later, you are dissatisfied. And you must choose another. You go through the same process all over again." Sometimes it seemed as if he was travelling inside language itself, passing through the veil to the deep inner world where all experience was stored. It felt as if I could see Al going deep into his mind to attempt to recover the unremembered, unlimited possibilities. His apparently limitless universe of words and accumulated images never ceases to amaze me. In his critical study of Coleridge's imagination, *The Road to Xanadu*, John Livingston Lowes introduced the concept of a "plastic and energetic function of memory," from which, "by some alchemical process of association, selection, [and] accretion," experience is shared and authored forth (Whalley 64). I should have liked to have seen Al's brain, to have asked a brain anatomist to extract it, his cerebral cortex (was Al *in* there?), to float it in formalin to reveal his huge brain-library of twenty million volumes, its hundred million neurons, for the benefit of science, and for those university professors eager to discover the formula for writing poetry so they could do it themselves. Walt Whitman once boasted that "the poet's brain is the ultimate brain" and had his donated to the American Anthropometric Society (qtd. in Sheppard 191). After one of our morning sessions, Al remarked that the end result of having pushed past the grey-white matter that impeded his poetic talent left him, rather than exhausted, with "a sort of exalted feeling." The sheer satisfaction of writing defined his life.

It was not possible to be around Al for any length of time and not be concerned about the nature of his poetic imagination. I was party to seeing Al at work on many occasions during our collaborations on Lawrence and John Donne, and on our proposed "translation" of *The Epic of Gilgamesh*. Robert Lowell had named such translations "imitations"; Al preferred the word "transliterations," but whatever they were, we agreed that I would begin by taking a line and offering up a personal contemporary prose translation.[1] (For *The Epic of Gilgamesh*, or "Gil," as Al loved to call it, I made use of the N.K. Sandars Penguin prose translation.[2]) I was then instructed to fall silent while Al worked on creating a parallel poetic line. We sat facing each other in comfortable armchairs in Al's living room in Sidney, and I watched Al and waited. And waited. And waited, as the silence extended itself, sometimes for a quarter of an hour – or more. Often, I was certain he had fallen asleep. Desperate for some human contact, I reshaped the prose line I'd given him and blurted out a variation. The dark eyes opened, and Al would bellow the worst insult he could think of: "Hey, Professor, how do you expect me to create when you're always interrupting?!" Silence was once more the order of the day, a quietude in which to reach the inexpressible, until it would finally be broken by that hoarse, honking voice announcing a line of belated beauty. In contrast, I can never forget his conscious cry of anguish the day I pointed out in a review of mine that McClelland & Stewart's edition of *The Collected Poems* (1986), edited by Russell Brown, had inadvertently omitted the last three lines of "The Darkness."[3]

The "zoom perspectives" in "The Darkness," as Dennis Lee named them (383), are typical of Al's most evocative writing. He moves from that particular porcupine – the poem, grounded in the particulars of this world – to all mythic, totemic animals, back to the particular "I" or "eye" and out to the cosmological or universal, then back again to the personal, bobbing and weaving, in and out – all in the first twenty-seven lines. But it is the "muscle memory" of it all, the apparent ease, the effortless naturalness of the intersections (intercessions) that take the breath away. "The Darkness" flows at a level above and beyond the words of the poem. It's as if another line is being imagined between the lines, creating a resonance over and above the written words, the poet like a jazz musician who plays the melody, then improvises on it, thereby creating music, a sound between the two lines creating a middle space between the spirit and the heart, between the invisible and the visible worlds, evoking the ineffable. In sum, a sacramental poetry.

Then there are the ironic self-deflations ("[t]hen I laugh"), the metaphysical unease ("some lost kind of coherence"), and the final, inevitable movement upward ("Look down on me / spirit of everyplace") contrasted with the resulting self-deflation of the modern poet ("even tho I am of little importance") who waits in this world

> until the dark velvet curtains
> are drawn and the scrap of darkness
> I clutched in my hand
> has changed to light[.]

This process, which Stan Dragland referred to as the poet's quest for "a lost kind of coherence" (17) and which Dennis Lee called Al's "*mysterium tremendum*," taking the phrase from Rudolph Otto ("Poetry" 385), owes much to Mircea Eliade, whose *Cosmos and History: The Myth of the Eternal Return* was a seminal influence on Al's evolution from a romantic versifier to modern poet. A.M. Klein and E.J. Pratt were about in the mid-1950s and, of course, Bliss Carman, but Al was more drawn to the Georgian versifiers like Kipling, John Masefield, A.E. Housman, Walter de la Mare, and Alfred Noyes. From *The Enchanted Echo* of 1944 to *The Blur in Between* of 1962, Al realized that something was amiss. In the mid-1950s, in the A-frame at Ameliasburgh, Al went into a hibernation that lasted over a year. He read the classics, beginning with *Gilgamesh* and going on to Homer, Ovid, Horace, Virgil, and *Beowulf*. In addition, Al spent the summer of 1956 sleeping on Layton's living-room floor, drinking in everything Irving had to offer. At that time, as he wrote in "Letter to Morley Callaghan" (ws 75–7), Al saw Irving as a kind of Hemingway figure, Louis Dudek as Robert McAlmon, and "Montreal as the City of Light." For the man from Ameliasburgh, Montreal was a movable, mini-Parisian feast.

Did Layton recommend Eliade, his fellow Romanian? Whatever the case, the influential religious scholar's basic idea that the cosmos and society are periodically regenerated became sacred text to Al. Furthermore, Eliade gave Al the confidence that, by writing poetry, he was capable of creating "a 'sacred history' preserved and transmitted through myths" (viii). According to Eliade, all that was "'revealed' at the beginning of time" had a "transcendental origin" (xxviii). If you gave what you experienced *intrinsic* value and made it real, that reality would transcend itself by the act of poetry, and your poem would become "a micro-cosmic imitation of the Creation" (11). Al's "thirst for being" (11) became unquenchable: whenever and wherever he walked was "the centre of the Earth" (17). In his best poems, Al "lived in harmony with the cosmic rhythms" (95). He became what he appeared to be: "a cosmic giant" (20).

In his essay "On the Relation of Analytical Psychology to Poetry," Carl Jung describes the poet as a force of nature, "wholly at one with the creative process" (72). Jung sees this poetic state of being as a "suprapersonal" process, in which artistic creation is a mystery (75). "Perhaps," he wonders, "art has no 'meaning' ... Perhaps it is like nature, which simply *is* and 'means' nothing beyond that" (77). He goes on to describe the poet as, quite simply, apathetic to conscious interest and activity, so that there occurs "a regressive development of the conscious functions ... [T]he instinctual side of the personality prevails over the ethical, the infantile over the mature, the unadapted over the adapted" (79), resulting in "a ruthless passion for creation" (102). Al was certainly devoted to his art, and gave it all his energy. Accessing this deep inner self gave Al a voice that was greater than his own – if that were possible. However, the result was that it "drain[ed] him of his humanity" (102). The moment Al attended to a poem, he left the land of the living for the world of the imagination. There was a cost; others paid it.

Al created a pantheon of poets, a tiny temple that was a memorial to those he considered truly great. Lawrence, of course, was in it, and also Layton, who first introduced Al to D.H.L. It was a delight to be around Al when he enthused about Lawrence the poet. He often referred to the Englishman not simply as a great writer but as a prophet and a priest. Al's favourite Lawrentian image was of the she-goat up in an almond tree, "looking down like some hairy horrid God the Father in a William Blake imagination" ("She-Goat," *Poems* 1.337). If, in conversation, Al sensed an opportunity to let this line loose, he would let it go with his patented surreal honk and hoot in raucous celebration of Lawrence's esoteric flight.

A third, rarely mentioned, influence was James Dickey, whose *Buckdancer's Choice* came out in 1965, the same year as *The Cariboo Horses*. Dickey's first collected poems appeared two years later.[4] One long evening dinner at Al's with Dennis Lee centred on Dickey. Al spoke passionately about the American's open, unfolding poetry – what Dickey dismissed as his "country surrealism." But it was much more than that. Al seldom attempted Dickey's split-line technique, but he was greatly influenced by how Dickey's poetic voice, the characteristic I (eye) of the poem, was transfigured into a visionary witness and, from that otherworldly place or space, brought together the particular and the universal, the human and nature, the personal and the cosmological, into a transcendent wholeness. Sitting cross-table, Dennis and I could only bobble our heads in agreement.

Al was a pure, intuitive poet. In his seminal essay "Poetry and Unknowing," in *Body Music* (1998), Lee defines the word "intuition" as meaning that "you're engaging with something that to all intents and purposes isn't there" (180). Al felt comfortable in such surroundings. For him, writing poetry was the only way of knowing. Dennis has a line in his book-length poem *Riffs* that reads: "if I deny the luminous presence – / something goes numb at the core" (33).

Yet in our Age of Death (think of words like *Holocaust*, *Hiroshima*, *Gulag*) it has become fashionable to defy transcendence, as it is to deny words like *excellence* or *canon*. Or *truth*, *goodness*, and *beauty*, for that matter, as understandable as this may be, given our history. All is relative in our secular world, everything held to be simply subjective, a matter of opinion. Such reductionist secularism and rational scientism may embrace momentary *values*, but not *virtues*. We no longer hold to *beliefs*, but rather *ideas*, ideas that can alter over time – like societies and cultures. As Anthony Esolen put it in a recent essay, "our schools have largely abandoned poetry in general and English literature written before yesterday afternoon."

In an essay entitled "A Place for Transcendence?" (we must forgive the question mark), Charles Taylor offers several reasons why transcendence has lost its, well, transcendence. We can no longer entertain Coleridge's "willing suspension of disbelief." According to John Milbank, in the modern world, transcendence has been replaced by the immanence of the human mind, "the cosmos by the universe," as Taylor writes (5). Taylor sees that our world, once "bathed in light," is now "lost in darkness" (6), the Christian religion seen as "a black box" (1). In our quest for "an exclusive humanism," we have reduced the transcendent to mere social relation (see Taylor 4–6). Christianity, as C.S. Lewis wrote, is "a discarded image" (see Dart).

But Taylor finds hope in the love that we are capable of showing to other human beings, in our eternal quest for meaning, and in the search for "new forms of spirituality" (9). As the noted philosopher makes clear, we transcend ourselves by unifying acts of love. However, "other human beings" did not take the place of Al's devotion to the craft and sullen art. I think of the work of spiritual poets who, through myth and metaphor, follow in the footprints of Donne, Gerard Manley Hopkins, Rainer Maria Rilke, T.S. Eliot, Lawrence, Lowell, Kenneth Rexroth, and Everson, such as Al's Canadian contemporaries: Dennis Lee, Don McKay, Robert Bringhurst, Tim Lilburn, and Barbara Colebrook Peace, among others, poets who are circling toward new pathways and "places where transcendence can reappear" (9).

We limit ourselves – and our appreciation of Purdy's poetry – when we turn our attention to Al's most popular pieces, like "Home-Made Beer," "At the Quinte Hotel," and "Birdwatching at the Equator." These serve as a necessary and welcome introduction, but they are a way into the poet rather than his poetry. In contrast, Al's transcendent poems offer the discerning reader compassion and hope, a liberation of the helping spirit, and a questing sense of meaningfulness. Beyond remembering, there will always be rooms for rent in the outer planets.

Perhaps Monsignor Peter Wilkinson, in commenting on Al as a transcendent poet, put it best:

> People don't have to be religious to create transcendent art. I think of Rowland Hilder, an English landscape artist who had a natural talent for drawing and watercolour painting and whose best work achieves transcendence. Listen to Ralph Vaughan Williams' Fifth Symphony. From what you tell me, as a young boy Al saw God as a watchful demon and so he can have no relation to God. However, you would be searching for God if you were searching for truth, goodness, and beauty. It may be a kind of *via negativa*, a default exploration only because he can't explain what it is he experiences – for, like all of us, he cannot express the inexpressible. Like poets who attain a higher, imaginative state, Al is attempting to change chaos into cosmos by creating metaphors that bear truth, that lead to a contemplation well beyond the rational order of things, a transcendence that offers a sense of

inner fullness and wholeness. Indeed, in this condition you could move from beauty to goodness to truth. And poetry might well get you there in the end.

The Stone Bird, published on New Year's Day, 1981, opens with "The Dead Poet," Al's audacious attempt to illuminate the source "where the words come from," that place "when everything becomes one thing" (BR 324, 323). The yellowed cover image comes from Al's mid-1960s Arctic sojourn. It depicts a bird carved by Tudlik, a Cape Dorset artist. The bird is often a transformative messenger in flight between two worlds. It flies up to the moon, to the spirit realm. The poem "Moonspell" begins: "I have forgotten English / in order to talk to pelicans / plunging into tomorrow" (BR 337). There is no denying that Al had a hawk-like look about him when he was writing.

Tradition has it that the initial poem is the best in the book, while the final poem offers an indication of what the unforeseen future may conjure up. The earthly landscape travelled by *The Stone Bird* is vast: in Part One, the poet is in Mexico and the Galápagos, with occasional shifts to Spain, Italy, and Uzbekistan. Part Two brings him closer to home: Hastings County, Ameliasburgh, Vancouver Island, the poems written "in the ovens of creation" ("Bestiary," BR 328), in "that far darkness / another kind of light" ("Moonspell," BR 338). And the poem immediately before "The Darkness" ends "in the disposable darkness / where I await my discoverer" ("Mantis," BR 352).

The last line of the last poem Al wished to be remembered by in *Beyond Remembering*, "Her Gates Both East and West," has the aging poet "looking outward into the night sky" (BR 591). I'd like to know how he reached beyond himself, how he imagined death. Some of his last poems have the quality of prayer: they contain repeated references to the wobbling spirit, the "calendar Christ," "the Apostle Paul," a god, the god, (Lawrence's) "million names of God."[5] Words and phrases such as these resonate like leitmotifs throughout Al's most numinous work. And he would repeat the line "I didn't know his God," from Lawrence's poem "Fish," whenever and wherever he could work it into the conversation.[6]

You can run away from something and, unconsciously, still be seeking it. At best, Purdy attained the transcendent realm but didn't understand the truth of where he was. At worst, he was a healthy skeptic. Try as he might to hide it from himself, he could never shake his religious foundation. Many of us can't. It haunts us still, as it haunted Al. The more he tried to free himself from his religious upbringing, the more he wrote out of it. For Al, God was a name for something he couldn't explain. I believe that "The Darkness" and the other epiphanies I have highlighted in this essay constitute an open-hearted search for a state of permanence and grace, the "eternal *now*" as Dennis Lee says ("Poetry" 384). They constitute a sphere of the sacred, a circle of deep inner mystery. In "In the Snow," Purdy muses: "I wonder if that footfall / outside my door might be god" (*SB* 71). Al was doing nothing less than waiting on God – even though he would deny it. His transcendent light shines in "The Darkness."

NOTES

1 See Robert Lowell, *Imitations* (New York: Farrar, Straus, and Cudahy, 1961).
2 N.K. Sandars, *The Epic of Gilgamesh: An English Version with an Introduction* (1960; New York: Penguin, 1972).
3 See *SB* 83–4; *CP* 277–8; *BR* 346–8.
4 James Dickey, *Poems, 1957–1967* (1967).
5 "wobbling": "when the spirit seen by no human / makes its presence known / and I can't describe its 'wobble'" ("Untitled," *BR* 536). "calendar Christ": "On the Death of F.R. Scott" (*BR* 462). "Apostle Paul": "Transvestite" (*BR* 575). "million names of God": "D.H. Lawrence at Lake Chapala" (*BR* 328).
6 "I didn't know his God, / I didn't know his God. // Which is perhaps the last admission that life has to wring out of us" (Lawrence, *Poems* 1.292).

REFERENCES

Beardsley, Doug. "Reflections on a Dynamic Collaboration." In *The Ivory Thought: Essays on Al Purdy*, edited by Gerald Lynch, Shoshannah Ganz, and Josephene T.M. Kealey, 221–6. Ottawa: University of Ottawa Press, 2008.
Blackmur, R.P. "Humanism and Symbolic Imagination: Notes on Re-reading Irving Babbitt." *Southern Review* 7, no. 2 (Autumn 1941): 309–26.
Dart, Ron. *White Gulls & Wilds Birds: Essays on C.S. Lewis, Inklings and Friends & Thomas Merton*. Abbotsford, BC: St Macrina Press, 2015.
Dragland, Stan. "Al Purdy's Poetic Openings." In *Al Purdy: Essays on His Works*, edited by Linda Rogers, 15–57. Toronto: Guernica Editions, 2002.
Eliade, Mircea. *Cosmos and History: The Myth of the Eternal Return*. Translated by Willard R. Trask. Princeton, NJ: Princeton University Press, 1959.
Esolen, Anthony. "Where Is the Religious Instruction?" *The Catholic Thing*, 30 January 2017, https://www.thecatholicthing.org/2017/01/30/where-is-the-religious-instruction/.
Jung, C.G. *The Spirit in Man, Art, and Literature*. New York: Pantheon, 1978.

Lawrence, D.H. *The Poems*. Edited by Christopher Pollnitz. 3 vols. Cambridge: Cambridge University Press, 2013–18.
Lee, Dennis. "The Poetry of Al Purdy: An Afterword." In *The Collected Poems of Al Purdy*, edited by Russell Brown, 371–91. Toronto: McClelland & Stewart, 1986.
– "Poetry and Unknowing." In *Body Music*, by Dennis Lee, 179–96. Toronto: House of Anansi Press, 1998.
– *Riffs*. London, ON: Brick Books, 1993.
Milbank, John. "Sublimity: The Modern Transcendent." In Schwartz, *Transcendence*, 207–30.
Purdy, Al. *Beyond Remembering: The Collected Poems of Al Purdy*. Edited by Al Purdy and Sam Solecki. Madeira Park, BC: Harbour Publishing, 2000.
– *The Collected Poems of Al Purdy*. Edited by Russell Brown. Toronto: McClelland & Stewart, 1986.
– *The Stone Bird*. Toronto: McClelland & Stewart, 1981.
– *The Woman on the Shore*. Toronto: McClelland & Stewart, 1990.
Schwartz, Regina, ed. *Transcendence: Philosophy, Literature, and Theology Approach the Beyond*. New York: Routledge, 2004.
Sheppard, Christian. "Walt Whitman's Mystic Deliria." In Schwartz, *Transcendence*, 191–206.
Taylor, Charles. "A Place for Transcendence?" Translated from the French by Damian Treffs. In Schwartz, *Transcendence*, 1–10.
Whalley, George. *Poetic Process*. London: Routledge, 1953.
Wilkinson, Monsignor Peter. Personal interview. 26 August 2016.

2

His Muses, *a mensa et toro*

Linda Rogers

Damn, he was diagnosed at eighty, when he had already decided he'd outlived the illnesses that had taken friends: cancer, heart disease, and despair. He had given up his cigarettes and cigars for slivers of the true cross, the ubiquitous toothpicks he held onto like a child way past the age limit for sucking his thumb. And this is appropriate. Alfred Wellington Purdy was always a boy, his mother's boy, the only, his prior womb-mate, like that of Elvis, another famous singer of his generation, having failed to survive the first ride to the light. In "The Dead Poet," he wrote:

> I was altered in the placenta
> by the dead brother before me
> who built a place in the womb
> knowing I was coming:
> he wrote words on the walls of flesh
> painting a woman inside a woman
> whispering a faint lullaby
> that sings in my blind heart still[.] (BR 323)

Mother, the stern Ontario church lady he lost on a shopping trip and found again thanks to amazing grace, was his first muse. But infancy is the shortest narrative arc. It wasn't long before Al gave up on his childish things, with prayer, the language of his childhood, among them, and moved on to poetry, never really admitting there might be no difference, that the angel messengers are as happy to transport poetic messages and imprecations as they are requests for grace. In "At Roblin Lake," he wrote:

> This tangential backyard universe
> I inhabit with sidereal aplomb,
> tho troubled with midnight debate
> by frog theologians, bogged
> down in dialectics and original
> sin of discursiveness
> (the god of boredom at one remove,
> discreetly subsidized on wooden plates) –[.] (BR 31)

Although Purdy physically left his holy mother, she retained the brain space taken up by first love, his first passage to the light, and never shared because he still needed all of her, all the attention, all the affection of his phenomenal angel. This first muse space he defended jealously. He was the alpha. The prior womb-death of his only sibling was not infanticide, but that is what it amounted to in Al's metaphorical journey. All his life, he killed his darlings and required personal angels to carry him off the battlefield. It is a history of cruel separation, his mother being first: "inept christian that she was, / bumbling among the granite colossi / searching for her redeemer" ("Evergreen Cemetery," BR 48).

In "On Being Human," Purdy describes the pain of separation, when he betrayed his first mother for his new goddess. This is atonement: "but I remember those last words / list them first / among the things I'm ashamed of" (BR 508). In the home of repair, the library where he was a monk in his singular devotion, poetry replaced the parables and homilies of his boyhood. The original model was Bliss Carman, from whom he borrowed good and bad habits, anachronistic prosody, the music he began to fill with awesome breath, the stamina of an articulate wonderer, and the muse, still a woman, Mother Nature.

"Make me over, mother April, / When the sap begins to stir!" Those lines from Carman's "Spring Song," much parodied, rang true for the country boy who had loved and then refused plainsong, his mother's church language, and was searching for his own voice, just as he was coming to sexual maturity. Poetry was his new mother, his goddess, his lover, and his muse. How many times did the greater poet repeat Carman's supplications to the muse they shared? That would be a number in the same range as slivers from the true cross that he held between his teeth:

> Only make me over, April,
> When the sap begins to stir!
> Make me man or make me woman,
> Make me oaf or ape or human,

> Cup of flower or cone of fir;
> Make me anything but neuter
> When the sap begins to stir!

The comforts of home left behind, the poet, part oaf, part human, looking for his personal songline, empirical evidence of his cultural history and geophysical entitlement, began the great walkabout that ended only when he did, every piece of it described in the arioso, the operatic language of a man with a great stride and even greater breath, until, ironically, that breath was stolen by one of his bad habits, a false bride that had satisfied his oral need.

There were many brides, many "soft fermenting syllables / in the brain's hall closet," invoked in "Say the Names," his last great poem, which is a conflation of all the feminine parts, from Tulameen to Similkameen, he had touched over decades of wandering, alone and in the company of his virtual wife (see BR 579). Eurithe rode bitch across the continents of his imagination, always sitting behind, serving her husband and a greater muse, the woman who lay in the king-sized bedrock of the Canadian Shield and beyond. From "Where the Moment Is": "Certainly you are the world / I am not done with, / until I dispense with words –" (BR 27–8).

In visual terms, Purdy was poetry's Group of Seven, his gestalt a singing line that linked geographical past to present, his language as clear as glacial water, deliberately clear because the self-avowed autodidact was fervently anti-intellectual. He was apparently a plain man who hid his baroque intelligence. Because of this simple(ton) mask, the mask of the guy who drank beer from the bottle and got in brawls, he was a better poet than prose writer. In his fiction and literary writing, he affected an artificial populist tone that never resonated as authentic. Al was too well informed to pass as the gee-shucks hick persona of his essays and stories. It was the purity of the landscape, the unornamented song of the folk storyteller, the Post-Impressionist painter, that appealed to his appetite for truth and engaged his pure gift for poetry. No fancy women for Al Purdy, his ideal shaped like a brown bottle of beer and tasting as honest as hops in creek water. This, from what passes as a love song, "Song of the Impermanent Husband":

> And you you
>   bitch no irritating
> questions re love and permanence only
>   an unrolling lifetime here
> between your rocking thighs
>
>   and the semblance of motion (BR 62–3)

– where there is no commitment except to context, the journey that never ends.

Loving the journey and his phenomenal world, defining its vast expanse in the language of White-comers, he became the Voice of the Land, a title bestowed by the League of Poets, thanks to an anonymous donor (with myself as president-surrogate, accompanied by my husband, Rick, Eurithe, poet Doug Beardsley, and journalist David Grierson, himself a lover of poetry about to die prematurely). There were others who campaigned shamelessly for the title, as poets will, after his death, but no one has deserved it like Purdy. No one loved the land as he did. No one had the breath control to round every dizzy curve in the national railways he tramped on, or sing the names of souls lost among the mountains. His was a true anthropomorphic love affair, every hill a breast, every valley a mons pubis.

In "Arctic Rhododendrons" he wrote,

> flowers were their conversation
> and love the sound of a colour
> that lasts two weeks in August
> and then dies[.] (BR 100)

"Love," as applied to enduring human affection, was a word Purdy despised as much as he abhorred sentimentality, affectation that caused him to snap his toothpicks in half. He might appreciate but not love the man-made (his eyes narrowed, his hand circling the neck of the aforementioned brown maiden), a great piece of music (usually sung by a tenor), lines of verse that met his criteria, or asparagus, stolen Bonnie-and-Clyde style with Eurithe at the wheel, engine running, poached from the ditches around Ameliasburgh. Love was the endgame, the goal, the perfect moment when he would lie down to sleep with Mother Nature. Once attained, it would mean the end of his quest; the romance that was his spirit life should only end on his terms, when he was written out, running on empty. The "Necropsy of Love" asserts

> . No, I do not love you
>   hate the word,
> that private tyranny inside a public sound,
> your freedom's yours and not my own:
> but hold my separate madness like a sword,
> and plunge it in your body all night long. (BR 68)

And then came the invasion, cancer – what an ugly word. Not a muse. Al was not amused. He was not done. There was more asparagus to capture, more poetry to trap in his mindful net. Much has been made of the recent, and inappropriate, revelations about Al's assisted death, but death had not been his desideratum, and it would have no dominion. He wrestled his fake muse, death, to the ground, taking control because his magnificent breath could not be stolen, not by mere mortality and certainly not by the lesser poets who scrambled to take his place. He was going to live and write as long as he could, and then he wouldn't. It was only then that he relented and said the name we'd all been waiting to hear. From "Alive or Not":

> As I grow older and older
> my speed afoot increases
> each time I am running and reach
> the place before she falls every time
> I am running too fast to stop
> I run past her farther and farther
> it's almost like a story
> as an orchid dies in the Brazilian jungle
> and there is a certain amount of horror[.] (BR 286)

Purdy continued to receive poetry, his own and the words that came from friends in the mail. The glacier melted, and the rocks in the great Canadian Shield moved aside for the great revelator, who, in his final days, finally said the name for the mortal love who was always there. Eurithe. When he was under house arrest, she who had been teased in poems that described her as the mother of irony became his kitchen goddess. Acknowledged.

Eurithe, the enabling muse, had to struggle in her role as mother. A stoic, also descended from Ontario farm people, she endured the everlasting boyness of her only-child husband, occasionally punctuating his misbehaviour with the perfect defining comment. Al was a great poet, a great thinker (I still can't say "intellectual," because when I, a woman, read "Say the Names" in a church in Halifax, God, his fingers greased with lightning, reached down and nearly tore the roof off), but he had certain weaknesses. A woman writer had to be an Amazon to truly earn his approval, an Atwood who matched his criteria for irony and sent flowers to his hospital room that literally refused to die, so he could acknowledge her supernatural powers, a Laurence with a deeper mastery of storytelling, or a humanist as expansive as Bronwen Wallace, who died after a cancerous assault on her gifted tongue. You could count them on one hand. The rest were pretty much acolytes to his enduring muse. The confessional "Married Man's Song" reports,

> she stands above him as a stone goddess
> weeping tears and honey
> she is half his age and far older
> and how can a man tell his wife this? (BR 181)

How indeed?

And children had to be neither seen nor heard. One of life's more brilliant moments happened when Al's friend David Day commented on the children playing on his statue in Queen's Park in Toronto. Maybe *crawling* and *mauling* would be more appropriate verbs? Al did not suffer the little children. They were definitely not muses. His muse was jealous and vengeful, tolerating practical wives, but eating up little boys, two of whom should have been near and dear to him.

His sons: Brian from an interim relationship, during a period of separation from Eurithe, and Jim, her child, hardly there in the poetry, except as an irritant that puts itself between the poet and his obsessions. His wife and surrogate mother suffered when Purdy banished the boys to the outer districts of intimacy. Other children were barely endured. He was the centre of his child universe. My eldest son, tolerated, but not exempted, because of his angelic voice, would sing on demand and disappear. Others were ignored until some of them grew up and joined the gifted cohort of passionate friends who loved the written word as much as he did.

Jim was not appreciated, but Brian, having similar gifts, might have slipped under the wire. He is, himself, a poet and bibliophile, his muse inherited. That is the tragic bass line of the poet's life and the burden his wife carried, except for one rebellious moment when she left Al's bedside when both husband and child were embarking on their final illnesses, a space filled up by Atwood's enormous immortal bouquet.

A student once told me that of all the genres offered in his creative writing classes, poetry was the most difficult for him because it was the most personally demanding. Like a cat that knows whether or not you are a cat person, poetry is the writer's lie detector. Purdy had to be honest in verse, and he may not have been able to say the word *love* for a pure reason, his superstitious belief that the magic would abandon his phenomenal life once he gave it a name. Love was for a different chakra, the view from Olympus. His poetry is suffused with love, his adoration of the rock and soil from which he sprang like a wildflower pushing through a crack, and his love of music, songs with and without words. The "Man without a Country" says:

> tho poems speak names which are only words
> and what words *are* there that you have not said yourself
> which we must always go beyond
> and arrive there naked
> as it was in the beginning[.] (PB 62)

The Voice of the Land had to leave his first muse behind because rural Ontario with its Methodisms restricted his vast search for truth and beauty. Nevertheless, he maintained its Calvinist rigour. In his canon, sex and death are sanctified, never vulgarized or betrayed in cheap sentimentality. In "At Roblin Lake," he makes his case for discretion:

> The pike and bass are admirably silent
> about such things, and keep their
> erotic moments *a mensa et toro*
> in cold water. (BR 30)

He did not swear and he did not want to stray from the muse that nurtured his single-minded pursuit of truth and beauty. She was demanding and he was worthy, home at last inside the pages of the granite book my husband designed to mark his grave:

> This is where I came to
> when my body left its body
> and my spirit stayed
> in its spirit home[.] ("Her Gates Both East and West," BR 588)

Eurithe, who responded with a smile when he circled her wrist with his fingers, his mortal bracelet, and said, "I act, she reacts," because she knew differently, has bought the plot next door to his and abandoned her plan to have her ashes laid on top of his – a final edit. He can choose, his imagination free to stay with her or fly off and make another allegiance with another muse, but the smart money, handled by Eurithe, mortal manager, says he won't.

REFERENCES

Purdy, Al. *Beyond Remembering: The Collected Poems of Al Purdy*. Edited by Al Purdy and Sam Solecki. Madeira Park, BC: Harbour Publishing, 2000.
– *Piling Blood*. Toronto: McClelland & Stewart, 1984.

3

Purdy's Mock Love Poetry: Misogyny, Nation, and Progress

Shane Neilson

In 1996, at the age of twenty-one, as a first-year medical student at Dalhousie University, I read the Al Purdy greatest-hits collection entitled *Rooms for Rent in the Outer Planets* during lectures. Renal physiology took a back seat to this poet with a tough persona. Sporting Van Gogh's *Café Terrace at Night* on the cover, that best-of collection took pole position in my bedroom, too. I read my girlfriend poem after poem night after night.

Ah! One can really get back into old habits of toxic masculinity. But I digress: the quality of Purdy's verse that I most admired – an insightful profundity masked by a put-on toughness and complicated by affect – worked in the bedroom, sure, but less for that toughness and more for my own enthusiasm for beauty. I've sat with Purdy's work for twenty years now, and the young man so excited by the persona has grown up. Though I haven't grown out of Purdy, exactly, I have stopped overlooking his flaws.

As D.M.R. Bentley has pointed out, "[b]y no means can all literary texts ... meet the exacting standards of contemporary tolerance" ("Colonial" 20). Though I endorse Purdy as a poet to read, I also suggest that the habitual misogyny of the Purdy persona accounts, in a genealogical-spiritual sense, for the noticeable lack of love poems on the part of a "national" poet. Why is it that Canada's so-called "most Canadian" poet hasn't written an outright love poem to a fully realized person? Does this lack say something about national preferences and tastes?

I begin by establishing the bona fides of Purdy as national champion. There are the state honours, of course: Purdy is a two-time winner of the Governor General's Award for Poetry and was awarded the Order of Ontario and the Order of Canada. Instances equating Purdy and his work with "nation" are distressing in their frequency, having been made so often that there is now a canon of skeptical Purdy-canonizing summaries that can be identified by the era of their production. Let's start with a useful meta-summary from Robert Lecker's *Keepers of the Code*:

> On the first page of the only book-length study of Al Purdy, George Bowering writes that "Al Purdy is the world's most Canadian poet." The first sentence of George Woodcock's introduction to Purdy's 1972 *Selected Poems* is "Al Purdy's writing fits Canada like a glove; you can feel the fingers of the land working through his poems" ... Following the familiar pattern, Clara Thomas, in *Our Nature–Our Voices: A Guidebook to English-Canadian Literature*, presents Purdy as our poet: "To hear him read is to hear the country speak. With his rolled-up shirt sleeves, untended hair, Cuban cigar, authentic pride, six foot four body that could (but never would) fit into a Mountie uniform ... he puts on a performance that only Leonard Cohen or Gwendolyn MacEwen can match[.]" (244)

The above are some choice chestnuts, albeit dated. Following in their wake is Sam Solecki's *The Last Canadian Poet: An Essay on Al Purdy*, from 1999, and an anthology of scholarly essays, *The Ivory Thought: Essays on Al Purdy*, from 2008.

Solecki's study argues "that Al Purdy is the major and perhaps last writer of ... the Canadian nation; to go further, that he is the major or central poet of our experience, the one who has given the strongest, most comprehensive, and most original voice to the country's cultural, historical, and political experiences and aspirations that have been at the heart of our various nationalist discourses since Confederation" (10). A couple of years after Purdy's death, Frank Davey took a long windup at Solecki's blimpish argument by first (ritually) summarizing Purdy's national hosannas:

> His death was the lead story on Canadian network television news, a front-page story in the nationally published newspaper the *Globe and Mail*, and the subject of a full-page obituary by journalist Val Ross in the *Globe* two days following. The front page story was titled "Canadian master poet succumbs to cancer" ... and Ross's somewhat longer obituary "National icon was larger than life[.]" (46)

Davey goes on to recapitulate the breathless testimonials to Purdy's importance by leading Canadian poets of the day (Robert Bringhurst, Susan Musgrave, Dennis Lee). Purdy, this consensus bleats, is A GREAT CANADIAN! Bentley has written that Purdy has acquired "near-mythogenic status" ("Conclusion" 239), and it is this myth that I find destructive in a material way when it comes to efforts to preserve his A-frame home in Ameliasburgh – but more on this later. Some scholarship has been written on the teleology of the construction in which Purdy's specific representations of nation promoted a kind of literary nationalism in a reciprocal relationship (see van der Marel, Solway), but for this essay, one need only recognize that a great amount of money and effort has been invested in presenting Purdy, for good or for ill, as "our guy."

Our guy is, of course, a flawed human being – like me, and like the audience for this chapter. In "The People's Poet: Al Purdy as Organic Intellectual," an essay from 2013 in the online journal *Lemonhound*, Rob Winger states in Purdy's defence that Purdy "never presented himself as simplistically nationalist" or "unknowingly chauvinist," which are "all qualities attributed to him since he's been posthumously proclaimed 'the people's poet'" (n.p.). Winger intimates that flaws take on greater significance the more the canonization machine is made to work to defy the law of political correctness – to work against the grain, as it were, of contemporary social mores. This is how canonization works nowadays, coincident with reciprocal counter-canonization. I remain an admirer of Purdy, especially of his more complex work, but the selection of Purdy as a "national poet" is problematic for reasons in excess of those that would apply to other poets of his generation, the generation of Canadian literary nationalism.

Winger invites discussion of such problems in a lone footnote to his essay: "Purdy's longstanding exhibition of male violence and various gender stereotypes in his poetry remains a useful exemplar of both historical and contemporary heterosexism and male privilege, and ought to be discussed, I think, *not* as outrageously misogynistic, but intentionally demonstrative of the need for continued social activism for women's rights." This diagnosis strikes me as being both as accurate and as reductive as a point Winger makes in the same footnote: "any theory of Purdy's work as a singular, supposedly 'masculine' poetics is at least partially reductionist." Indicting Purdy solely on the basis of his representations of women would be limited, but so is reading Purdy and suggesting *only* that Canadian poetry as a field needs to do more work on inclusivity and representation. Purdy constitutes a real problem for the nation that picked him.

I will summarize the "Problem of National Purdy" hinted at above because I want to spend the bulk of this essay considering Purdy's poetry less in terms of identity politics and more in terms of the emotional limitations of his work due to his speaker's attitudes, if such a distinction can be made. Mark Silverberg has written of "Song of the Impermanent Husband" as a poem with a speaker espousing "blatant misogyny" (237). This point can be made – acknowledging an obfuscating layer of self-mockery and irony – of the *bulk* of Purdy's work. Davey indicts that same poem too and adds that the

> relatively few women in Purdy's reflective lyrics are often similarly dehumanized, such as the native women, "Beaver or Carrier women maybe / or Blackfoot squaws" he 'celebrates' in "The Cariboo Horses" for having had "whiskey-coloured eyes" and having been sexually ridden like "equine rebels" –
> such women as once fell dead with their lovers
> with fire in their heads and slippery froth on thighs (7)
> Here the collocation of native women with animals, whiskey, and reckless passion is as extreme and lamentable as any in our literature. This is the title poem of the collection for which Purdy was given his first Governor-General's Award. (53)

The insinuation here is that Al Purdy is a flawed man who has racist and misogynist attitudes, and certainly more could be said about the designation of Purdy by the League of Canadian Poets as "The Voice of the Land." The voice of the land for whom? Surely not Indigenous peoples. By asking such questions, am I engaging in a de-canonizing impulse as strong as the canonizing one? (And which of those will prove to be the lesser evil for the greater good?) Davey might acknowledge some of Purdy's good poems before he makes his airtight prosecutor's case, but to be fair to Davey, prosecutors aren't supposed to defend their quarry or to mitigate the attack when the quarry is so open to indictment. Indeed, Purdy wrote from a particular "macho" stance – and there's no avoiding that. Ditto his representations of race, which come from the zone of whiteness. His sins against political correctness appear to a contemporary reader – and certainly to the academy – much like his duds did to onlookers in the 1990s. (Purdy wore the flapping loose clothes of an old, out-of-touch man.)

I forgive all these things. After all, the man wrote some transcendent pieces. But there is a consequence of the misogyny in his work that I conceive of as Purdy's great failing as a poet. Because Purdy is our national champion, this failing says something about us, too. An outside observer of our poetry – perhaps already possessed by stereotypes of frigid igloos – upon meeting the officially sanctioned edifice of Al Purdy, could be forgiven for thinking Canada a rather cold, loveless country. Once again, Davey is a great entry point:

> The masculinism implicit in the terms of Solecki's praise of Purdy has a long history in Western poetry that it is unnecessary to outline here. The general assumptions of the lyric at the beginning of the 1960s were still those of the courtly love tradition – men wrote or recited, as in Bowering's "Inside the Tulip" (*The Man in the Yellow Boots*, 1965: 16), women read or listened. The lyric was at once an instrument of courtship – and it was men who did the courting – and one of reflection. (52)

Welllllll – wait a minute. Although the rumours are numerous concerning Purdy and the reading circuit, and though I don't dispute the overwhelmingly masculine tenor of that decade, I have great difficulty thinking of Purdy reading poems themselves as instruments of courtship. He woos women with *what* poems, exactly?

Bards are expected to devote at least some of their output to two great subjects: love and war. Purdy was able to write serviceable poems about war – he even wrote a whole book about Japan's nuclear aftermath in *Hiroshima Poems* (1972) – but he was constitutionally unable to write love poetry. And as a poet, Purdy had a *duty* to write love poetry. He tried to fulfill this duty, writing dozens of poems that attempt to square themselves with the ethereality of love. Most degenerate into a jokey self-parody, a haw-haw kind of snickering at the embarrassment of unmanly, "flowery" stuff. As Davey and Silverberg remark about the case of the "Song of the Impermanent Husband," Purdy's other "love" poems laugh at themselves; they wink at their reader, swaggering in a self-mockery that disables the very idea of them as love poetry. If love somehow is always in earnest, then love is not present in poems like "Home-Made Beer":

> Whereupon my wife appeared from the bathroom
> where she had been brooding for days
> over the injustice of being a woman and
> attacked me with a broom –
> With commendable savoir faire I broke
> the broom across my knee (it hurt too) and
> then she grabbed the breadknife and made
> for me with fairly obvious intentions –

> I tore open my shirt and told her calmly
> with bared breast and a minimum of boredom
>   "Go ahead! Strike! Go ahead!"
> Icicles dropped from her fiery eyes as she
> snarled
>   "I wouldn't want to go to jail
>   for killing a thing like you!" (BR 74)

Yes, you're *supposed* to laugh. This is both the poem's intended effect *and* crucial weakness. I do not mean that love poetry cannot be knowing or humorous; lovers can laugh at themselves, but Purdy's love poetry has a habitual parodic stance that, in making fun of the mystery of love, demystifies the poem. Conveying that bizarre, baffling, and compelling mystery is the trick and achievement of the good love poem.

Unsurprisingly, the parodic stance of the poetry was reflected in biography too. In "Moths in the Iron Curtain, or Roaming in the USSR with Al Purdy and Ralph Gustafson," Victor Pogostin, then their interpreter, relays this anecdote:

> In October of 1976, Al Purdy and Ralph Gustafson were
> parachuted behind the Iron Curtain under the aegis of an
> agreement between the Canadian Department of External
> Affairs and the Kremlin, with the USSR Writers' Union playing
> the host. Their wives, Eurithe and Betty, introduced to me
> by Al as "the female chauvinist chaperones," and by Ralph as
> "the indispensable," came along. (197)

The difference between "indispensable" and "female chauvinist chaperones" is vast. In life and in his work, Purdy's stock defence against sentimentality is parody. Yet constitutive jokiness is a hard path to success in love poems – the disrespect shown to the love object and the self has a negative register that keeps the door from opening. So many Purdy poems read as if the poet approached the vat of sentiment and, in order to prevent a dousing in treacle, backtracked by yukking it up. Purdy himself made his method clear in "On Being Romantic": he didn't want to evoke "the euphoric dreams of lovers" but "the ridiculousity [*sic*] inherent in the whole comic disease" (LB 10). Unlike many other male poets of his generation who did accomplish the task, such as Irving Layton in "Divinity," Earle Birney in "She Is," Milton Acorn in "Live with Me on Earth under the Invisible Daylight Moon," Alden Nowlan in "For Claudine Because I Love Her," and Leonard Cohen too many times to mention, the fact being obvious.

Purdy had another escape mechanism when writing his love poems. Love poetry, when not hamstrung by sentiment, often falls victim to narcissism. Purdy's way to avoid this was to leaven his poems with pessimism; much of his poetry has an anti-love stance. Here are Purdy's own words to this effect: "[In love poetry I capture] the mordant happiness of despair as well. Pain and its red blot and the brain, sorrow that things end, fade into little rags of memory that haunt us in their absence" (*LB* 10). Why did he have such a pessimistic outlook on love? It may be that he was congenitally incapable of the emotion; love just might not have been part of his repertoire of feelings, a condition hinted at in his autobiographical writings. Before his marriage, Purdy says, he never experienced love for another human being. Even love for his mother (his father died very early in his life) was absent, an absence documented in his poem "On Being Human" (*BR* 507–8) and in the following passage from his autobiography:

> There is no excuse for me that I didn't respond to her requests, importunities and demands for love, even if they were unspoken. I should have faked it, even as a child. That would have meant I had some idea of the torture, pain and ecstasy of people who can actually love. I should have faked it, leaned my head against the bony decaying skullface of love and pretended to be human. (*RBS* 37)

Purdy had a famously standoffish relationship with Eurithe, and could never quite claim in print that he loved her. About as close as he ever got to expressing his affection for his wife in the two hundred and ninety-six pages of his autobiography comes in the following passage: "Our personal relations were somewhat wary and careful. Volcanic quarrels would be succeeded by armed truce, or a disguised tenderness. Sexual relations were always nocturnal, occasionally resembled combat in their hostile preliminaries. But – let us say – there was love, although I avoided such words" (*RBS* 157–8). Exactly. The hedged bet of "let us say" tells readers all they need to know. Purdy – remember that this is autobiography, not poetry with the pleasant fiction of a "speaker" – just didn't possess that part of the human apparatus; he could only hypothesize it. To understand just how inadequate a declaration of love this is, imagine facing your own lover and saying unto them, "Let us say, I love you." Purdy's ruthlessness in this regard is somewhat shocking: he likely had his wife read the manuscript for his autobiography, so Eurithe would have had to see those lines and live with them in print. To round out the family, so to speak, Purdy mentions his son in passing a total of two times in his autobiography, one of these invocations a description of how his wife was solely responsible for the child's upbringing.

Purdy's absent capacity made for a famous anecdote in Canadian literature. As competitive as the next poet, Purdy was especially jealous of Irving Layton. When Layton published *Love Where the Nights Are Long* (1962), an anthology of love poetry illustrated by Harold Town, Purdy thought that he should do the same. He proposed to Jack McClelland that he gather together all of his own love poems for publication, and that this book also be illustrated by Town. McClelland agreed, and Purdy set to work. After submitting the manuscript, Purdy heard nothing for many months. Eventually McClelland and Town came to visit Purdy in Ameliasburgh. The encounter, as related by Purdy with typical candour, went like this:

> When I met them to talk about the book, both were a little embarrassed about their change of heart re Town doing the illustrations. After a long pause, during which we tried to read one another's minds, McClelland said, "Your poems are hard-boiled. We had expected them to be romantic."
> Now my wife has the same complaint about me ...
> "Romantic," I said.
> "No, hard-boiled," Jack McClelland said.
> Harold Town nodded in agreement. "You're just not romantic," he said with a kind look, drawing his cloak closer to him. (LB 10)

Salvaged out of this false start was *Love in a Burning Building*, Purdy's non-illustrated book of love poems that actually reads like a treatise on how to commit arson. Consider the finale of "Song of the Impermanent Husband," in which the poet offers his mate the following command:

> And you you
>   bitch no irritating
> questions re love and permanence only
>   an unrolling lifetime here
> between your rocking thighs
>
>   and the semblance of motion[.] (BR 62–3)

Here the very "question" of love is "irritating," and the only "semblance" of purpose can be found between "rocking thighs" – meaning sexual congress. A cruder development of this theme comes in the mock-romantic "Side Effect":

> The Muse has thighs of moonlight and silver
> her cunt is frozen gold
> and that is why if any mortal woman need ask
> my hands are always cold[.] (LB 37)

This kind of carnal carny atmosphere is pervasive in *Love in a Burning Building*; straining to be funny, Purdy comes off instead as a versifying Benny Hill.

Perhaps the foremost instance of Purdy's jaundiced use of the word *love* is in "Necropsy of Love" (BR 68), one of Purdy's best – and best-known – poems. This poem's title is perhaps the most cogent comment one could make about Purdy's "love" poetry: "necropsy" is defined as "1. a post mortem examination, an autopsy" (OED). With this word Purdy is saying that, for him, love is dead, that this poem is an autopsy of love *as a corpse*. This theme is developed further in the poem's first stanza:

> If it came about you died
> it might be said I loved you:
> love is an absolute as death is,
> and neither bears false witness to the other –
> but you remain alive.

Note the hesitation of "it might be said," and the qualification "but": the reader is served notice of equivocation by a poet with serious reservations about the very word – "let us say" redux. Indeed, the next stanza considers "love" as a word, not an act:

> No, I do not love you
>   hate the word,
> that private tyranny inside a public sound,
> your freedom's yours and not my own:
> but hold my separate madness like a sword,
> and plunge it in your body all night long.

This is not a tender reflection on word or deed; rather, it reads more like a violent refutation – a "separate madness like a sword" plunged in a consort's "body all night long." The sexual connotations here are obvious; it is as if Purdy is saying that the *impossibility* of love should be met with carnal resignation, that sex is all we have in the end. In his poetry, sex was as close as he could come to sacrament: something intrinsic to the man prevented him from writing about love unreservedly. The poem continues:

> If death shall strip our bones of all but bones,
> then here's the flesh and flesh that's drunken-sweet
> as wine cups in deceptive lunar light:
> reach up your hand and turn the moonlight off,
> and maybe it was never there at all,
> so never promise anything to me:
> but reach across the darkness with your hand,
> reach across the distance of tonight,
> and touch the moving moment once again
>   before you fall asleep –

In this final stanza, Purdy purposely invokes the trappings of romance, namely "wine cups" and "lunar light," and calls them "deceptive." He even goes so far as to say that the moonlight might never have been "there at all." This means that *love* might not have been there at all, that it might not exist. The poem ends with a shrug toward sex, that temporizing anaesthetic of touch. This is also the most positive and "moving moment" in the poem – the place where the poet tries to reconcile himself with the given conditions and at least parleys with the feminine opposition.

Purdy disliked the word *love*. There is much to admire in the Purdy oeuvre, including the taciturn lyricism of "Necropsy of Love," but one can't help but think that he was hampered by a mind that couldn't – or wouldn't – love. Perhaps I'm reading too much into the work. Maybe Purdy was writing about himself when he wrote this about Charles Bukowski, another self-consciously "tough" poet: "[I]sn't all this toughness and machine-gun language, even in its cumulative effect – isn't that only part of a man ... I certainly wouldn't go into the business of naming the parts of which a man of many parts should be composed. (I dislike even my own strictures)" (*SA* 191). I admit that I may be reading only the parts that Purdy wished to name. But if this is so, why does Purdy finish the preceding passage with: "But certainly the sum-total impression of the portrait painted in these poems is that of a living stance, a leaning attitude." Indeed – a stance *against*, and not *for*. Forgive me, but I feel like our national poet's inability to write love poetry straight should knock him off the venerable pedestal – a fitting enough consequence for the attitudes he held, perhaps?

Though there is a more pressing matter in the present. The very public activities of the Al Purdy A-frame Association are conducted with the purpose of preserving the Purdy homestead as a national literary monument. As Brooke Pratt writes in "'Preserving the echoing rooms of yesterday': Al Purdy's A-Frame and the Place of Writers' Houses in

Canada," almost "all public expressions of support for the preservation of the A-frame ... equate its potential destruction with the destruction of Canadian culture more broadly" (88). Margaret Atwood, Dennis Lee, and many other white writers are on record making the same connection to Purdy's wooden structure – as Lee puts it, "the house itself has become a living password, a concrete reminder of who and what we are. It would be folly to lose a totem of such power; we can't afford such cultural amnesia" (17). I beg to differ in a visceral way. When asked by a poet friend if I intended to apply to the A-frame residency myself based on my ability to recite swaths of Purdy's verse, my response surprised me in its vehemence. "Why would I?" I asked back. "The best I can tell, he wrote many of his great poems there, but it's also the place where he neglected his wife and the place from which he banished his son." Speaking less personally, and in conclusion: what will be the effect of state and community support for a residency grafted onto a site in which the darker forces of nation coalesced?

REFERENCES

Bentley, D.M.R. "Colonial Colonizing: An Introductory Survey of the Canadian Long Poem." In *Bolder Flights: Essays on the Canadian Long Poem*, edited by Frank M. Tierney and Angela Robbeson, 7–29. Ottawa: University of Ottawa Press, 1998.

– "Conclusion, Retrospective, and Prospective." In *The Ivory Thought: Essays on Al Purdy*, edited by Gerald Lynch, Shoshannah Ganz, and Josephene T.M. Kealey, 239–46. Ottawa: University of Ottawa Press, 2008.

Davey, Frank. "Al Purdy, Sam Solecki, and the Poetics of the 1960s." *Canadian Poetry: Studies, Documents, Reviews*, no. 51 (Fall–Winter 2002): 39–55.

Lecker, Robert. *Keepers of the Code: English-Canadian Literary Anthologies and the Representation of Nation*. Toronto: University of Toronto Press, 2013.

Lee, Dennis. "Till the House Was Real." In *The Al Purdy A-Frame Anthology*, edited by Paul Vermeersch, 11–17. Madeira Park, BC: Harbour Publishing, 2009.

Lynch, Gerald, Shoshannah Ganz, and Josephene T.M. Kealey, eds. *The Ivory Thought: Essays on Al Purdy*. Ottawa: University of Ottawa Press, 2008.

"necropsy, n." OED *Online*. Oxford University Press, June 2017.

Pogostin, Victor. "Moths in the Iron Curtain, or Roaming in the USSR with Al Purdy and Ralph Gustafson." *Canadian Literature*, no. 212 (Spring 2012): 197–202.

Pratt, Brooke. "Preserving 'the echoing rooms of yesterday': Al Purdy's A-Frame and the Place of Writers' Houses in Canada." In *Canadian*

Literature and Cultural Memory, edited by Cynthia Sugars and Eleanor Ty, 84–99. Don Mills, ON: Oxford University Press, 2014.

Purdy, Al. *Beyond Remembering: The Collected Poems of Al Purdy*. Edited by Al Purdy and Sam Solecki. Madeira Park, BC: Harbour Publishing, 2000.

– *Love in a Burning Building*. Toronto: McClelland & Stewart, 1970.

– *Reaching for the Beaufort Sea: An Autobiography*. Edited by Alex Widen. Madeira Park, BC: Harbour Publishing, 1993.

– *Starting from Ameliasburgh: The Collected Prose of Al Purdy*. Edited by Sam Solecki. Madeira Park, BC: Harbour Publishing, 1995.

Silverberg, Mark. "The Can(adi)onization of Al Purdy." *Essays on Canadian Writing*, no. 70 (Spring 2000): 226–51.

Solecki, Sam. *The Last Canadian Poet: An Essay on Al Purdy*. Toronto: University of Toronto Press, 1999.

Solway, David. "Standard Average Canadian." In *Director's Cut*, by David Solway, 87–100. Erin, ON: The Porcupine's Quill, 2003.

van der Marel, L. Camille. "Unsettling *North of Summer*: Anxieties of Ownership in the Politics and Poetics of the Canadian North." *ARIEL: A Review of International English Literature* 44, no. 4 (October 2013): 13–47.

Winger, Rob. "The People's Poet: Al Purdy as Organic Intellectual." *Lemonhound*, 24 April 2013, https://lemonhound.com/2013/04/24/rob-winger-on-al-purdy/.

PART TWO

Land Claims:
Al Purdy and the
Unpeaceable Kingdom

4

The Too Easily Kept Illusions: Myth-making, Private Canons, and Patterns of Exclusion

J.A. Weingarten

Scholars enjoy myths. We enjoy most, perhaps, the myths we make for ourselves – by which I mean the stories scholars tell about the writers they prize. There are many myths about Al Purdy, some of which have endured for decades, and these stories are much more revealing of Purdy's critics than of himself: he has been the "most Canadian poet" (Bowering 1), "the first" to accomplish a "native mapping" of Canada (Lee, "Running" 16), and the "central poet of our experience" (Solecki, *LCP* 10). This representation of Purdy persists. A book of tribute called *And Left a Place to Stand On* (2009), for example, includes a long list of poems that celebrate Purdy's embodiment of Canada, while Donna Allard and Nat Hall write that to tear down Purdy's A-frame home is akin to "tear[ing] the roots of Canadian poetry" and "felling the maple tree" (45). However relevant these portrayals may have been to critics of the post-1960 era, they are much less useful today, more than a century after Purdy's birth and two decades after his death. The challenge of reading Purdy today – with fuller awareness of the many progressive political movements ever emerging since 1960 – is that doing so requires scholars (including me) to go beyond these long-running myths, each of which (whether we realize it or not) impedes our ability to reflect more deeply on what is surely a complicated legacy.

The reality of this challenge was driven home for me several years ago when I first read Robert Budde's introduction to *The More Easily Kept Illusions: The Poetry of Al Purdy* (2006), in which he describes Purdy's "mythic presence" (ix) as a "quintessentially Canadian" poet (viii). At the same time, Budde is quite selective in his edition when it comes to Purdy's poetry. While he argues that Purdy embodies Canada, he also remarks that he "find[s] some of Purdy's poems offensive – 'offensive' in the sense that they have the potential to cause harm and to misrepresent. They contain, in short, racist and sexist elements" (xiv). "I have chosen," Budde continues, "not to include many poems that are considered Purdy's best because of these racist and sexist elements" (xiv). Here is a basic tension in Purdy criticism, one well represented by, though not unique to, Budde's book: a sacrosanct reverence for Purdy's contributions to Canadian literature and a recognition of the obvious fact that his writing and thinking are sometimes utterly incompatible with the contemporary political milieu of the liberal arts. This tension is one that Budde mostly avoids by declining to acknowledge the implication of aligning a "quintessentially Canadian" poet (viii) with "racist and sexist" writing (xiv). That implication, however, is worth exploring, because it unintentionally proves that predominating concepts of "Canadian" identity – and, relatedly, the writing of those who represent such concepts – have, indeed, been historically inseparable from racist and sexist ideologies. Dodging that conundrum and refusing to engage with poems that exemplify those qualities of Purdy's writing, Budde denies his audience opportunities to reflect on those concerns in any meaningful way.

The issue here is neither one editor's characterization of Purdy nor even the broader use of nationalist rhetoric in Purdy criticism over the last fifty years. The issue with which I am grappling is the ease with which scholars simplify legacies, first by removing poets from broader contexts, and then by guarding them from challenging debates. In such scholarship, critics craft – purposely or unconsciously – inflexible literary histories. There are consequences to these oversimplifications: the complexity of poets and their politics is lost, connections (even if conflictual ones) among writers become invisible, and scholarly or pedagogical opportunities to explore those unexpected and instructive connections are missed.

Before I say more about those consequences, let me elaborate on that widely adopted and wholly illusive reading of Purdy as "quintessentially Canadian," because it represents a hopeful search that has much more to do with national insecurities than with Purdy; the motif belongs to a particular generation of critics, and it has, in some cases, been inherited by later scholars. By the 1960s, cultural pride among English-descended Canadians was booming. Confederation lit a fuse that stretched for nearly a century: the "Great Coalition" of the 1860s seemed to promise national unity; members of the late-nineteenth-century Canada First movement spoke passionately of a unified national identity (and intolerantly of immigration and diversity); Canadian acts of valour during the First World War and the formation of the League of Nations in

1919 convinced Canadians of their place on the world stage; the country's vital service in the Second World War further bolstered national pride; a growing arts community after the 1957 founding of the Canada Council for the Arts promised a richer Canadian culture; federal talk of a national flag provided a fresh instance of iconography behind which many Canadians could rally; and the approaching 1967 Centennial churned widespread excitement through celebrations and funding for art installations and events. For all kinds of reasons (economic, cultural, artistic, governmental, symbolic), the "Canada" that English Canadians represented (perhaps the only Canada they knew at the time) seemed widely embraced, well defined, and invigorated.

Sharing in this enthusiasm, some literary critics spoke romantically of the inevitability of a Canadian poet who could realize E.K. Brown's 1943 prediction: "our Whitman," Brown famously said, "is in the future" (20). These critics wanted a poet who would, as Walt Whitman had done for the United States in the nineteenth century, traverse the country, contain multitudes, and embody and speak for the common man. My gendered language here is a deliberate nod to William Wordsworth's modelling of the "real language of men," a concept that captures some of the exclusionary thinking typical of romantic "national bard" formulations. Nevertheless, critics like Brown regarded those romantic bards as necessary to the nation – its rich past, its eager present, its promising future.[1] The arrival of a deliberately anti-romantic and cosmopolitan modernism in Canada during the 1920s – a literary movement that regarded nationalistic and emotional lyrics such as Whitman's as self-indulgent and sentimental – lessened the chances that a Whitman or Wordsworth figure embodying such doctrines would emerge in this country. To be sure, by 1950, romantic nationalism was passé.

Yet, as a writer who knew little, if anything, about this modernism until the 1950s (when he was approaching forty), Purdy wrote between two traditions. He was simultaneously romantic and modern, a characterization that Margaret Atwood captures wonderfully when she describes him as "both sentimental and obscene" ("Foreword" 17). Purdy was, in some respects, the romantic wanderer of Canada, mapping the country from Newfoundland to Baffin Island to the British Columbian coast. He wandered not just through space, but also through time; many of his poems explore historical events. His poems of the sixties and seventies emphasized Canadian history at an opportune moment: as Canada celebrated its Centennial, Purdy gestured to the historical foundation that explained the significance of what risked seeming to many an unremarkable point in time. To the pleasure of English-Canadian nationalists, he gave shape and weight to Canada's past in ways that no other English-language poet had done: he surveyed the distant past of Viking settlements on the East Coast, conjured up narrative fragments connected to sites of great personal or regional significance (Kispiox, Batoche, Ameliasburgh), and even gathered pieces of his own family history in a long poem, *In Search of Owen Roblin* (1974).[2]

In such works, Purdy writes evocatively of small towns "a little adjacent to where the world is" ("The Country North of Belleville," BR 80), the modern world that the dead left for us "to stand on" ("Roblin's Mills [II]," BR 157), the distant aural echoes of pasts "whispering across the fields of eternity" ("The Battlefield at Batoche," BR 222), the magnificence of "permanent" cave paintings ("The Horseman of Agawa," BR 209), and memories of "torn down" mills ("Inside the Old Mill," BR 278). These poems epitomize what most readers of the 1960s found between the covers of Purdy's books: an energetic poet rejecting an emotionless modernism and writing unabashedly of Canada and its past, revelling in the local, the familiar, and the familial. And yet he did so with a modern flair: his philosophical skepticism, scientific grasp of geological time and evolution, self-reflexive questioning, New Left bent, brazen sexuality, resistance to closure, and seeming atheism signalled his modernness. But most appealing of all, Purdy was *readable*. His coarse and familiar voice charmed readers, offering them something recognizable and rare: "the insistent, untidy drunk" (Atwood, "Foreword" 17) who could wax poetic about, and then extract a philosophical exquisiteness from, even the most quotidian scene.

"At the Quinte Hotel" (1968; BR 130–1) nicely captures that romantic and modern duality in Purdy's writing. He imagines a poet-figure with many of the tics and traits typical of his own poetry over the next several decades, a figure at once humble, brash, comical, arrogant, clever, and insightful:

> I am drinking
> I am drinking beer with yellow flowers
> in underground sunlight
> and you can see that I am a sensitive man
> And I notice that the bartender is a sensitive man too
> so I tell him about his beer
> I tell him the beer he draws
> is half fart and half horse piss
> and all wonderful yellow flowers[.]

The scene scarcely evokes the sublime landscapes of romantic poetry, and in fact Purdy appears to parody those settings: the "flowers" are bubbles of third-rate beer, the "sunlight" is an artificial overhead bulb, and the only suggestion of wildlife is "horse piss." The scene is deliberately unromantic. So too is Purdy's persona. He imagines himself as "a sensitive" sentimentalist, but he later "knock[s] the shit" out of another patron on his way to "piss." He concludes the brawl by reading one of his poems aloud, and, although his work elicits an emotional response from the room, everyone falls silent when he proposes that his reading be repaid with beer:

> and it was brought home to me in the tavern
> that poems will not really buy beer or flowers
> or a goddam thing
> and I was sad
> for I am a sensitive man[.]

"At the Quinte Hotel" balances Purdy's jesting wit with his philosophical depth; there is something unpredictably profound in asking what, if any, value a poem has if it cannot even earn you a beer. Even if a poem has no monetary value, it certainly appears to have a more elusive, indefinable worth: the poet's reading pacifies a mass of hooligans and even brings them to "tears." The scene exemplifies Purdy's modern romanticism: he pairs natural imagery and emotional sensitivity (both typical of romantic bards) with the crudeness of a working-class figure who swears freely, drinks too much, and resorts too hastily to violence. The everydayness of this voice led critics such as Dennis Lee to characterize Purdy's poetry as representing the essence of Canada's "native idiom" ("Poetry" 390) and to call him "our Whitman" ("Running" 16); the label was, almost certainly, a nod to Brown's earlier prediction of a future Whitman. Scholars upheld Lee's characterization for decades.[3] That assessment, paired with Purdy's voice and an insistent attention to Canadian history in his most popular poems, established Purdy as a central figure in the country's literary canon.

Purdy, however, questioned these characterizations, and objected for decades to comparisons between him and Whitman. He once remarked, "I've been accused of being like [Whitman], but I don't like him" (Purdy and O'Brien 150), and he wrote to George Bowering in 1973 that he resented any comparison to Whitman, a poet who is, in Purdy's words, "monotonous, long-winded and fulla shit" (letter, 26 September 1973). Regardless of what he thought, though, the myth of Purdy as our Canadian Whitman, our quintessentially Canadian poet immortalizing the "native" Canadian voice and life, was so firmly entrenched in the critical discourse by the end of the 1970s that it proved difficult to dislodge. It crept into reviews, articles, encyclopedia entries, Purdy's various selecteds and collecteds, and full-length studies such as Bowering's *Al Purdy* (1970) and Sam Solecki's *The Last Canadian Poet* (1999).

While this history of Purdy's critical construction and his era may be too brief to be considered comprehensive, it provides enough of a glimpse to show how Purdy's role as the national bard is one part of much larger efforts to soften cultural insecurities and tensions seeded in the 1860s and blooming by the 1960s as the country approached the Centennial.

In 2000, Mark Silverberg published a spectacular article on this construction, in which he proposed that the "canonization of Purdy [has] simultaneously [been] a process of Canadianization" (226). Drawing on Robert Lecker's studies of canon formation, Silverberg rightly pointed out that "the national preoccupation with defining a Canadian identity translated into a (heavily government-sponsored) literary-critical industry whose purpose was to find or create images of that identity" (227).[4] Certainly, the key word here is "create," because romantic conceptions of national identity necessarily require invention and intervention – even at the level of government. Through such invention, criticism becomes, in Silverberg's view, a ventriloquist's act, whereby the poet is the puppet of the critic (233).[5] Silverberg thus concluded that critics have "reductively Canadianiz[ed] Purdy" and limited opportunities to see him "in other ways" (228).

Still, I question whether Silverberg goes far enough with his critique. While he is critical of romantic-nationalist readings of Purdy, he does not want "to contest Al Purdy's status"; he wants instead to propose alternative ways of reading Purdy's legacy (245). So, while Silverberg skilfully articulates a critical myopia in the field, he still characterizes Purdy as many nationalist critics have: as unquestionably "one of our most important poets," whose status may or may not be contestable (247). Granted, Silverberg is much less dramatic than Budde or Lee, but his phrase still betrays uncritical assumptions about who "we" are and why "we" should see Purdy as these critics and so many others do. If more pressure could be put on Silverberg's implied assumption that Purdy has universal appeal, then there would be an opportunity to draw out more complex conclusions about his significance to future readers. That questioning can be a productive tool in studying and teaching Canadian literature more generally, because this approach simply asks critics to read and speak of writers in broader contexts.

For now, though, let me conclude this line of thought by saying that while it has been comforting and convenient to use Purdy as an emblem of Canadian identity, it is also naive to do so – not only because, as

Silverberg argues, it neglects Purdy's other accomplishments as a poet, but also because the concept of a singular Canadian identity is illusory, as well as politically and culturally harmful. That identity has historically been imagined through processes of exclusion and built on policies that advanced discrimination and cultural assimilation: residential schools were, from the late nineteenth century to the late twentieth century, assaults on and denials of the dignity and importance of Indigenous languages and traditions;[6] the Trudeau government's reprehensible White Paper (*Statement of the Government of Canada on Indian Policy*, 1969) was a concerted effort to erase special status for Indigenous peoples;[7] until the 1960s, there were no language laws to protect the French language or to allow francophone politicians to speak French in Parliament;[8] and many other historical and contemporary instances of legislation, such as the Chinese Immigration Act (1885), fostered widespread social and economic inequality.[9] The concept of a united Canadian identity was further reinforced through the disenfranchisement of Indigenous peoples and by open discrimination against non-British-descended Canadians when it came to educational opportunities. For decades, Indigenous people had to forfeit their cultural identity in order to attend university, and institutions such as McGill University and the University of Toronto had strict quotas for Jews.[10]

These efforts were intended to control who participated in the construction of Canada: each action, in its own way, ensured that the building of Canada – in politics or in scholarly and creative narratives – would be denied for generations to those who were not (generally speaking) British-descended and Christian. In the absence of diverse representation, illusions of sameness became commonplace, and those illusions encouraged a search (at least among those privileged with academic careers) for representative literary icons in a country where universalizing representations *seemed* possible, even if they were and are not. That assessment of Canada is not cynicism about the country or about Canadian scholarship; it is simply the reality of this place, a reality that asks scholars to appreciate the sincere possibility that the future of Canadian criticism depends on their willingness to imagine a model of criticism that resists comfortable answers and exclusionary paradigms.

Many scholars predate me in this respect, including Budde. As a contrast to his introduction to *The More Easily Kept Illusions*, his insightful essay on postcolonialism (from 2004) observes "a Canadian ethos that has, since its inception, been founded on racist principles" ("Codes" 245). Exposing and exploring that "ethos," Budde says, "may disturb students ... it involves self-reflection, vulnerability, and an awareness of one's own conditional/conditioned language" (245–6). The historian Timothy

Stanley similarly questions the usefulness of a national identity that can be "claim[ed]" only by some Canadians: "By making Europeans and their activities the subject of the narratives ... the grand narrative makes it difficult for non-Europeans to claim membership in the imagined community that it purports to explain" (83). In a literary context, Laurie Kruk acknowledges the impossibility of one unifying identity, and therefore insists that scholars must interrogate – in the classroom and in scholarship – the term itself: "*Identity*, that fascinating word for our students, needs to be complicated inasmuch as our own self slides between what is given, what is (unconsciously) constructed, and what is self-created" (308). There again is that word: "created." Identity is a useful creation when it orients the self; it is destructive when it becomes a way of speaking for or excluding others.

Kruk's model has been missing from much Canadian criticism of the past fifty years, and the evidence of that absence can be found even by considering a favoured trope in that discourse: "the most important writer." Impossibly, many writers have earned this moniker: P.K. Page is "probably English Canada's most important poet of the last fifty years" (McNeilly 423); "E.J. Pratt is often considered Canada's most important poet" (Stouck 65); Earle Birney is "Canada's finest poet" and its "most important poet" (Nesbitt 1); "Margaret Atwood is, by many a count, Canada's most important writer" (Nischik 331); and Leonard Cohen is "potentially the most important writer that Canadian poetry has produced since 1950" (Milton Wilson, qtd. in Simmons 122). That this kind of assessment recurs so often is already a suggestion of its hollowness as a justification for studying specific writers; the trope enacts a conflation of "*my* favourite" or "the author who best reflects *my* values and identity" with "the *most* important" – with too little consideration of what "importance" means.

A critic can determine importance only by determining function, and the function of writers, as explained by critics, is always a reflection of the scholar's position – just as canons, as Lecker has long contended, are mirror "image[s] of [scholars] and their values" ("Canonization" 657). I agree with Lecker's basic point: personal values often determine literary worth. In the 1990s, Lecker was asking scholars to recognize their internalized prejudices and world views in order to dismantle monolithic canons and to facilitate more diverse ones.[11] Scholars such as Lorraine Weir seized this opportunity by expressing concern that the works most likely to be canonized were also the ones most likely to "be absorbed with least resistance or noise in the institution" (194). This skeptical perspective on canon formation gradually motivated some scholars to take greater editorial risks. Lecker, as a case in point, recently acknowledged Smaro Kamboureli's widely adopted anthology, *Making a Difference: Canadian Multicultural Literature* (1996, 2007), as "the end of canonical innocence" (*Keepers* 18). Whereas earlier anthologies symbolized, in Dermot McCarthy's words, "the authority of tradition" (30), an "instrument of national unity" (33), and a reconciliation of Canada's "contradictory [political and social] elements" (34), Kamboureli's anthology demonstrated iconoclasm and proved that a new generation of critics could radically, swiftly, and authoritatively upend existing canons.

In thinking about these deliberate reimaginings of the Canadian literary canon, Lecker has pointed out that the unceasing effort to add diversity to the Canadian canon (a process in which Kamboureli's anthology played a major part) has made "national literature anthologies" into "self-defeating" projects: "There can be no such thing as the accurate representation of the nation through a national literature anthology. Paradoxically, national literature anthologies underline the fact that nations are plural and unstable, unmappable in any form" (*Keepers* 8). At the very least, Lecker's argument is certainly true of Canada at large, a country in which a singular concept of nation – both culturally and literarily – has struggled to be believable and sustainable. Critics, therefore, can no longer placidly agree on the function or importance of authors in a canon that is arguably more diverse today than it has been in the past – so diverse, in fact, that Lecker argues that the canon no longer adheres to any discernible "code" or structure. Rather, canons are expressions of "personal choice," whereby "every teacher can become an anthologist" (*Keepers* 20). He argues that the canon appears to "shift rapidly from institution to institution and from instructor to instructor every year," and so claims for importance now rest with individuals working from their private canons (20).

That framework may seem freeing and appealing to progressive scholars attempting to overturn long-standing myths upheld by advocates of more conservative canons, but the private canon also risks insularity. Take, for instance, David Gilmour's infamous statement from 2011, an odious and extreme position: "When I [became a teacher] I said I would only teach the people that I truly, truly love. Unfortunately, none of those happen to be Chinese, or women" (Keeler). While Gilmour's statement is an outrageous example of a narcissistic (not to mention racist and sexist) insularity – insofar as he seems to be saying, "my canon and my experiences are the only ones worth teaching to a range of students" – it differs only in degree from the trope of "importance" that I'm interrogating here. Even if most scholars acknowledge diversity in ways that Gilmour refuses to do, our excessive claims for individual authors still obscure in comparable ways the value of that diversity by suggesting critical hierarchies.

What good is it to include, for instance, a variety of writers in the canon if I still tell my students, colleagues, and readers that Purdy is the most important or most representative Canadian writer among them? What good is that diversity if I position Purdy as the zenith of my private canon? Does doing so not implicitly devalue other literature, even as it is included in my courses and scholarship? Does doing so not signify a continuation of exclusionary illusions of "Canada," not to mention the conflation of "me" with "*we*"? There must be something more rigorous than these private canons, because while "the accessible canon" – that is, "those [canonical] works that remain in print" (Kelly 127) – may be more diverse and auspiciously unstable, as Lecker argues, instability hardly guarantees any genuine change.[12] There is no guarantee, in other words, that scholars will choose to approach diversity on any terms but those that have been handed down to them by a generation of critics whose practices mirror the monolithic nationalism of their era, and who were, therefore, constructing exclusionary frameworks for reading Canadian literature that continue what Daniel Coleman has called "the national project of building a British-based civility" that denigrates the values, knowledge, and literatures of other cultures (22). Indeed, it is impossible to argue that one writer is the most important or nationally representative without also suggesting that other writers – those less obviously aligned with what becomes the central myth of national identity or of private canons – are anomalous artists, whose contributions are somehow less deserving of attention.

Acknowledging diversity is an empty gesture if scholars fail to grasp what diversity offers: multiple positions from which to read and interpret the functions that underlie individual importance. Accepting the critical challenges those positions offer means rejecting the vertical mosaics embedded in much romantic-nationalist philosophy and, instead, considering the ways in which one author intersects with, connects to, disagrees with, or complements the positions of other writers of various backgrounds – without putting so much emphasis on value statements such as "best," "most," "finest," "foremost," and so forth. Those statements matter not at all if, as I am proposing here, the task of the literary critic is really to understand an *environment*, and not just an individual legacy.

To me, as an academic trained in a "Western" tradition, Purdy is certainly an important writer in Canadian literary history, and I can find much to appreciate, admire, study, and teach in his poems – but I cannot unequivocally grant him the status of "most important," because that would be true *only* from my specific perspective, which is, admittedly, very much informed by privileges and prejudices that I have only just begun to question and unsettle as a mature scholar. In part, that unsettling has come by way of incisive and eye-opening scholarship that encourages fuller mindfulness of one's privilege and place, and here I am deeply indebted to Deanna Reder's perceptive work: "identify and value your position," she has written, "which grants you a distinct perspective, even as it demands that you consider your intentions as you complete [your] work; imagine beyond the images and myths that saturate the field" (4). From Reder's work – and innumerable other critical and creative works – I have learned, again and again, something essential to both my life and my scholarship: genuine introspection assures change.[13] If I refuse self-critique, then I am unlikely to grow. Change is difficult only when we fail to look honestly at ourselves. But the moment I choose to acknowledge a vulnerability or critical oversight in my self and my work, then change becomes unavoidable. Then change becomes necessary. It precipitates new pursuits that affirm, in empowering ways, my ability to grow as a scholar and educator. We better understand those vulnerabilities by reading powerful and diverse literature, because doing so ensures that we resist reading individual writers like Purdy in vacuums that oversimplify their legacies. Earlier, I noted that Lorraine Weir believed that only literary works of relatively little "resistance or noise in the *institution*" (194; emphasis added) stroll effortlessly into the canon, but the proverbial and amorphous "institution" to which she refers is not solely at fault: individual scholars like Gilmour or Budde (and even myself) can be as resistant and remiss when building their private canons, and this is an issue of critical sensibility more than it is of institutional resistance.

Contemporary scholarship is therefore about more than just the *macro* (broad opportunities for canon formation); it is as much about the *micro* (the private canon and individual approaches to individual authors on smaller scales) and the realization that acknowledging diverse authors is insufficient while scholars still favour those who most resemble themselves. What, for instance, makes Atwood, Birney, Cohen, Page, Pratt, or Purdy more "important" to Canadian literature than Maria Campbell, whose *Halfbreed* (1973) led Gregory Scofield to regard her as his "friend, sister, and mother" (197), a claim that parallels those of other Indigenous authors?[14] Louise Bernice Halfe similarly recalls the overwhelming experience of reading Campbell's "courageous survival story" (email, 9 March 2017). In a telephone conversation with Halfe several years ago, I naively asked if Purdy's poetry had influenced her. Halfe told me, quite plainly, that she had not read him. Her statement caught me off guard because of assumptions I made, because of my position, about Purdy's legacy and impact. It was a revelatory moment for me, even if it seems somewhat silly in retrospect that I had so much difficulty comprehending that a poet like Halfe could write well and successfully in this country without reading Al Purdy.

In laying all of these issues bare, I am not suggesting that Purdy is unimportant or that he should be cut from broad or private canons; I stand by the general claims of my previous publications, each of which draws attention to Purdy's contributions to Canadian poetry as a mentor and as a groundbreaking poet.[15] I am, however, questioning the ways in which many scholars read and remember writers like Purdy by mythologizing them without deeply questioning their status and legacy from different perspectives.

Budde voices an analogous concern in his introduction to *The More Easily Kept Illusions*: "I think readers and students should look into this systemic racism and sexism in some of Purdy's work because it is indicative of prevailing thought that still exists in contemporary writing and needs revision. But here ... I have chosen poems that represent the best of Al Purdy, the style, themes, and energy that will be his legacy" (xv). The problem with Budde's statement, though, is that Purdy's casual racism and sexism are part of his legacy, and the decision to editorially circumvent those qualities of his work is not – as Budde might view it – evidence of an editor's sensitivity to theories and practices of decolonization or feminism. In fact, his approach is a variety of whitewashing: it relieves him of the challenging task of explaining, on the one hand, why poems such as "The Cariboo Horses" (his prime example of Purdy's racism) were celebrated in the mid-1960s and, on the other hand, why such poems can no longer be celebrated uncritically. In relieving himself of that editorial responsibility, Budde denies readers, students, and teachers opportunities to probe and question Purdy's politics, even as he half-heartedly encourages them to "look into" those issues further. This is not engaged or responsible scholarship; it represents an inadequate political gesture minimized further by Budde's assumption that "the best" qualities of writers and their work will, or should, compensate for their less desirable qualities.

Hence, we need to admit several things:

(1) Purdy is not quintessentially Canadian, even if he may be important to a specific idea of Canada, as other writers like Atwood, Birney, Campbell, Halfe, Page, and more have been important to specific frameworks within which we can study literature produced in this country;

(2) Reading Purdy or any author as "the most important" puts limits on what criteria determine importance and reinforces myths

of an illusory sameness in Canada, and the same trope surreptitiously replicates the more overt forms of exclusion that characterized early literary canons in Canada; and

(3) The critics who are unwilling to eject Purdy from new and more diverse canons – I am among them – need to engage with him, all of him, and not just "the best of Al Purdy."

If scholars accept those admissions, then they can look more critically at Purdy's work in ways that establish fruitful comparisons and explore productive contrasts with other writers whose literature has been of equal, if not greater, importance to readers living in or outside this country.

Now I have said everything but *how*. How does one preserve or teach Purdy without sidestepping the racism and sexism in his writing? One solution is to focus on more than Purdy in scholarship and in the classroom and, in so doing, to provide fuller and more thoughtful contexts for his work. I want to consider, briefly, two possible critical methods: *flexible influence* and *positional scholarship*.

A productive model of influence must be flexible in its assumptions about the ways in which authors receive each other. Critics can imagine influence as a critically engaged and dialogic act, rather than as a passive inheritance.[16] Susan Stanford Friedman challenges the myth of the latter model of influence: "Writers seldom duplicate their influential precursor(s); rather, they often work within a certain framework established by other writers or generic conventions, but vary aspects of it in significant ways" ("Weavings" 155). Variance is, as Friedman notes, one means of resisting straight mimicry, but influence needn't be strictly reverential; it can be an intricate negotiation. That is to say, influence often means the paradoxical acceptance and rejection of the precursor.

Consider Purdy's influence on Atwood, who belonged to a generation of writers inspired by Purdy's historiographic poetry. What I referred to earlier as his unabashed exploration of local Canadian history gave younger writers the confidence to undertake similar, prideful explorations of the past. In that regard, Laurie Ricou once wrote that Purdy exerted "more influence ... than ... any other Canadian writer" (8) in terms of both "subject-matter" and "form" (11–12). Ricou's potential hyperbole notwithstanding, one finds evidence of that inheritance in Atwood's writing. She wrote positively of Purdy's history poems in *Survival: A Thematic Guide to Canadian Literature* (1972): "There is a distinct archeological motif in Canadian literature – unearthing the buried and forgotten past – that for me is epitomized by Al Purdy's poems about poking around in the foundations of old Ontario farmhouses, graveyards, remains of Indian villages and other likely sites" (112). For writers of the post-1960 era, Purdy's "archeological" writing legitimated the history poems that younger writers undertook. Atwood hinted at Purdy's empowering model in a letter to him, in which she said that she was "glad" he liked her *Journals of Susanna Moodie* (1970): "if there was one Can. poet I'd dedicate it to," she continued, "it would be you" (letter, 26 March 1970). For a relatively young poet like Atwood, Purdy's approval clearly meant something.

This indebtedness, however, is complex. On the one hand, Atwood was very much a nationalist in an era of widespread cultural nationalism, and so she shared with Purdy the historical fascinations of his 1960s poetry. At the same time, her feminism aligned not at all with his deep-rooted misogyny. In his letters and poetry, Purdy often objectifies and/or denigrates women: Budde's example is the "maddening bitch" in "Song of the Impermanent Husband" (1965; *BR* 61), but we can also look at Purdy's comments about Atwood's Moodie, a woman he describes as "not quite human" and "a bitch" ("Atwood's" 83). In his review of Atwood's book, he goes further and condescends to Atwood herself: "I disagree with most of Atwood's viewpoints wholeheartedly, and the circumstances will never arrive when I can say the rest of this review to her personally (besides, she's a woman, even though very intelligent)" (84). These are examples of the kind of casual misogyny that would eventually lead Shirley Gibson to write suspiciously of male-authored Canadian poetry of the 1960s and 1970s, a body of work she felt was ruled by "that clutch of Canadian males, found mostly in the West, who drink beer, relieve themselves in the snow, scale the lower slopes of the Rockies and call plaintively to their fellow poets while 'woman throws wood on fire'" (34); and though I earlier praised "At the Quinte Hotel," Eurithe Purdy remembers it as an "off-putting" poem with an overly "macho tone" (52).

Atwood felt similarly about Purdy in more general ways: "For a young male poet of [the 1960s], [Purdy's] energy and [his] approach – casual, slangy, subversive of recent poetic convention – could be liberating and inspirational, and some found in him an ersatz father figure. But for a young female poet – well, this was not the sort of father figure it would be altogether steadying to have" ("Foreword" 17). While recognizing that Purdy's representation of masculinity made him a less than ideal mentor for young female poets, Atwood adds that she gradually realized "that the drunk in the bar was also a major storyteller ... he's above all an explorer ... digging up the bones and shards of a forgotten ancestral past" (17–18). Here is a model of influence consciously managed from positions of both acceptance and rejection: acceptance of Purdy's method and rejection of his politics. In such a model, his importance as a poet is heavily negotiated rather than uncritically assumed.

Atwood's central influence as she wrote *The Journals of Susanna Moodie* was, of course, not Purdy. Moodie was Atwood's "steadying" model, because of what she – a nineteenth-century pioneer, writer, and mother – had been able to do: "We read writing by women," Atwood said in 1990, because "we were curious about the *lives* of these women. How had they managed it? We knew about the problems; we wanted to know there were solutions ... It was comforting as well as exciting to read these writers ... It was more like a laying on of hands, a feeling that you too could do it because, look, it could be done" ("If" 17). Purdy could encourage a writer like Atwood to cultivate her historical curiosity, but he could never serve the function of a foremother like Moodie, who showed, in a wholly different way, that "it could be done." It is important to respect the complexity of that literary inheritance. This nuanced model of influence can be a catalyst for intricate, historically informed literary criticism and teaching. We can place poems from *The Cariboo Horses* (1965) alongside *The Journals of Susanna Moodie* with an eye to thematic or aesthetic continuities, as well as to evident political discontinuities.

Similarly, it would be rewarding to juxtapose "Roblin's Mills [II]" (1968) and "Joe Barr" (1968) with Margaret Laurence's *The Diviners* (1974), a novel that begins with the closing lines of "Roblin's Mills [II]" and whose Christie Logan bears a remarkable resemblance to Purdy's Barr, who tells "himself stories all day" and pushes "garbage with his stick" (BR 177). This was also the novel that irreparably damaged the friendship between Laurence and Purdy by generating between them heated debates about feminism. Laurence openly identified as a feminist, and she imagined *The Diviners* as a thorough exploration of that political consciousness. Laurence's self-reflexive protagonist, Morag, is inspired by Catharine Parr Traill's determination to be both mother and writer. She often wonders how Traill could ever have found time to write while weighed down by domestic duties: "Breakfast ... feed[ing] the chickens ... children's education hour ... Cleaning ... baking ... All before lunch" (108–9). Just as Moodie was a foremother to Atwood, Traill was a foremother to Laurence. Although Laurence was wary of Purdy's potential response to such aspects of *The Diviners*, she anxiously wanted him to read it. After months of hearing nothing from him about the book, she began to assume that her feminism discomforted Purdy. His delay in reading *The Diviners* effectively ended their friendship, and Purdy later recalled that he "felt pushed into a corner ... she thought

I felt threatened" ("Disconnections" 203). A breaking point came in December 1974, when an irritated Purdy wrote an angry reply to one of Laurence's phone calls: "I am continually on the defensive with you about [*The Diviners*]. I am charged with not liking it, not having read it, being threatened by it ... I do think you might dispense with that old cliché 'being threatened' – the prime favourite of all women's lib non-thinkers" (letter, 10 December 1974). This hostile response captures some of the tension between the two, as well as Purdy's evident skepticism about feminist thought (or what he perceived, quite narrowly, to be the absence of thought in feminism). While Purdy's poetry obviously influenced Laurence, this exchange, like Atwood's various exchanges with Purdy, is further evidence of the understandable ambivalence with which some writers received his literature and example.

Reading Purdy in relation to these writers enables critics to recognize his capacity to be a positive influence on younger authors, even as his politics run counter to their feminism. To read Purdy (or any writer) in this way presents an opportunity to portray intricate literary intersections that demonstrate thought-provoking departures and innovations in Canada's literary history without oversimplifying the impact, character, and legacy of any one author.

The other approach to Purdy's poetry that I suggest is *positional scholarship*, a term I derive from debates about literary canons and decolonization. For decades, there have been efforts to teach "positioning" as a response to diverse literary traditions in and outside Canada. One of the places in which I first encountered such efforts was Helen Hoy's brilliant introduction to *How Should I Read These?* (2001), in which she synthesizes works by Uma Narayan, Chandra Mohanty, and Susan Stanford Friedman in order to argue the importance of "[m]ethodological – or epistemological – humility and caution" (she draws the terms from Narayan specifically), which require readers to recognize their "insider" or "outsider" positions in relation to specific knowledge systems (18). For Hoy, this strategy is essential to non-Indigenous-authored scholarship on Indigenous literatures: we must be explicit about the place from which we begin our scholarship, especially when we are outsiders to the cultures about which we write.[17]

At the same time, I think this strategy is essential in more general contexts. Scholars should consider a broad readership. For instance, a critic arguing for a non-Indigenous writer's "importance" should be mindful of the potential impact that argument might have on, for instance, Indigenous readers. It is, indeed, important that academics test the validity of their arguments in the context of various political, social, economic, or cultural locations, rather than working strictly within their own. Too often scholars presuppose that the "self"/"other" binary is relevant only in cases where – to stick with Hoy's context – Indigenous literature is at the forefront of a study, despite the fact that the binary is, explicitly or implicitly, present in every study. The fact that I am situated within a specific system of knowledge does not simply become irrelevant because I undertake projects that limit my direct dialogue with communities whose knowledge systems and experiences differ from mine; if it were possible to live under such a rock, then academics could simply choose to avoid the most important and challenging questions currently shaping the field of which they claim to be a part. Therefore, if I make an argument for Purdy's importance – "our Whitman," the "quintessentially Canadian" poet, or "the central poet of our experience" – then I have to test the validity of that claim by imagining its reception by readers whose experiences and influences may be altogether different from my own. And if my claim fails that test, then I must be willing to qualify and complicate it without displacing that responsibility onto students, readers, or other scholars.

In order to better explain positional scholarship, I want to build on Budde's introduction to *The More Easily Kept Illusions*, in which he rightly points out that Purdy makes careless assumptions about and offers reductive stereotypes of Indigenous peoples in poems such as "The Cariboo Horses" and, I would add, others like the shockingly offensive "R.C.M.P. Post"; in the latter, Purdy's speaker observes a "drunk Indian" and says, "I wonder if when he's sober / he reverts back to being a man" (*SD* 44). In an article published a decade ago, I noted another example of such carelessness in Purdy's "The Battlefield at Batoche" (1972; *BR* 219–22), in which he dismisses the existence of contemporary Métis communities by stating that the "Métis nation was born and died" in 1885. That article outlined the general features of Purdy's aesthetics and philosophical style as they were manifested in that poem, features I argued (and still argue) to be markers of his poetic sophistication: "self-reflexive authority, regionalism, a fragmentation/wholeness binary, and epistemological apprehension" (Weingarten, "Coherence" 147). Thereafter, I posed a concluding and unanswered question: "is [Purdy's] historiographic critique complicit in or positioned against a colonial history of Canada?" (147). At the time, I was unable (or, more likely, unwilling) to offer an answer.

The answer seems much simpler to me now: Purdy's poem *is* complicit in perpetuating the mythologizing and erasure often found in settler-authored histories of the Métis. My praise for "The Battlefield at Batoche" is as genuine now as when I published that article in 2010, but I cannot dismiss the fact that Purdy's portrayal of the Métis is reductive insofar as he blatantly rejects the possibility of a resolute community with an enduring political consciousness:

> In evening listening
> to the duplicate rain-sound on the roof
> of our camped trailer it seems
> that I was wrong about my motives
> and the dark girls mourning at Batoche
> the dead men in shallow rifle pits
> these mean something
> the rain speaks to them
> the seasons pass
> just outside their hearing
> but what they died for has faded away
> and become something quite different
> past justice and injustice[.]

I teach "The Battlefield at Batoche" as a model of Purdy's poetic ear and meditations on history: the sparse gerunds and participles offer faint echoes within the poem that parallel the aural distance the speaker notes between a past that "whisper[s] across the fields of eternity" and the present, in which the speaker, "listening," admits that he can hear only the rain. Because he can hear only *his* present, his knowledge of the past is flawed or, at the very least, incomplete. Purdy's implicit admission is sensible, given how easily he elides the history of the Métis by speaking of them wholly in the past tense: their cause has "faded away" and the injustices of the era are in "the past." Like his claim that "the Métis nation was born and died" at Batoche, these lines reinforce long-running myths in Canadian history and literature of the "vanishing race," and they demonstrate Purdy's privilege: he possesses the unearned confidence to write or unwrite an entire people, disregarding the fact that these "injustice[s]" persisted in 1972 – and persist today. That scene is evidence of one of Purdy's greatest shortcomings as a writer: his romanticizing, to the point of complete distortion, of the lastness and lostness of peoples and things. He meditatively revels in the sombreness of a future in which "the Ojibway are all dead" ("The Horseman of Agawa," BR 210), the past in which the "last Dorset" carves an ivory swan for his absent family ("Lament for the Dorsets," BR 161), the "broken consonants" of a seemingly vanished people ("Remains of an Indian Village," BR 53), and the "Dead Beothucks of Newfoundland" ("Joint Account," BR 183). These are the kind of poems that led Margery Fee to argue in the 1980s that Canadian literature prefers "dead Indians" to "contemporary [living] Indians" ("Romantic" 16). However well the above lines from "The Battlefield at Batoche" capture some of Purdy's philosophical depth, they also capture his problematic assumptions about cultures of which he had too little knowledge and to which he evidently had no connection.

To read a poem like "The Battlefield at Batoche" responsibly means placing it alongside other works of literature that approach this history from a wholly different position. The opportunity to interrogate and topple the prejudices of long-celebrated poets like Purdy is *why* I still teach such a problematic poem. Published a year after Purdy's poem, Maria Campbell's *Halfbreed* perfectly captures the ease with which one can undermine Purdy's assessment of the past: Campbell recalls that her grandmother "never accepted defeat at Batoche, and she would always say, 'Because they killed Riel they think they have killed us too, but some day, my girl, it will be different'" (11). There are other fruitful comparisons that similarly challenge Purdy's narrative of the Métis, such as Marilyn Dumont's "Letter to Sir John A. Macdonald" (1996):

> Dear John: I'm still here and halfbreed,
> after all these years
> you're dead, funny thing,
> that railway you wanted so badly,
> there was talk a year ago
> of shutting it down
> and part of it was shut down
> the dayliner at least,
> "from sea to shining sea,"
> and you know, John,
> after all that shuffling us around to suit the settlers,
> we're still here and Métis. (52)

In that first stanza, Dumont's speaker twice insists on presence, with slightly different connotations underlying each phrase: "I'm still here and halfbreed" focuses specifically on her "I" and claims the racialist language of colonizers to identify her. The second iteration of her sentiment – "we're still here and Métis" – has grander implications. First, it suggests community ("we"), and it replaces the racializing and lower-case "halfbreed" with the upper-case proper noun "Métis," a better indication of self-definition than the English pejorative "halfbreed." That second announcement of both self and community, with its connotations of continuity and survival, contrasts with Purdy's image of a Métis nation that died with Riel.

In fact, whereas Purdy's poem presents a rather powerless people – reminiscent, if only loosely, of the historian George Stanley's thoughtless portrayal of the Métis as a people whose "self-confidence" has been lost and can "never [be] possess[ed] again" (4) – Dumont's poem uses the cliché of a "Dear John" letter with powerful and comic irony. A typical "Dear John" letter would have been used by a wife to acknowledge her desertion of her husband (the history of the letter has its roots in announcements of wartime breakups sent by post) and is therefore a promise of absence (i.e., "when you get home, I won't be here"). Dumont's "Dear John," however, is an assertion of her *presence* and "John's" absence: "you're gone," she insists throughout her poem, "and I'm still here." And much more than "John" is gone. His legacy is also fading: the railway has been partially "shut down," and his efforts to displace and fragment the Métis have evidently failed. They are, Dumont reminds him, still here, a reminder repeated in much Métis-authored literature since the 1970s.[18] Purdy writes away the Métis by too presumptuously conflating Riel's death with a nation's death; Dumont, however, writes that "Riel is dead, / but he just keeps coming back" (70).

I teach Dumont's "Letter to Sir John A. Macdonald" because it offers something that Purdy's poetry cannot: it shows the resilience of the Métis and demonstrates that poetic language can announce and empower people in the present as much as it can be used (as Purdy does) to elegize a dynamic past. That perspective on history is as vital, if not more so, to the classroom and to Canadian scholarship as Purdy's ghostly mills and family histories.

This is the kind of pressure that needs to be put on claims about Purdy's legacy – because he matured as a writer during a tumultuous era in Canadian history, an era so politically divided that it would be impossible to assume that any one writer adequately captures the social directions, political fervour, and competing definitions of *nation* during that period or after. This was an era that proves the recent claim of Adam Chapnick and Norman Hillmer that there can "be no single or static twentieth-century Canadian nationalist ideology ... The meanings given to 'Canada' [over the twentieth century] were multiple, fluid, and contradictory" (5). It is therefore fruitless and frankly irresponsible to explore literature produced in Canada under the assumption that any writer can be anything more than a narrative pivot in a very large and multi-faceted story.

It is worth adding, too, that those critical narratives often end up sidestepping authors' self-portrayals. A case in point: vague hints of my argument are peppered throughout Purdy's own writing. While critics may be able to write off his self-reflexive questioning as playfully comic in poems such as "House Guest" ("I guess I was wrong," BR 130) and "Home-Made Beer" ("PS, I was wrong –," BR 74), his introspective writing in "The Peaceable Kingdom" (1970; BR 230–3) is unmistakably solemn, even elegiac.[19] He wrote the poem in the wake of the October Crisis in 1970, during which Pierre Laporte was murdered by nationalist revolutionaries affiliated with the Front de Libération du Québec. To Purdy, that event epitomized his rethinking of national unity and national discontent. His doubt about such ideals permeates the poem, as he finds himself "thinking of the change come over us / and by us I mean the country / our character and conception of ourselves." He says more of his revelation in his closing section:

> ... bubbles break as we join
> the mainstream of history
> with detention camps and the smell of blood
> and valid reasons for writing great novels
> in the future the past closing around
> and leaving us where I never wanted to be
> in a different country from the one
> where I grew up[.]

Here, Purdy's Canada is no longer aligned with Pierre Trudeau's "Peaceable Kingdom"; it is as implicated in the history of colonialism, genocide, and oppression as any other country. He leaves it ambiguous whether or not this revelation denotes a change in the country or simply a change in his perspective, but I suspect that most readers today, knowledgeable of what the nationalist project of Canada has looked like since its beginning, would recognize the latter interpretation to be the more sensible position for Purdy to adopt. This is a seldom-anthologized poem that offers a rare sight in Purdy's oeuvre: rather than his typically comic and oafish reaction to his own ignorance (as in "At the Quinte Hotel"), here he portrays his sombre shock at an evidently painful epiphany, one that brings him to challenge, in ways he seems to have long resisted, his own quixotic vision of Canada. It is an unfamiliar stance for Purdy to adopt, and the publication of this particular poem coincides (perhaps accidentally, perhaps not) with a phase of his career during which he began to write less about Canadian history and more about his travels across the world, from Italy to Japan to the Galápagos – and that cosmopolitanism, too, has been of much less interest to critics than his poems of the 1960s.

If scholars nevertheless wish to return to Purdy's poems about Canada, then it is essential to understand his writing as an opportunity for scholarship that teaches readers how to engage with, rather than shy away from, the complexity inherent in studies of national, cultural, and individual identities. The model of scholarship I am imagining resists the insularity of a private canon and attends to variations in perspectives and in literature. To believe that ethical and responsible teachers and scholars can do otherwise is the easiest and most convenient illusion to hold on to. No perspective is all-encompassing or incontestable, and no legacy is unambiguous or immune to fruitful challenges. Difficult though it may be, it is also fulfilling and necessary to negotiate and balance our judgments of writers, politics, and history, and to produce scholarship that recognizes critical challenges in problematic literature, even as we encourage audiences to be drawn into our passion for the arts. This is especially important in the classroom. Teachers must be willing to encourage students to think critically, even about the books they love, and that can be done without denying either teachers or students the chance to continue loving them.

I love Purdy's poetry. I can forget neither my experience as an undergraduate watching a professor weep while reading "The Country North of Belleville," nor the dented stomach I feel when I read "On Being Human" aloud. But I also don't mistake those memories or feelings for evidence of something universal in the experience of reading Purdy's writing. His legacy is not one thing and cannot be regarded in just one way. The same is true of any other writer. The more we deny authors their range – their talent, flaws, prejudices, and successes, and the intricacy of their politics – and their connections to or disconnections from writers of different positions, the more we deny our students and colleagues the opportunity for truly prodigious engagements with a field finally appreciating a range of valid knowledge systems and inclusive world views.

NOTES

1 Daniel Coleman has written extensively about the growth of such ideas in Canada, noting that these "nineteenth-century romantic-nationalist idea[s] ... equated each nation with a single culture" (4). In this model of national development, "some societies [are] farther ahead on the single timeline of civilization, while others [are] 'backward' or delayed" (11).
2 Purdy's pivotal experiments in fusing history and poetry, especially in the 1960s, laid the groundwork for many subsequent poets who would continue and develop these experiments: Atwood, John Newlove, Barry McKinnon, and Andrew Suknaski each produced historically conscious poetry that, to one degree or another, emulated Purdy's writing of the sixties. These are just a handful of names on a much longer list of poets whom Purdy influenced. For further consideration of Purdy's influence, see Lane, Ricou, and Atwood, *Survival*.

3 The trope of "Canada's Whitman" was deployed frequently from the 1940s to the 1980s. Patrick Lane, for instance, connects the work of several Canadian poets to Whitman: "William Carlos Williams's frustration with Pound and Eliot was based upon what he saw as a betrayal of the American voice in favour of a European one. What Williams demanded was a cadence and a measure uniquely American, a poetry built of 'a local pride.' In that sense his poetic was as great as Whitman's. It is the same for Purdy, Newlove, Atwood, Suknaski, and others. Theirs has been a new making, something never seen before, done at great risk" (64).
4 See Lecker, "Canonization."
5 Others have made similar remarks. Robert Kroetsch, for instance, proposes that "Solecki's Purdy [in *The Last Canadian Poet*] is the fulfillment of Solecki's own migrant dream" (21).
6 From Volume 5 of *Canada's Residential Schools: The Final Report of the Truth and Reconciliation Commission of Canada*:
> Over a century of cultural genocide has left most Aboriginal languages on the verge of extinction. The disproportionate apprehension of Aboriginal children by child welfare agencies and the disproportionate imprisonment and victimization of Aboriginal people are all part of the legacy of the way that Aboriginal children were treated in residential schools. Many students were permanently damaged by residential schools. Separated from their parents, they grew up knowing neither respect nor affection. A school system that mocked and suppressed their families' cultures and traditions destroyed their sense of self-worth. Poorly trained teachers working with an irrelevant curriculum left students feeling branded as failures. Children who had been bullied and abused carried a burden of shame and anger for the rest of their lives. Overwhelmed by this legacy, many succumbed to despair and depression. Countless lives were lost to alcohol and drugs. Families were destroyed, children were displaced by the child welfare system ... The legacy has also profoundly affected [survivors'] partners, their children, their grandchildren, their extended families, and their communities. (3)
7 The White Paper advocated "the gradual elimination of reserves," which effectively meant that all Indigenous groups would be responsible strictly to Canadian laws and government and that all Indigenous peoples would lose special status (Finkel 249). In 1970, the "Indian Chiefs of Alberta" replied with what came to be known as the "Red Paper," which rejected the premise of the White Paper and its efforts to assimilate Indigenous peoples (Newhouse 290–1). Under pressure, Pierre Trudeau's government withdrew the White Paper in 1971.
8 Until 1969, most, if not all, government communication was entirely in English. It was not until the Official Languages Act (1969) that the Canadian

government officially recognized the right of francophone politicians to conduct business in French.

9 The Chinese Immigration Act (1885) ensured that each Chinese immigrant entering Canada would be required to pay fifty dollars to complete the immigration process. Those responsible for the "head tax" based their model on a Royal Commission report that proposed a ten-dollar tax, which the federal government believed was too small.

10 From the Indian Act (1867; relevant section amended 1876): "Any Indian who may be admitted to the degree of Doctor of Medicine, or to any other degree by any University of Learning, or who may be admitted in any Province of the Dominion to practice law either as an Advocate or as a Barrister or Counsellor or Solicitor or Attorney or to be a Notary Public, or who may enter Holy Orders or who may be licensed by any denomination of Christians as a Minister of the Gospel, shall *ipso facto* become enfranchised and be under this Act" (86.1). On Jewish quotas, see Tulchinsky: "Ira Mackay, dean of arts [at McGill University], acted on the view that 'the simple obvious truth is that the Jewish people are of no use to us in this country'" (318).

11 Lecker returns to this article in his *Keepers of the Code: English-Canadian Literary Anthologies and the Representation of Nation* (2013): "In attempting [in 1990] to explain the mimetic bias of the Canadian canon and the majority of its critics, I made no mention of Canadian anthologists, arguably the most influential group of all when it comes to defining the English-Canadian canon" (5).

12 Peggy Kelly's invocation of this concept comes from Alastair Fowler's *Kinds of Literature* (1982):

> The literary canon in the broadest sense comprises the entire written corpus, together with all surviving oral literature. But much of this potential canon remains in practice inaccessible for a variety of reasons, such as the rarity of its records, which may be sequestered in large libraries. Hence the more limited accessible canon. Accessible literature is very much narrower than the *New Cambridge Bibliography of English Literature* might suggest. (Fowler 214–15)

13 I recommend the following critical works: Cynthia Sugars's *Home-Work: Postcolonialism, Pedagogy, and Canadian Literature* (2004), Laura Moss's *Is Canada Postcolonial? Unsettling Canadian Literature* (2003), Bryan Palmer's *Canada's 1960s: The Ironies of Identity in a Rebellious Era* (2009), and Deanna Reder and Linda M. Morra's *Learn, Teach, Challenge: Approaching Indigenous Literatures* (2016). Some of the most enlightening works I have read have been memoirs – including Maria Campbell's *Halfbreed* (1973) and Gregory Scofield's *Thunder through My Veins: Memories of a Métis Childhood* (2000) – as

well as poetry and fiction by Indigenous writers. At the same time, the realizations I note in this chapter have also come from reading works by many non-Indigenous writers: Madeleine Thien's *Simple Recipes* (2001), Souvankham Thammavongsa's *Found* (2007), and Renée Sarojini Saklikar's *Children of Air India* (2013) are only a few examples.

14 I use "Canadian literature" to denote literature produced in the country of Canada (which, of course, will include a range of more specific national literatures), including literatures that contest the historical concepts of "Canadian" as an identity. I am, however, willing to leave that interpretation of the term open to debate. "Other Indigenous authors": consider, for instance, the suggestion that "Daniel David Moses uses a metaphor of kinship to assert that Aboriginal writers in Canada experience Campbell as an active influence, calling her '[t]he mother of us all[,]' and Lenore Keeshig-Tobias agrees, '[s]he is. Of course she is'" (Fagan et al. 267).

15 See, for instance, Weingarten, "'Stories.'"

16 See Weingarten, *Sharing the Past*.

17 As a non-Indigenous scholar, I find Hoy's discussions regarding positioning particularly resonant, but I draw attention once again to the work of Reder, who has edited (with Morra) an anthology – *Learn, Teach, Challenge* – that, I suspect, will be a permanent fixture in the Canadian critical canon: it offers essential readings in the decolonization of literature and ruminates on widely applicable reading and teaching strategies in the context of Indigenous literatures.

18 "We are still here" is a recurring phrase and sentiment. It is, for example, the first sentence of Ute Lischke and David T. McNab's introduction to *The Long Journey of a Forgotten People: Métis Identities and Family Histories* (2007), and Christine Welsh uses the phrase in "*Women in the Shadows*: Reclaiming a Métis Heritage" (1996): "For our words and music and images are testaments to the remarkable fact that we are still here – that we have survived near-annihilation and that we continue to resist – and though they necessarily give voice to our pain, they also express our vision for the future, and in so doing they become tools for healing, for empowerment, and for change" (66).

19 Purdy initially published "The Peaceable Kingdom" as a broadside (1970), though it appeared later in *Sex and Death* (1973).

ARCHIVAL SOURCES

Margaret Atwood Papers. MS. Coll. 335. Thomas Fisher Rare Book Library, University of Toronto.
    Letter from Margaret Atwood to Purdy, 26 March 1970, Box 76.

Margaret Laurence Fonds. 1980-001. Clara Thomas Archives and Special Collections, York University.
    Letter from Purdy to Margaret Laurence, 10 December 1974, Box 4, Folder 103C.

Al Purdy Fonds. 2071b. Queen's University Archives.
    Letter from Purdy to George Bowering, 26 September 1973, Box 2, Folder 43.

REFERENCES

Allard, Donna, and Nat Hall. "Where Poetry Is More than Just Words." In *And Left a Place to Stand On: Poems and Essays on Al Purdy*, edited by Allan Briesmaster, 45. Brighton, ON: Hidden Book, 2009.

Atwood, Margaret. Foreword to *Beyond Remembering: The Collected Poems of Al Purdy*, edited by Al Purdy and Sam Solecki, 17–18. Madeira Park, BC: Harbour Publishing, 2000.

– "If You Can't Say Something Nice, Don't Say Anything at All." In *Language in Her Eye: Views on Writing and Gender by Canadian Women Writing in English*, edited by Libby Scheier et al., 15–25. Toronto: Coach House, 1990.

– *The Journals of Susanna Moodie*. Toronto: Oxford University Press, 1970.

– *Survival: A Thematic Guide to Canadian Literature*. Toronto: House of Anansi Press, 1972.

Bowering, George. *Al Purdy*. Toronto: Copp Clark, 1970.

Brown, E.K. *On Canadian Poetry*. Toronto: Ryerson Press, 1943.

Budde, Robert. "Codes of Canadian Racism: Anglocentric and Assimilationist Cultural Rhetoric." In *Home-Work: Postcolonialism, Pedagogy, and Canadian Literature*, edited by Cynthia Sugars, 245–56. Ottawa: University of Ottawa Press, 2004.

– Introduction to *The More Easily Kept Illusions: The Poetry of Al Purdy*, edited by Robert Budde, vii–xv. Waterloo, ON: Wilfrid Laurier University Press, 2006.

–, ed. *The More Easily Kept Illusions: The Poetry of Al Purdy*. Waterloo, ON: Wilfrid Laurier University Press, 2006.

Campbell, Maria. *Halfbreed*. Toronto: McClelland & Stewart, 1973.

Canada's Residential Schools: The Final Report of the Truth and Reconciliation Commission of Canada. Vol. 5. Montreal and Kingston: McGill-Queen's University Press, 2015.

Chapnick, Adam, and Norman Hillmer. "Introduction: An Abundance of Nationalisms." In *Canadas of the Mind: The Making and Unmaking of Canadian Nationalisms in the Twentieth Century*, edited by Adam Chapnick and Norman Hillmer, 3–14. Montreal and Kingston: McGill-Queen's University Press, 2007.

Coleman, Daniel. *White Civility: The Literary Project of English Canada.*
  Toronto: University of Toronto Press, 2006.
Dumont, Marilyn. *A Really Good Brown Girl.* 1996. London, ON: Brick Books,
  2015.
Fagan, Kristina, et al. "Reading the Reception of Maria Campbell's *Halfbreed*."
  Canadian Journal of Native Studies 29, no. 1–2 (2009): 257–81.
Fee, Margery. *Literary Land Claims: The "Indian Land Question" from Pontiac's
  War to Attawapiskat.* Waterloo, ON: Wilfrid Laurier University Press, 2015.
– "Romantic Nationalism and the Image of Native People in Contemporary
  English-Canadian Literature." In *The Native in Literature,* edited by Cheryl
  Calver et al., 15–33. Oakville, ON: ECW Press, 1987.
Finkel, Alvin. *Our Lives: Canada after 1945.* Toronto: Lorimer, 1997.
Fowler, Alastair. *Kinds of Literature: An Introduction to the Theory of Genres and
  Modes.* Cambridge, MA: Harvard University Press, 1982.
Friedman, Susan Stanford. "Beyond White and Other: Relationality and Narra-
  tives of Race in Feminist Discourse." *Signs* 21, no. 1 (Autumn 1995): 1–49.
– "Weavings: Intertextuality and the (Re)Birth of the Author." In *Influence and
  Intertextuality in Literary History,* edited by Jay Clayton and Eric Rothstein,
  146–80. Madison: University of Wisconsin Press, 1991.
Gibson, Shirley. "Blessed Be Macho's Lack." *Globe and Mail,* 26 June 1976: 34.
Hoy, Helen. *How Should I Read These? Native Women Writers in Canada.*
  Toronto: University of Toronto Press, 2001.
Keeler, Emily M. "The Gilmour Transcript." *Hazlitt,* 25 September 2013,
  http://hazlitt.net/blog/gilmour-transcript.
Kelly, Peggy. "Anthologies and the Canonization Process: A Case Study of the
  English-Canadian Literary Field, 1920–1950." In *Anthologizing Canadian
  Literature: Theoretical and Cultural Perspectives,* edited by Robert Lecker,
  127–44. Waterloo, ON: Wilfrid Laurier University Press, 2015.
Kroetsch, Robert. "Reading Solecki Reading Purdy: A Digressive Review."
  Review of *The Last Canadian Poet: An Essay on Al Purdy,* by Sam Solecki.
  The Fiddlehead, no. 204 (Summer 2000): 20–3.
Kruk, Laurie. "'Outsiders' and 'Insiders': Teaching Native/Canadian Literature
  as Meeting Place." In *Home-Work: Postcolonialism, Pedagogy, and Canadian
  Literature,* edited by Cynthia Sugars, 301–20. Ottawa: University of Ottawa
  Press, 2004.
Lane, Patrick. "The Unyielding Phrase." *Canadian Literature,* no. 122–3
  (Autumn–Winter 1989): 57–64.
Laurence, Margaret. *The Diviners.* Toronto: McClelland & Stewart, 1974.
Lecker, Robert. "The Canonization of Canadian Literature: An Inquiry into
  Value." *Critical Inquiry* 16, no. 3 (Spring 1990): 656–71.
– *Keepers of the Code: English-Canadian Literary Anthologies and the
  Representation of Nation.* Toronto: University of Toronto Press, 2013.

Lee, Dennis. "The Poetry of Al Purdy: An Afterword." In *The Collected Poems of Al Purdy*, edited by Russell Brown, 371–91. Toronto: McClelland & Stewart, 1986.
– "Running and Dwelling: Homage to Al Purdy." *Saturday Night*, September 1972: 14–16.
Lischke, Ute, and David T. McNab. "We Are Still Here." In *The Long Journey of a Forgotten People: Métis Identities and Family Histories*, edited by Ute Lischke and David T. McNab, 1–9. Waterloo, ON: Wilfrid Laurier University Press, 2007.
McCarthy, Dermot. "Early Canadian Literary Histories and the Function of a Canon." In *Canadian Canons: Essays in Literary Value*, edited by Robert Lecker, 30–45. Toronto: University of Toronto Press, 1992.
McNeilly, Kevin. "Poetry." In *The Cambridge History of Canadian Literature*, edited by Coral Ann Howells and Eva-Marie Kröller, 422–40. Cambridge: Cambridge University Press, 2009.
Mohanty, Chandra Talpade. "On Race and Voice: Challenges for Liberal Education in the 1990s." *Cultural Critique*, no. 14 (Winter 1989–90): 179–208.
Narayan, Uma. "Contesting Cultures: 'Westernization,' Respect for Cultures, and Third-World Feminists." In *The Second Wave: A Reader in Feminist Theory*, edited by Linda Nicholson, 396–414. New York: Routledge, 1997.
Nesbitt, Bruce. *Earle Birney*. Toronto: McGraw-Hill Ryerson, 1974.
Newhouse, David. "Aboriginal Identities and the New Indian Problem." In *Canadas of the Mind: The Making and Unmaking of Canadian Nationalisms in the Twentieth Century*, edited by Norman Hillmer and Adam Chapnick, 287–99. Montreal and Kingston: McGill-Queen's University Press, 2007.
Nischik, Reingard M. "'The Translation of the World into Words' and the Female Tradition: Margaret Atwood, 'Significant Moments in the Life of My Mother.'" 1983. In *The Canadian Short Story: Interpretations*, edited by Reingard M. Nischik, 331–40. Rochester, NY: Camden House, 2010.
Purdy, Al. "Atwood's Moodie." *Canadian Literature*, no. 47 (Winter 1971): 80–4.
– *Beyond Remembering: The Collected Poems of Al Purdy*. Edited by Al Purdy and Sam Solecki. Madeira Park, BC: Harbour Publishing, 2000.
– *The Cariboo Horses*. Toronto: McClelland & Stewart, 1965.
– *In Search of Owen Roblin*. Toronto: McClelland & Stewart, 1974.
– "An Interview with Al Purdy." Interview by Peter O'Brien. *Essays on Canadian Writing*, no. 49 (Summer 1993): 147–62.
– *Sex and Death*. Toronto: McClelland & Stewart, 1973.
Purdy, Eurithe. "If Those Walls Could Talk: A Reminiscence by Eurithe Purdy." In *The Al Purdy A-Frame Anthology*, edited by Paul Vermeersch, 39–53. Madeira Park, BC: Harbour Publishing, 2009.

Reder, Deanna, and Linda Morra. Introduction to *Learn, Teach, Challenge: Approaching Indigenous Literatures*, edited by Deanna Reder and Linda M. Morra, 1–4. Waterloo, ON: Wilfrid Laurier University Press, 2016.

Ricou, Laurie. "Poetry." In *Literary History of Canada*. Vol. 4: *Canadian Literature in English*, edited by W.H. New, 3–45. Toronto: University of Toronto Press, 1990.

Scofield, Gregory. *Thunder through My Veins: Memories of a Métis Childhood*. Toronto: Harper, 2000.

Silverberg, Mark. "The Can(adi)onization of Al Purdy." *Essays on Canadian Writing*, no. 70 (Spring 2000): 226–51.

Simmons, Sylvie. *I'm Your Man: The Life of Leonard Cohen*. New York: HarperCollins, 2012.

Solecki, Sam. *The Last Canadian Poet: An Essay on Al Purdy*. Toronto: University of Toronto Press, 1999.

Stanley, George. *Louis Riel: Patriot or Rebel?* Ottawa: Canadian Historical Association, 1954.

Stanley, Timothy. "Why I Killed Canadian History: Towards an Anti-Racist History in Canada." *Histoire Sociale–Social History* 33, no. 65 (May 2000): 79–103.

Stouck, David. *Major Canadian Authors: A Critical Introduction*. Lincoln: University of Nebraska Press, 1988.

Tulchinsky, Gerald. *Canada's Jews: A People's Journey*. Toronto: University of Toronto Press, 2008.

Weingarten, J.A. "'The Coherence of Canadian History Was Lost': Al Purdy, George Bowering, and the Factitious Louis Riel." *Open Letter* 14, no. 4 (Fall 2010): 131–51.

– *Sharing the Past: The Reinvention of History in Canadian Poetry since 1960*. Toronto: University of Toronto Press, 2019.

– "'Stories in the Poems': Al Purdy's Editing of Andrew Suknaski's *Wood Mountain Poems*." *Canadian Poetry: Studies, Documents, Reviews*, no. 71 (Fall–Winter 2012): 68–87.

Weir, Lorraine. "Normalizing the Subject: Linda Hutcheon and the English-Canadian Postmodern." In *Canadian Canons: Essays in Literary Value*, edited by Robert Lecker, 180–95. Toronto: University of Toronto Press, 1992.

Welsh, Christine. "*Women in the Shadows*: Reclaiming a Métis Heritage." In *New Contexts of Canadian Criticism*, edited by Ajay Heble et al., 56–66. Peterborough, ON: Broadview Press, 1997.

Unsettling the North: Shame in *North of Summer*

Misao Dean

Al Purdy's *North of Summer* (1967) features some of his most admired and anthologized work. Poems such as "Arctic Rhododendrons" and "The Country of the Young" are among those that provide the basis for his canonization as, in Tom Marshall's phrase, Canada's "first truly native poet" (90). *North of Summer* exemplifies the development of the distinctive Purdy persona, characterized by "an idiom and voice whose rhythm, syntax, and texture sound Canadian and offer what Dennis Lee calls 'the local nature of cadence'" (Solecki, LCP 12). These poems seem to claim for Purdy the title of, in Sam Solecki's phrase, "the last Canadian poet" (Solecki, LCP). An additional characteristic of the Purdy "voice" is its goal of articulating the nation, not just in idiom but also in its awareness of place and history, in poems that aim to speak the settler experience from a variety of specific landscapes and histories to claim the vastness of the nation for an articulate nationalism.

But this "voice" is not merely discursive: it is embodied in *North of Summer* through the language of emotions. Embarrassment, shame, love, longing, and loneliness are the mechanisms whereby the Wordsworthian romantic aesthetic of "emotion recollected in tranquillity" that characterizes the entire collection is undercut and ironized. Emotions play a much larger role in *North of Summer* than is often acknowledged by critics, who tend to analyze the discourse of emotion in the poems as technique.[1] I propose in this chapter to perform the opposite move, to embody the "voice" of the poems by reading it through theories of the way that affect and emotion construct the self. Shame in particular – described by affect theorists such as Silvan Tomkins and Martha Nussbaum as foundational to the construction of the self, of bodily boundaries, and of consequent self-consciousness and guilt – is the emotion that dominates the collection. But shame in settler communities has a further significance when considered as an affect that circulates through economies of apology and reparation: Purdy's settler shame is personal, not national, though *North of Summer* might be considered, along with other modernist texts such as Margaret Atwood's *Surfacing* (1972) or W.O. Mitchell's *The Vanishing Point* (1973), part of the "prehistory" of Truth and Reconciliation in Canada.

According to Tomkins, shame is the first affect a child experiences, and the foundation of the self.[2] In Tomkins's system, shame (like all affects, as he describes them) is hard-wired into the neural system and observable in children as young as seven months. An infant's desire to act, and its inevitable frustration by bodily limitation, result in the involuntary adoption of "the attitude of shame": "the lowering of the eyelids, the lowering of the eyes, the hanging of the head" (Sedgwick and Frank, "Shame" 518). Simultaneous desire and frustration prompt the child to experience a sense of powerlessness, "drawing a boundary line or barrier" (520) that creates "the space wherein a sense of self will develop" (501). This affect is experienced in the adult as "an inner torment, a sickness of the soul" (Tomkins 133). While Tomkins's theory of affects as located in the body and as involuntary responses to stimuli is very different from more conventional Freudian theories of emotion as constructed through drives, the function of shame in both systems is similar. As Nussbaum recounts, shame arises from an infant's realization of its helplessness and dependency, coupled with its desire for omnipotence: "Shame involves the realization that one is weak and needy in some way in which one expects oneself to be adequate" (*Upheavals* 196). The realization that one's desire has been frustrated as a result of some personal inadequacy is the basic structure of shame in both systems.

A key poem for reading the function of bodily shame in the construction of the self in *North of Summer* is "When I Sat Down to Play the Piano" (*NS* 43–5; *BR* 112–14), a mock-heroic description of the very low-comedy problem of how to attend to one's bodily needs in the North. Most critics of Purdy's work identify this poem as a contribution to his comic repertoire; like "At the Quinte Hotel," it adopts a self-deprecating and self-mocking tone, contrasting the prosaic life of the Purdy-speaker with the conventional expectation that poetry will be elevated in both language and subject. But "When I Sat Down to Play the Piano" is more than just comic relief, and attending to its emphasis on shame and the vulnerability of the body provides a different way to read the collection as a whole. The speaker uses a mocking parody of historical literary language to describe his actions: "He cometh forth hurriedly from his tent / and looketh for a quiet sequestered vale," accompanied by a paperback book and a roll of "violet toilet tissue." He seeks a privacy that is more or less unattainable, not only because the landscape is flat and treeless, but also because he is followed by the many dogs that belong to his Inuit hosts. He has engaged a young boy to drive off the dogs by throwing stones at them, but the boy is only partially successful, and laughs when "a big black husky dashes in / swift as an enemy submarine / white teeth snapping at anus." The speaker describes in detail how his body is both visible and vulnerable in this landscape, but only in the comically elevated language of parody: historical references proliferate as he describes the boy, his champion in the fight with the dogs, as "Montcalm at Quebec / Horatius at the bridge / Leonidas at Thermopylae," Custer, and finally the Biblical David facing Goliath. Eventually the frustrated speaker, like "Achilles[,] retreateth without honour." As with the archetypal self in Tomkins's system, his bodily needs and inadequacies are obvious; that his humiliation is very public is indicated by the specific readers addressed in the poem:

> Dear Ann Landers,
> what would you do?
> Dear Perry Mason
> what would you do
> in a case like this?[3]

"When I Sat Down to Play the Piano" describes a circumstance in which the body's vulnerability forces a literal self-consciousness, consciousness of self; the speaker's sense of self as autonomous and independent is undermined by his own need, and "it does not matter whether the humiliated one has been shamed by derisive laughter or whether he mocks himself. In either event he feels himself naked, defeated, alienated, lacking in dignity or worth" (Tomkins 133). His final, resentful salvo in his fight with the dogs – "p.s. Next time I'm gonna take a gun" – expresses directly how the experience of "[s]hame then causes the real vulnerable self to hide," and an "inauthentic 'false self'" of aggression and revenge "to come to the fore" (Nussbaum, *Upheavals* 197).

"When I Sat Down to Play the Piano" is a reminder of the quotidian problem of bodily shame in the Arctic landscape for visitors from the South. Early European explorers and travellers were often unaccustomed to a diet completely composed of meat (or fish), and therefore travelled with noticeable internal as well as external discomfort. In the Protestant tradition of his time, Ernest Thompson Seton, who visited the Arctic in 1907, was obsessed by his bowels; he carried "rhubarb pills," which he also dispensed ad hoc to people in remote settlements who asked him for medication for their illnesses. John Hornby, who starved to death on the Thelon River in 1927 along with his companions, Harold Adlard and Edgar Christian, gave himself enemas in his final days.[4] Contemporary practitioners of "no trace camping" confront their bodies daily by lining their latrines with plastic receptacles and packing their waste out of remote areas, activating Tomkins's affect of disgust as well as shame; other wilderness campers pack among their essentials a Ziploc bag containing a roll of toilet paper and a cigarette lighter, anticipating the moment when they will stand, with their trousers lowered, among the shrubs and tree trunks, attempting to burn the evidence. The body in the North insists on recognition of its vulnerability, and this recognition, Nussbaum suggests, is accompanied by "a primitive shame at one's weakness and impotence" (*Upheavals* 197). "When I Sat Down to Play the Piano" demonstrates the way this acknowledgment constructs the space of the self through the affect of bodily shame.

"Dead Seal" (*NS* 58–9; *BR* 115–16) is a puzzling poem that also represents the speaker's feelings of disgust and shame, this time in reference to the body of a dead seal on the beach, the product of a hunting trip undertaken by his hosts. The seal, anthropomorphized not only as a clown but also as "a fat little old man" and (conversely) a baby, is an "other" who is also the same, blurring the boundary between human and animal. Despite his longing to pet the seal, the speaker is also disgusted by the idea of touching the "dark slow worm of blood" that marks this object as dead. He intellectualizes this affect, suggesting that he is responding to a taboo against killing ("'Thou Shalt Not'") imposed in Western cultures. In the second part of the poem, "curiosity" overcomes his revulsion, and he "reach[es] out" to touch the seal "as if the head were electric / with a death-taboo invisibly attached." He finds it not only "sticky where the bullet touched," but also, frighteningly, "smooth elsewhere like an intimate part of the human body." This blurring of the human-animal boundary – "they unsure of what being an animal consists of / I equally unsure of what a human being is supposed to be" – creates a shock of shame; he realizes that this body should be "touched with delight in living," not "curiosity and defiance of breaking rules."

The speaker embodies the confusion and ambivalence of the city-dwelling meat eater, unwilling to acknowledge the way humanity in the North survives almost completely on what filmmaker John Houston calls a "Diet of Souls."[5] As Purdy later stated in his essay "Arctic Poems and Prose" (1966), "when you're jerked directly from modern city to a hunting culture it makes you realize how important environment can be" (5). The intimacy and materiality of death, of dead animals, touch him momentarily; he is implicated in these processes of the natural world, and the boundaries between animal and human that he evoked earlier in the poem are challenged. But the speaker recoils in order to reinstall these boundaries, drawing another one not just between human and animal, but between his hosts and himself. He retreats to his tent, declaring "I am not a hunter" and wondering "what got into me." His momentary feeling of connection to the seal and the sealers, and his material implication in the processes of life that they represent, are replaced by a hierarchy governed by feelings of alienation and disgust, perhaps linked with the imagery of the poem "Aspects," which associates the blood left on the beach by hunters with garbage and discarded menstrual pads (NS 56).

In some ways, reading these poems in order to highlight their representations of shame follows in the wake of formalist readings that have already noted the way many of the poems set up the speaker for a fall, for failure, by evoking heroic stereotypes or rash prejudgments and then ironically undercutting them. This pattern is reinforced by an analysis of the language, which Dennis Lee notes is a "middle style" (386) that mixes high and low vocabulary in poems that, according to Janice Fiamengo, often "foreground their verbal inadequacies before they risk a lyrical flight" (161). This account of the poems is largely accurate, but incomplete. It leaves out the way the poems foreground negative emotions, especially shame, as the primary way in which the speaker responds to the landscape and the people he encounters. Disorientation, misunderstanding, self-consciousness, bodily and emotional vulnerability, disgust, and loneliness are the feelings the speaker names in both "When I Sat Down to Play the Piano" and "Dead Seal," yet he is unable to fully acknowledge these feelings, and in both cases he ends the poem with a withdrawal into resentment and defensiveness. These poems are not the passive "set of binoculars" that allows readers to see the North, as Purdy claims in the "Postscript" to *North of Summer*, or even a more specifically Purdified "optic glass" that presents his particular view of the North (NS 84). Instead, the poems record the shame and defensiveness of a white Canadian body when confronted with the challenging physical landscapes and the legacy of colonialism in the Canadian North of the 1960s.

Reading the poems that constitute *North of Summer* through their representation of the speaker's feelings demonstrates the way they are almost uniformly structured by a contrast between the speaker's omnipotent self-regard and his ultimate frustration and resulting self-consciousness, which is an almost textbook definition of the workings of shame. In "Trees at the Arctic Circle" (NS 29–30; BR 102–4), the speaker compares the dwarf trees, less than eighteen inches tall, with their southern counterparts, the "great Douglas firs / ... tall maples waving green / and oaks like gods in autumn gold" of the boreal and coastal forests. His gaze determined by the tall trees he expects to find, the speaker judges Arctic trees to be "coward trees," whose small stature is "grovelling" and fearful. However, when he looks "close up," he revises this "confident dismissive judgement" (Solecki, LCP 100); he finds instead that the "seed pods glow / like tiny delicate earrings," and he admires their persistence in the Arctic cold. Finally, he admits that he was "carried away in [his] scorn … most foolish in [his] judgments," and declares:

> I have been stupid in a poem
> I will not alter the poem
> but let the stupidity remain permanent
> as the trees are[.]

For Sam Solecki, "'Trees at the Arctic Circle' is an example of a poem trying to allow the reader to enter into 'the process' or experience as it is being lived through by a speaker who records or enacts his changes of attitude" (LCP 98), and a demonstration of Purdy's attempt to "open up the lyric form from within" (102). Alternatively, the poem might be read as a confrontation with the Arctic as "other," which results in a positive recognition of the difference the trees represent. But the poem also documents the speaker's own self-judgment, his sense of embarrassment at his mistake, and he publicly castigates himself not only as "stupid," but also as "foolish," "the Pontifex Maximus / of nullity" whose self is defined by its limitations. Similarly, poems like "At the Movies" (NS 77–8; BR 120–1) frustrate the poet's ambition by refusing to yield up their "meaning": "The point I'd hoped to separate / from all these factual things stubbornly / resists me and I walk home feeling stupid" with "the beginnings of a headache." "Still Life in a Tent" (NS 47–9; BR 109–11) almost wholly consists of the speaker's complaints and miseries as he languishes alone and ill in his tent, experiencing "the shame of allowing his needy dependent self to emerge" (Nussbaum, *Upheavals* 197): "Oh misery me misery me / I am sick as hell / and so sorry for me" (NS 48; BR 110). The poem abruptly shifts as the speaker declares that he is

> so glad to be here
> with the chance that comes but once
> to any man in his lifetime
> to travel deep in himself
> to meet himself as a stranger[.] (NS 49; BR 111)

The ending resolves the speaker's feelings of shame by evoking the code of the introspective artist who endures suffering for self-knowledge: his humiliating illness, the poem states, will be worth it, because it allows him to grow as a person. Each of these poems relies upon the language of feelings to describe not only the encounter of the self with the North, but also the foundational encounter of the self with its limitations, and the way that "[a]ny ideal to which one holds oneself has shame as its permanent possibility" (Nussbaum, *Upheavals* 198).

What might be gained from calling these poems manifestations of shame, rather than analyzing them, as Solecki does, as examples of an aesthetics of process that defines a characteristic poetic achievement? Certainly historical and formal analyses have much to say about *North of Summer* and the individual poems in it, about Purdy's measured and deliberate construction of a speaker who disclaims cultural authority and the formal requirements of lyric poetry as a strategy for reinscribing both in a new way. In the context of claims for Purdy's centrality to the definition of a specifically Canadian literary voice, conventional literary analyses focus on supporting these claims through emphasis on the openness and self-consciousness of the speaker, his transparent project of observing and understanding the North as other, and the undeniable literary achievement of the poems. Frank Davey identifies these readings as located within the ideology of "high modernism ... [that saw] the poem as a complex, allusive, aesthetic object, that attested to the skill and Eurocentric erudition of the writer," and argues that the characterization of Purdy as the voice of the nation is "marked discursively by a nostalgia for a period before industrialization and its multiplying of the power of mass culture" (40). For Davey, formalist readings of *North of Summer* are morally reprehensible; his is among the more critical analyses that have challenged the colonialist politics implicit in the speaker's representations of the Indigenous people of the eastern Arctic as Canadian, and in his assumption that he can understand not only the land but also the people of the North.[6] Undoubtedly, *North of Summer* constructs Baffin Island through what John Urry has called the "tourist gaze," and poems such as "Girl," "Hunter, New Style," and "At the Movies" interpellate the reader as a visitor who gazes at Indigenous people who are equally a part of an exotic landscape offered to the tourist gaze.[7] This landscape reproduces the distortions of empire: Davey notes that "the relatively few women in Purdy's reflective lyrics are ... dehumanized" (52), and dismisses the whole book as a "romantic documentar[y] of Canadian difference" (40), while Lorraine York concludes that in these poems "the North becomes a huge, white narcissistic playground, passively offering up to us the image of our imposing selves" (48–9).

Reading *North of Summer* through the affect of shame allows the reintegration of these contradictory readings, and suggests a way to build a new relationship between settler subjects and the North by allowing settler readers to attend to their own implication in colonialist histories.[8] Rather than interpreting the speaker's failures to understand the North as a literary technique for destabilizing the lyric, or as a comic one that undercuts the authority of the heroic modern explorer with postmodernist irony, reading these poems for shame unsettles settler subjects by asking them to feel the guilt and shame that must attend any face-to-face meeting between settlers and Indigenous peoples in the full light of history. Rather than defending *North of Summer* as a literary accomplishment, lamenting it as a nostalgic evocation of a Canadianness lost (or never attained), or attacking it as evidence of settler colonialism and state power, the settler subject who understands *North of Summer* as an articulation of shame may be able to enter what Sedgwick (following Melanie Klein) labels the depressive position, the position from which new kinds of filiations and communities can emerge.[9]

The possibility of such new relationships is one of the conventional motives for travel, and *North of Summer* is organized as a travel narrative, with the first major poem, "The Turning Point," narrating Purdy's flight to Frobisher Bay (now known as Iqaluit), and the subsequent poems – "The North West Passage," "Arctic River," and "Girl" – describing his layover there, including his visit to the local tourist attraction, the Sylvia Grinnell River, now a popular park. The following six poems are set in Pangnirtung, which was Purdy's next stop after Iqaluit, and where he spent most of his time. "Metrics" introduces a sequence of fifteen poems describing a two-week trip to the Kikastan Islands with an Inuit family, organized for him by the local federal government administrator in Pangnirtung. These poems, which I.S. MacLaren describes as the "centre of *North of Summer*" (125), are followed by five poems again located in Pangnirtung. The concluding poem, "The Country of the Young," provides an opportunity to meditate on the experience of "seeing" the North, with its injunction to "'Look here ... Look again'" (*NS* 79; *BR* 126). The book is about equally divided between poems written about the Kikastan Islands trip and those set in the communities of Iqaluit and Pangnirtung, suggesting a more or less equal division between representations of life in settled northern communities and representations of traditional life on the land; the poems are arranged to emphasize the chronological order of a trip from the populated South to the unpopulated North and back again. John Van Rys agrees that the book as a whole evokes the genre of the contemporary travel narrative by figuring the poems as letters or postcards written "*from* Baffin Island, poems sent from afar" to an implied reader (8).[10]

The book's arrangement and Purdy's statement that the poems are "like a set of binoculars" that the reader can use to view the North ("Postscript," NS 83) suggest Urry's idea of "the tourist gaze" as an analytical tool. The "tourist gaze" is characterized by "much greater sensitivity to visual elements of landscape or townscape than is normally found in everyday life" (*Consuming* 132), but because the objects of the gaze have already been constructed as sites of tourist interest, "what is then seen is interpreted according to these pre-given categories" (132). Rather than representing new experience, the tourist gaze reaffirms what is already known, and further allows reinterpretation of everything seen "as a sign of itself" (Jonathan Culler, qtd. in Urry, *Consuming* 133), as a typical or essential representation of otherness. Thus the "tourist gaze" can also function as a mechanism for managing or diverting the uncomfortable feelings that are prompted by shame. Purdy's preconceptions about the North – his desire to see "the pictures in my head / of what I'd expected things to be like / start to come true" ("Metrics," NS 38; BR 105) – lead to the shame of unfulfilled expectations, but also allow the speaker to experience the triumph of identification and "authentic" experience without, in essence, changing his mind. In "The Sculptors" (NS 75–6; BR 118–19), the speaker hunts through a pile of discarded carvings, looking for one that he can take home as a gift, but finds only rejects, "tusk broken," "ivory inlay gone," carvings of animals that look

> broken
>   bent
>   misshapen
> failed animals
> with vital parts missing[.]

"I'm a little ashamed of myself / for being impatient with them," he admits, but his shame inspires a moment in which he claims that he "can see and feel / what it was like to be them / the tb out-patients" who carved these animals, "losers and failures / who never do anything right." He expects to find works of art and tourist souvenirs, but the carvings are evidence of age, injury, suffering, and disease – evidence of the vulnerability of the human body that he shares with the carvers. The poem ends as he once again defensively retreats to the "inauthentic self" of difference and distance, reinscribing his position of privilege by avowing that he would "like to buy every damn case" of the maimed carvings to express his sympathy for the Inuit, rather than linger further in his experience of their impotence.

Confusion and disorientation are the feelings that most aptly characterize the poems that attempt to locate the North in relation to other places, both geographically and temporally. Purdy wrote in "Arctic Poems and Prose" that the midnight sun "gave [him] a strange feeling, like being drunk while seeing Niagara Falls on your third honeymoon" (1). The second poem in the collection, "The North West Passage" (NS 20–1; BR 97–9), achieves this feeling by depicting the speaker consulting a map and identifying places both geographically and temporally by referring to the history of their names. But for Purdy, the map-reading is superfluous; he is only going as far as someone else is willing to take him, and he never sees the locations he cites. The poem does not so much end as peter out, as the speaker discards the map and speculates about "strawberries and ice cream for dinner." "South" (NS 60–3), a poem in the Kikastan Islands section, imagines the speaker at the top of the world, looking south, where "the continents reeling away / far beneath me" create the "illusion of upness / which has no east or west or anything." But while "South" acknowledges that the speaker's sense of "upness" is an illusion, it still orients the traveller according to the norms of a conventional map – above and looking down on the rest of the world. The speaker sits in the hunting boat with his guide Jonesee: "the world shrinks away" from him and "gathers itself as a ghostly premise" that exists only in abstractions, "objectively mixed together / without correlatives."

The title of Van Rys's article, "Alfred in Baffin Land," conveys the sense of reversal, the "through the looking glass" nature of Purdy's North. However, the point of this reversal is not just Bakhtinian carnival, as Van Rys suggests, but also the exoticism and difference of life on Baffin Island. Poems like "What Can't Be Said," "Innuit" [sic], and "At the Movies" reinforce the idea that, as the speaker says in "At the Movies," "[t]he setting is really unreal" (NS 77; BR 120), mixing elements of traditional lifeways with the popular and commercial culture of the South, the traditional culture being impenetrable to the speaker and associated with "the race-soul of The People" ("Innuit," NS 33). The North remains resolutely *there* as opposed to *here*, and the poems convey no sense that what is happening *there* – garbage on the beach, destruction of the culture – has anything to do with the speaker or with what is happening *here*. Instead the poem suggests the affect of dizziness, disorientation, and disgust that plagues the tourist.

In "Track Meet at Pangnirtung" (NS 70–1), the speaker is similarly figured as a tourist witnessing a sort of "games day" celebration presided over by the "Anglican minister," whose presence evokes the legacy of the Canadian residential-schools policy and the devastation it wrought in Indigenous communities. The poem embodies shame by situating the speaker as an audience for the laughter and smiles of community members. Success and failure at the childish competitions and races figure individual members of the community as mainly "losers," "now weaponless," whose joy compensates for their material lack and cultural loss: "no one seems to mind losing here / for losing is a kind of pleasure ... and laughter is / a red filling between the hours." The poem includes an ambiguous vignette as an emblem of joy. It describes a scene involving another visitor to the North:

> A white construction worker gives
> one old woman a package of cigarettes as
> payment for taking her picture so
> she smiles[,]

allowing both the worker and the poet to take her smile "away ... into the leapfrog future." This scene takes the joy of the elderly woman as licence to reduce her, in her proper person (a fellow Canadian, as nationalist readings of *North of Summer* would have it), to a tourist attraction, a postcard image; it also becomes a kind of permission for the poet to reproduce the scene in his poem as a typical or essential representation of the human. The smile becomes the alibi that disguises the power difference between the two, just as "laughter is the / ignorant wisdom of the young" – in contrast to their idle elders, who are "still / in the running." The poem's positive message about the endurance and knowledge of the elders who understand the race of life seems wrung by force from a set of images that reveal, despite themselves, the results of colonialist policies and cultural genocide.[11]

The organization of *North of Summer* as a travel narrative prompts the comparison of the poet as a contemporary traveller to historical travellers like Franklin and Frobisher, as well as mythical travellers like Odysseus, with a resultant representation of emotional vulnerability and self-consciousness. In "The Turning Point" (NS 18–19), the speaker describes "Baffin" as "[a] club-shaped word" he has "remembered since childhood." Baffin Island is associated with "a warm kind of wonder" that he "used to be ashamed of" because it marked him off as an artist. In "The North West Passage" (NS 20–1; BR 97–9), the heroic circumstances of early travel in the North are contrasted with modern contempt for the North – "ICBM computers [could] make a quarter inch error / and destroy the illusion of paradise by mistake," while "[t]he Beaufort Sea and Ellesmereland" are "places to drop cigarette butts in." The speaker recognizes that modernity undervalues his imaginative vision of the North and its history; he knows that the "Terror and Erebus sank long ago" and are now irrelevant, and the poem peters out because the speaker "can't think of anything more to say."

In fact, many of the poems represent the speaker's growing realization that he has little to say about the North. In "Metrics" (NS 37–9; BR 104–7), which recounts the first day of his trip to the Kikastan Islands with Jonesee and his family, the speaker tries to quell his "heavy loneliness" and "lost feelings" by setting up his typewriter in his tent "for an 'order of things.'" As he sits in the twilight, the raucous noise of oldsquaw ducks

>   gathers everything
> all the self-deception and phoniness
> of my lifetime into an empty place
> and the RUNNER IN THE SKIES
> I invented
>   as symbol of the human spirit
>   crashes like a housefly

– while he realizes that the "echo of cosmic emptiness" he was trying to articulate is completely inauthentic. The only meaning inherent in his feelings is that

>   some damfool ducks
> are having a ball out there
>   far out
>   there
>   where I can't join them

– and this realization prompts him to write what he considers to be the real poem. The poet's encounter with his own pretensions is a common trope in *North of Summer*, and its effect is not just to ironize or undercut the voice of the speaker, or to document the way an inner monologue constructs a self; instead, the speaker in "Metrics" is lonely and afraid, aware of the way he has made his feelings and failures public, and determined to salvage a poem from the confusion and failure to measure up to his ambition. He's ashamed.

Another source of embarrassment and disorientation that recurs in several poems is the speaker's inability to communicate with his hosts. "English is not spoken here" ("Metrics," NS 37; BR 104): he is unable to politely decline a proffered cup of tea, and is reduced to "mak[ing] a face" to communicate his distaste ("Odysseus in Kikastan," NS 40), while in "What Can't Be Said," he is left behind to socialize with the women, and the group just "sit[s] there like a bunch of monkeys / about as phoney as you can get" (NS 46; BR 114). In "Washday" (NS 64–6; BR 121–3), this moment of self-consciousness becomes the centrepiece of the poem when the speaker recognizes his own name among the syllables spoken by the people around him, and realizes that they are talking about him:

>   she adds my name
>   to the weightless sounds
>   breathed out
>   some of the "me" I am
>   removed
>   the walled self
>   defenses down
>   altered[.]

This is the view from the outside, the moment of shame that constructs the self: "I'm given to the air / then back to myself / like a gift from her." He responds to what he experiences as a peak moment by speaking her name, "Leah," which, minus the context of his own feelings, makes no social sense – "she looks at me / queerly" – and silence ensues. In the following poem, "Kikastan Communications" (NS 67), the speaker hunts for ways to communicate and recognizes that his inability to speak their language makes him a child in the eyes of his hosts and "a puzzle to myself." While he is able to observe and document his surroundings, his inability to speak means that he can never really communicate with his hosts beyond his human needs – for food, shelter, heat, and companionship – in other words, beyond their recognition of his bodily vulnerability.

Thus Purdy's main way to interact with the people he meets in the North is through the "tourist gaze," rather than through speech. Poems that are merely portraits of the people that Purdy met (such as "Girl," "Hunter, New Style," and "Innuit") are problematic for a contemporary reader and rarely anthologized: they prompt a feeling of shame in the reader because of their embarrassing presumption that they have understood the people they only describe. These poems most directly represent the way that the "tourist gaze" manages Purdy's shame – because tourism gives him licence to describe the way people look without any knowledge of their thoughts, and with no real relationship with them. "Girl" (NS 24–5) describes a light-skinned teenager employed as a typist in Iqaluit; her appearance suggests to the speaker that the mix of her "white blood boiling red / under the not-brown skin" is the result of historical and "accidental" connections between Inuit women and white sailors.

The references to "blood" and "skin" evoke the histories of rape and exploitation that still determine the lives of many Indigenous women, and the readerly recognition that these judgments are expressed in idiomatic Canadian speech makes the common caveat that excuses racism in literature – something like, "It's not his fault; this is the way they thought in those days" – even less acceptable. The speaker claims to know what the "Girl" is thinking, positioning her as culturally between two worlds, one where "[n]o thought of a non-Christian past / enters her working head" and another where "she sits in the tents of her people sewing / skins." The poem distorts the reality that indeed this "Girl," like most contemporary Indigenous people, actually lives in one world – one that includes both modernity and traditional knowledge, colonialism and agency, typewriters and hide tents – and it erases the histories of violence and theft that created this world. Similarly, the poem "Innuit" (NS 32–3) describes an Indigenous carver who is "unknowable" not because, as we know, the speaker can't talk to him, but because he is an "other." Instead of interacting with the old man, the speaker claims that, by looking "in his faded eyes," he can see the "race-soul" of the Indigenous people of the region, "the Dorset and pre-Dorset cultures[,] ... that reaches into the past / but touches an old man still living." What Purdy claims to find presented to his gaze when he looks at the inhabitants of Pangnirtung and Iqaluit is the history that prompted him to come to the North "moving somewhere behind his eyes" in

>   secret vaults
>   and catacombs of marrow
>   bone rooms
>   that reveal nothing

to "white men." This poem relegates the old man to the anachronistic space of a romanticized Indigenous past that continues, somehow, to exist in the present. It documents little more than the poet's use of his encounter with the man as an occasion for the particular poem he wants to write, and, more poignantly, his failed attempt to recognize and greet the other with compassion.

Reading these poems in order to highlight their representations of shame is a way of dissenting from the interpretation of *North of Summer* as a work of nationalist celebration. Purdy himself claimed to feel elated by the sensation of coming home when he arrived in the North: "Why I'm home! This is Canada," he wrote later in an article for *The Beaver* ("Arctic" 1). I.S. MacLaren ably summarizes this interpretation, which he attributes partially to the historical moment in which the collection was published and partially to the promotional activities of Purdy's publisher, Jack McClelland, who ensured that the Arctic trip was reported in major news media: "Despite being only infrequently national, patriotic, or heroic, by the time that it had appeared in the spring of the nation's centennial year, *North of Summer* had become what one reviewer called 'a public event'" (MacLaren 121) – one among many other celebrations of Canada's North in 1967. MacLaren elucidates the logic of this reception: because the Arctic was a vast and challenging landscape, "it made heroes of men who engaged it; Al Purdy, whose poems' settings had already covered an impressive geographical portion of Canada, had engaged it; ergo Al Purdy was heroic, Canada's first, best, and, later, last Canadian poet" (122–3). However, MacLaren persuasively argues that reading the volume for its evidence of Purdy's "humanization of the North" is a more rewarding and inclusive approach: "at its core *North of Summer* possesses a humanism residing in and issuing from a community of Inuit and their dogs pursuing a way of life that Canada had not yet wholly brought to an end" (125). MacLaren's focus on the representation of Inuit lifeways in the Kikastan Island poems wonderfully demonstrates Purdy's humanism, yet sees the value in the poems as focused outwardly, rather than on the feelings of the speaker himself.

Viewing these poems as failures to interpret Indigenous lifeways for a southern audience suggests an obvious reaction: shaming and rejection. Sara Ahmed, in *The Cultural Politics of Emotion*, argues that collective shaming in response to growing calls for acknowledgment and reform of colonialist practices can in fact reinforce such practices by allowing the nation to reform around the shared performance of shame. Ahmed argues that public "declarations of shame can bring 'the nation' into existence as a felt community" (100) because, rather than feeling individual shame, "[i]ndividuals become implicated in national shame, [only] insofar as they already belong to the nation" (102). In the cases she cites, the ritual of public and collective shaming (which in another context might result in expunging Purdy's poetry from the canon) is what reinforces the boundaries of the nation and allows individuals to evade acceptance of their own guilt and responsibility. Certainly "Girl" and "Innuit" are examples of the few poems in *North of Summer* that seem easy to dismiss because their racism is so obvious. "Girl," in particular, is sadly comparable to Duncan Campbell Scott's "The Half-Breed Girl" and "The Onondaga Madonna," poems which similarly use the trope of "the blood" to figure cultural hybridity as biological. But Scott's poems are now over a hundred years old, and notoriously dramatize his support for the implementation of the genocidal residential-schools policy; reading the same sentiments from Purdy, with less historical distance to excuse them, might prompt a contemporary reader to reject these poems, and the man who wrote them, and in so doing enact that feeling of glib superiority described by Ahmed as a form of public shaming.

Alternatively, one might relate the shame and vulnerability that the speaker feels to the form of melancholia that occurs when settlers are forced to integrate shame and responsibility into their sense of themselves as national subjects. Haydie Gooder and Jane M. Jacobs argue that melancholia results when

> there is a refusal to break the original attachment to the lost object or ideal. Rather, the trace of the lost object/ideal becomes internalized. It is drawn into the ego and within this inner world the ego absorbs both the love and the rage felt towards the lost object/ideal. This reconfiguration of the "topography of the ego" results in self-beratement and guilt (a form of narcissism). (235)

While Purdy's poems use the distance afforded by the "tourist gaze" and a strategic retreat into defensiveness to redraw boundaries that stabilize the self, perhaps these distances are less available to his readers. Lyric poetry involves a different practice of reading than a government declaration or apology; the intimate encounter with the printed text, the conventional emphasis on the construction of an inner self that an engaged reading practice requires, creates the experience of witnessing, and even an imagined communion with, the shamed self. Thus, while lyric poetry might seem to refuse the easy jump over collective shame into collective consensus that Ahmed describes, it might also encourage the destabilization of the self and a certain willingness to linger with negative feelings that Gooder and Jacobs identify as a form of settler narcissism. This fraying of the self under the gaze of the other, and the willingness to remain frayed, to continue to "feel bad," may in their way be just as counterproductive as jumping to easy solutions.

These poems recall other modernist writers who have represented their own feelings of shame in reaction to the effects of colonialism and racism. F.R. Scott, in "All the Spikes but the Last," chides E.J. Pratt for his refusal to acknowledge the contributions of Chinese workers to the building of the Canadian Pacific Railway: "Is all Canada has to say to them written in the Chinese Immigration Act?" (194). Atwood's nameless narrator in *Surfacing* (1972) sees children on the side of the highway selling blueberries, and recognizes, in hindsight, that her family's back-to-the-land lifestyle probably threatened the livelihood of their Indigenous neighbours. For Atwood, the personal was political: feelings, the most intimate ways that individuals construct their identities, are in themselves political acts. Feeling personally implicated in colonialism is the first step to unsettling the world view of rational certainty and technological omnipotence that led to disastrous outcomes for Indigenous peoples and people of colour in Canada. In contrast, Emily Carr aestheticizes Indigenous poverty in *Klee Wyck* (1941), and never seems to connect her own privilege to the want she sees around her. She rarely feels ashamed among her Indigenous "friends," and maybe she should. Reading Purdy's poems for their representation of emotions, and especially negative emotions, can be the basis of a new way of teaching Canadian literature, especially works from the modern period. The speaker of the poems admits the bafflement, disgust, and shame he feels when forced by circumstances and by social interactions to recognize his own limitations and vulnerability, modelling for the reader how non-Indigenous Canadians have been repulsed and shamed by the results of their interventions in Indigenous lives and cultures. The poems suggest how Canadians often retreat to little jokes and disclaimers, refusals to see, in order to escape the loneliness and despair we feel when forced to face our own legacy of power and our current inability to understand. *North of Summer* is in many ways a collection of poems of "white fragility," of the negative feelings that result when settler people, with perhaps what they perceive as innocent good intentions, try to see clearly where and among whom they live, and then retreat in confusion and misunderstanding.[12] In this sense, they represent the possibility of what Sedgwick calls a reparative reading, a reading practice that, by dwelling on negative feelings, might result in acceptance of the role of nationalism and racism in the construction of Canadian nationality without minimizing the emotional effects of that realization. Rather than rejecting these poems as artifacts of colonialism (in Sedgwick's "paranoid" mode), a reparative reading can become the basis for a new understanding of what a Canadian is and strive to move beyond it to a new relationship with Indigenous neighbours. Nussbaum suggests that "primitive shame – a shame closely connected to an infantile demand for omnipotence and the unwillingness to accept neediness – is, like disgust, a way of hiding from our humanity" that finally constrains us as individuals and as a society (*Hiding* 15). Denial of this primitive shame and self-consciousness represents an unwillingness to acknowledge the vulnerability that we hold in common with all other humans, and leads to the "unwillingness to recognize the rights and needs of others" that has marked the internal colonialism of Canada's relationship with the North (Nussbaum, *Hiding* 15). Reading Purdy for emotions acknowledges ways in which settler Canadians share his vulnerability – as a first step to opposing the way that colonialisms of the past continue to be enacted in the present.[13]

NOTES

1 "Technique": see Fiamengo, Van Rys, and Lahey, for example.
2 As described by Eve Kosofsky Sedgwick and Adam Frank in "Shame in the Cybernetic Fold," Tomkins "offers a kind of origin myth (in the shame of the infant) for a genetic narrative of the individual and filiation of the self" (501).
3 In *Beyond Remembering* (2000), the reference is not to Perry Mason (*NS* 43), but to the "Galloping Gourmet" (*BR* 112) – i.e., Graham Kerr.
4 Seton: see *Arctic Prairies* (1911); see also *Trail of an Artist-Naturalist* (1941) for information about his strange attitude to his body. Hornby: see *Unflinching: A Diary of Tragic Adventure* (1937), by Edgar Christian. Many books about the North suggest that recreational travel under northern conditions forces tourists to acknowledge the primacy of the body, sometimes for the first time; see, for example, *Out of the Whirlwind* (1995), by M.T. Kelly, or *Snowman* (1976), by Thomas York. While Mordecai Richler's *Solomon Gursky Was Here* (1989) also focuses on eating and elimination as important elements of life in the North, I would argue that, rather than using these elements solely to embody his characters, Richler primarily uses them symbolically.
5 In Houston's *Diet of Souls* (2004), Inuit hunters explain the precariousness and uncertainty of traditional lifeways, which they attribute to the fact that their diet consists wholly of other living beings, which themselves have souls.
6 See also, for example, van der Marel, York.
7 Urry defines the tourist gaze as one that is constructed through popular and high culture, and suggests that it structures the experiences of people who travel in order to "see" particular landscapes, events, and objects previously marked off as worthy of "seeing." The tourist gaze constructs these experiences as different and helps sustain for travellers the distance between the everyday and the exotic.
8 This reading practice is suggested by Sedgwick; see Sedgwick, "Teaching/Depression" and Sedgwick, *Touching Feeling*.
9 Sedgwick discusses the difference between the paranoid and depressive positions in *Touching Feeling*. In her view, a defensive and inflexible reactivity against others can be broken by moving into the "depressive position" as defined by Klein, a psychological state that is unstable and so able to recover and remake relationships with lost objects.
10 Van Rys: "Moreover, the volume offers a consistent play with concepts of the travel book. As the title indicates, these are poems *from* Baffin Island, poems sent from afar; they comprise a personal journey, a diary, and an explorer's journal in the vein of Samuel Hearne. Purdy consistently plays with the idea of poems as postcards or letters, as the prose postscript to the volume suggests. Each poem is postmarked with its place of origin" (8).
11 It might be objected that this reading of the poem is ahistorical because the abuses perpetrated by the residential-schools system and the Christian

churches that ran them would not have been known to Purdy. However, I would suggest that the problems of residential schools were known to many in the settler community by 1967. For example, Emily Carr wrote about the role of the schools in spreading tuberculosis and destroying Indigenous cultures in *Klee Wyck* in 1941.

12 Robin DiAngelo describes "white fragility" as an exaggerated reaction of emotional insult, hurt, guilt, and hostility expressed by white audiences when confronted with the idea of white privilege and ongoing colonialism (see DiAngelo).

13 Thanks to Nicole Shukin for her valuable suggestions for improving this chapter, and to Conrad Leibel for help with proofreading and documentation.

REFERENCES

Ahmed, Sara. *The Cultural Politics of Emotion*. Edinburgh: Edinburgh University Press, 2004.

Davey, Frank. "Al Purdy, Sam Solecki, and the Poetics of the 1960s." *Canadian Poetry: Studies, Documents, Reviews*, no. 51 (Fall–Winter 2002): 39–55.

DiAngelo, Robin. "White Fragility." *International Journal of Critical Pedagogy* 3, no. 3 (2011): 54–70.

Fiamengo, Janice. "Kind of ludicrous or kind of beautiful I guess: Al Purdy's Rhetoric of Failure." In Lynch, Ganz, and Kealey, *Ivory Thought*, 159–72.

Gooder, Haydie, and Jane M. Jacobs. "'On the Border of the Unsayable': The Apology in Postcolonizing Australia." *Interventions: International Journal of Postcolonial Studies* 2, no. 2 (2000): 229–47.

Grace, Sherrill E. *Canada and the Idea of North*. Montreal and Kingston: McGill-Queen's University Press, 2002.

Lahey, Ernestine. "Seeing the Forest for the Trees in Al Purdy's *North of Summer*." *Belgian Essays on Language and Literature*, no. 1 (2003): 73–83.

Lee, Dennis. "The Poetry of Al Purdy: An Afterword." In *The Collected Poems of Al Purdy*, edited by Russell Brown, 371–91. Toronto: McClelland & Stewart, 1986.

Lynch, Gerald, Shoshannah Ganz, and Josephene T.M. Kealey, eds. *The Ivory Thought: Essays on Al Purdy*. Ottawa: University of Ottawa Press, 2008.

MacLaren, I.S. "Arctic Al: Purdy's Humanist Vision of the North." In Lynch, Ganz, and Kealey, *Ivory Thought*, 119–36.

Marshall, Tom. *Harsh and Lovely Land: The Major Canadian Poets and the Making of a Canadian Tradition*. Vancouver: University of British Columbia Press, 1979.

McNish, Jill L. "Failure, Then Failure: Shame and William James's 'Sick Soul.'" *CrossCurrents* 53, no. 3 (Fall 2003): 389–403.

Nussbaum, Martha. *Hiding Our Humanity: Disgust, Shame, and the Law.* Princeton, NJ: Princeton University Press, 2004.
– *Upheavals of Thought: The Intelligence of Emotions.* Cambridge: Cambridge University Press, 2003.
Purdy, Al. "Arctic Poems and Prose." 1966. Typescript of an essay published in *The Beaver.* MSS 4/7 I.E.1. University of Saskatchewan Archives and Special Collections. A.W. Purdy Digital Archive, http://canlit.library.usask.ca/islandora/object/purdy%3A1104.
– *Beyond Remembering: The Collected Poems of Al Purdy.* Edited by Al Purdy and Sam Solecki. Madeira Park, BC: Harbour Publishing, 2000.
– *North of Summer: Poems from Baffin Island.* Toronto: McClelland & Stewart, 1967.
Scott, F.R. *The Collected Poems of F.R. Scott.* Toronto: McClelland & Stewart, 1981.
Sedgwick, Eve Kosofsky. "Teaching/Depression." *Scholar & Feminist Online* 4, no. 2 (Spring 2006): 1–6, http://sfonline.barnard.edu/heilbrun/sedgwick_01.htm.
– *Touching Feeling: Affect, Pedagogy, Performativity.* Durham, NC: Duke University Press, 2003.
Sedgwick, Eve Kosofsky, and Adam Frank. "Shame in the Cybernetic Fold: Reading Silvan Tomkins." *Critical Inquiry* 21, no. 2 (Winter 1995): 496–522.
Solecki, Sam. *The Last Canadian Poet: An Essay on Al Purdy.* Toronto: University of Toronto Press, 1999.
Tomkins, Silvan. *Shame and Its Sisters: A Silvan Tomkins Reader.* Edited by Eve Kosofsky Sedgwick and Adam Frank. Durham, NC: Duke University Press, 1995.
Urry, John. *Consuming Places.* London: Routledge, 1995.
– *The Tourist Gaze.* 1990. London: Sage, 2002.
van der Marel, L. Camille. "Unsettling *North of Summer*: Anxieties of Ownership in the Politics and Poetics of the Canadian North." *ARIEL: A Review of International English Literature* 44, no. 4 (October 2013): 13–47.
Van Rys, John. "Alfred in Baffin Land: Carnival Traces in Purdy's *North of Summer.*" *Canadian Poetry: Studies, Documents, Reviews*, no. 26 (Spring–Summer 1990): 1–18.
York, Lorraine. "The Ivory Thought: The North as a Poetic Icon in Al Purdy and Patrick Lane." *Essays on Canadian Writing*, no. 49 (Summer 1993): 45–56.

6

Rune and Riddle in "The Runners"

Ian Rae

Al Purdy's poem "The Runners" (*WG* 110–11; *BR* 162–4), from his 1968 collection *Wild Grape Wine*, extrapolates from a fragment of *Erick the Red's Saga* (c. 1250 CE) that describes how two minor characters, the Gaels Haki and Haekia, are instructed by their Norse masters to explore "Vinland," on what was probably the northeast coast of Canada, around 1004 CE.[1] According to Purdy's epigraph, the Norse command the fleet-footed Gaels to *"return ... before the end of the third half-day"* (*BR* 162) with a scouting report, and, in the saga, the Gaels execute this task by returning with wild grapes and wheat as proof that they "had found good land" (Magnusson and Palsson 95).[2] However, Purdy's poem imagines the temptation of the brother and sister to flee their Norse masters and adopt this "Wine land" as their refuge. "The Runners" builds on the scant details of the Gaels' lives in *Erick the Red's Saga* to develop an Anglo-Celt fantasy that positions the Gaels as the first European colonizers of North America, thereby taking priority away from the Norse, Basque, Spanish, and French. But Purdy's conclusion avoids asserting definitively whether the siblings remain in Vinland or return with the Norse, who threaten the Gaels with the "strong magic" of "the runes they carve on wood and stone" (*BR* 163). From its title to its closing refrain, "The Runners" plays with orthographic and etymological connections between "run," "rune," "riddle," and "read" to transform the siblings' running into a brand of rune-making – that is, the poem dramatizes the question of whether or not the siblings can find a way, through words, to counteract the Norse runes and contrive their freedom in Vinland. The poem thereby creates an unorthodox "neck riddle," a question that will determine the addressee's life or death, by fashioning an open-ended conclusion that compels readers to participate in responding to the neck riddle and deciding the siblings' fate.

To understand the significance of my broader argument about Purdy's riddle and its open-ended conclusion, I must first clarify the anomalous status of "The Runners" within the poet's oeuvre and its critical reception. For an influential (and predominantly male) generation of critics who came of age in the 1960s, Purdy functioned as an exemplary figure, the very voice and embodiment of Canada in English (Budde vii–viii). This critical framing of Purdy as "unofficial Canadian poet laureate" (Lynch, Ganz, and Kealey, "Introduction" 1) helps to explain the statue of Purdy (2008) in Toronto's Queen's Park, site of the Ontario government, with the inscription: "Voice of the Land." This epithet "is also the name of an award created by the League of Canadian Poets to honour Purdy's contribution to Canada" (Canadian Press). As D.M.R. Bentley quips in his conclusion to *The Ivory Thought: Essays on Al Purdy* (2008), "[f]ew Canadian poets have attained the near-mythological status of Al Purdy and none has been accorded the dubious distinction of being described as the 'most,' 'first,' and 'last' Canadian poet" (239). Bentley alludes to the fact that, at the outset of George Bowering's 1970 monograph on Purdy, Bowering, who would later become Canada's first modern Poet Laureate, hails Purdy as the "world's most Canadian poet" (*Al Purdy* 1). When Purdy died of lung cancer in 2000, Robert Bringhurst eulogized him as "the very epitome of Canadian poetry" (qtd. in Davey 47). Likewise, in *The Last Canadian Poet: An Essay on Al Purdy* (1999), Sam Solecki laments the diminishing importance of the white, male Canada of British descent that Purdy represents, in comparison to the more multicultural – and in Solecki's opinion, diffuse – definitions of national identity that became commonplace in the late twentieth century (*LCP* 4–7).

However, Frank Davey (55) and David Solway (18–20) contest Purdy's representative status, in part because Purdy's poems mourn the passing of the Loyalist, Upper-Canadian traits that he is said to embody, but which represent only an influential fraction of the Canadian population. Indeed, right after Bowering utters his superlative claim for Purdy, he proceeds to note that Purdy's persona as the barroom bard evolved alongside the more urbane persona of Leonard Cohen, and it was the Jewish Montrealer who won the informal *Globe and Mail* poll for Canada's inaugural parliamentary poet-laureate post in 2001, not Bowering or Purdy (Anderssen).[3] Moreover, George Elliott Clarke, Canada's seventh Parliamentary Poet Laureate, had to unlearn the wry understatement of Purdy and the terseness of Margaret Atwood – what he was taught to understand as Canadian poetry – in order to liberate his own ebullient mixture of "Africadian" orality and blues, and to thereby articulate the experiences of his Black Nova Scotian community, whose founding was roughly contemporaneous with the arrival of Purdy's ancestors in Ontario in the 1780s (Clarke; Lee 371).

The critical tradition that constructs Purdy as "the People's Poet" and "the Voice of the Land" also has limited explanatory power for understanding "The Runners." On the one hand, ethnicity influences "The Runners" because the poem nationalizes the popular Vinland myth by severing Norse proprietorship and substituting a proto-Canadian couple who convert the failed episode of Norse colonization on the East Coast into a potentially successful Gaelic one. This Anglo-Celt fantasy is, in some ways, an expression of Purdy's identity: the name "Purdy" is English in origin, but it flourished in Northern Ireland before migrating to Ontario ("Purdy"), where it claims a village and a lake north of Belleville. Yet, on the other hand, any critical emphasis on Purdy as "representative man" (Solecki, *LCP* 10), in which the poet becomes "the voice of the Canadian vernacular" (Atwood, "Foreword" 18), fails to make sense of "The Runners," which abandons the first-person persona of the clowning lyricist in favour of a dialogue between two Gaelic speakers (presumably in translation) that is earnest, unironic, and alternately rhapsodic and urgent. "The Runners" forsakes the "hinterland idiom" (Lee 391; cf. 389–91) of masculine camaraderie, avoids the "droning cadences of tavern cusses" (Brockwell 10), and outpaces the "rangy, loping gait which ha[s] become [Purdy's] signature" (Lee 375; cf. 378). The absence of irony in a Purdy poem from the 1960s is particularly striking: one expects a quip, a clever piece of colloquial double-talk. Indeed, Søren Kierkegaard argues that the structure of ironic speech is akin to that of riddling speech: "the ironic figure of speech cancels itself; it is like a riddle to which one at the same time has the solution" (248). Yet a neck riddle is no joke, and thus Purdy avoids his usual antics in "The Runners," which develops a single literary reference over the length of the poem instead of interspersing archaic references into a larger meditation. The tone of "The Runners" is breathless (they are running for their lives) and elevated (they are trying to talk themselves into a heroic gesture). Furthermore, potential clues to the siblings' fate are encoded in the title and in the body of the poem in a cryptic fashion that is uncommon for the barroom bard, but revealing of an erudition that has always undergirded Purdy's jokey persona.

Purdy's own critical reflections would seem to relegate the story of Haki and Haekia to the trash heap of his early writings, for in his autobiography he recalls being repulsed by encountering "the sort of heroic drivel I was writing myself with Robin Hood and the Norse myths"

(Purdy, qtd. in Rogers, "What" 131). The antiquated diction and cadences of Purdy's early verse (e.g., the poems in *The Enchanted Echo* [1944]) still make appearances in his mature writing, but they are invoked ironically, ridiculed as absurd, attached to an object Purdy wishes to elegize, or doused with alcohol and humour. This is the much-anthologized voice of "The Country North of Belleville," "The Cariboo Horses," "At the Quinte Hotel," "Lament for the Dorsets," and other canonical works that contrast the vernacular present with an earlier, more heroic, but ultimately lost age. And yet "The Runners" has survived Purdy's legendary break with inherited poetic models (Lee 372). It makes the short list of Purdy's *Selected Poems* (1972), gets performed on his audio cassette (*The Collected Poems of Al Purdy*, 1990), and appears in standard anthologies of Canadian verse, such as Gary Geddes's *15 Canadian Poets x 3* (2001).

What, then, if not the stagy dialogue between Haki and Haekia, appeals to Canadian readers about this poem? Certainly the Vinland legend is a popular one, and it looms large in the title of *Wild Grape Wine*, as well as in poems such as "The Winemaker's Beat-Étude," where the speaker harvests wild grapes in Prince Edward County, Purdy's own personal "Wine land" and now a major viniculture destination in Ontario. But Purdy also addresses Norse colonization in other poems, such as the typically colloquial and anecdotal "Over the Hills in the Rain, My Dear," also from *Wild Grape Wine*, and critics generally overlook these poems. I would argue, then, that in place of typical CanLit markers, such as mimesis of place or an identifiably Canadian voice, the chief attraction of "The Runners" is its enactment of Canadian identity as a riddle, a formulation that was common in literary circles in the 1960s, as I will demonstrate in the final third of this chapter.

PURDY'S NECK RIDDLE

There is a special urgency in the Gaels' deliberations, because the runners seem to be in a predicament in which all paths lead to death. Three half-days have already passed, and Haki warns his reluctant sister that "If we are away longer, / the Northmen will beat us with thongs, / until we cry for death" (BR 163). On the other hand, if the pair run away, Haki predicts that "we should die slowly, / the beasts would gnaw at our bodies, / the rains whiten our bones" (BR 163). The Gaels could return to the ships immediately, but *Erick the Red's Saga* makes clear that half of the exploratory Vinland party departed after a hard winter and "ran into fierce headwinds and were driven right across to Ireland. There they were brutally beaten and enslaved" (Magnusson and Palsson 97). The historically informed reader is thus aware that none of the conventional answers to the Gaels' predicament are good. The Gaels must invent a new perspective to safeguard their bodies and futures. Purdy makes use of the riddle genre to dramatize this predicament, but his riddle is unusual in the way that it tries to evoke potential answers to its central conundrum instead of settling upon any final answers.

Purdy's method of riddling is fourfold. First, the poem's diction alludes to Northrop Frye's famous assertion in his conclusion to the *Literary History of Canada* (1965) that the central question of Canadian literature is "some such riddle as 'Where is here?'" ("Conclusion" 2.338). Second, Purdy uses the archaic setting of Karlsefni's Vinland expedition to turn the Centennial-era trope of giving voice to place into a life-or-death predicament analogous to a neck riddle. Third, the conclusion to "The Runners" is highly enigmatic – from the Greek *aenigma*, "riddle" – and demands that readers sort through a variety of clues (mythological, socio-cultural, rhetorical, tonal) to decide for themselves whether or not the siblings adopt Haekia's plan to "stay here" (BR 163). Finally, the clues that suggest that the siblings remain in Vinland form a network of verbal echoes according to an etymological design that ties the siblings' fate to Vinland. The latter reading hinges on the proposition that the seemingly innocuous repetition of the poem's concluding lines – "while we are running / while we are running" (BR 164) – is not simple repetition but rather a punning play on words that converts "running" into "rune-ing." Purdy's poem thus belongs to the print tradition of riddles, not to the oral one of folk tales, because it depends for its effect on the visual pun in the orthography of "run/rune," as well as on some knowledge of etymology.

The Old Norse and Old English spelling of "rune" is "r-ú-n," meaning "whisper" or "mystery": a "character of the earliest Germanic alphabet, *run* denoted a cryptic sign signifying something secret, mysterious or pertaining to hidden lore" (Cuddon 592–3). The term later came to denote "charms, healing formulas, and incantations," as well as "any secret means of communication," including poems with encrypted messages (Harmon 425). Unlike the riddle, the rune, as a poetic genre, does not have a well-defined form, but rather depends on these archaic associations with magic and encryption. Thus the narrative movement of Purdy's poem, from conspiratorial whispers to communion with mystery, follows the etymological evolution of the word "rune" by tracing the runners' transformation from whispering captives to rune-makers of their own. Indeed, one connotation of "rune" is "secret counsel" (*Princeton* 1101) and Purdy both portrays the secret counsel of the siblings and enacts a secret counsel through the way in which the poem's visual puns and etymological connections offer the reader clues to its ambiguous conclusion. As if to confirm Purdy's interest in such archaic signifiers, the *Oxford English Dictionary* states that an obsolete meaning of the noun *rune* means "[c]ourse, onward movement, esp. of a celestial object; (also) rapid movement, running, esp. of a person." When the reader knows these etymologies, the reiterated phrase of the third- and second-last lines in Purdy's poem emerges as a synthesis of the poem's key themes: running, rune-making, whispering, and fashioning a secret identity.

The way in which Purdy adapts aspects of the formally well-defined riddle genre, with its interplay of question and answer, to the mysterious ends of runic inscription is also fascinating and unusual. For example, in "Toward a Theory of the Literary Riddle," Dan Pagis draws on the folk-tale tradition when he argues that a riddle should be constructed as a question, and that it should employ stock words and phrases to mark its status as a riddle and thereby prompt an answer from the reader: "a riddle is only that text ... whose author, or later riddler, deliberately presents it to the reader as a challenge; and, naturally, a riddle is a text ... suited to being a challenge, encoded through various devices, but still soluble through the hints it contains" (81). Purdy's poem, in contrast, is structured around an implicit question; it formulates no direct challenges; and it offers no clear-cut answers. If it did, the poem would include a question marker (usually "who" or "what"), followed by a chain of propositions (usually paradoxical), punctuated by a question mark.

One could rewrite Purdy's poem as a more conventional riddle by following Pagis's genre definition and rendering the poem as:

Who run to remain here,
whisper to stay silent,
and make runes to end magic?

The answer to this riddle would be Haki and Haekia, and thus Purdy's title would give away the answer to the riddle. However, riddles cannot tolerate anticlimactic conclusions, as Anne Carson explains: "good riddles do not say what they mean. It is an innately stingy form of discourse, disguising its data and begrudging its truth. 'You know the riddle advertises all the techniques that the joke conceals,' says Freud. The riddle advertises everything except its own punchline" (23). Instead of developing "The Runners" toward a comic punchline, Purdy links his riddle to the unsaid, to the "silence inside silence" that Haekia perceives in the landscape (*BR* 163), and to the unstated decisions made after propositions introduced by the Gaels in phrases that frequently terminate in ellipses or dashes. Purdy's use of run-on sentences – the poem's second sentence traverses fifteen line breaks, three stanza breaks, and three changes of speaker – dramatizes the siblings' urgent attempts to respond to the neck riddle, while visual puns partly conceal important data related to their potential responses. A contest of words and wills is thus established, as in the riddle tradition ("What's black and white and red all over?"). However, explication ("The newspaper!") is withheld, as in the runic tradition.

Purdy's ambiguous conclusion exploits the fact that the challenge of the riddle, as it is posed by the author or speaker to the reader or addressee, elicits a variety of potential responses and causes different levels of discourse to intersect, as Galit Hasan-Rokem and David Shulman explain:

> The riddle's form is dialogic, requiring the interaction of self
> and other. Two levels are joined in the question, only to be
> disentangled in the answer. The process involved is inherently
> enigmatic and also transformative: the transition effected
> leaves reality changed, restructured, its basic categories restated,
> recognized, affirmed. This is no less true for the inner reality
> of consciousness than for any external, objectified world.
> ("Introduction" 3)

However, Purdy's conclusion is notable for its refusal to "disentangle" the different levels of discourse or to provide readers with a definitive answer to his neck riddle. Purdy treats the riddle as generative, rather than reductive, and in so doing departs from most critical definitions of the genre.

For example, according to Frye, whose shadow looms large over Purdy's generation of writers, "the idea of the riddle is descriptive containment": "the subject is not described but circumscribed, a circle of words drawn around it. In simple riddles, the central subject is an image, and the reader feels impelled to guess, that is, to equate the poem to the name or sign-symbol of its image" (*Anatomy* 300). Purdy plays with this idea of descriptive containment in the crucial fifth stanza of his nine-stanza poem, when Haekia comes to suspect that her brother's physical strength cannot protect her from the dangers she faces: "Brother, a cold wind touched me, / tho I stand in your arms' circle: / perhaps the Northmen's runes have found us" (BR 163). Threatened by supernatural forces, Haekia resolves that the Gaels must instead draw a circle of words around themselves for protection. She adopts a strategy of descriptive containment to circumscribe, but not quite describe, a method of escape.

She suggests that this method must connect words to the evocative silence of the stones and tangled forests, as well as the criss-crossing animal trails. Unlike the angular Norse runes, then, which were meant to be cut in wood and stone with knives, Haekia envisions a form of language that connects the local topography to the interlacing patterns of vines, serpents' tails, and human limbs in Celtic and Scandinavian art of the pre-Christian and early Christian periods, around the turn of the millennium (e.g., Viking stave churches, the Sutton Hoo metalwork). Likewise, the overall movement of Purdy's poem, from action to inscription, seems to follow Haekia's proposed poetic method.[4]

This kind of involuted design is also characteristic of the diction and logic of riddles in the Nordic tradition that Frye elucidates in *Anatomy of Criticism* (1957). For example, Frye notes that Old English riddle poems, whose elemental diction Purdy echoes, "belong to a culture in which such a phrase as 'curiously inwrought' is a favourite aesthetic judgement" (*Anatomy* 280). Haekia's vision of emancipation produces this "curiously inwrought" effect through its logic and diction. Haekia initially perceives the alien land as animate and malevolent: "I think the land knows we are here. / I think the land knows we are strangers" (BR 162). Yet she is captivated by the aura of mystery in the landscape, whose "magic" (BR 162) seems to emerge from "another silence inside silence" (BR 163). This paradox, which ties the poem's early parallelisms into a verbal knot, strikes Haekia as the means to counteract the Northmen's magic, and hence, in the fifth stanza, she prophesies:

> But there are berries and fish here,
> and small animals by the sea's edge
> that crouch and tremble and listen ...
> If we join our thoughts to the silence,
> if our trails join the animal trails,
> and the sun remembers what the moon forgets ...
> Brother, it comes to me now,
> the long ship must sail without us,
> we stay here –[.] (BR 163)

Haekia thus connects voice to place as part of her survival strategy, which is a common theme in Purdy's poetry. The Gaels cannot outrun the Norse magic, but joining "*words* to the silence" might be a way to counteract (or ruin) the power of the Norse runes. Hence the siblings' fragmentary dialogue frequently trails away into ellipses and dashes to connect words to silence. Yet Purdy's long, complex sentences propel the broken dialogue onward and make the poem feel as if the siblings are being swept into something vast, energetic, and powerful. Finally, the double syntax of "and listen" (BR 163), which might describe the listening animals or might be an imperative verb commanding Haki's attention before Haekia articulates her vision of the future, enacts the human-animal interface that the vision describes.

Despite Haekia's vision of the future, in which she tries to use the present tense "stay" as a performative verb to make the future start now, the siblings' ultimate fate in Vinland is uncertain. This lack of narrative closure in the poem might frustrate readers accustomed to Aristotelian forms of narrative. However, Purdy's conclusion draws on the non-narrative poetic forms that M. Travis Lane describes:

> Narrative assumes and implies chronology and causality, with their structural implications. And the beginning and the end of a narrative are defined by the choice of a subject. The hero dies, or the war is over, what comes next is a different story.
>
> It is easy to think of narrative as being the essential form of all writing, the ur-text of all poetry. Yet some of our oldest poems are not narrative: praise, prayer, tirade, persuasion, argument, instruction, description, riddle, and rune. Non-narrative forms of poetry differ from narrative poetry in a very significant way: their ends are not primarily selected and defined by the choice of subject. (145)

As a case in point, the end of "The Runners" is not defined by the predictable outcome of its narrative sequence, but rather by the etymological nuances of its title and keywords. In modern English, for example, the mystery of the runic alphabet is enhanced by the fact that the Old English alphabet initially adopted the runic characters for aspirated and unaspirated pronunciations of "th," and these characters have since disappeared. A trace of this runic influence nonetheless lingers in the first word of Purdy's title. The erudite aspects of Purdy's riddling poem, then, are very unlike his picturesque poems, of which Robert Stacey observes that there is "a purposeful under-deployment of literary skill, a tactical maladroitness that bespeaks a desire to forfeit absolute control over one's means of expression" (114). "The Runners," in contrast, forfeits control over its conclusion, but otherwise is cleverly wrought. If anything, the maladroit repetition of "running" in its third- and second-last lines functions as a cipher of Purdy's cunning.

The open-ended conclusion defies conventions of the riddle genre. For example, in *Untying the Knot: On Riddles and Other Enigmatic Modes*,

Hasan-Rokem and Shulman argue that the mystery of a riddle must ultimately be soluble:

> there is a structure of encoding, or enchantment, or doubling (erotic suggestion), which entails a block to perception or a knotted conflation of domains (often with elements of linguistic paronomasia or visual punning); the solution removes the block, unties the knot, and usually also disenchants. By definition, this process unfolds in the social context of a challenge; the challenger controls the answer, which is always overdetermined. An initial act of calculated ambiguation – seemingly underdetermined, superficially permitting multiple answers on the basis of the clues supplied – moves toward the disambiguating, singular conclusion. ("Afterword" 316)

Purdy's conclusion, in contrast, refuses to disambiguate. The poem's final line, which consists solely of the word "Sister –," might mean that the Northmen's runes have taken effect: Haki has been silenced in mid-conversation and cast into oblivion. Or perhaps Haki is calling for his sister as predators drag her away. Or perhaps the open dash signifies that the brother falls mute because he has no argument to counter Haekia's plan to stay in Vinland, effectively giving her the last word in their debate. Or the dash might be a visual pun, inviting the reader to fill in the blank. In any case, the open-ended conclusion holds several possible outcomes in riddling suspension. Rather than resolving these ambiguities, Purdy's poem prefers to emphasize that moment of challenge and potential response in the riddle that "can reveal in a brief flash an excluded cosmos, a non-world or topsy-turvy world lurking just beneath our properly ordered and familiar one" (Hasan-Rokem and Shulman, "Introduction" 4).

For example, the element of erotic suggestion in "The Runners" adds a menacing scenario to the series of possible conclusions, one that might involve incest, rape, and/or abduction. Whereas Haekia sees her salvation in the evocative silence of the vast territory, Haki insists on physical proximity as a defence against all dangers. His first words in the second stanza read like a series of euphemisms for sexual congress: "Sister, we must share our strength between us, / until the heat of our bodies makes a single flame" (BR 163). Rereading the poem from this erotic angle makes one wonder whether Haekia's discussion of the landscape is an attempt to direct her brother's attention away from his early fixation on their bodily union: the "one that we are is more than two that we were," Haki says in *Wild Grape Wine* (110), in a line that Purdy cut from *Beyond*

Remembering: The Collected Poems of Al Purdy (163). In both editions, Haki continues: "and the sun knows only our double heartbeat, / and the rain does not come between –" (BR 163). Incestuous union is typical of creation myths about founding couples (e.g., Zeus and Rhea, Isis and Osiris), and emphasizes the first couple's power to defy social taboos, establish a new order, and overcome the threat of oblivion.

Purdy arguably positions Haki and Haekia as the first people of a landscape that the author has evacuated of Indigenous presence – unlike *Erick the Red's Saga*, where the "Skraelings" defend their territory (Magnusson and Palsson 99–101), and unlike Purdy's "Lament for the Dorsets," where "the Dorset giants / ... dr[i]ve the Vikings back to their ships" (BR 160). However, in "The Runners," images of Haekia's sudden chill in her brother's arms make one wonder whether this closeness is consensual and whether "Sister –," without a response from Haekia, is the sound of her forcible abduction. As Claude Lévi-Strauss demonstrates in his structuralist analyses, riddles and incest exhibit a strong correlation across a wide variety of cultures and historical periods (e.g., Oedipus and the Sphinx) because they tend to conjoin taboo concepts (35–9). The phonic similarity of "Haki" and "Haekia" seems to invite confusion in the reader, one that might produce such a conjunction.

Alternatively, if Haekia's will prevails and her identity is not subsumed by her brother's, then the poem has a progressive gender dynamic that positions the woman as the heroic character. Richard Bauman explains that tales oriented around riddles deal "with two different spheres of power, institutional versus interactional, which, while they are frequently related, are potentially separable from one another; a person who is structurally subordinate in institutional terms may nevertheless dominate a structurally superordinate person in a given interaction by force of wit, rhetorical skill, or some other interactional means" (67). Put simply, riddles give protagonists the opportunity to overcome authority by contorting linguistic and logical categories in order to produce new and compelling forms of sense. Usually, the protagonists are challenged to outwit a male authority figure at his own game. For example, neck riddles often feature a clever reversal of the riddler's challenge, in which a "prisoner ... saves his neck by propounding a riddle which his executioner cannot answer" (Roger D. Abrahams, qtd. in Bauman 75).

Purdy's poem creates the opportunity for a power reversal between the Gaels and King Olaf Tryggvason of Norway, who lent the Gaels to the Vinland explorer Leif the Lucky, who then lent them to Karlsefni for the latter's colonization venture. Norse settlements often used Gaels as slaves (Larrington 18), and it is very likely that Haki and Haekia are not willing members of Karlsefni's expedition. At the very least, the Gaels are controlled by instruments of royal power (ships, weapons, decrees, writing). Haki becomes the spokesperson for royal power in the siblings' dialogue as he pleads with Haekia to maintain the status quo. However, Haekia's defiance of these institutional and familial pressures makes her decision to "stay here" (BR 163) feel even bolder.

Toying with the power dynamics of gender roles in this manner can enhance the suspense and mystery of riddles. Pagis demonstrates that one of the best-known examples of a neck riddle is the unorthodox "story of the gnome Rumpelstiltskin, who puts the king's wife in great distress and is willing to release her only if she guesses his bizarre name; at the last moment she succeeds" (95). The Rumpelstiltskin story initially deviates from the Authority-Subordinate formula of the riddle genre by making the Queen answerable to the underclass of gnomes. The story ultimately reifies institutional power by allowing the Queen to get the correct answer and to maintain order in the kingdom, but the suspense of the story hinges upon Rumpelstiltskin's temporary usurpation of power and his threat to primogeniture (he demands the Queen's first-born child). Haekia, who fears that "cunning dwarves at the roots of darkness / shall seize and drag us down" (BR 162) if she defies the Northmen's runes, faces an equally life-threatening predicament. However, her response can potentially upset the established order by contravening imperial decree and overruling the protestations of her brother, who represents patriarchal norms.

Frye outlines two further generic definitions of the riddle that help to make sense of Purdy's atmospheric use of the genre: "A slightly more complicated form of riddle is the emblematic vision ... [and the] connection of the emblematic vision with the heraldic image of modern fiction is easy to see. In *symbolisme* we have a third form of riddle where it is normally a mood rather than an object that is contained" (*Anatomy* 300). While most of "The Runners" is more dramatic than symbolist, the mood of the poem, as it relates to the emblematic vision of the pair running for freedom, is crucial to the poem's effect. The early mood is claustrophobic, as the speakers feel confined by a land that is both animate and malevolent. Their initial response is to run, then to huddle together, then to run again. Yet the air of mystery in the land, which initially oppresses Haekia, later seems to empower her. The end of the poem gestures toward an embrace of the vast territory and its plenitude. Haekia's catalogue of the observable world gradually rises toward a vision of emancipation that draws on a felt, but unseen, power. Her declaration that they should "stay here" comes in a moment of rapture and defies the logic of self-preservation (BR 163). Although Haki makes a pragmatic case for obeying the Northmen's commands, his suggestion seems to be overruled by the rhetorical force of Haekia's vision. Still, ambiguity haunts the ending of "The Runners" because Haekia's vision might be foolhardy. Purdy, after all, considered his readership "those citizens of a second-class nation who are unable to comprehend their own subservience or their own naive stupidity" ("Introduction" iv). The tension between lyrical flight and mundane practicality in Purdy's poetry often leads to a "doubtfully affirmative vision," rather than a full-blown epiphany or a decisive course of action, as Stan Dragland observes (qtd. in Fiamengo 165). Readers must decide for themselves what to make of the Gaels' renewed running in the final stanzas, and have little more than mood and etymological clues to use as the basis of their judgments.

This emphasis on mood, rather than narrative outcome, places the reader in the position that W.B. Yeats describes in "Symbolism in Painting," in which the Irish poet argues that the non-narrative resources of art can be marshalled to facilitate constant questioning in the viewer and reader: "All art that is not mere story-telling, or mere portraiture, is symbolic, and has the purpose of those symbolic talismans which medieval magicians made with complex colours and forms, and bade their patients ponder over daily, and guard with holy secrecy; for it entangles, in complex colours and forms, a part of the Divine Essence" (148). Purdy held Yeats in great esteem (Solecki, "Al" 109–10), yet the complex tangle of cultural referents and choices in "The Runners" seems to capture not Divine Essence but the crux of many Centennial-era deliberations over the fate of Canadian settlers and artists. The poem's fixation on place, as well as the tension between embracing and rejecting one's cultural history (e.g., Haekia's nostalgia for the "home islands" [BR 163]), is appropriate for the decision facing the Gaels, but it also suits a period of Canadian history when Atwood would famously claim: "This country is something that must be chosen – it is so easy to leave – and if we do choose it we are still choosing a violent duality" (*Journals* 62). "The Runners" is a poem about choices and violent consequences; it is meant to be "ponder[ed] over," to catalyze personal and national self-reflection, rather than to be resolved. Indeed, narrative resolution in poetry had come to be seen as overvalued by the late 1960s, as Dragland argues of Purdy's "The Dead Poet": "Finding a key is not the same as finding a solution, but the key may certainly be a talisman – pure energy – to hold onto while you wrestle with the possibilities it suddenly opens up" (16). Hence, Lee praises the way in which "The Runners" explores "a deep and positive ambivalence in the Canadian makeup" without trying to "master" the place or situation (389). Purdy constructs the challenge, but does not control the answer.

CANADIAN CRITICAL BACKGROUND

Purdy's unorthodox treatment of the riddle genre might have been influenced by his literary milieu. The notion that Canadian identity is at once riddling, place-based, and marked by cultural diversity in its human aspect was common in nationalist literary circles in Purdy's formative years, at least in what Bowering derisively calls the "Anglo-Saxon halls of learning in Ontario and Quebec" ("Purdy" 65).[5] For example, James Reaney's 1957 essay "The Canadian Poet's Predicament" compares Canadian literature with Indigenous art and poetry and finds that canonical Canadian art lacks the geographical specificity and stylistic distinctiveness of Indigenous productions:

> The totem poles and mounds seem so effortlessly to come out of the look of the country; but our culture, as yet, doesn't. When you compare Michelangelo's gigantic statues of Day and Night, Twilight and Dawn, when you compare them with the tense coloured oblongs by which in their ritual sand paintings the [West Coast] Indians describe the same eternal truths, the difference between the genius of this continent and the genius of Europe becomes evident with a flash. And that difference contains the answer to the riddle of being an artist in this country. (120–1)

Reaney uses the term "riddle" as a common synonym for "mystery" here, but it is notable how the vision of escape for Purdy's runners is tied to a place-based notion of artistry, and how leaving this place altogether is also an option for the settler. Reaney, one of the country's most ardent regionalists, maintains that Canada is "a country to stay in, and not to stay in. When you start to write a poem in Canada and think of the British Museum Reading Room you almost go mad because the great tradition of English literature, the glare of its brilliant modern representatives seems so oppressively and crushingly great" (119–20). The Canadian poet, then, is in a position akin to that of Haekia, who needs to devise a new voice and form language to counteract the authority of the runic tradition, yet who is simultaneously overawed by the allure of the landscape and the magnitude of the task.

Frye, Reaney's mentor at the University of Toronto, updates Reaney's poetic predicament for the age of mass communications in his conclusion to the second edition of the *Literary History of Canada*. Frye considers the struggle of the artist to define place as part of a larger Canadian struggle to maintain cultural identity in a globalized environment:

> Canadian writers are, even now, still trying to assimilate a Canadian environment at a time when new techniques of communication, many of which, like television, constitute a verbal market, are annihilating the boundaries of that environment ... It seems to me that Canadian sensibility has been profoundly disturbed, not so much by our famous problem of identity, important as that is, as by a series of paradoxes in what confronts that identity. It is less perplexed by the question "Who am I?" than by some such riddle as "Where is here?" ("Conclusion" 2.338)

Like any good riddle, Frye's formulation asks a question that is not easily soluble, and thus elicits many answers. *Essays on Canadian Writing* devoted a special issue to suggesting answers to Frye's riddle in 2000 (see Lecker). Annick Hillger devotes an entire chapter, "The Sphinx of the Unknown Land," to the impact of Frye's riddle on Michael Ondaatje in *Not Needing All the Words: Michael Ondaatje's Literature of Silence* (2006). Peter Dickinson wittily echoes Frye's riddle in the title of *Here Is Queer: Nationalisms, Sexualities, and the Literatures of Canada* (1999), and recent riffs of this sort include Robert McGill's *War Is Here: Canadian Literature and the Vietnam War* (2017). The Canadian Sphinx, it seems, is looking for a plethora of plausible answers, not *the* answer.

Frye's formulation of the riddle is truer to genre conventions than Reaney's because Frye uses internal rhyme to mimic some of the formal properties of the riddle. Frye's question marker "where" includes within it the clue "here," which makes the logic of the phrase circle back on itself and seem to restate the question as soon as it is answered. Frye's pithy question thus becomes a vehicle of nationalism in the post-Centennial era by encouraging respondents to use words to establish national boundaries in a borderless electronic environment and to generate new definitions of Canada. Purdy's open-ended conclusion resembles Frye's riddle in this generative aspect, effectively challenging readers to explain how, why, and if the Gaels "stay here" (*BR* 163). The readerly involvement that the poem's perplexing conclusion demands should remind critics that the word "[r]iddle was originally the cognate object of read, and the riddle seems intimately involved with the whole process of reducing language to visible form, a process which runs through such by-forms of riddle as hieroglyph and ideogram" (Frye, *Anatomy* 280). One could add *rune* to this list. Purdy's poem, then, finds common generic ground between the riddle and rune in the sense that both genres involve cryptic sign systems that demand careful deciphering, but that may not necessarily be resolved.

Although the riddle genre is interrogative, only one question mark appears in "The Runners," right before Haekia articulates her vision, when she falls silent and her brother asks: "Why do you stare at nothing?" (BR 163). This confrontation with "nothing" recalls Purdy's engagement with existentialist philosophy in his previous collection of poems, *North of Summer* (1967), where the answer to most philosophical conundrums can be found in the simple lessons of the Arctic landscape, such as the resilience of the "dwarf" "Trees at the Arctic Circle" that "spend their time / unbothered by any human opinion / just digging in here and now" (BR 103). Yet Eli Mandel argues in his introduction to *Poets of Contemporary Canada (1960–1970)* that Canadian writers must progress beyond an obsession with landscape to become "historians of the soul" (xiii). He therefore selects poems from ten writers, beginning with Purdy, and offers them as "clues to that always unsolved mystery in Canada, the nature of our cultural history or at least its present form" (xii). The mythic landscape in "The Runners" is thus only part of the solution to the siblings' problem. They must look inward and confront their own fears and failings before they free themselves.

The siblings' interrogation of "nothing" in "The Runners" is also a confrontation with the perceptual bias of the colonist, who sees very little that is familiar (grapes, wheat) and much that is unfamiliar, which produces a sense of dread and void. However, when the Gaels take a hard look at the fertile land in the second half of the poem, they realize that it teems with animal and vegetal life as well as new human possibilities. In keeping with the modernist tradition that influenced Purdy's development during his Montreal phase, the siblings are invited to negate "nothing," and thereby create new forms of life and consciousness. The riddle becomes Purdy's means of negating the perceptual (seeing "nothing"), verbal (silence), and historical (failed migration) negations informing "The Runners." But at the same time, the ambivalent conclusion of "The Runners" offers a glimpse of Purdy's poetic "soul," in that it highlights a psychological continuity that Solecki traces across the breadth of Purdy's mature writing: "Dramatic self-assertions and visions of grandeur trip over radical self-doubt, lacerating self-criticism, and awareness of bad faith" ("Materials" 19). Perhaps Canadian readers are attracted to "The Runners" because this glimpse into the underlying psychological structures of the writer offers Canadians clues to the "nature of our cultural history" over the past one hundred and fifty years (Mandel xii).

Another interpretation of the poem's appeal, one that helps to contextualize the dialogic qualities of "The Runners," arises out of Robert

Kroetsch's review of *The Last Canadian Poet*, in which he argues that Solecki draws flawed conclusions about Purdy's mature poetry:

> Solecki recognizes but cannot quite admit the paradox that the poet who sings Ameliasburg is the poet who lets us into our multiplicities. Purdy, undoing Bakhtin's reservations about the lyric poet, becomes the lyric poet who can speak beyond the monologue and voice our polyphony, our carnival many. And Purdy is surely a carnival poet; in so being he gains presence by upsetting presence. Solecki dreams an enduring authority. Purdy swings open wide the door, the gate. (21)

To his credit, Solecki cites this passage in *The Ivory Thought* and agrees with the "studhorse man ... to a point" ("Materials" 26). I think the future viability of Purdy's poetry in a multicultural Canada depends on this critical shift from Solecki's bardic interpretation of Purdy to Kroetsch's multiplicitous one (see also Van Rys), which is partly why Purdy's atypical poems interest me. The conclusion to "The Runners" certainly "swings open wide the door" to a variety of possible interpretations, as well as opening up the generic frameworks of the rune and riddle to multiplicitous effect. Thus Purdy's riddling style in "The Runners" is not single-voiced but requires new forms of critical interpretation (see, for example, Silverberg 247). Mark Silverberg is correct that by "reductively Canadianizing Purdy, critics and anthologists have effectively hidden much of what is good and bad in his work. As we are encouraged to see Purdy only as 'one of us,' a representative Canadian big enough to fill a Mountie's uniform, we are also discouraged from seeing him in other ways" (228). For example, "The Runners" seems politically progressive in that it sidelines the poetic persona of the "learned hick" (Budde ix) in favour of a dialogue driven by a forceful female speaker, but it also erases Indigenous presence in the coastal territory and in the collective "we," as does Reaney's notion of "our culture" (121). Recent scholarship suggests that the hide-covered canoes used by the "Skraelings" resemble those used by "Algonquin-speaking" peoples in the Gulf of St Lawrence (Wallace 25). Archaeologists have shown that there were "many Indigenous occupations of the site" at L'Anse aux Meadows (25), and the "reason given in the sagas for abandoning Vinland is that the new land was already inhabited and the Norse were outnumbered and sure to lose in any kind of conflict" (29). Still, if Linda Rogers is correct that Purdy's poems are "the chart of our progress to a culture" ("Introduction" 11), then "The Runners" is a different kind of chart than "At the Quinte Hotel." Inquiring into atypical Purdy poems might provoke critics to think about Canada and Canadian literature in generative ways that do not necessitate a reductive notion of collective identity.

NOTES

1 The version of the poem in *Wild Grape Wine* is different from the slightly longer version in *Being Alive* (1978), *The Collected Poems of Al Purdy* (1986), and *Beyond Remembering* (2000).
2 In this chapter I use the spellings and the details of the saga excerpted by Purdy as an epigraph to his poem. The translation of *Erick the Red's Saga* supplied by Magnus Magnusson and Hermann Palsson in *The Vinland Sagas: The Norse Discovery of America* spells Erick as "Eirik" and Haekia as "Hekja," and states that the Gaels were instructed to return to the Viking ships within "three days" (95), not three half-days.
3 In fact, neither Purdy nor Bowering received a nomination in the *Globe* poll.
4 I am grateful to an anonymous assessor of this chapter for this suggestion.
5 This tradition persists, for example, in the "Where Am I?" series of Discover Ontario commercials that played extensively on television in 2017. The commercials consisted of a barrage of place images that inundated the audience with signs of the province's geographical and cultural diversity, while a voice-over intoned: "I'm a question wrapped in history inside a country. Where am I? More water than land, fewer people than trees. Where am I? Ice formed me, a giant lives inside me. [Sound of Niagara Falls rushing.] I'm the riddle you have yet to solve. Where am I?"

REFERENCES

Anderssen, Erin. "Parliamentary Poet Wanted." *Globe and Mail*, 7 February 2001, https://www.theglobeandmail.ca.
Atwood, Margaret. Foreword to *Beyond Remembering: The Collected Poems of Al Purdy*, edited by Al Purdy and Sam Solecki, 17–18. Madeira Park, BC: Harbour Publishing, 2000.
– *The Journals of Susanna Moodie*. Toronto: Oxford University Press, 1970.
Bauman, Richard. "'I'll Give You Three Guesses': The Dynamics of Genre in the Riddle-Tale." In Hasan-Rokem and Shulman, *Untying the Knot*, 62–77.
Bentley, D.M.R. "Conclusion, Retrospective, and Prospective." In Lynch, Ganz, and Kealey, *Ivory Thought*, 239–46.
Bowering, George. *Al Purdy*. Toronto: Copp Clark, 1970.
– "Purdy among the Tombs." In Lynch, Ganz, and Kealey, *Ivory Thought*, 63–70.

Brockwell, Stephen. "Ingredients for Certain Poems by Al Purdy." In Lynch, Ganz, and Kealey, *Ivory Thought*, 9–12.
Budde, Robert. Introduction to *The More Easily Kept Illusions: The Poetry of Al Purdy*, edited by Robert Budde, vii–xv. Waterloo, ON: Wilfrid Laurier University Press, 2006.
Canadian Press. "'People's Poet' Al Purdy's Statue Unveiled." CTV News, 21 May 2008, http://www.ctvnews.ca/people-s-poet-al-purdy-s-statue-unveiled-1.297237.
Carson, Anne. *Economy of the Unlost*. Princeton, NJ: Princeton University Press, 1999.
Clarke, George Elliott, ed. *Fire on the Water: An Anthology of Black Nova Scotian Writing*. Porter's Lake, NS: Pottersfield, 1991.
Cuddon, J.A. *A Dictionary of Literary Terms*. 1977. New York: Penguin, 1979.
Davey, Frank. "Al Purdy, Sam Solecki, and the Poetics of the 1960s." *Canadian Poetry: Studies, Documents, Reviews*, no. 51 (Fall–Winter 2002): 39–57.
Dickinson, Peter. *Here Is Queer: Nationalisms, Sexualities, and the Literatures of Canada*. Toronto: University of Toronto Press, 1999.
Dragland, Stan. "Al Purdy's Poetry: Openings." In Rogers, *Al Purdy*, 15–57.
Fiamengo, Janice. "'Kind of ludicrous or kind of beautiful I guess': Al Purdy's Rhetoric of Failure." In Lynch, Ganz, and Kealey, *Ivory Thought*, 159–72.
Frye, Northrop. *Anatomy of Criticism: Four Essays*. 1957. Princeton, NJ: Princeton University Press, 1990.
– "Conclusion." In *Literary History of Canada: Canadian Literature in English*, edited by Carl F. Klinck, 2.333–61. 2nd ed. 3 vols. Toronto: University of Toronto Press, 1976.
Geddes, Gary, ed. *Canadian Poets x 3*. 4th ed. Toronto: Oxford University Press, 2001.
Harmon, William. *A Handbook to Literature*. 12th ed. Glenview, IL: Pearson, 2012.
Hasan-Rokem, Galit, and David Shulman. Afterword to Hasan-Rokem and Shulman, *Untying the Knot*, 316–20.
– Introduction to Hasan-Rokem and Shulman, *Untying the Knot*, 3–9.
–, eds. *Untying the Knot: On Riddles and Other Enigmatic Modes*. New York: Oxford University Press, 1996.
Hillger, Annick. *Not Needing All the Words: Michael Ondaatje's Literature of Silence*. Montreal and Kingston: McGill-Queen's University Press, 2006.
Kierkegaard, Søren. *On the Concept of Irony, with Continual Reference to Socrates*. 1841. Edited and translated by Howard V. Hong and Edna H. Hong. Princeton, NJ: Princeton University Press, 1989.
Kroetsch, Robert. "Reading Solecki Reading Purdy: A Digressive Review." Review of *The Last Canadian Poet: An Essay on Al Purdy*, by Sam Solecki. *The Fiddlehead*, no. 204 (Summer 2000): 20–3.

Lane, M. Travis. "Alternatives to Narrative: The Structuring Concept." *Open Letter* 6, no. 2–3 (Summer–Fall 1985): 145–51.

Larrington, Carolyne. *The Norse Myths: A Guide to the Gods and Heroes*. London: Thames and Hudson, 2017.

Lecker, Robert. "Where Is Here Now?" *Essays on Canadian Writing*, no. 71 (Fall 2000): 6–15.

Lee, Dennis. "The Poetry of Al Purdy: An Afterword." In *The Collected Poems of Al Purdy*, edited by Russell Brown, 371–91. Toronto: McClelland & Stewart, 1986.

Lévi-Strauss, Claude. *The Scope of Anthropology*. Translated by Sherry Ortner Paul and Robert A. Paul. London: Jonathan Cape, 1974.

Lynch, Gerald, Shoshannah Ganz, and Josephene T.M. Kealey. Introduction to Lynch, Ganz, and Kealey, *Ivory Thought*, 1–8.

–, eds. *The Ivory Thought: Essays on Al Purdy*. Ottawa: University of Ottawa Press, 2008.

Magnusson, Magnus, and Hermann Palsson. *The Vinland Sagas: The Norse Discovery of America*. New York: New York University Press, 1966.

Mandel, Eli, ed. *Poets of Contemporary Canada (1960–1970)*. Toronto: McClelland & Stewart, 1972.

McGill, Robert. *War Is Here: The Vietnam War and Canadian Literature*. Montreal and Kingston: McGill-Queen's University Press, 2017.

Pagis, Dan. "Toward a Theory of the Literary Riddle." In Hasan-Rokem and Shulman, *Untying the Knot*, 81–108.

"Purdy." *Dictionary of American Family Names*. Edited by Patrick Hanks. Oxford: Oxford University Press, 2006.

Purdy, Al. *Beyond Remembering: The Collected Poems of Al Purdy*. Edited by Al Purdy and Sam Solecki. Madeira Park, BC: Harbour Publishing, 2000.

– *The Collected Poems of Al Purdy*. Edited by Russell Brown. Toronto: McClelland & Stewart, 1986.

– *The Collected Poems of Al Purdy*. Audio cassette. Audio Encore, 1990.

– Introduction to *The New Romans: Candid Canadian Opinions of the U.S.*, edited by Al Purdy, i–iv. Edmonton: Hurtig, 1968.

– *North of Summer: Poems from Baffin Island*. Toronto: McClelland & Stewart, 1967.

– *Selected Poems*. Toronto: McClelland & Stewart, 1972.

– *Wild Grape Wine*. Toronto: McClelland & Stewart, 1968.

Reaney, James. "The Canadian Poet's Predicament." In *Masks of Poetry: Canadian Criticism on Canadian Verse*, edited by A.J.M. Smith, 110–22. Toronto: McClelland & Stewart, 1968.

Rogers, Linda, ed. *Al Purdy: Essays on His Works*. Toronto: Guernica Editions, 2002.

– "Introduction: Reaching for the Beaufort Sea." In Rogers, *Al Purdy*, 9–14.

– "What a Life." In Rogers, *Al Purdy*, 128–38.
"Rune." *Oxford English Dictionary*. 3rd ed. (March 2011). Online.
"Rune." In *The New Princeton Encyclopedia of Poetry and Poetics*, edited by Alex Preminger and T.V.F. Brogan, 1101. Princeton, NJ: Princeton University Press, 2013.
Silverberg, Mark. "The Can(adi)onization of Al Purdy." *Essays on Canadian Writing*, no. 70 (Spring 2000): 226–51.
Solecki, Sam. "Al Purdy among the Poets." In Rogers, *Al Purdy*, 108–27.
– *The Last Canadian Poet: An Essay on Al Purdy*. Toronto: University of Toronto Press, 1999.
– "Materials for a Biography of Al Purdy." In Lynch, Ganz, and Kealey, *Ivory Thought*, 13–30.
Solway, David. "Standard Average Canadian, or the Influence of Al Purdy." *Canadian Notes and Queries*, no. 59 (Spring–Summer 2001): 18–20.
Stacey, Robert David. "Purdy's Ruins: *In Search of Owen Roblin*, Literary Power, and the Poetics of the Picturesque." In Lynch, Ganz, and Kealey, *Ivory Thought*, 103–18.
Van Rys, John. "Alfred in Baffin Land: Carnival Traces in Purdy's *North of Summer*." *Canadian Poetry: Studies, Documents, Reviews*, no. 26 (Spring–Summer 1990): 1–18.
Wallace, Birgitta. "Finding Vinland: The Evidence Appears Overwhelming for the Location of the Legendary Norse Settlement." *Canada's History*, February–March 2018: 20–9.
Yeats, W.B. "Symbolism in Painting." In *Essays and Introductions*, by W.B. Yeats, 146–52. London: Macmillan, 1961.

7

The Poet and the Ethnographer: Purdy, Marius Barbeau, and the Poetry of Myth

Nicholas Bradley

Al Purdy was phenomenally prolific. From the 1960s until the end of the century, it was unusual if more than a few years passed without the arrival of a substantial volume of his poems, and the results of his sustained productivity are milestones in the history of Canadian poetry: *Poems for All the Annettes* (1962), *The Cariboo Horses* (1965), *North of Summer* (1967), *Wild Grape Wine* (1968), *Sex and Death* (1973), *In Search of Owen Roblin* (1974), and so on.[1] The list only concludes with *Beyond Remembering: The Collected Poems of Al Purdy*, the retrospective anthology published shortly after his death in 2000. Purdy's works appeared frequently in literary journals, popular magazines, and newspapers, and only a small number of Canadian authors, poets or otherwise, matched the public reputation he enjoyed at the height of his celebrity; by the time of his death, he had become venerated, an institution himself. From 1965 until 1994, his major collections of poetry were issued by McClelland & Stewart, the country's most prominent literary publisher.[2] Readers of the *Globe and Mail* might have noticed "The Horseman of Agawa" or "A Handful of Earth" in the newspaper's pages, and subscribers to *Maclean's* magazine could have followed Purdy's dispatches from his travels across Canada.[3] Few Canadian cultural institutions escaped Purdy's gravity, or he theirs; he was involved at various times with the Canadian Broadcasting Corporation, the National Film Board, and even the Hudson's Bay Company.[4] Although Purdy's titanic oeuvre has not been examined exhaustively, no little attention has been devoted to his poetry and his seemingly permanent place in Canadian letters. From George Bowering's *Al Purdy* (1970), the first long study, to Sam Solecki's *The Last Canadian Poet* (1999), the most comprehensive account of the poetry, Purdy's works have been treated relatively often, and in some cases thoroughly.

Given his record of publication and the scholarly reception of his works, it is somewhat surprising that any of Purdy's literary efforts remain to be discovered. His archives have been explored, but they nonetheless conceal a host of unnoticed compositions in addition to an immense amount of biographical information. Several volumes could be assembled of his unpublished poems, and his correspondence and writing in other genres (essays and radio plays, for instance) await critical scrutiny, editorial care, and compilation. Any serious author would be expected, over the course of a long career, to abandon projects – not every image leads to an immortal lyric, nor every thought to an insightful meditation – and Purdy's papers divulge innumerable failed poems. But one forsaken manuscript stands apart because of its divergence from his habitual style and subjects: "Yehl the Raven and Other Creation Myths of the Haida." The unpublished sequence of poems illustrates Purdy's ethnographic interests and represents a point of contact between modern Canadian literature and mid-century anthropology. Early in the 1960s, Purdy wrote his "Creation Myths" by adapting narratives found in the studies of Marius Barbeau (1883–1969), the Canadian folklorist and ethnographer. He attempted to publish the resultant poems as a short book. "Yehl the Raven" never appeared in print, however, and although the manuscript has not been utterly invisible to Purdy's colleagues and critics, it has been mischaracterized, unappreciated, and essentially overlooked. Nor have its origins and virtual disappearance yet been explained.

In what follows, I aim to describe the manuscript and to suggest that it merits perusal, not because of the excellence of the poetry, but because it enriches understandings of Purdy's early career, especially in terms of biographical detail, and confirms that Purdy was, to a degree not previously apprehended, a fervid reader of ethnographic writing. I also provide an account of the manuscript's place in Purdy's archives in order to illustrate the challenges that his papers, dispersed and seemingly endless, pose to researchers. Purdy's enormous body of published poetry beggars the synoptic reader's efforts to understand his literary life as a whole, and the unpublished papers only compound the critical problems engendered by nearly limitless words. But "Yehl the Raven," an obscurity of dubious aesthetic accomplishment, offers to clarify aspects of Purdy's creative life that have been all but ignored, including certain incipient intellectual passions and artistic false starts. At the same time, "Yehl the Raven" shows that, at the outset of his career as a mature writer, Purdy was determined to render his poetry a means of exploring Canadian history and geography, in which he included Indigenous cultures, even if doing so took him away from personal experience and his home in southern Ontario. In other words, what

Purdy took as appropriate subjects and modes for a Canadian writer was more expansive than his typical characterization as a regionalist would indicate. His assumption that the "Creation Myths" fell within his purview reflects a desire to find in Indigenous cultures an authentically Canadian heritage, while his inability to do considerably more than rearrange Barbeau's texts, or to rewrite them in a stilted oratorical style, suggests Purdy's uneasy relation to the source material. In attempting to make the stories his own, he inadvertently signalled his distance from the cultures that fascinated him.

In *Al Purdy*, Bowering announced, with customary irreverence, his subject's early interest in Barbeau:

> In 1960 Purdy received his first Canada Council fellowship, and typically he decided not to live off the money in Spain or France, but rather to head for the Cariboo, which he had visited while he was in the air force. He had all kinds of grandiose ideas about his project, such as writing an opera about the life of the Indians, and it was around this time that he was often reported to be writing an epic based on Haida myths as described in the works of Marius Barbeau and published by the Canadian government. Very Canadian stuff. All that has surfaced from this time are Purdy's poems about the northern interior of British Columbia, but they are enough to pay off the Canada Council investment. (8)

Bowering gave no indication that the "epic" was anything more than an unfulfilled ambition – evidence, that is, of Purdy's wayward fascinations. Concentrating instead on Purdy's published works, he did not mention the "Haida myths" again, and the possible or actual existence of the epic – to say nothing of the opera – has not been taken seriously by later commentators.

In *The Last Canadian Poet*, Solecki referred in passing to Purdy's "unpublished translations of Haida myths" (43), and the correspondence gathered in Purdy's *Collected Letters* (2004) includes two partially clarifying passages. In 1990 Purdy wrote, in a letter to the author Steven Heighton, that he had found among his own papers "a manuscript of Indian myths adapted from Marius Barbeau in 1963," which he newly wanted to publish (YA 453).[5] Solecki observed in his editorial note that the "versions of Barbeau's transcriptions of 'Indian myths' have not been published" (YA 453 n2). And in 1991 Purdy told George Woodcock – the Canadian man of letters was an influential supporter of Purdy's writing – that the unearthed manuscript, having been sent to the Oberon Press to no avail, was soon to be brought out by Harbour Publishing (YA 460).[6] Evidently he revised the manuscript between July 1990 and the following April. Yet no book was published, as Solecki wrote again, and the adaptations have not to my knowledge been noted elsewhere (*YA* 460 n1). "Yehl" is a name essentially unfamiliar to Purdy's readers.

The documents that provide the necessary explanatory details have languished unread. The poet's archive, made up of collections at several Canadian universities, is so extensive and labyrinthine that an accurate picture of the complete corpus is vexingly difficult to obtain. Purdy was an idiosyncratic organizer of his papers (literary, financial, and personal). In 1969 he wrote, in a letter to Douglas O. Spettigue, a professor of English at Queen's University involved in the acquisition of Purdy's files, that "the papers themselves are contained in seven cardboard cartons, each approximately the size of a liquor case" (qtd. in Heil 32).[7] Decades later he included, in a similar message to the archivist Shirley Spragge, an important consideration: "The boxes I mentioned are mostly whiskey boxes, not from my drinking I hasten to assure you. One picks them up free at the Belleville liquor store" (qtd. in Heil 33 n9). Over time, the seven cartons became a vast, nearly chaotic, accumulation of documents at Queen's, and the challenge of discerning order in that collection and the others has literary-historical consequences: even Purdy's most loyal readers do not know the extent of his writing.

Alex Widen was a friend of the poet's in the early 1990s, and for a time he served as an unofficial researcher on Purdy's behalf. Widen edited Purdy's *Reaching for the Beaufort Sea: An Autobiography* (1993) and collaborated with him on the publication of *Cougar Hunter: A Memoir of Roderick Haig-Brown* (1992); financial matters related to the latter book led to disagreement and brought the relationship to an unhappy close. Correspondence between Widen and Eurithe Purdy indicates that Widen found "Yehl the Raven" in the Queen's University Archives in 1990, and that Purdy had him send a revised version of the poetic sequence to Harbour Publishing the following year.[8] Widen also stumbled upon a version of "Yehl the Raven" at the University of British Columbia.[9] Although in 1990 Purdy drafted a new preface and made minor alterations to the poems, the manuscript was not published by Harbour – nor by any other press – and for more than twenty-five years it has lingered quietly and undisturbed amid his archived papers. Because Purdy revised the poems that Widen exhumed, "Yehl the Raven" now exists in several versions – two from the 1960s and a third from 1990–91.

The University of Saskatchewan holds a typescript sent by Purdy (from Ameliasburgh, Ontario) to Barbeau (in Ottawa), who returned it; that copy is, I believe, the oldest surviving version of "Yehl the Raven." It is composed of Purdy's preface, on which he wrote by hand a brief note to Barbeau, and eighteen typewritten pages of poetry. And it is accompanied by a perfunctory letter, dated 5 August 1963, from Barbeau to Purdy.[10] The manuscript at the University of British Columbia was revised by Purdy in 1966.[11] Various copies of "Yehl the Raven" are held at Queen's. One file contains a copy of the Saskatchewan manuscript and the letter from Barbeau.[12] Another file includes a copy of the Saskatchewan manuscript without the letter.[13] A third file includes a copy of Barbeau's letter, the revised preface of 1990, twenty-five pages of revised and retyped poems, and the same poems composed on a computer, as opposed to Purdy's typewriter.[14] Yet another file contains what I assume to be the original typewritten pages of the revised poems of 1990.[15] The confusing existence of numerous documents, originals as well as duplicates, is due to the many hands engaged in the manuscript's near-publication – first Purdy, and then Purdy and Widen, and then, after Al Purdy's death, Widen and Eurithe Purdy. Additional copies of Purdy's renderings of the "Creation Myths" may yet be located at Queen's or elsewhere.

The early version of "Yehl the Raven" – the Saskatchewan typescript and the copies thereof – bears the typewritten title "Yehl the Raven and Other Myths of the Haida": Purdy added the word "Creation" by hand before "Myths."[16] In addition to the brief preface in prose, there are thirteen poems: "Prologue," "Haida Genesis," "How Yehl Stole the Sun and Moon," "How Yehl Brought Water to the People," "How Yehl Gave the People Salmon," "Bear-Mother," "Strong-Man," "Nanasimgat," "Salmon-Eater," "The Woodworm of Masset," "Thunderbird," "Dzelarhons," and "Epilogue." The "Prologue" concerns the revelation of Yehl the Raven to Charles Edenshaw – called "Charley" in the poem – a Haida artist about whom Barbeau wrote. (Purdy and Barbeau used the spelling *Edensaw*.) The following eleven poems are, as the preface suggests, adaptations of myths that Purdy encountered in Barbeau's books, which he did not name. The poems are not in fact translations, as Solecki stated in a pardonable slip (*LCP* 43). The "Epilogue" depicts the sordid skid row of contemporary Vancouver and the grim reality of "the last carver"; the poem is comparable to Purdy's other works of the time, which often attend to urban extremity in a hard-boiled manner:

> In the streets of Vancouver
> there is a last Edensaw,
> the last carver become a garage mechanic,
> listening to the missing innards of a Chevrolet,
> grease on his fingers, grained in his marvellous old fingers –
> ...
> There is a time of ending for the last Edensaw[.][17]

Although there is more to the "Epilogue" than the stereotype of the vanishing Indian, the poem is likely to strike readers today as, if not an outright *bêtise*, an objectionable expression of the misconception that traditional cultures were on the verge of disappearance. But if Purdy imagined Haida culture to exist in a state of decline as a consequence of colonization, he also allowed, in his fashion, for the possibility of revival. The poem concludes by suggesting that "Yehl the Raven" was "waiting to be alive again –[.]"

The preface to "Yehl the Raven" provides some indication of Purdy's ambitions, his anthropological interests, and his method of adaptation:

> My intention in this book is to relate the Haida myths as simply and entertainingly as possible. Also by intention, I've left my own fingerprints on each of them. Such an obvious anomaly as "from the sea bottom ooze of human beginnings" in the Salmon Eater myth must be forgiven. For "human beginnings" stemmed from a clam shell in one of the creation myths of Yehl the Raven.
>
> All of these myths are taken from books by Marius Barbeau, published by the National Museum of Canada. And I think there are no other books that can in any way match those of Barbeau for the richness and detail of their information. Any farther [*sic*] study must inevitably send the reader back to this admirable source.
>
> Among my reasons for re-telling these myths at all is their own multiplicity. Some of them are given in a dozen versions, like bewildering palimpsests with slight variations of incident and language. To add to the general confusion the Haida myths are mostly borrowed from other tribes on the mainland, principally Tsimsyan. The Haida carvers appropriated these old stories and embodie[d] them in scrimshawed argillite, a slate-like stone found in a mountain quarry near Skidegate in the Queen Charlottes. Charley Edensaw was one of the best of these carvers in argillite. Barbeau regards him as a master, and what can I do but concur in that judgment. Edensaw was a chief among his people. He died at the age of 85 in 1924 –
>
> One more thing: the Prologue and Epilogue of this volume are entirely my own invention. And again, may I say to Marius Barbeau: thank you.

The remarkable nature of the manuscript is immediately apparent: the contents show that in the years before his first true literary successes and his concomitant celebrity, Purdy wrote a series of poems altogether different, both in topic and style, from his other works – poems, that is, written not in the bluff, personal-anecdotal mode for which he became notorious, but instead in an oratorical register. "Yehl the Raven" reveals him to have been a more attentive reader of ethnographic literature than has been acknowledged, and a more enthusiastic student of the mythology of the Northwest Coast, even if he struggled to transform his source material into consistently satisfying poetry.

Also immediately apparent in this preface is Purdy's obliviousness to his larger debt. Although he thanks Barbeau, he does not thank Indigenous storytellers or artists, either individually or in the collective. It is impossible to know whether this oversight is a reflection of the historical view that the stories were part of a shared heritage and therefore freely available for adaptation – and not intangible cultural heritage governed by specific protocols for dissemination – or whether it is merely Purdy's individual negligence. Either way, Purdy gives no indication that he saw any cultural or ethical barriers to his use of Barbeau's texts. He was demonstrably a curious reader, but he was a reader above all: the manuscript provides no evidence that he sought to dispense with Barbeau as an intermediary, and to engage directly living members of Indigenous communities. It is plainly true that, from a contemporary perspective, Purdy's method was unsatisfactory, and that his gratitude to Barbeau was, if not misdirected, then all too narrowly shared; it is also the case that Purdy, whether unwittingly or not, reflected the assumptions of his time in deferring to the expertise of the anthropologist.

Although his preface refers only generally to "books by Marius Barbeau, published by the National Museum of Canada," Purdy's discussion of argillite suggests that his primary source was Barbeau's *Haida Myths Illustrated in Argillite Carvings* (1953). The poems correspond closely to sections of that book, their similarities lexical as well as narrative and thematic. Barbeau's *Haida Carvers in Argillite* (1957) is also clearly relevant. Both volumes were published by the National Museum of Canada – "[v]ery Canadian stuff" indeed (Bowering 8). *Haida Myths* is at once a catalogue, commentary, and compendium of myths, both in the author's paraphrase and as related by ethnographic informants. Barbeau used photographs of Haida sculptures to illustrate myths narrated, in large measure, not on the Queen Charlotte Islands (as Haida Gwaii was then known) but on the mainland of British Columbia, by storytellers who were not themselves Haida.[18] He wrote that carving in argillite was a recently developed practice that originated in coastal trade, and proposed that art in argillite was intrinsically modern because of its "purely commercial nature": "Seen under this light, argillite carving can no longer be considered the legacy of the dim unrecorded past; and the carvers responsible for it, nameless Red Men of prehistory" (178). The vocabulary ("Red Men") will seem clumsy if not offensive to contemporary sensibilities, but Barbeau's point is clear: the works in question and their creators belong to the recent past. If he relied for his anthropological information on *Haida Myths*, then it is likely that Purdy recognized that ostensibly timeless myths are always expressed in historical time.

Purdy's poems often depart only slightly from Barbeau's texts. It is almost impossible to say whether he borrowed phrases deliberately or inadvertently, or whether he would have relinquished the loan words had he further revised the poems for publication in the 1960s; but there can be no doubt that the poetry in its unfinished state is highly derivative. (There are, however, enough alterations of Barbeau's texts to indicate that Purdy was not attempting simply to rearrange the found ethnographic text into lines of poetry, as John Robert Colombo made poetry from William Lyon Mackenzie's speeches in *The Mackenzie Poems* [1966].)[19] Here, for example, are the first lines of "How Yehl Stole the Sun and Moon":

> The Raven, in his wanderings among the islands,
> heard of an old fisherman living with his daughter
> on North Island – in a lodge on a rocky island.
> The old man kept two bright balls of light
>   called the sun and moon
> hidden away in a box beside his lodge by the sea:
> a greater light and a lesser light,
> of which one should rule the day
> and the other rule the night.
> These were marvellous tales to Yehl the Raven,
> who loved all brightness.

Barbeau included in *Haida Myths* a précis of the story of "how the Raven stole the Sun or the Moon and cast it into the sky where it has stayed as a luminary ever since" (167), which he deemed a "crucial episode of the beginning of the world" (169). Purdy's verse is highly similar to the prose of Barbeau's text, which was attributed to "'Captain' Andrew Brown of Massett" (167). Barbeau's version begins: "One day Raven learned that the old fisherman living alone with his daughter at North Island kept a ball of bright light, called the moon, hidden in his lodge by the sea. He craved its possession" (167). Purdy did not leave his source material unchanged, but neither is his adaptation especially original. If he was captivated by the myths, and if he sensed that the narratives could be told effectively in verse, it appears that he also failed to find his own idiom for their retelling. Purdy's own faults are likewise undeniable. The poems are repetitious and, although they strive for solemnity, they carry a whiff of Kipling's *Just So Stories*. They remained important to their author, however, perhaps because they represented a link to his memorable experiences in British Columbia.

Other anthropological works may have figured in Purdy's reading. *The Indian Speaks* (1943), by Barbeau and Grace Melvin, includes texts related culturally and geographically to Purdy's adaptations. Among them are "The Last Pagan," derived "[f]rom songs and records of the Nass River" (48); "Ananai!," adapted "[f]rom a story told in 1939, at Massett, Queen Charlotte Islands, by Peter Hill, a Haida" (53); and "The Owl," derived "[f]rom a Gitksan song, recorded in 1920, on the upper Skeena River" (57).[20] Still other texts in *The Indian Speaks* are directly connected to Purdy's poems: "Thunderbird," derived "[f]rom rituals and songs of the Nass and Skeena River Indians" (56); "Yehl," as "[t]old, in 1939, by Ot'iwans, Big-Eagle – whose surname [sic] is Captain Andrew Brown – of the Haida tribe of Massett" (114); and "Raven Steals the Moon," derived "[f]rom a narrative recorded in 1939; narrator: Captain Andrew Brown, a Haida of the Queen Charlotte Islands" (117).[21] In the rendition of Barbeau and Melvin, "Yehl" begins in a mode that evokes the Book of Genesis: "Yehl – Raven, in the beginning, was like a god; he called things forth out of nothing, and many, many of them came to be" (113). Purdy may have drawn on this story in writing his "Haida Genesis," in which the Biblical parallel is explicit, or he may simply have shared with Barbeau and Melvin the opinion that the stories of Raven deserved, or even demanded, an exalted tone. (The poem's Biblical title and motif may also stem from *Haida Myths*; Barbeau used the phrase "Haida Genesis" repeatedly [see, for example, 158, 167].) Other close correspondences occur. Barbeau and Melvin wrote in "Yehl" that "[a] tiny human face appeared in the center of the shell" (113), and Purdy wrote comparably in "Haida Genesis" that "a small human face appeared in the opening shell." The shared subject excuses a general sameness, but distinctly similar phrasings, in this poem as elsewhere, intimate that Purdy read Barbeau's books not wisely but too well.

In general, the poems in the "Yehl the Raven" manuscript betray Purdy's debts. In "How Yehl Brought Water to the People" and "How Yehl Gave the People Salmon," as well as in "Haida Genesis," he used the formulaic phrase that plainly suggests the Old Testament: "In the beginning…" Other hints of Genesis are found throughout the sequence, and the "Epilogue" echoes Ecclesiastes 3:1-8:

> There is a time of ending for the last Edensaw,
> a time for not carving any more at all,
> a time for not taking in marriage,
> a time for not conceiving and not being born,
> and not even living any longer,
> a time for nothing.

Some of Purdy's possible borrowings are less obvious. The term "nightstars" (in "How Yehl Gave the People Salmon") resembles other compounds in the "Yehl the Raven" sequence, but the poeticism may originate in the literary past – in Shelley, for example: "Till the night-stars shone through the cloudless air" (112).[22] – or it could simply be a case of pleonasm for effect, an attempt to grant the poem a sophisticated tone. Either way, the poetry suggests that Purdy was straining to find the appropriate style. Does the phrase "stones in a stopped throat" (in "Strong-Man") allude to Parmenides? Was "sea roads" (in "Nanasimgat") intended to summon up *whale-road*, the famous Anglo-Saxon kenning? Purdy probably did not recall lines from Robert Lowell's "The Quaker Graveyard in Nantucket" – "This is the end of the whaleroad and the whale / Who spewed Nantucket bones on the thrashed swell" (11) – but, given his admitted fondness for G.K. Chesterton's poetry, conceivably he knew "sea-roads" from "Lepanto" (17).[23] Earle Birney's "Mappemounde," which would seem a likely source because of Purdy's well-established appreciation of his poetry, does not contain the word, although it includes "whalehall" (*Strait* 4).[24] Birney's "Beyond the Meadhall" does use "whaleroad" (see Solecki, *LCP* 3), but the poem was written long after "Yehl the Raven."[25] Identifying allusions is often a speculative practice, one subject to the limitations of the individual critic's eye and ear. A thorough study or a critical edition will, in due course, explicate such resemblances, whether Biblical or secular, and trace any possible similarities to Purdy's mature poetry. The repetition in these lines from "Shoeshine Boys on the Avenida Juarez," from *Wild Grape Wine*, is not altogether unlike the typical style of the poetry in "Yehl the Raven":

> And all down the Avenida Juarez
> the grins have faded out completely,
> and probably only I shall remember
> (and the CIA man twenty steps behind me)
> being crazy as hell one morning,
> and writing a poem about it,
> and writing about writing a poem about it,
> and making it into the echo of a poem,

> the echo of a grin on the Avenida Juarez,
> the echo of being alive once,
> the echo of dying on the Avenida Juarez. (WG 26; BR 142)

At the time of the composition of "Yehl the Raven," Barbeau was a venerable figure, and Purdy must have believed that he was drawing on the authoritative scholarship of an eminence. Readers today may be less accepting of Barbeau's works, not least because of what they partly conceal. Although *Haida Myths Illustrated in Argillite Carvings* and related volumes were published under Barbeau's name, they were not the result of his labours alone. "William Beynon, the author's Tsimsyan assistant in the field since 1915," Barbeau wrote in his acknowledgments in *Haida Myths*, "has either interpreted or recorded most of the narratives, unless they were from printed sources as quoted" (viii).[26] Ralph Maud observed of *Haida Myths* that "Barbeau has seven stories to Beynon's twenty-three" (129): Beynon (1888–1958) was a major contributor to the ethnography of the Northwest Coast, but his collaboration with Barbeau was consigned to the background in *Haida Myths* and other studies, even when his importance was granted. Recent commentators have tended not to view him as a subordinate figure but instead, as Charles R. Menzies writes, as "the unsung hero of Tsimshianic research" (24).[27]

An additional problem is ideological. Barbeau thought that Northwestern traditions formed part of a global store of ancient stories. That presumption suggests, at present, not a benign ecumenism but instead the dire history of anthropological salvage:

> Although the myths or tales all belong to the Haida, they are not their monopoly. They form only a minor branch on a huge mythological tree which belongs to most of humanity. This cultural growth at first germinated and developed in the Old World – Asia and Europe; then, during the last millenia [*sic*], it spread by oral transmission in migratory tribes to the New World at large, and then to the Haida on the Queen Charlotte Islands in the North Pacific. (vii)[28]

Barbeau's reductive language and universalizing perspective are obviously inadequate; no myths are only "a minor branch" from the perspective of the culture to which they belong. More to the point, the view that the "tree" "belongs to most of humanity" serves to justify projects of cultural appropriation such as Purdy's. "Yehl the Raven" is unquestionably a work of the 1960s, the poetry like all literature indisputably of its time. Purdy's licence to adapt the myths was assumed, although he did not claim to have anthropological expertise, and the question of consent from the community did not arise. Yet Purdy's writing, whatever its faults, implies that he understood well enough that Indigenous peoples had not disappeared from British Columbia or from Canada at large, and that he was forever a foreigner in the Haida and Tsimshian worlds, even if the mythology seemed to offer an enticing solution to a Canadian cultural "problem" that Birney identified in "Pacific Door": "that there is no clear Strait of Anian / to lead us easy back to Europe" (*Strait* 37). The manuscript in its miscellaneous forms may not accord with contemporary tastes and values, but "Yehl the Raven" evinces an interest and admiration that, if nothing else, show Purdy to have been attracted to the possibility of cross-cultural understanding.

For a time, Purdy was regularly described as having some acquaintance with Indigenous peoples. Bowering suggested, for instance, that Purdy's sympathy for "the Tsimsyan Indians" was tied to his characteristic resistance to authority: "He is deeply and habitually allied with the underdogs in a country and a world that allow bosses to ignore or suppress the underdogs. So Purdy is seen with the mattress workers, with the Tsimsyan Indians of the British Columbia interior, with the Sons of Freedom on their freedom march to Agassiz prison, with the Eskimo hunters of Baffin Island" (7). A similar characterization was advanced in the cover copy of *The Cariboo Horses*, which likewise referred to "the Tsimsyan Indians": "Alfred Purdy has travelled widely in Canada and has published in many Canadian literary magazines. Born in Wooler, Ontario, he spent six years with the RCAF, owned a taxi business in Belleville, tried introducing a union into a Vancouver mattress factory, and lived with the Tsimsyan Indians in the interior of British Columbia." Such portraits of the author take his experiences in northern British Columbia as one manifestation among many of his arch-Canadian identity, and as an illustration of his curious background, but the "Yehl the Raven" manuscript indicates, I believe, that Purdy had more than a passing interest in the myths in question. The textual evidence shows that he cared enough about them to write and revise a manuscript that he attempted at some length to publish. The taxi business and "the Tsimsyan Indians," in short, were not perfectly equivalent elements in Purdy's imagination.

Purdy's published poetry at times depicts encounters with living Indigenous people, and is not wholly in keeping with the view, which lingered in the 1950s, that Indigenous peoples existed in a post-lapsarian state of cultural contamination. Homer G. Barnett's description of the "Status of the Old Culture" in *The Coast Salish of British Columbia* (1955), for example, emphasizes loss rather than continuity, adaptation, and resilience, and fails to mention the obvious causes of whatever cultural changes may be observed:

At present the old culture is practically dead. There has been very little displacement of the Indian population, and reserves for the most part comprise the traditional village locations; but the material basis, the technology, and the spirit of the aboriginal economy are gone ... Dugout canoes are still made, but "gas boats" and row boats have taken the field. Houses are built in the modern manner. The ancient handicrafts are modified or have ceased altogether to be practiced. (2)

Poems such as "Hazelton, B.C.," "The Cariboo Horses," and even "Kispiox Indian Village" show that Purdy was capable of quasi-realistic portrayals of contemporary Indigenous lives; although he emphasized poverty and dereliction, and at times used essentially racist language, he did not simply elide Indigenous people from his vision of British Columbia. I raise this point not to defend Purdy or his poetry, but simply to observe that although his reliance on Barbeau's writing, and his reading of other anthropological works, led him to a narrow perspective on cultural change, in his travels he sought a touch of the real. "Yehl the Raven," in contrast, subscribes to the notion that genuine Indigenous cultures had vanished.

As I noted, Purdy revised his preface to "Yehl the Raven" in 1990. The poems themselves remained essentially the same as in the 1960s, but the new beginning emphasized his regard for his sources: "I hope the spirit of my intentions shows my respect for the Haida, as they respected the bear spirit and the salmon spirit among the vast tribe of living creatures on the earth."[29] Ultimately, however, "Yehl the Raven" was left incomplete and unpublished, and how the poems would have been received had they been issued, and what new creative endeavours might have succeeded them, can only be imagined. Purdy's career ran in other directions instead, yet he portrayed Barbeau in a late collection, *To Paris Never Again* (1997). "Marius Barbeau: 1883–1969" begins with a recollection that foregrounds the ethnographer's eccentricity:

In 1968
a little old man dancing
at home near downtown Ottawa
demonstrating western Indian dances
out of courtesy to a visitor – :

wearing a feathered headdress
and beaded buckskin jacket
ducking his head and beating a drum
chanting *HI-yah HI-yah HI-yah*

> the sound part animal part human
> circling the dark dinner table
> and old-fashioned sideboard
> his feet tremulous
> age too much for him[.] (TP 31; BR 533)

The performance was unorthodox – today it appears scandalously improper – and the speaker (a version of Purdy) remembers being "slightly embarrassed for him" (TP 31; BR 534). But in the poem's lyric present, the speaker admits to feeling "embarrassed that I was embarrassed," for he realizes that Barbeau was profoundly moved, and even entranced, by the people and landscapes of Tsimshian and Gitxsan country – as was the speaker himself: "faintly in my own lifetime / [I] have glimpsed the shining mountains" (TP 31; BR 534).[30] And here any distinction between poet and persona threatens to vanish. Purdy spent part of the Second World War stationed in northern British Columbia, and he returned as a tourist; his experiences of the region, on the evidence of his writing, stayed with him throughout his life (see RBS 98–9). If "Yehl the Raven" led away from what became his typical mode and his perennial subject, the manuscript and its ethnographic impulse were also entwined with that very theme – himself.

Purdy's attempt at what elsewhere came to be called "ethnopoetics" saw his sympathetic interest in Indigenous texts greatly exceed his cultural knowledge and, at least in the early 1960s, his poetic technique – not technique *tout court*, but the ability to find an appropriate style and register with which to render Indigenous narratives. Except in a general sense, this assessment is not a criticism of Purdy himself; it is unlikely that any Canadian poet at the time would have been successful according to contemporary aesthetic standards or protocols for embarking on an ethical project of adaptation. Had Purdy known about the roughly contemporary efforts of (American) figures such as Jerome Rothenberg, Dennis Tedlock, and Dell Hymes – *Alcheringa*, a notable journal of ethnopoetics, first appeared in 1970 – perhaps his engagement with Barbeau's texts might have been fruitful, but that is cause for speculation. Purdy's abandoned manuscripts enrich our understanding of his imaginative range and his fascination with other cultures, and in particular they suggest that, even if it lacks nuance in certain contexts, his conception of Canada was broader than is allowed by the stereotype of the bard of Ameliasburgh. As a suite of poems, however, "Yehl the Raven" is at best a limited success.

The poems in the forgotten manuscript also point outward, however, linking Purdy to other writers who have similarly drawn upon the ethnographic record. These connections suggest the remarkable degree to which modern and contemporary Canadian authors have, with varying degrees of rigour and expertise, sought to engage Indigenous cultures, often as a means of establishing a purportedly authentic Canadian tradition running continuously from the pre-colonial past to the present.[31] Purdy's "Haida poems" are not unlike those in *Songs of the Western Islands* (1945) and *The Arrow-maker's Daughter and Other Haida Chants* (1957), both by Hermia Harris Fraser and published by the estimable Ryerson Press of Toronto. Although Harris's poems are "bogus," in at least one expert's estimation (Bringhurst, "Reading" 30, 228 n9), they were discussed approvingly until relatively recently. A.J.M. Smith wrote in 1968, for instance, that "Only very late – after the work of anthropologists like [Edward] Sapir, Barbeau, and Alfred Bailey – has it become possible to make genuine poetry out of the native mythology of Canada, as for example in the translations of Haida poems by Hermia Harris Fraser or a few of the poems of Alfred Bailey, or to deal dramatically and sympathetically with the Indian, as in John Newlove's moving poem 'The Pride'" (8). Smith's term of praise, "genuine," now rings false, and his very premise, that non-Indigenous writers were free to draw upon "native mythology," is dubious in the extreme; yet this was the cultural climate, damningly full of good intentions, in which Purdy the would-be ethnopoet wrote.

Purdy's verse renditions may also be compared, less uncharitably, to more sophisticated adaptations, such as those of the American poet David Wagoner in *Who Shall Be the Sun? Poems Based on the Lore, Legends, and Myths of Northwest Coast and Plateau Indians* (1978), or to Robert Bringhurst's translations of Haida myths, the book-length introduction to which is *A Story as Sharp as a Knife: The Classical Haida Mythtellers and Their World* (1999, 2011). It is important, however, not to repeat the error of describing Purdy's poems as translations (as in Solecki, LCP 43), and although Bringhurst's editing and translation of, and commentary on, Haida texts have attracted strong criticism, his linguistic and scholarly competence set him apart from Purdy, a complete amateur.[32]

Gwendolyn MacEwen's *Noman* (1972), a collection of stories, draws on anthropological material similar to that on which Purdy relied; her sources are possibly the same as his, in fact. In "House of the Whale," the narrator, Lucas George, a young Haida man, describes argillite carving: "When I was young some of our people still carved argillite to earn extra money. It was a dying art even then, but the little slate figures always brought something on the commercial market. The Slatechuk [*sic*] quarry up Slatechuk creek wasn't far from Skidegate; and there was an almost inexhaustible supply of the beautiful black stone, which got shaped into the countless figures of our myths" (7). Lucas George's reference to "myth-hunters" – "museum researchers and writers from the mainland" (8) – may be an oblique reference to Barbeau; if not, it nonetheless hints at the frenzy of anthropological activity on the Northwest Coast in the early and mid-century.[33]

The most unlikely and most intriguing connection, perhaps, is between Purdy and the contemporary Nisga'a author Jordan Abel, whose age – he was born in 1985 – and poetic methods would otherwise suggest little relation to Purdy. The two poets' respective adaptations of Barbeau's writing, however, place them in an unlikely intertextual conversation. Abel has quickly emerged as a leading poet in Canada (which is not necessarily to say "in Canadian poetry"): his first book, *The Place of Scraps* (2013), won the Dorothy Livesay Poetry Prize, for the best book of poetry by a writer from British Columbia, and his third book, *Injun* (2016), won the Griffin Poetry Prize, the most lucrative and arguably the most prestigious such award in Canada. Abel uses techniques including erasure and digital manipulation to modify his source texts in order to reveal their ideological suppositions and latent ironies; he is not a creative writer in the usual sense, but rather an "uncreative writer" (see Goldsmith).[34] His poetry, more visually oriented than aurally, and resistant to quotation or paraphrase, bears little obvious relation to Purdy's typical approximations of ordinary speech. In *The Place of Scraps*, Abel adapts, or pillages, Barbeau's *Totem Poles* (1950), salvaging poetry from a work of anthropological salvage that is both the substance of Abel's poetry and its target of attack.[35] As Sophie McCall writes, Abel "transforms Barbeau's writings into visual poetry that invokes landscapes, maps, and shorelines, and that carves the source texts into scattered words, letters, blank spaces, and brackets ... Layering and remixing Barbeau's words, recordings, images of poles, and tattered archival documents through a variety of formats and media, Abel reverses the political implications of 'salvage' anthropology in an act of repatriation" (502).[36]

If Purdy and Abel are rendered unlikely fellow-travellers by their incongruous engagements with Barbeau's works, what McCall terms the "political implications" (502) of *The Place of Scraps* throw into relief the unpalatable aspects of "Yehl the Raven," the political implications of which do not flatter Purdy. His attempt to create poetry from anthropological writing must be considered a failure by contemporary measures: working from source texts of questionable accuracy and which represent synecdochically the broader salvage-anthropological intervention, Purdy perpetuated the assumptions of that enterprise, wrote without credible knowledge of the cultures from which the texts emerged, presumed that he had authority to adapt the texts, and certainly did not embark on a process of collaboration with Indigenous experts, as might be done today. Yet Purdy and Abel are conjoined by their interest in Barbeau. I do not mean to force a comparison between fundamentally dissimilar poets, but their juxtaposition bespeaks an essential tension in Canadian literature: namely the perennial and heated question of the place of Indigenous cultures, if any, within a specifically Canadian tradition. Or, to put the matter differently but more pointedly, the question of who can claim, and on what grounds, to speak of, or to make art from, the cultures that Canada strove to suppress, and ultimately to eradicate.

NOTES

1 Milestones, but not necessarily monuments. Purdy revised and recycled his poems routinely, and not every book was wholly original.
2 Books, broadsides, and other rarities by Purdy were published by small presses throughout his career. He travelled in the moonless, ephemeral world inhabited by most poets, but the works for which he is best known circulated in the mainstream of Canadian letters; his poetry was uncommonly visible.
3 "The Horseman of Agawa" was published in the *Globe Magazine* (25 July 1970), and "A Handful of Earth" in the *Globe and Mail* (26 November 1977). For a partial list of his magazine articles, see SA 391.
4 Purdy's "Arctic Rhododendrons" (a poem collected in *North of Summer*) and "Whoever You Are" (a poem collected in the 1968 edition of *Poems for All the Annettes*) were purchased by The Bay as part of a literary patronage scheme. See Ross and York 37, 46–7, 50–1.
5 The letter's date is 5 July 1990.
6 The date of Purdy's letter to Woodcock is 9 April 1991. The letter is therefore not included in *The Purdy-Woodcock Letters* (1988).
7 Purdy's papers are not held exclusively by Queen's, but the principles of archival collection and organization that Jeremy Heil examines are broadly relevant.
8 Alex Widen, letter to Eurithe Purdy, 12 September 2011. Al Purdy Fonds, Queen's University Archives: Location 2210.4, Box 1, Folder 8.
9 Alex Widen, letter to Al Purdy and Eurithe Purdy, n.d. [1990]. Al Purdy Fonds, Queen's University Archives: Location 5002.5, Box 2, Folder 6.
10 Al Purdy, "Yehl the Raven and Other [Creation] Myths of the Haida." Al Purdy Papers, University Archives and Special Collections, University of Saskatchewan: MSS 4, Box 5, Folder 15.
11 Alfred Purdy Fonds, University of British Columbia Rare Books and Special Collections: RBSC-ARC-1452, File 1.
12 Al Purdy Fonds, Queen's University Archives: Location 2210.4, Box 1, Folder 8.

13 Ibid.: Location 2071, Box 11, Folder 3 [marked 89].
14 Ibid.: Location 5002.5, Box 2, Folder 25.
15 Ibid.: Location 5147, Box 10, Folder 4. Copies of the documents herein are found in another file (Location 5002.5, Box 2, Folder 25).
16 Purdy, "Yehl the Raven," University of Saskatchewan: MSS 4, Box 5, Folder 15. Subsequent quotations of "Yehl the Raven" are drawn from this manuscript.
17 "Urban extremity": "The Machines" and "Towns" are illustrative. Both poems were gathered in *The Blur in Between: Poems, 1960–61* (1962). "Hard-boiled": from "For Curt Lang": "your hard-boiled friend Purdy" (BR 586). See also LB 10, Atwood 98.
18 The name "Yehl" appears outside the Haida context as well. See Cruikshank: "Tlingit reportedly interpreted these first European ships to arrive at Lituya Bay as the return of White Raven, Yéil, the world-maker who had promised to be reborn" (135).
19 I am grateful to an anonymous reviewer for this suggestion.
20 The italicized phrases appear here as they do in the original.
21 "Raven Steals the Moon": the passage from this story in *Haida Myths*, which I quoted earlier, is found in *The Indian Speaks* in a slightly different form (Barbeau and Melvin 115).
22 The line from Shelley occurs in a poem ("Ballad") from *St. Irvyne; or, The Rosicrucian: A Romance*.
23 Purdy was a great admirer of Chesterton's writing – an unfashionable influence, but important regardless (see RBS 135, 215, 285–6, and Solecki, LCP 57, 224, 232, 275 n16).
24 "Appreciation": see Birney and Purdy. Purdy's friendship with Birney spanned decades.
25 In *Last Makings* the poem is dated 1985. See Toswell, 12–14, 30.
26 Compare Menzies: Beynon was "an ethnographer who was both a member and an observer of Coast Tsimshian society" (22).
27 Margery Fee writes, for example, that although Beynon and George Hunt were "[r]ecruited as interpreters, both are now regarded as anthropologists in their own right" (17). Beynon's distinctive significance as an ethnographer is made apparent in *Potlatch at Gitsegukla: William Beynon's 1945 Field Notebooks*, edited by Margaret Anderson and Marjorie Halpin.
28 "Anthropological salvage": see Wakeham. On the ethical and editorial difficulties posed by Barbeau's texts, see Fortin. How a contemporary edition of "Yehl the Raven" might be undertaken appropriately, or whether one should exist at all, remains to be explored.
29 Purdy dated the revised preface: 28 July 1990 (Al Purdy, "Yehl the Raven and Other Creation Myths of the Haida [1990]," Al Purdy Fonds, Queen's University Archives: Location 5002.5, Box 2, Folder 6). The year before Purdy made his alterations, Mordecai Richler published the satirical novel *Solomon

Gursky Was Here, in which he drew on Haida mythology: "'According to the Haidas, of the unfortunately named Queen Charlotte Islands, more properly Haida Gwai [*sic*], the Islands of the People,' Sir Hyman once said to Moses, 'according to them, before there was anything, before the great flood had covered the earth and receded, before the animals walked the earth or the trees covered the land or the birds flew between the trees, there was the raven'" (Richler [2005] 479). In his Author's Note, Richler wrote that he was "indebted to *The Raven Steals the Light* [1984], by Bill Reid and Robert Bringhurst, for the Haida myths" (540). The note appeared in the paperback edition of 1990, but not in the first edition of the novel (Richler [1989] 559). Whether Purdy and Alex Widen perceived the coincidence, or any unintended connection between "Yehl the Raven" and Richler's novel, their correspondence does not disclose. On the Haida stories in *Solomon Gursky Was Here*, see Morra 83–6.

30 Purdy's readers will recognize this poetic self-reproach. The move from embarrassment to understanding in "Marius Barbeau: 1883–1969" is a variation on the self-criticism of "Trees at the Arctic Circle," from *North of Summer*: "I have been stupid in a poem / I will not alter the poem / but let the stupidity remain permanent" (NS 30; BR 104).

31 See Lecker 17–18 on Ralph Gustafson's use of "Haida songs," translated by Constance Lindsay Skinner (Bringhurst, "Reading" 228 n9), in his *Anthology of Canadian Poetry* (1942): "Gustafson was presenting indigenous work in translation, a gesture that replicated the colonization of the very people whose language set them apart from the tradition that was now annexing them" (17).

32 See also *The Raven Steals the Light* (1984), by Bill Reid and Robert Bringhurst. For an overview of Bringhurst's extended project of translation from the Haida, see Bradley, and for a succinct autobiographical account of his encounter with Haida literature, see Bringhurst, "Air," especially 219–24.

33 Compare the title of Nansi Swayze's *The Man Hunters: Jenness, Barbeau, Wintemberg* (1960).

34 As Sarah Dowling writes, "Abel is the author of three books relying heavily, if not completely, on practices of appropriation and re-presentation [*sic*] closely aligned with what Marjorie Perloff describes as the poetics of unoriginality" (199 n23).

35 For a sustained analysis of *The Place of Scraps*, see Karpinski.

36 In this regard, according to McCall, Abel is part of a wider endeavour: "contemporary Indigenous artists and writers like Nisga'a poet Jordan Abel in *The Place of Scraps*, Métis Dene playwright Marie Clements in *The Edward Curtis Project*, Cree scholar and poet Neal McLeod in *Cree Narrative Memory*, and Garry Thomas Morse in *Discovery Passages* (a book of poems that explores his mother's Kwakwaka'wakw ancestry), are revisiting their own

families' encounters with anthropologists and collectors of stories, images, and material culture" (501). For Morse, Franz Boas fulfills a role analogous to that played by Barbeau for Abel; Boas is depicted dancing (104ff–13) as the dancing Barbeau appears in Purdy's "Marius Barbeau: 1883–1969."

ARCHIVAL SOURCES

Alfred Purdy Fonds, University of British Columbia Rare Books and Special Collections.
> RBSC-ARC-1452, File 1.

Al Purdy Fonds, Queen's University Archives.
> Al Purdy, "Yehl the Raven and Other Creation Myths of the Haida," QUA Location 2071, Box 11, Folder 3 [marked 89].
> – "Yehl the Raven and Other Creation Myths of the Haida," QUA Location 2210.4, Box 1, Folder 8.
> – "Yehl the Raven and Other Creation Myths of the Haida," QUA Location 5002.5, Box 2, Folder 25.
> – "Yehl the Raven and Other Creation Myths of the Haida," QUA Location 5147, Box 10, Folder 4.
> – "Yehl the Raven and Other Creation Myths of the Haida [1990]," QUA Location 5002.5, Box 2, Folder 6.
> Alex Widen, letter to Al Purdy and Eurithe Purdy, n.d. [1990], QUA Location 5002.5, Box 2, Folder 6.
> Alex Widen, letter to Eurithe Purdy, 12 September 2011, QUA Location 2210.4, Box 1, Folder 8.

Al Purdy Papers, University Archives and Special Collections, University of Saskatchewan.
> Al Purdy, "Yehl the Raven and Other [Creation] Myths of the Haida," MSS 4, Box 5, Folder 15.

REFERENCES

Abel, Jordan. *The Place of Scraps*. Vancouver: Talonbooks, 2013.
Atwood, Margaret. *Second Words: Selected Critical Prose*. Toronto: House of Anansi Press, 1982.
Barbeau, Marius. *Haida Myths Illustrated in Argillite Carvings*. Ottawa: National Museum of Canada, 1953.
Barbeau, Marius, and Grace Melvin. *The Indian Speaks*. Toronto: Macmillan, 1943.
Barnett, Homer G. *The Coast Salish of British Columbia*. Eugene: University of Oregon, 1955.
Beynon, William. *Potlatch at Gitsegukla: William Beynon's 1945 Field Notebooks*. Edited by Margaret Anderson and Marjorie Halpin. Vancouver: University of British Columbia Press, 2000.

Birney, Earle. *Last Makings*. Toronto: McClelland & Stewart, 1991.
– *The Strait of Anian: Selected Poems*. Toronto: Ryerson Press, 1948.
Birney, Earle, and Al Purdy. *We Go Far Back in Time: The Letters of Earle Birney and Al Purdy, 1947–1987*. Edited by Nicholas Bradley. Madeira Park, BC: Harbour Publishing, 2014.
Bowering, George. *Al Purdy*. Toronto: Copp Clark, 1970.
Bradley, Nicholas. "At Land's End: *Masterworks of the Classical Haida Mythtellers*." In *Listening for the Heartbeat of Being: The Arts of Robert Bringhurst*, edited by Brent Wood and Mark Dickinson, 194–223. Montreal and Kingston: McGill-Queen's University Press, 2015.
Bringhurst, Robert. "Air, Water, Land, Light, and Language: Reflections on the Commons and Its Contents." In *Editing as Cultural Practice in Canada*, edited by Dean Irvine and Smaro Kamboureli, 211–24. Waterloo, ON: Wilfrid Laurier University Press, 2016.
– "Reading between the Books: Northrop Frye and the Cartography of Literature." In *Educating the Imagination: Northrop Frye, Past, Present, and Future*, edited by Alan Bewell, Neil ten Kortenaar, and Germaine Warkentin, 16–35. Montreal and Kingston: McGill-Queen's University Press, 2015.
– *A Story as Sharp as a Knife: The Classical Haida Mythtellers and Their World*. Vancouver: Douglas and McIntyre, 1999. 2nd ed. 2011.
Cruikshank, Julie. *Do Glaciers Listen? Local Knowledge, Colonial Encounters, and Social Imagination*. Vancouver: University of British Columbia Press, 2005.
Dowling, Sarah. *Translingual Poetics: Writing Personhood under Settler Colonialism*. Iowa City: University of Iowa Press, 2018.
Fee, Margery. "Rewriting Anthropology and Identifications on the North Pacific Coast: The Work of George Hunt, William Beynon, Franz Boas, and Marius Barbeau." *Australian Literary Studies* 25, no. 4 (2010): 17–32.
Fortin, Marc André. "'Ought We to Teach These?': Ethical, Responsible, and Aboriginal Cultural Protocols in the Classroom." In *Learn, Teach, Challenge: Approaching Indigenous Literatures*, edited by Deanna Reder and Linda M. Morra, 459–65. Waterloo, ON: Wilfrid Laurier University Press, 2016.
Goldsmith, Kenneth. *Uncreative Writing: Managing Language in the Digital Age*. New York: Columbia University Press, 2011.
Heil, Jeremy M. "The Procrustean Bed: A History of the Arrangement of the Al Purdy Fonds." *Archivaria*, no. 76 (Fall 2013): 27–54.
Karpinski, Max. "'Split with the Kind Knife': Salvage Ethnography and Poetics of Appropriation in Jordan Abel's *The Place of Scraps*." *Canadian Literature*, no. 230–1 (Autumn–Winter 2016): 65–84.
Lecker, Robert. Introduction to *Anthologizing Canadian Literature: Theoretical and Cultural Perspectives*, edited by Robert Lecker, 1–33. Waterloo, ON: Wilfrid Laurier University Press, 2015.
Lowell, Robert. *Lord Weary's Castle*. New York: Harcourt, Brace, 1946.

MacEwen, Gwendolyn. *Noman*. Ottawa: Oberon, 1972.
Maud, Ralph. *A Guide to B.C. Indian Myth and Legend: A Short History of Myth-Collecting and a Survey of Published Texts*. Vancouver: Talonbooks, 1982.
McCall, Sophie. "Positioning Knowledges, Building Relationships, Practising Self-Reflection, Collaborating across Differences." In *Learn, Teach, Challenge: Approaching Indigenous Literatures*, edited by Deanna Reder and Linda M. Morra, 499–502. Waterloo, ON: Wilfrid Laurier University Press, 2016.
Menzies, Charles R. *People of the Saltwater: An Ethnography of Git lax m'oon*. Lincoln: University of Nebraska Press, 2016.
Morra, Linda. "The Anti-Trickster in the Work of Sheila Watson, Mordecai Richler, and Gail Anderson-Dargatz." In *Troubling Tricksters: Revisioning Critical Conversations*, edited by Deanna Reder and Linda M. Morra, 77–91. Waterloo, ON: Wilfrid Laurier University Press, 2010.
Morse, Garry Thomas. *Discovery Passages*. Vancouver: Talonbooks, 2011.
Purdy, Al. *Beyond Remembering: The Collected Poems of Al Purdy*. Edited by Al Purdy and Sam Solecki. Madeira Park, BC: Harbour Publishing, 2000.
– *The Cariboo Horses*. Toronto: McClelland & Stewart, 1965.
– *North of Summer: Poems from Baffin Island*. Toronto: McClelland & Stewart, 1967.
– *Reaching for the Beaufort Sea: An Autobiography*. Edited by Alex Widen. Madeira Park, BC: Harbour Publishing, 1993.
– *Starting from Ameliasburgh: The Collected Prose of Al Purdy*. Edited by Sam Solecki. Madeira Park, BC: Harbour Publishing, 1995.
– *To Paris Never Again*. Madeira Park, BC: Harbour Publishing, 1997.
– *Yours, Al: The Collected Letters of Al Purdy*. Edited by Sam Solecki. Madeira Park, BC: Harbour Publishing, 2004.
Reid, Bill, and Robert Bringhurst. *The Raven Steals the Light*. Vancouver: Douglas and McIntyre, 1984.
Richler, Mordecai. *Solomon Gursky Was Here*. Markham, ON: Viking, 1989.
– *Solomon Gursky Was Here*. Toronto: Penguin, 2005.
Ross, Michael, and Lorraine York. "Imperial Commerce and the Canadian Muse: The Hudson's Bay Company's Poetic Advertising Campaign of 1966–1972." *Canadian Literature*, no. 220 (Spring 2014): 37–53.
Shelley, Percy Bysshe. *The Complete Poetry of Percy Bysshe Shelley*. Vol. 1. Edited by Donald H. Reiman and Neil Fraistat. Baltimore: Johns Hopkins University Press, 2000.
Smith, A.J.M. "The Canadian Poet: Part I: To Confederation." *Canadian Literature*, no. 37 (Summer 1968): 6–14.
Solecki, Sam. *The Last Canadian Poet: An Essay on Al Purdy*. Toronto: University of Toronto Press, 1999.

Toswell, M.J. "Earle Birney as Anglo-Saxon Scop: A Canadian 'Shaper' of Poetry?" *Canadian Poetry: Studies, Documents, Reviews*, no. 54 (Spring–Summer 2004): 12–36.

Wagoner, David. *Who Shall Be the Sun? Poems Based on the Lore, Legends, and Myths of Northwest Coast and Plateau Indians*. Bloomington: Indiana University Press, 1978.

Wakeham, Pauline. "Salvaging Sound at Last Sight: Marius Barbeau and the Anthropological 'Rescue' of *Nass River Indians*." *English Studies in Canada* 30, no. 3 (September 2004): 57–88.

PART THREE

Myths, Masks, and Texts: Al Purdy's Entangled Lives and Works

8

Scholarly Editing:
A Way to Read "House Guest"

Eli MacLaren

Besides a biography of Purdy, we need scholarly editions of his work. Many of his poems change substantially from one printing to another. The latest editions of his work, including *Beyond Remembering: The Collected Poems of Al Purdy* (2000), co-edited by Purdy and Sam Solecki, tend to obscure this fact, presenting new "final" versions of the poems rather than exposing their revision over time, with a rare exception or two. The purpose of the following essay is to argue the benefits of beginning to read Purdy through the lens of textual scholarship.

Editing Purdy to bibliographical standards is a daunting task because of his propensity to revise, which, given the poet's signature irreverence, might even be deemed a deliberate flouting of the code of book publishing. If publication tries to fix texts so that the world can discuss them exactly, it is quickly apparent that Purdy's published texts defy this rule, changing to a greater or lesser extent according to the decisions of a given editorial moment. One need only open the three editions of *Poems for All the Annettes* (1962, 1968, 1973) side by side to discover blatant inconsistencies, beginning with the table of contents. Over a decade ago, Dean Irvine surveyed the editing of Purdy, both the record to date and the challenges to come. He observes that early on Purdy developed a "revisionist practice that would become standard for his subsequent selected and collected editions" (73). This revisionist practice was in play when Purdy co-edited *The Collected Poems of Al Purdy* (1986) with Russell Brown and *Beyond Remembering* with Solecki. Since fewer than half of the poems that Purdy had published appeared in those books (262 and 321, respectively, of approximately 700 total), Irvine argues that they represent the poet's oeuvre more as he wished to see it at those late moments in his career than as it had, in fact, accumulated over time: "With just three poems from his first three volumes included in the first collected, and none whatsoever in the second, Purdy and his editors effectively effaced the beginnings of his career" (77). Russell Brown persuaded the poet to include more poems than originally planned, and these inclusions "mark an important turn in the representation of Purdy's poetry, for they tentatively gesture towards a non-evaluative, literary-historical method of editing a poet's collected works" (Irvine 80). Nevertheless, Purdy's impulse to recreate his poems with each republication, an artistic prerogative that his co-editors respected, generally drew the collections to the goal of proliferating chosen poems afresh, rather than documenting the train of their existence – let alone compiling all of the poems ever published or, harder still, written.

Critical appraisal constitutes one motive for editing, and it is the one that has dominated the editions of Purdy's poetry so far. In this paradigm, dismissing the early writing is a tactic to shore up the later work. Solecki casts Purdy's career as pivoting on a typically modernist epiphany, a reforging of the poetic self in which daring twentieth-century realism broke in on and consumed a vacuous nineteenth-century sentimentalism: "It is conventional wisdom, encouraged by some of Purdy's own comments in his letters and essays (see 'Disconnections,' *Reaching for the Beaufort Sea*, and Dennis Lee's 'Afterword' to the *Collected Poems*), that [Bliss] Carman and the kind of poetry he represents were completely left behind when Purdy remade himself as a writer through the 1940s and 1950s" (LCP 56). As he says, Purdy himself promulgated this narrative: "Up to that time my literary gods were Bliss Carman, G.K. Chesterton, W.J. Turner, etc. ... But suddenly I found myself reading T.S. Eliot, Dylan Thomas, W.B. Yeats, Ezra Pound and others. I had realized that my own writings were, if not precisely mediocre, certainly not immortal literature either" (RBS 135; qtd. in Solecki, "Chronology" 12). Solecki draws a line between failure and success at about 1960: "He [Purdy] pauses repeatedly in the autobiography to wonder how the man who had failed at almost everything – including poetry – until the age of forty could also have written *Poems for All the Annettes* (1962) and *The Cariboo Horses* (1965) and won the Governor General's Award" ("Chronology" 17). Editorially, *Beyond Remembering* is based on this line, omitting, as Irvine remarked, all the poems from Purdy's first three printed chapbooks (at first glance, anyway), from his early periodical publications, and from his half-dozen typescript compilations archived at the University of Saskatchewan. The rationale for this choice is that it will promote the reading of his best, his most enduring, work, at least among readers who accept the given definition of "the best."

Textual scholarship offers a different route into a writer's work. Although it too endeavours to provide the reader with what an editor judges to be the author's best text, it explicitly compares different copies of a work in order to illuminate rather than conceal their discrepancies. This approach, which Irvine designates "a non-evaluative, literary-historical method of editing," has been amply fleshed out over decades of commentary. (David Greetham offers an excellent entry point.) Textual scholarship is non-evaluative insofar as it strives to present variants objectively, but it is highly evaluative (even to the point of calling itself a mode of "criticism," too) in that it manifests an editor's judgment in the ordering and presentation of variants. Such judgment impinges on the edited text, whether one variant is privileged to form the main reading text while others are consigned to notes, or all variants are judged equally authoritative and displayed in parallel. It is fair to say that textual scholarship is historical, in the sense that it works to understand the past iterations of a work and the alterations it has undergone, whereas literary criticism is more concerned with the present and future interpretation of the work. Most importantly, Irvine is right to note that Purdy's oeuvre is now ripe for textual scholarship. He makes the interesting point that "the critical archive [i.e., academic commentary] reveals a far greater interest in reading Purdy's early (pre-1962) poetry than his selected and collected editions permit" (81).

There are many examples of this last point. D.M.R. Bentley historically recuperates Purdy's first book, *The Enchanted Echo* (1944), which is ignored by *Beyond Remembering*, as an important milestone in Purdy's career ("Unremembered"). He argues that Purdy's Vancouver friend and fellow poet, Joan Buckley, and her admiration of the kind of poetry practised by the Confederation poets, were instrumental in the publication of *The Enchanted Echo*, and hence fundamental to whatever Purdy subsequently went on to do. Despite lambasting Carman as a "ventriloquist" and a "dead end," Solecki essentially makes a similar point, not only by devoting a whole chapter to Purdy's wrestling with Carman's shadow, but also by specifically conceding "the persistence of a relatively conservative prosody in Purdy's mature work" (*LCP* 53, 75, 71). Moreover, he grants that "Purdy is one of the few contemporary poets writing predominantly in free verse who is nostalgic for the past, saddened by the fact that his poems – because of free verse – cannot be memorized and recited and therefore cannot be literally as memorable as the poems of his first model [Carman]" (*LCP* 59). Sandra Djwa likens Purdy's oeuvre to a geological plot of ground, in which the top layers obscure those lying beneath; specifically, she asserts Purdy's debt to the mythopoeia of E.J. Pratt: "In his impulse towards romantic myth-making and his insistence on the primacy of the human imagination (especially on the function of poetry in creating the world we live in), Purdy, like Pratt, is a modern romantic, but one who invokes realism, irony, and humour in his stance as a national poet" (60). I.S. MacLaren has pointed out Purdy's incorrigible recourse to Robert Service as late as 1979 in "Ballad of the Arctic," a poem with a rollicking iambic tetrameter, which Purdy later revised into the much shorter free-verse poem, "Arctic Places" (130–4). Rather than following *Beyond Remembering* in bypassing the early work and the early influences, these studies fold them into understandings of Purdy as an author who distinguished himself not merely by writing good poetry, but by crossing between different orders of good poetry in the course of his life, adapting old habits to new regimes of judgment, while carrying much along with him essentially unchanged. Showing the stages of revision to Purdy's poetry in a scholarly, rather than a critical, edition will facilitate further work in this vein, revealing the spectrum of his growth.

Purdy's poetry may be ready for scholarly editing, but the practical dimensions of the undertaking present a formidable obstacle. Irvine estimates that publishing a scholarly edition of Purdy's complete poems "would probably require extensive editorial collaboration ... [and] major financial support from granting agencies" (88). However, if this practical challenge is the principal reason why the work has not yet occurred, despite academic interest in Purdy's growth as an author, then the answer is to make an honest start. Irvine imagines different ways to construct a scholarly edition of Purdy's poetry, all of them grand, ranging from a diplomatic reprinting of all of Purdy's books, with the poems in the order in which they originally appeared, combined into one giant volume, to a genetic edition of all of the poems, arranged by date of composition or publication, with variant words or phrases provided in an apparatus, and variant versions of entire poems appended either in print or online (85–7). The scope of these visions may be part of the problem. Versioning, especially, exposes itself to charges of horrendous excess, even in digital form: it simply heaps too many texts on the reader, who, asked to read all, instead reads none. No new edition can completely replace the library of all Purdy's original books, but since these can generally be consulted in universities across the country, or even still purchased from dealers, it is not yet necessary to make any such attempt. What the study of Purdy's poetry needs acutely is elucidation of the specific ways in which his poems change. This elucidation can start without impediment, one poem at a time, for textual scholarship is finally more than an overweening quest for editorial mastery. It may mine documents for empirical data in the form of textual variants, and it may dream of presenting them, accurate and complete, at one fell swoop, but these are not its purposes. Scholarly editing draws the reader into a deeper and more delightful contemplation of the work in all its forms. Scholarly editing is a way of knowing Canadian poetry. To indicate the ends for literary studies of this bibliographical and historical way is what the following discussion of Purdy's "House Guest" intends. The case is a new one, but the overall point is ancient: to understand the author, we must compare the copies of his or her work.

House Guest

> For two months we quarrelled* over socialism   poetry   how
>   to boil water†
> doing the dishes   carpentry   Russian steel production
>   figures and whether
> you could believe them and whether Toronto Leafs‡ would
>   take it all
> that year and maybe hockey was rather like a good jazz
>   combo
> 5 never knowing what came next
> Listening
> how the new house built§ with salvaged old lumber
> bent a little in the wind and dreamt of the trees it came from
> the time it was travelling thru
> 10 and the world of snow moving all night in its blowing sleep
> while we discussed ultimate responsibility for a pile of dirty
>   dishes
> Jews in the Negev   the Bible as mythic literature   Peking
>   Man
> and in early morning looking outside to see the pink shapes
>   of wind¶
> printed on snow and a red sun tumbling upward almost
>   touching the house

---

* quarrelled *throughout in 1972, 1976, 1978, 1986, 1996, 2000*] quarreled *throughout in 1968, 1973*

† poetry how to boil water *single line of verse 1968, 1973, 1986, 1996, 2000*] poetry / [centred:] how to boil water *1972, 1976, 1978; in these three editions, sixteen other long lines of verse are likewise broken into two lines of type positioned variously on the page.*

‡ Leafs *1972, 1976, 1978, 1986, 1996, 2000*] Maple Leafs *1968, 1973*

§ built *1972, 1978, 1986, 1996, 2000*] made *1968, 1973*; build *1976*

¶ *line 13 appears twice in 1976, before and after line 12*

15   and fretwork tracks of rabbits outside where the window light
      had lain
   last night an audience
   watching in wonderment the odd human argument
   that uses words instead of teeth
   and got bored and went away*

20   Of course there was wild grape wine and a stove full of
      Douglas fir
   (railway salvage) and lake ice cracking its knuckles in hard
      Ontario weather
   and working with saw and hammer at the house all winter
      afternoon
   disagreeing about how to pound nails
   arguing vehemently over how to make good coffee
25   Marcus Aurelius   Spartacus   Plato and François† Villon
   And it used to frustrate him terribly
   that even when I was wrong he couldn't prove it
   and when I agreed with him he was always suspicious
   and thought he must be wrong because I said he was right
30   Every night the house shook from his snoring
   a great motor driving us on into daylight
   and the vibration was terrible
   Every morning I'd get up and say "Look‡ at the nails –
   you snored them out half an inch in the night –"
35   He'd believe me at first and look and get mad and glare
   and stare angrily out the window while I watched 10 minutes
      of irritation
   drain from his eyes onto fields and farms and miles and miles
      of snow§
   We quarrelled over how dour I was in early morning
   and how cheerful he was for counterpoint
40   and I argued that a million years of evolution
   from snarling apeman had¶ to be traversed before noon
   and the desirability of murder in a case like his

---

*   away // Of *1968, 1972, 1973, 1976, 1978, 1996*] away / Of *1986, 2000*
†   François *all other editions*] Francois *1976*
‡   "Look *double quotation marks throughout in 1972, 1976, 1978, 1986, 1996, 2000*] *single quotation marks throughout in 1968, 1973*
§   snow / We *1973, 1986, 1996, 2000*] snow // We *1968, 1972, 1976, 1978*
¶   had *1968, 1973*] have *1972, 1976, 1978, 1986, 1996, 2000*

        and whether the Etruscans were really Semites
        the Celtic invasion of Britain   European languages   Roman
          law
45   we argued about white being white (prove it dammit)
          & cockroaches
        bedbugs in Montreal   separatism   Nietzsche   Iroquois
          horsebreakers on the prairie
        death of the individual and the ultimate destiny of man
        and one night we quarrelled over how to cook eggs
        In the morning driving to town we hardly spoke
50   and water poured downhill outside all day for it was spring
        when we were gone with frogs mentioning lyrically
        Russian steel production figures on Roblin Lake which were
          almost nil
        I left him hitchhiking* on #2 Highway to Montreal
        and I guess I was wrong about those eggs

"House Guest" is an important Purdy poem. Appearing in at least nine of his books, it belongs to the corpus that commonly defines Purdy as an author. One of the reasons for its broad appeal is doubtless its bearing witness to the achievement of building the Purdy A-frame near Ameliasburgh – an achievement that verges on national myth, because the A-frame was and remains a house of Canadian poetry. A writer-in-residence program aims to keep the A-frame a place where poetry is written ("A-frame").

    In 1957, Al and Eurithe bought the plot of land and began to build with the help of Eurithe's father, Jim Parkhurst, reusing wood from the Canadian Pacific Railway (Solecki, "Chronology" 13). Al and Eurithe's hospitality to fellow writers made the A-frame a hub of literary creativity, perpetuating the hospitality that Al himself had earlier received at Malcolm Lowry's cottage – "a sort of driftwood house ... built atop log pilings on the beach, and look[ing] almost like a houseboat" – at Dollarton, outside Vancouver (RBS 137). "Even while the A-frame was being built, it became a meeting place – for poets, for poetry lovers, for those aspiring to be poets" – from Earle Birney, Milton Acorn, and Patrick Lane to Margaret Atwood, Michael Ondaatje, and Steven Heighton ("A-frame"). "House Guest" is also a record of Purdy's friendship with fellow poet Milton Acorn (YA 157). In 1974, Mike Doyle admired "the finely realized concreteness" of the poem, singling it out as one of Purdy's best in his critical review of the oeuvre to date (12). "House

---

*   hitchhiking 2000] hitch hiking *1968, 1972, 1973, 1978, 1986*; hitch-hiking *1976, 1996*

Guest" was one of the seventy-five poems selected for *Rooms for Rent in the Outer Planets: Selected Poems, 1962–1996* (1996), the slim volume aimed at putting Purdy's lifetime-best work in the hands of the general reader, an aim that was to some extent realized when Susan Musgrave defended it in the Canada Reads competition of 2006. "House Guest" is one of the handful of poems featured prominently in Brian D. Johnson's documentary film *Al Purdy Was Here* (2015). If Al Purdy succeeded in rebuilding the house of Canadian poetry with salvaged materials, "House Guest" has come to stand for this feat.

"House Guest" figures quarrelling as constructive. For two months, the speaker and his guest bicker about everything under the sun, "socialism   poetry   how to boil water / doing the dishes   carpentry   Russian steel production figures" (ll. 1–2), while working together on the house that shelters them each night. They are equals: they both know enough about poetry, for example, to fight over it. Their relationship is antagonistic yet co-operative: they labour together "with saw and hammer at the house all winter afternoon / disagreeing about how to pound nails / arguing vehemently over how to make good coffee" (22–4). In fact, their hostility is a measure of their intimacy, for their friendship stands clear at the end. After leaving his guest at the highway, the speaker admits his own error in the last dispute (how to cook eggs), admitting his guest into that innermost room of the home, his own heart.

On a further level, the structure built by the argument between the two men is the poem itself, for like the physical building, the verbal one is made from any old material lying at hand ("bedbugs in Montreal   separatism   Nietzsche   Iroquois horsebreakers on the prairie" [46]). Both buildings make sound and invite "Listening" (6); both dream (8); both endure, "travelling thru" "time" (9). Every poetic house is an instance of "the odd human argument / that uses words instead of teeth" (17–18); every poem is built by a quarrel between author and skeptical reader, whose skepticism softens only when the struggle to discover the meaning (the form) is finished. If "House Guest" begins with a quarrel, it ends with the transformation of that quarrel into poetry. The binary character of this quarrel between host and guest, between writer and audience, is manifest in the particular highway named ("#2"), the period of time spent together ("two months"), the transition between two seasons (from winter to spring), mention of the Cold War (capitalism versus communism), suggestions of Canadian biculturalism ("Toronto," "Montreal," "separatism"), the two-word title, and the arrangement of the poem on the page in two sections of free verse.

This binary pattern bespeaks the fluid dualism that Purdy contemplates throughout his oeuvre. Fraser Sutherland judges his poems "saturated with religious belief, inasmuch as they are perpetually involved in the process of transforming matter into spirit (transcendence), and spirit into matter (immanence)" (*YA* 508). Quoting Sutherland, Tim Heath argues that Purdy's style consists of a profound willingness to alternate between opposites: his poems centre on "relics and reliquaries[, which] assert the possibility that a seemingly worthless object possesses special value, so much so that the very idea of precious refuse troubles such binaries as worthless/invaluable, sacred/profane, spiritual/material, and immanent/transcendent" (192). Whether the centre of a poem is a live contrast between the present and the past, love and violence, departure and return, mind and body, or truth and illusion, the binary pattern manifests itself across Purdy's work, not as a hierarchy but rather as a dynamic in which the poet's own humility causes a restless fluctuation. In "House Guest," this centre is the quarrel, a binary interaction between self and other.

If "House Guest" salvages seemingly random words and phrases for purposeful reuse, it likewise treats prior Canadian poetry as a relic in Heath's sense, indicating the larger structure of the national canon. Purdy's poem culminates with "frogs mentioning lyrically / Russian steel production figures on Roblin Lake which were almost nil" (51–2), a metaphor of the springing of the poem from the mud of an argument. This metaphor – poet as frog – recalls Archibald Lampman's "The Frogs," a sonnet sequence that uses the same figure to assert the invulnerability of poetry to decay. Lampman's frogs are

> Breathers of wisdom won without a quest,
> Quaint uncouth dreamers, voices high and strange;
> Flutists of lands where beauty hath no change,
> And wintry grief is a forgotten guest. ("The Frogs" ll. 1–4)

The romantic trope is constant: both poems represent frogs as lyrical voices that naturally express a transcendent spiritual phenomenon, whether "beauty" in imaginary "lands" or an impossibly located "production" that would be reckoned as "nil" if measured only physically. Purdy knew Lampman's poem: in "Bullfrogs" in *The Blur in Between* (1962), he wrote of "just plain frogs" that

>   their counterpoint
> would move Bliss Carman
> to iambic hexameter;
>
> rouse Archibald Lampman
> to competitive fever[.] (16)

Frogs are poets for Purdy, as they were for the Confederation poets. Furthermore, both "House Guest" and "The Frogs" pair the passing of winter with the departure of a guest. The invocation of Lampman also raises the question of scansion. In Purdy's poem, should we hear three spondees emphasizing the pouring of spring rain "downhill outside all day" (50)? This unusual rhythm would be climactic if, as with Lampman, reading the poem entailed scanning it.

"House Guest" supports later Canadian poetry, too. Gordon Johnston has taken inspiration from the visit of two poets. In "Visiting Poet," he adds himself into the mix:

Visiting Poet

The poet is putting up a visiting
poet overnight, his wife none too pleased.
I've brought them a sleeping bag
but in the jumble in the back of the car
I only find the little blankets
from my granddaughter's crib.
I'll have to go back, but first
I remember I've bought the poets something,
a bottle of Crown Royal.
When I find it, the top has broken off;
it has crashed against
a bottle of scotch: a crazed shape
inside a fancy shopping bag.
We're remembering the broken glass
the last time this poet visited;
someone drank wine
from a glass with a crack in it.
My hands are covered with tiny splinters of glass
and I want to ask if I may wash them, please.
"What is the shape of this?" I ask. The poet host confides,
"Our friendship grew in the shadow
of my mother's death, which pulled on it like a moon."

Johnston's poem invokes the boozing and the literary hospitality for which the Purdy A-frame became renowned. Like Purdy's poem, "Visiting Poet" is about friendship between poets, figured again as one staying at another's house, with a third now entering bearing a gift. Like Purdy's (scrambled?) eggs, Johnston's bottles of whiskey have cracked open and congealed into a "crazed shape"; this original and puzzling shape, emphasized by the repetition toward the end of the poem, is a metaphor of friendship and of poetry. Love, like art, involves a unique breaking of the glass barrier between spirits. "What is the shape of this?" is the reader's question for every poem, and in every poem, "friendship" is the author's answer. Moreover, if whiskey, with an alcohol content of 40 per cent, freezes around minus 26°C, then the visit described here must also take place in the winter. Johnston's allusions suggest that Purdy's "House Guest" continues to build the house of Canadian poetry, both on its own and in a larger context.

What, however, *is* the shape of this poem? Purdy saw "House Guest" republished several times during his life, and each edition presented an opportunity for revision. Consequently, the text has accumulated a number of variants, and the poem should now ideally be read in light of them. Quite a different version of the poem, with the same title, "House Guest," appeared in Purdy's early collection *Pressed on Sand* (1955), a Ryerson Poetry Chap-Book edited by Lorne Pierce and published two years before the building of the A-frame commenced. The second and more familiar version of "House Guest" first appeared in the revised edition of *Poems for All the Annettes*, and appeared again in the third edition of that book. Retrospective selections of Purdy's work have kept this second version in print, in one form or another: *Selected Poems* (1972); *The Poems of Al Purdy* (1976), a New Canadian Library paperback, under the general editorship of Malcolm Ross; *Being Alive*, edited by Purdy and Dennis Lee (1978) (for Lee's role, see Irvine 75); and *The Collected Poems of Al Purdy*, *Rooms for Rent in the Outer Planets*, and *Beyond Remembering*, mentioned above. Comparing these texts – all of them published, all of them authoritative – not only raises questions that only a scholarly edition of the poem can treat properly, but also reveals the expansion of Purdy's concept of poetry.

Some of the variants are straightforward improvements made by the author or a trustworthy editor. The central verb, "quarrelled," which appears three times in the poem, originally spelled with one *l* (1, 38, 48), has been brought into line in later editions with what the *Canadian Oxford Dictionary* (COD) now recognizes as standard Canadian spelling. Single quotation marks, similarly, have been replaced with double, and "hitch hiking" (53) has become "hitch-hiking" and finally "hitchhiking," as preferred by the COD. Harmlessly, "Toronto Maple Leafs" (3) has been shortened to "Toronto Leafs." The passage that introduces the self-reflexive conceit (that the poem, too, is a house composed through quarrel) first read "the new house *made* with salvaged old lumber" (7; emphasis added) instead of "built." This substitution emphasizes the labour and achievement of construction, and probably little fuss need be made over it.

If trust in the final authorized edition resolves such conflicts, a real textual crux surfaces in the "snarling apeman" passage. The 1968 and 1973 editions, published by House of Anansi Press, read as follows: "I argued that a million years of evolution / from snarling apeman *had* to be traversed before noon / and the desirability of murder in a case like his" (38–42; emphasis added). By contrast, all of the editions published by McClelland & Stewart and by Harbour change the last subordinate clause to the present tense: "and I argued that a million years of evolution / from snarling apeman *have* to be traversed before noon / and the desirability of murder in a case like his" (emphasis added). With the first variant, the past tense emphasizes the particular relation between speaker and guest. Each morning, the house guest wakes up in a bad mood as big as a prehistoric epoch; his paleolithic crabbiness, which does not abate until lunch, is grounds for murder. This accusation continues the speaker's tone of hostile mockery toward his guest, and is therefore in keeping with the antagonism that persists until the final line of the poem. With the second variant, this accusation softens into a general remark allowing that everyone is grumpy in the morning.[1] The difference is slight but significant, and the earlier variant is preferable.

Further trouble stems from the arrangement of the poem on the page, which affects perceptions of the overall structure. In the first edition of the poem, the lines of verse are all justified on the left margin. However, several, including line 1, are too long for a single line of type and so extend onto a second line; where this occurs, the extra words are uniformly indented 1.2 cm, indicating that, poetically, they belong to the prior line. (See Figure 8.1.) Overall, the poem is divided into three sections of roughly equal length, with stanza breaks after lines 19 ("and got bored and went away") and 37 ("drain from his eyes onto fields and farms and miles and miles of snow"). This tripartite structure suggests patterns that enhance the poem's proposition of the fruit of quarrel – familiar patterns, such as architectural stability (triangles, tripods), classical dialectics (thesis, antithesis, synthesis), procreation (self, other, child), or divinity (the Trinity). *Selected Poems* (1972) and *Being Alive* (1978) followed this overall structure, but centred the indented ends of long lines. (See Figure 8.2.) *The Poems of Al Purdy* (1976) mistook these ends for new lines of verse, floating them around the middle of the page, but not uniformly; the result is a poem that appears to have seventy-one lines (rather than fifty-four), seventeen of which have a strange emphasis due to their shortness and their scattered position. This layout gives rise to false questions of interpretation: one might ponder in vain why the phrase "how to boil water" has a unique position on the page, rather than attending to the metaphorical resonance of the more important line, "Listening." (See Figure 8.3.) By contrast, in the third edition of *Poems for All the Annettes* (1973), there are only two sections, with a break after line 19, and the long lines are treated correctly. The bipartite structure emphasizes the quarrel itself – dualism, struggle, cohabitation, relation – in ways that resonate with several details of the poem, including, in addition to those discussed above, the contrast between people and animals. Any product of the argument is left subtler, more to be inferred. Then *The Collected Poems of Al Purdy* (1986) removed the section breaks altogether, rendering the poem as an undivided whole – an arrangement that does not so much suggest unity as simply eclipse the question of formal structure altogether, obviating the analysis of parts. *Rooms for Rent in the Outer Planets* (1996) reverted to the bipartite arrangement. *Beyond Remembering* (2000), following 1986, also merged the sections into one. As far as stanzaic form is concerned, the 1973 and 1996 editions of "House Guest" seem to offer the richest structure; however, readers will wish to be aware of all the possibilities in judging of this issue for themselves.

In addition to these variants, there is the first version of "House Guest," published in *Pressed on Sand* (1955). Is it simply a different poem, or is it a prior phase in the process of creating one poem? Lexically, it is almost entirely different, but thematically, it strongly resembles the second version:

House Guest

    I have an artist in the house for one week.
    And expect to be discommoded, uncomfortable sometimes,
    For I know him – the effeminate child,
    With some stigmata of greatness that strikes
5 Violently at the world's hypocrisy; chill blue gleams
    Of pure malignity: love soured and love grown old.

    I expect pastels on the floor and numerous friends,
    And mincing swear words and tentative
    Veiled overtures without commitment;
10 Mild pronunciamentoes that spend
    Gusto like a miser's purse, and save*
    A bottom potential the mind will not decant.

    But what is the relationship? I must know

---

*   save] saves *1955*

> Why this pale man I have studied for six months,
> 15 Why his pictures live, what life returns again.
> Is there a difference basically
> Underlying mine like a Byzantine plinth,
> And growing into another world – a gossamer one?

This poem, like the second version, presents a conflict between host and guest, a conflict that turns toward sympathy at the end. This speaker seems more patient. Rather than contradicting and mocking his guest, he only "expects[s] to be discommoded, uncomfortable," and the "swear words" are all on one side. The "relationship" at the centre of this poem is not obviously one of equality. The speaker is not, or not yet, an artist, whereas the guest possesses (genuinely or sarcastically) "some stigmata of greatness" marking his prophetic vocation. There is of course no mention of co-operatively building the A-frame, that undertaking still lying two or three years in the future. Nevertheless, this first version of the poem, like the second, culminates with one admitting the other into his heart. Their antagonism dissolves as the speaker generously reverses their relation, imagining himself inside the artist's house – the artwork – with pillars stretching from their bases into a loftier world. The "life" that enfolds the speaker at the end is triply emphasized, through two figures of speech – anacoluthon, the changing of grammatical structure mid-sentence ("Why this pale man I have studied for six months, / Why his pictures live") and polyptoton, the repetition of a word with a different suffix or grammatical inflection ("live"/"life") – as well as through the difficulty of the pronoun "mine," which must stand for *my life*. Moreover, the final effect is metapoetic, for as the speaker has entered into the picture, so the reader has entered into the poem. Like the second version, the first version of "House Guest" self-reflexively figures poetry as the act of hosting.

Recovering the first version of "House Guest" reveals another phase of poetry, another stylistic register of Purdy's, lying at some remove from the common-speech free verse of "The Country North of Belleville," "Still Life in a Tent," "At the Quinte Hotel," and his other famous poems of the 1960s, and yet not unconnected with it. "I'm still changing and watching myself change," wrote Purdy to Earle Birney on 30 June 1959, "like diving into successive pools of water and seeing your own reflection in each. But damned if I know where I'm going, or whether my stuff is any good. I can see some difference in what I write now and what's in the Ryerson book [*The Crafte So Longe to Lerne*, 1959], and that's just 2–3 months ago" (YA 53–4). If Purdy's practical understanding of poetry was evolving in the 1950s and 1960s, the 1955 text of "House Guest" allows us to recover

HOUSE GUEST

For two months we quarreled over socialism   poetry   how to
       boil water
doing the dishes   carpentry   Russian steel production figures
       and whether
you could believe them and whether Toronto Maple Leafs
       would take it all
that year and maybe hockey was rather like a good jazz combo
never knowing what came next
Listening
how the new house made with salvaged old lumber
bent a little in the wind and dreamt of the trees it came from
the time it was travelling thru
and the world of snow moving all night in its blowing sleep
while we discussed ultimate responsibility for a pile of dirty
       dishes
Jews in the Negev   the Bible as mythic literature   Peking Man
and in early morning looking outside to see the pink shapes of
       wind
printed on snow and a red sun tumbling upward almost touching
       the house
and fretwork tracks of rabbits outside where the window light
       had lain
last night an audience
watching in wonderment the odd human argument
that uses words instead of teeth
and got bored and went away

Of course there was wild grape wine and a stove full of
       Douglas fir

Figure 8.1 The first page of "House Guest" in the revised edition of *Poems for All the Annettes* (1968). Several long lines of verse extend onto a second line of type. Author copy.

HOUSE GUEST

For two months we quarrelled over socialism   poetry
                how to boil water
doing the dishes   carpentry   Russian steel production
                figures and whether
you could believe them and whether Toronto Leafs would
                take it all
that year and maybe hockey was rather like a good jazz combo
never knowing what came next
Listening
how the new house built with salvaged old lumber
bent a little in the wind and dreamt of the trees it came from
the time it was travelling thru
and the world of snow moving all night in its blowing sleep
while we discussed ultimate responsibility for a pile of dirty
                dishes
Jews in the Negev   the Bible as mythic literature
                Peking Man
and in early morning looking outside to see the pink shapes
                of wind
printed on snow and a red sun tumbling upward almost
                touching the house
and fretwork tracks of rabbits outside where the window light
                had lain
last night an audience
watching in wonderment the odd human argument
that uses words instead of teeth
and got bored and went away

Of course there was wild grape wine and a stove full
                of Douglas fir
(railway salvage) and lake ice cracking its knuckles in hard
                Ontario weather
and working with saw and hammer at the house all winter
                afternoon
disagreeing about how to pound nails
arguing vehemently over how to make good coffee
Marcus Aurelius   Spartacus   Plato and Francois Villon

Figure 8.2 The first page of "House Guest" in *Selected Poems* (1972). The ends of long lines are indented to the centre of the page.
Courtesy of McGill Library, Rare Books and Special Collections.

HOUSE GUEST

For two months we quarrelled over socialism   poetry
                how to boil water
doing the dishes   carpentry   Russian steel production
                figures and whether
you could believe them and whether Toronto Leafs would
                take it all
that year and maybe hockey was rather like a good jazz combo
never knowing what came next
Listening
how the new house build with salvaged old lumber
bent a little in the wind and dreamt of the trees it came from
the time it was travelling thru
and the world of snow moving all night in its blowing sleep
while we discussed ultimate responsibility for a pile of dirty
                dishes

Figure 8.3 The first page of "House Guest" in *The Poems of Al Purdy* (1976). The line ends from 1972 have been mistaken for new lines of their own and scattered about the middle of the page, creating a false emphasis.
Courtesy of McGill Library.

a step in his development. The diction ("discommoded," "malignity," "plinth," "gossamer") is refined and elevated, chosen as much for the rare sound as the sense. A neologism, blending *pronunciation* and *mementoes*, pushes this interest in the aural artifice of poetry still further.[2] Similarly, the rhythm twists away from any conventionally predictable metre toward unique emphasis, such as the three consecutive stresses of "chill blue gleams" or the anapest with which the poem finishes. Moreover, the poem subtly fulfills a six-line stanza with half-rhymes (*abcabc*): "week"/"strikes," "sometimes"/"gleams," "child"/"old," etc. (Line 16 enacts its "difference" by breaking from the rhyme scheme.) Internal rhyme ("hypocrisy"/"malignity") and alliteration ("pale man"/"pictures," "growing"/"gossamer") further enhance the aural design. These details are evidence of a mode of poetry still centred on the original assembly of sounds.

    Poets of the generation prior to Purdy, such as W.B. Yeats, Charles G.D. Roberts, and E.J. Pratt, held rhythm and rhyme to be inexhaustible. "House Guest" allies itself with them through allusion, positioning Purdy as their heir. His "Byzantine" pillar "growing into another world," for example, brings to mind Yeats's "Sailing to Byzantium," in which the speaker has "sailed the seas and come / To the holy city of Byzantium" (ll. 15–16). Purdy's "gossamer" world of art recalls the climax of Roberts's "The Tantramar Revisited," in which poetry metaphorically replaces old fishing nets:

> Then, as the blue day mounts, and the low-shot shafts of the sunlight
> Glance from the tide to the shore, gossamers jewelled with dew
> Sparkle and wave, where late sea-spoiling fathoms of drift-net
> Myriad-meshed, uploomed sombrely over the land. (ll. 47–50)

If romanticism cherishes the musicality of poetry and its adumbration of the sublime, then the first version of "House Guest" shows a poet steeped in it, but turning to modern effects, such as irregular rhythm and experimentally subtle rhyme.

The romantic facets of this poem accord with the general character of the Ryerson Poetry Chap-Books. In 1955, this series was still edited by Lorne Pierce, who had founded it thirty years prior with guidance from an elderly Charles G.D. Roberts. Although the Ryerson Poetry Chap-Books had by this time opened up to contributions by Dorothy Livesay (1950), Raymond Souster (1951), Louis Dudek (1952), and other writers more or less affiliated with Canadian modernism, the Ruskinian character of the editor, forged long before, continued to make itself felt. In her biography of Pierce, Sandra Campbell describes his idealism as a resilient conviction, rooted in his rural childhood in a strictly Methodist home, the philosophy of idealistic service imparted by John Watson and other professors at Queen's University during his BA before the First World War, his harrowing work as a minister-in-training in impoverished immigrant communities on the Prairies, his admiration for nineteenth-century Russian literature, and his lifelong fight against lupus. In a report dated April 1952, Pierce wrote: "In a time of bewilderment and violence and vulgarity, we shall more than ever dedicate ourselves to integrity, to decency, to justice, to the inner law and the higher freedom, without which life is impossible" (qtd. in Campbell 472). Between 1942 and 1952, Ryerson had printed four books of poetry by Birney, Purdy's mentor. Purdy's following this lead with his own Ryerson Poetry Chap-Books in 1955 and 1959 signifies compatibility between his authorial and Pierce's editorial goals. The Ryerson Poetry Chap-Books exemplify a tenacious, backward-looking, Toronto-centric culture of Canadian poetry that cannot be reduced to the modernism of the McGill Group, with which they were contemporary, and this culture contributed to Purdy's formation as a poet.

Purdy was invigorated by his discovery of Irving Layton and other Montreal poets in the mid-1950s, and there is no reason to doubt that the publication of the first edition of *Poems for All the Annettes* by Contact Press in Montreal should continue to be viewed as a significant step in his career. However, viewing the literary and bibliographical evidence of Purdy's debt to romanticism multiplies his colours, encouraging readings that grasp the persistence of a host of factors in his work – rhythm, rhyme, stanzaic structure, pastoral recourse to the natural world, idealism – that go well beyond the modernist assertion of historic rupture. A scholarly edition of Purdy's poems would reveal his development as a writer, an extent that has more stages than a "bad" period followed by a "good" one. A whole view of Purdy would show us a modern texture shot through with older poetic influences.

Purdy's poems, even the most celebrated ones, abound with variants. "The Country North of Belleville" has at least four passages varying substantively between the first edition in *The Cariboo Horses* (1965) and later editions. For example, the Sisyphean farmer in that poem spends "days in the sun" (CH 74, l. 14) – or is it "backbreaking days / in the sun and rain" (BA 22, ll. 14–15)? The land he works is "a lean land / not fat" (CH 75, ll. 20–1); later, it is "a lean land / not like the fat south" (BA 22, ll. 21–2), an addition which invites a deeper political interpretation of the whole poem. Bentley, whose reading of "The Country North of Belleville" reveals its metapoetic conceit (*Gay* 209–12), and Solecki, who extends this reading (LCP 148–52), both situate the poem as a work of the 1960s: "Had he not written a poem after the appearance of *Wild Grape Wine* in 1968 his reputation would be secure on the basis of 'Elegy for a Grandfather,' 'The Country North of Belleville,' 'Transient,' [etc.]" (LCP 145). Both critics, however, quote and discuss the text as published in 1986 in *The Collected Poems of Al Purdy*, following the second variants in the passages quoted above. If "The Country North of Belleville" is "one of the finest poems in Canadian literature" (147), then it merits a scholarly edition that clarifies its form down to the last hyphen.

"At the Quinte Hotel," arguably the most famous of Purdy's poems, especially since Douglas Bensadoun adapted it into a short film starring Gord Downie in 2002, is quite consistent from one publication to the next. Still, an intriguing hermeneutic issue arises from the one obvious variant. In the revised edition of *Poems for All the Annettes* (1968), the poem includes a dedication immediately below the title: "*(for Alan Pearson)*" (95). As Purdy explained in a 1996 letter, Alan Pearson was his drinking companion:

> I had a friend named Alan Pearson with me on this occasion (very long ago), and when this little ex-boxer (which I didn't know at the time) started to beat up on these two older guys – I think both of them a little drunk – it made me feel indignant that the waiters did nothing to stop it ... And I did feel a bit like a damn fool for standing up and challenging the little prick. Pearson just sat there and watched me somewhat unbelievingly, perhaps thinking I was showing off – which in a sense I was. But anyway, as the poem intimates, I knocked him down with my charge and sat on him, and the waiters threw him out to my great relief. The bit about reading him a poem, is of course sheer embroidery. (YA 519)

The dedication to a real personal acquaintance anchors the poem in historical particulars. The proper noun has a literal and limited significance that is opaque to the uninformed reader but appropriate to the author's style, which frequently incorporates mundane details from his own life. Later editions of "At the Quinte Hotel," including that in *Beyond Remembering*, omit the dedication. It has no figurative significance; the reader does not need it in order to arrive at the insight of the poem, the paradoxical worth and worthlessness of poetry, beside which the name may seem mere biographical clutter. Moreover, dedications in poems frequently have an allusive literary function, but since Alan Pearson is not "a highly recognizable" author, deleting this one could be legitimated as a way of making the poem more poetic. Interpreting "At the Quinte Hotel" thus forks at the dedication: on the right hand, there is a more concrete reading; on the left, a more abstract one.

If textual scholarship will incrementally improve the reading of Purdy's most famous poems, it will greatly affect the discussion of others, which vary far more than the sample discussed so far. In *In Search of Owen Roblin* (1974), "Elegy for a Grandfather" has thirty-five different lines than it does in the *Collected Poems*. *Rooms for Rent in the Outer Planets* includes four poems under the heading "*Poems for All the Annettes* (1962)" (7), but none of them appears as it did in 1962. "Spring Song," for example, originally started with twenty-nine other lines, including a decisive condemnation of the "followers of sickening Nietzsche" (PA 27, l. 26), and had nothing about frogs singing Beethoven or the hourglass having a feminine shape. Similarly, fourteen lines were added to "Remains of an Indian Village" after the first edition in 1962. Readers of Purdy must dispense with the cardinal assumption of print culture, namely that published texts are fixed texts. In his case, the starting point should instead be the opposite assumption – that one copy of a poem will not exactly match the next.

Criticism will go awry if it is based on unscholarly texts. One example will suffice to conclude. In his generally admirable article, Mike Doyle quotes the last five lines of "At Evergreen Cemetery" as "perhaps the key moment of *The Crafte So Longe to Lerne*" (10). He uses them to articulate his argument that Purdy's first three decades of published work show a course of development, or a capacity for metamorphosis, that indicates real potential. This is his poetic "eclecticism, his protean personality" (9) as a poet:

> Myself, having the sense of something going
> on without my knowledge, changes taking place
> that I should be concerned with,
> sit motionless in the black car behind the hearse
> waiting to re-enter a different world. (Qtd. in Doyle 10)

The argument is sound but the evidence faulty, for these lines are from the text of the poem as published in the revised edition of *Poems for All the Annettes* (1968), a poem consisting of twenty-five lines. In *The Crafte So Longe to Lerne* (1959), "At Evergreen Cemetery" has only eighteen lines, and ends thus:

> And I, having the sense of something going on
> Without my knowledge, changes taking place
> That I should be concerned with,
> Sit motionless in the black car behind the hearse,
> Waiting to re-enter the world. (CSL 20)

The change in the last line is pivotal. Without the word "different," the passage no longer illustrates Doyle's argument especially well; in fact, the lines could be used to argue that a stubborn stasis attaches to the speaker, regardless of the ethereal changes happening, and that the world he re-enters will be substantially the same.

Textual variation is the chief reason for a scholarly edition of Purdy's poems. Several differing, equally authoritative, editions of a poem exist, but as yet none gathers these inconsistencies together to reveal and assess them. At present, readers must hunt for variants across Purdy's many books, or hope that their interpretations of a single copy will transcend confusion and contradiction. To compile a synoptic edition of Purdy's unruly texts will not be easy, but it does not have to be colossally overwhelming. The bibliographical way will be a rich avenue into every poem.

NOTES

1 For comparison, consider the following: *He said, "The sky is blue."* Reported indirectly, this sentence would become *He said that the sky was blue*, a rendering that emphasizes an observation at a given moment and hence a particular conversation. By contrast, reporting the speech as *He said that the sky is blue* would emphasize a general truth. Granted, one could also read the "snarling apeman" passage as confessional self-criticism by the speaker, but this interpretation would dilute the quarrel between the two men, whereas the thrust of the poem is, until the final line, to intensify it.

2 This passage, no matter which way you turn it, seems to contain an error, however. If it is read as a noun, "saves" (11) makes little sense. If a verb, "saves" (singular) is hard to link to any subject other than "that" (10) (plural, referring to "pronunciamentoes") and should therefore be "save." This emendation yields the sense, "the artist uses words sparingly, reserving potential emotions/thoughts for his own ends." Textual variation is the main reason for editorial intervention advanced by this essay, but correcting errors is traditionally another important reason.

REFERENCES

"The A-Frame." *The Al-Purdy A-frame Association*, www.alpurdy.ca.
Bensadoun, Douglas, dir. *At the Quinte Hotel*. Bravo!FACT, 2002. *YouTube*, 6 October 2006.
Bentley, D.M.R. *The Gay]Grey Moose: Essays on the Ecologies and Mythologies of Canadian Poetry, 1690–1990*. Ottawa: University of Ottawa Press, 1992.
– "Unremembered and Learning Much: LAC Alfred W. Purdy." In Lynch, Ganz, and Kealey, *Ivory Thought*, 31–50.
Birney, Earle. *David and Other Poems*. Toronto: Ryerson Press, 1942.
– *Now Is Time*. Toronto: Ryerson Press, 1945.
– *The Strait of Anian*. Toronto: Ryerson Press, 1948.
– *Trial of a City, and Other Verse*. Toronto: Ryerson Press, 1952.
Campbell, Sandra. *Both Hands: A Life of Lorne Pierce of Ryerson Press*. Montreal and Kingston: McGill-Queen's University Press, 2013.
Canadian Oxford Dictionary. 2nd ed. Edited by Katherine Barber. Toronto: Oxford University Press, 2004.
Djwa, Sandra. "Al Purdy: Ivory Thots and the Last Romantic." In Lynch, Ganz, and Kealey, *Ivory Thought*, 51–62.
Doyle, Mike. "Proteus at Roblin Lake." *Canadian Literature*, no. 61 (Summer 1974): 7–23.
Greetham, David. "What Is Textual Scholarship?" In *A Companion to the History of the Book*, edited by Simon Eliot and Jonathan Rose, 21–32. Oxford: Blackwell, 2007.

Heath, Tim. "Buried Bones and Ornaments and Stuff: Purdy's Reliquary Poetics." In Lynch, Ganz, and Kealey, *Ivory Thought*, 191–211.

Irvine, Dean. "Beyond Forgetting: Editing Purdy] Purdy Editing." In Lynch, Ganz, and Kealey, *Ivory Thought*, 71–90.

Johnston, Gordon. "Visiting Poet." In *But for Now*, by Gordon Johnston, 10. Montreal and Kingston: McGill-Queen's University Press, 2013.

Lampman, Archibald. "The Frogs." 1888. In *The Poems of Archibald Lampman*, 7–10. Toronto: University of Toronto Press, 1974.

Lynch, Gerald, Shoshannah Ganz, and Josephine T.M. Kealey, eds. *The Ivory Thought: Essays on Al Purdy*. Ottawa: University of Ottawa Press, 2008.

MacLaren, I.S. "Arctic Al: Purdy's Humanist Vision of the North." In Lynch, Ganz, and Kealey, *Ivory Thought*, 119–36.

Purdy, Al. *Being Alive: Poems, 1958–78*. Toronto: McClelland & Stewart, 1978.

– *Beyond Remembering: The Collected Poems of Al Purdy*. Edited by Al Purdy and Sam Solecki. Madeira Park, BC: Harbour Publishing, 2000.

– *The Blur in Between: Poems, 1960–61*. Toronto: Emblem, 1962.

– *The Cariboo Horses*. Toronto: McClelland & Stewart, 1965.

– *The Collected Poems of Al Purdy*. Edited by Russell Brown. Toronto: McClelland & Stewart, 1986.

– *The Crafte So Longe to Lerne*. Ryerson Poetry Chap-Books 186. Toronto: Ryerson Press, 1959.

– *In Search of Owen Roblin*. Toronto: McClelland & Stewart, 1974.

– *Poems for All the Annettes*. Toronto: Contact Press, 1962.

– *Poems for All the Annettes*. 2nd ed. Toronto: House of Anansi Press, 1968.

– *Poems for All the Annettes*. 3rd ed. Toronto: House of Anansi Press, 1973.

– *The Poems of Al Purdy*. Toronto: McClelland & Stewart, 1976.

– *Pressed on Sand*. Ryerson Poetry Chap-Books 157. Toronto: Ryerson Press, 1955.

– *Reaching for the Beaufort Sea: An Autobiography*. Edited by Alex Widen. Madeira Park, BC: Harbour Publishing, 1993.

– *Rooms for Rent in the Outer Planets: Selected Poems, 1962–1996*. Edited by Al Purdy and Sam Solecki. Madeira Park, BC: Harbour Publishing, 1996.

– *Selected Poems*. Toronto: McClelland & Stewart, 1972.

– *Yours, Al: The Collected Letters of Al Purdy*. Edited by Sam Solecki. Madeira Park, BC: Harbour Publishing, 2004.

Roberts, Charles G.D. "The Tantramar Revisited." 1883. In *Selected Poetry and Critical Prose*, edited by W.J. Keith, 51–3. Toronto: University of Toronto Press, 1974.

Solecki, Sam. "Chronology." In *Yours, Al: The Collected Letters of Al Purdy*, edited by Sam Solecki, 11–17. Madeira Park, BC: Harbour Publishing, 2004.

– *The Last Canadian Poet: An Essay on Al Purdy*. Toronto: University of Toronto Press, 1999.

Yeats, W.B. "Sailing to Byzantium." 1927. In *The Norton Introduction to Poetry*, edited by J. Paul Hunter, Alison Booth, and Kelly J. Mays, 595–6. 9th ed. New York: W.W. Norton, 2007.

9

Six Ways of Looking at "Elegy for a Grandfather"

Jamie Dopp

In *The Last Canadian Poet: An Essay on Al Purdy* (1999), Sam Solecki summarizes the importance of Ridley Neville Purdy in the work of his grandson Al: "Naming and honouring 'Rid' is both paradigm and prelude to the extended imaginative engagement with regional and national history that we encounter in Purdy's major work. The emotional and mnemonic wrestle with the almost mythic grandfather helps Purdy to find the voice that will 'name' his place, his ancestors, and ... [ultimately] himself" (*LCP* 146). Traces of the life of Old Rid appear in a number of Al Purdy's poems, including such well-known works as "My Grandfather Talking – 30 Years Ago" (1965), "My Grandfather's Country" (1968), and I*n Search of Owen Roblin* (1974), as well as in the novel *A Splinter in the Heart* (1990). Passages in Purdy's autobiographies, *Morning and It's Summer* (1983) and *Reaching for the Beaufort Sea* (1993), are also devoted to his grandfather. Of all the texts that name and honour Old Rid, however, the most distinguished is "Elegy for a Grandfather" – one of Purdy's finest poems. It first appeared in the 1956 collection *Emu, Remember!* After this, it reappeared, in no fewer than five revised versions, in five later collections; the final text appears in *Beyond Remembering*, the collected poems of 2000. The fact that Purdy rewrote and republished the poem so many times speaks to the importance it holds in his canon. Indeed, as I hope to show, the poem operates very much in the way Solecki claims, as a "paradigm and prelude ... [to] Purdy's major work," and a study of the different versions is an excellent way to understand some of the central elements, both formal and thematic, that define Purdy's poetic achievement.

The 1956 version of "Elegy for a Grandfather" is notable for the regularity of its form. As found in *Emu, Remember!*, the poem consists of three stanzas of seven lines each, the lines of similar length and mostly end-stopped, with an almost regular pattern of six stresses per line in groups of three, divided by a caesura. The poem contains end-rhyme throughout, mostly of the off-rhyme variety, and concludes with the repetition of "With a deck of cards in his pocket and a Presbyterian grin," which creates a ring of finality characteristic of a traditional closed-form poem. Here is the first stanza in full:

> Well, he died, didn't he? They said he did.
> His wide whalebone hips will make a prehistoric barrow,
> A kitchen midden for mice under the rough sod,
> Where relatives stood in real and pretended sorrow
> For the dearly beloved gone at last to God,
> After a bad century – a tough, turbulent Pharaoh
> With a deck of cards in his pocket and a Presbyterian grin. (ER 2)

Note the implied pauses after "hips," "mice," and "real" in the second to fourth lines above. These pauses, in combination with the six stresses, hint at the Alexandrine of classical verse. There may be a homage in the form to Charles G.D. Roberts's "The Tantramar Revisited," but a more likely influence is Dylan Thomas, whom Purdy acknowledged as a major influence in this period.[1]

A Thomas-like quality becomes more evident in the second stanza, which takes on a kind of lilting rhythm:

> Well, maybe he did die, but the boy didn't see it.
> The man knows now and the whimsical tale is told
> Of a lying lumberjack with a fist like a piece of suet,
> A temper like toppling timber and splintering words to scald
> The holy ears of an angel – and a beautiful man in a riot.
> But a bright, bragging boy's hero with a pocketful of gold.
> Like a neolith [sic] swear word from the opposite end of time. (ER 2)

Compare "Of a lying lumberjack with a fist like a piece of suet" with the six-stress line that is the rhythmic anchor of "Fern Hill" (from *Deaths and Entrances*, 1946): "Now as I was young and easy under the apple boughs" (*Collected* 150). Another possible source is Alfred Noyes's "The Highwayman," a favourite early poem of Purdy's, which contains not only a six-stress line but also many examples of alliteration: "The wind was a torrent of darkness among the gusty trees. / The moon was a ghostly galleon tossed upon cloudy seas" (373). The alliteration in the 1956 version of Purdy's "Elegy" has a hint of Old English about it, which, as Solecki points out, is likely a testament to the influence of Earle Birney, a mentor for Purdy in the 1950s (LCP 229).

The most irregular line in the 1956 version, from a rhythmical point of view, is the first. To find six stresses in that line, you have to force three stresses upon "They said he did" – a stretch. More likely, a stress is missing, which gives the line an anticlimactic feeling, as if it is part of a continuing argument, and the implied speaker is reluctantly conceding a point. The halting rhythm introduces halting content, for the half-rhetorical, half-defensive question ("Well, he died, didn't he?") emphasizes the difficulty of understanding or believing in the grandfather's death that is a key theme in the poem.

One formal oddity of the first version has to do with its use of rhyme. The first two stanzas keep to a regular *abababc* rhyme scheme ("did"/"sod"/"God," "barrow"/"sorrow"/"Pharoah," and "grin" in the first stanza; "see it"/"suet"/"riot," "told"/"scald"/"gold," and "time" in the second stanza). In the third stanza, however, the pattern breaks down, the rhymes less distinctly noticeable:

> No doubt at all that he's dead: a sadly virtuous voice
> Folded tragedy sideways and glossed his glittering sins.
> Old in his ancient barrow and no one could ever guess
> If the shy fox people play with his gnarled grey bones,
> Or a green Glengarry river sluices his grave and sighs.
> And earth has another tenant involved in her muttering plans,
> With a deck of cards in his pocket and a Presbyterian grin. (ER 2)

It's hard to know what to make of this difference. It's tempting to suggest that it reflects a lack of technical skill – this is an apprentice-poem, after all – but there is no way of legitimately asserting that. Perhaps it's an early, subtle, or unconscious example of Purdy's tendency to undercut his poems when they appear to be becoming too polished or beautiful-seeming. Robert Stacey makes a strong case that Purdy's mature work has elements of the picturesque in it, with its valuing of "roughness" and "irregularity" over polished form, and its attraction to imperfection as a source of poetic value (104). Later versions of the "Elegy," as we shall see, counterbalance the mythologizing of Old Rid evident in the 1956 version with a stress on the grandfather's imperfection. Perhaps the apparent falling apart of the 1956 rhyme scheme anticipates this process of counterbalancing.

The near-regular form of the 1956 "Elegy" is common in mid-twentieth-century modernist verse. Many poems from this era contain traditional elements that are de-emphasized in various ways, sometimes to the point where you have to be an especially attentive reader to notice their presence. Irving Layton, another important influence on Purdy in the 1950s, uses modernized traditional elements in a number of poems of the 1950s and early 1960s – see "Sacrament by the Water" (1956), "Whatever Else Poetry Is Freedom" (1958), and "Keine Lazarovitch 1870–1959" (1961). Birney also uses modernized traditional elements in "David" (from *David and Other Poems*, 1942), perhaps the best-known Canadian poem of the 1940s, with its brilliant succession of near-inaudible half-rhymes and its flexible five-stress line. Though traditional elements are de-emphasized in this kind of writing, something of their historical function remains. Most significantly for "Elegy for a Grandfather," the elements work to elevate the subject matter. Elegies, by definition, lend themselves to greater formality and a higher tone. Purdy's first version of the elegy for Old Rid combines the sense of elevation caused by the form with a thematic elevation of the grandfather into a near-mythic figure. That Old Rid is larger than life magnifies the boy's difficulty in comprehending his death – how could such a godlike figure end up dead? It also helps to underline another key question raised by the poem, which has to do with how such figures do or don't live on in those they leave behind.

It's tempting to summarize the significance of the 1956 "Elegy" by saying that it illustrates the kind of poetry Purdy will leave behind. Purdy is famous for the violence of his disavowal of his early work. Of his poems from the 1956–57 period, he has written that they were "pretentiously nonmeaningful, ambiguous ... in the manner of William Empson," with an overall result that was "disastrous" ("Disconnections" 207). There is some truth to this assessment when it comes to most of the poems in *Emu, Remember!* And yet, as we'll see from later versions of the "Elegy," it's a mistake to think that there is a total break between Purdy's poems of the 1950s and his later work. Some formal elements persist, and some key themes appear in embryo in the early poems. This is particularly true of the 1956 version of the elegy for Old Rid.

The second version of "Elegy for a Grandfather" appeared in 1968 in *Wild Grape Wine*. The first two stanzas look similar to the original poem, except that they have eight lines each instead of seven and contain some variation in line length. Here are the new first two stanzas in full:

Well, he died I guess. They said he did.
His wide whalebone hips will make a prehistoric barrow
men of the future may find and perhaps may not:
where this man's relatives ducked their heads
in real and pretended sorrow

> for the dearly beloved gone thank Christ to God,
> after a bad century: a tough big-bellied Pharoah,
> with a deck of cards in his pocket and a Presbyterian grin –
>
> Maybe he did die, but the boy didn't understand it,
> the man knows now and the scandal never grows old
> of a happy lumberjack who lived on rotten whiskey,
> and died of sin and Quaker oats age 90 or so.
> But all he was was too much for any man to be,
> a life so full he couldn't include one more thing,
> nor tell the same story twice if he'd wanted to,
> and didn't and didn't –[.] (WG 36)

There is an interesting hybrid quality to the free verse in these stanzas. Although there is no longer a regular pattern of rhyme, rhythm, or stanza form, the six-stress line persists in unchanged lines, as well as in lines, like the sixth of the first stanza, whose changed wording does not alter the underlying rhythm. There is something apt about this mix of change and continuity. As Solecki points out, the free verse characteristic of Purdy's mature poetry tends to retain rhythmical traces of his long apprenticeship in traditional forms: "the general influence [of the traditional forms] is there in the simple fact that Purdy's poems are closer to *vers libéré* than *vers libre*, since there is often a residue of traditional metre in them" (LCP 58). This is a subtle distinction but a valuable one. It implies the difference between things born free and things once captive but now liberated, the latter inevitably carrying the history of their captivity within them. Various details in this version of the "Elegy," including the appearance of the final dash (which suggests informality and ongoing process), suggest Purdy's embrace of greater poetic freedom; none of these details, however, erase the regularity that remains in the underlying rhythm, traces of which persist in all subsequent versions of the poem.

Another notable change in 1968 has to do with the introduction of a persona. The revision of "didn't he?" to "I guess" signals a shift away from an impersonal, T.S. Eliot–like mode to a mix of mythic and realist or subjective elements. The persona itself, of course, is very significant. What Dennis Lee calls the "quantum-leap" in Purdy's poetry of the early 1960s is directly related to Purdy's embrace of his distinctive persona, that half-autobiographical, half-fictional character with the colloquial, sometimes gruff, often joking, self-mocking, masculine voice (373). The persona is not deployed in the "Elegy" in the exuberant manner of "At the Quinte Hotel," but it does motivate revisions consistent with

Purdy's later assumed voice. Gone are the trace romantic elements of the 1956 version (ER 2), the references to mice and "the shy fox people," the characterization of the grandfather's story as "a whimsical tale," and the invocation of "a green Glengarry river" that "sighs" over the grandfather's grave. Gone also are a number of more formal and abstract passages. In the first stanza, for example, "gone at last to God" becomes "gone thank Christ to God" – a formulation at once more colloquial and more gruff; and in the second stanza, the abstract "sputtering words to scald / The holy ears of an angel" is replaced with concrete details about how Old Rid "lived on rotten whiskey, / and died of sin and Quaker oats age 90 or so."

A subtle effect of these changes is to align the voice in the poem more closely with the imagined voice of Old Rid himself. In the 1956 version, with its formal and almost euphemistic language, the voice of the poem seems aligned at times with the townspeople, as if, like them, the speaker (still unacknowledged, in keeping with the impersonal mode of Eliot) observes and judges the grandfather from a distance. The formal changes to the version of 1968 emphasize the affinity between Purdy the speaker and the Old Rid he speaks about, an affinity that becomes the explicit thematic focus of the new third stanza.

Another notable feature of the 1968 version is the way the original third stanza has been expanded into two; indeed, at twenty-six lines in total, the new third and fourth stanzas are longer than the entire 1956 poem. The first few lines of the new third stanza look similar to the original, but eventually the stanza is taken over by shorter lines. Here is the opening of the new third stanza:

> Just the same he's dead. A sticky religious voice
> folded his century sideways to get it out of sight,
> and lowered him into the ground like someone still alive
> who made other people uncomfortable[.] (WG 36)

The content here is the same as the 1956 version – a reassertion of the fact of the grandfather's death – but now the phrasing is more direct and the rhythm flat. The formal changes emphasize the speaker's sense of deflation when he must acknowledge the reality of the grandfather's death. "A sticky religious voice" replaces the "sadly virtuous voice" of the original (ER 2), and the burial of the grandfather is portrayed in more realistic detail than the single, abstract line of 1956 allowed ("Folded tragedy sideways and glossed his glittering sins," ER 2). The falling rhythm of "uncomfortable" extends the sense of deflation.

After the restatement of the grandfather's death, the stanza offers more details about his life: "barn raiser and backwoods farmer, / become an old man in a one-room apartment / over a drygoods store –" (WG 36). By conjuring up the image of Old Rid as the young Purdy knew him, these lines subtly reinforce the persona's resistance to accepting the grandfather's death. Almost as an acknowledgment of this reluctance, the stanza goes on to declare, for a third time, that the death of Old Rid really did happen:

> And earth takes him as it takes more beautiful things:
> populations of whole countries,
> museums and works of art,
> and women with such a glow
> it makes their background vanish
>   they vanish too,
> and Lesbia's singer in her sunny islands
> stopped when the sun went down –[.] (WG 36)

The newness of these lines is reflected in their form. Although "And earth takes him as it takes more beautiful things" has some affinity with the six-stress line of 1956, the shorter lines are different, not only in length but also in rhythm. The shorter lines tend to slow the reading down, and the irregular stresses create a more prose-like effect. The heavily indented "they vanish too" reads like a conversational interjection – almost an interruption. And, finally, the heavy enjambment of "islands / stopped" pushes the form toward versions of *vers libre* even more open than Purdy's own characteristic *vers libéré*.

The shorter lines of the new third stanza, and of the fourth stanza to follow, illustrate how the 1968 revisions undo or undercut the polished near-regularity of the 1956 "Elegy." At the same time, viewed as part of the poem as a whole, they attest to the coexistence in Purdy's writing of elements of free verse and elements of his conservative apprenticeship. From a rhetorical point of view, the shorter lines draw even more attention to the content of the third and fourth stanzas than those stanzas would have already because of their position at the end of the poem. There is also, I think, a thematic connection. The shorter lines formally emphasize Purdy's rejection of traditional beauty in poetry; at the same time, the content of the lines concerns the value of the "unbeautiful" Old Rid (WG 37). Form, then, reinforces content. Purdy's valuing of the unbeautiful complicates a reading of the third stanza, which, on the surface, seems to offer a conventional elegiac consolation in which the loss of the grandfather is portrayed as a tragedy lesser than the loss of other, more beautiful, people and things – and hence less to be mourned. If the unbeautiful is a source of value for Purdy, however, then the consolation of the third stanza is a rhetorical subterfuge. Indeed, the third stanza ultimately invokes things beautiful not to lower the value of Old Rid by comparison, but to stress the value of his being "decidedly unbeautiful."

Old Rid's persistence in the life of his grandson is made the explicit focus of the new fourth stanza:

> No, my grandfather was decidedly unbeautiful,
> 250 pounds of scarred slag.
> And I've somehow become his memory,
> taking on flesh and blood again
> the way he imagined me,
> floating among the pictures in his mind
> where his dead body is,
> laid deep in the earth –
> and such a relayed picture perhaps
> outlives any work of art,
> survives among its alternatives. (WG 37)

By the time this ending arrives, the 1968 version has already made clear that there are two main areas in which Old Rid persists. First, the grandfather represents, to his grandson, a model for living a full life. This meaning is implied in the 1956 version, but is made explicit by an important line in the 1968 "Elegy": "a life so full he couldn't include one more thing" (WG 36). At the same time, Old Rid becomes a muse figure. His way of telling stories becomes, at least in part, a model for Purdy's poetry. The unbeautiful, hypermasculine, transgressive voice that Purdy ascribes to Old Rid is akin to the voice that Purdy himself adopts at times, and Purdy's poetry, just like Old Rid's life and stories, works to unsettle Victorian niceties. The 1968 "Elegy," with its addition of the unbeautiful details about the grandfather and its overall substitution of elements consistent with the Purdy persona, formally enacts the poetic model implied by Old Rid.

The actual manner in which Old Rid persists is another question. The fourth stanza of the 1968 version offers, as an image of persistence, the grandfather, dead in the ground, imagining his grandson Al into existence. This image feels strained. Whether you read it as supernatural or surreal or fanciful, it seems out of keeping with the sensibility of the rest of the poem. Purdy himself seems to have been dissatisfied with the image, since it is the primary focus of subsequent revisions of the poem.

The phrase "250 pounds of scarred slag" is particularly revealing of Purdy's mature poetics. This line illustrates how the 1968 version stresses the specific over the abstract: the 1956 version describes Old Rid's size in various metaphorical ways, but now Purdy has put a number to it. "[S]carred slag" also illustrates a shift. No longer is there a hint of whimsy in the alliteration, as in the earlier "temper like toppling timber"; instead, an ugly mix of sibilance and the guttural underscores the "unbeautiful" quality of Old Rid. Also important to note is that the claim of "250 pounds" only *seems* realistic; in fact, the claim is not only a guess but also probably an exaggeration. Old Rid died when Purdy was a child. What Purdy knows about the physical size of his grandfather is the product of his own fragmentary memories and photographs like the one at the beginning of *Morning and It's Summer* (12). In the photograph, Old Rid is a large man, at least in comparison to the toddler seated beside him, but it is impossible to say that he really weighed two hundred and fifty pounds.

That "250 pounds of scarred slag" is probably an exaggeration reinforces the mythologizing of Old Rid in the "Elegy," a tendency that remains in the 1968 version, despite the revisions. At the same time, the line's apparently realistic quality, especially the emphasis on Old Rid's ugliness, illustrates Purdy's urge to undercut such mythologizing. So often in Purdy exaggeration coexists or competes with a desire to bring things and people back down to earth. This lowering occurs through self-effacement, in the case of his own exaggerated posturing, or by elements that deflate the mythically elevated, even as those same elements – like Old Rid's ugliness – tend to be recoded as positive, as expressing something real and authentic in opposition to a Victorian sensibility that might find them shocking.

One last point about the 1968 version: Old Rid's near-mythic stature is connected to his portrayal through the Purdy-child's eyes. The childlike perspective is stressed by the persistence of "the boy" in the second stanza, even as the rest of the poem is revised under the influence of the adult Purdy persona. Purdy's difficulty in comprehending or accepting his grandfather's death speaks to the persistence of this inner, childlike self, a persistence that is a feature of Purdy's persona generally and which adds a complicating other dimension to his often hypermasculine, Old Rid–like self-presentation. As Purdy himself puts it in *Morning and It's Summer*: "Some part of me still remains a child:

sitting on a pile of lumber behind Reddick's Sash & Door Factory in 1924, trying to explain to myself how I got here and what I'm going to do about it" (*MS* 11).

The 1968 version provides the template for the fourth and fifth versions of the "Elegy," which appeared in *Morning and It's Summer* (1983) and in the *Collected Poems* (1986), respectively. The 1986 version, in turn, is reprinted – as what I take to be the definitive version – in *Beyond Remembering*. The 1983 and 1986 versions, however, are bookended by two fascinatingly altered variations of the poem.

The first of these – and the third version of the "Elegy" overall – appeared in 1974 in *In Search of Owen Roblin*, which Solecki describes as Purdy's "most ambitious and sustained" attempt to explore "a past whose traces can still be found in the present" (*LCP* 152). Indeed, the book opens with an explicit meditation on the relationship between past and present, in which Purdy contemplates an album of ancestors that seems to offer a mirror for himself ("a temporal transvestite / wearing black old-fashioned clothes") while yet reminding him of the impenetrable mystery of the past ("frozen faces … [with] opaque bulging eyes") (*IS* n.p.; *BR* 238). The difficulty of knowing the past, along with the inevitable role of the interpreting subject, are crucial themes throughout *In Search of Owen Roblin*, even as the text as a whole makes an argument for the importance of knowing the past.

Excerpts from "Elegy for a Grandfather" form much of the second section of *In Search of Owen Roblin*. The excerpts are tied together with prose-like connecting passages, which flesh out certain elements and continue the meditation on the relationship between past and present begun in the opening. Here is the transition to the excerpts from the "Elegy":

> First my grandfather
> his name was Ridley Neville Purdy
> said in full for no part was separable
> With only a short plunge back
> thru time I can locate him
> just before 1930
> the year he died age 90
> standing in my mother's living room
> a giant among the knick-knacks
> a monster among the lace doilies
> his moustache like the ram on a bulldozer
> wearing clothes made of sheet iron
> built to last forever in 1930[.] (*IS* n.p.; *BR* 239–40)

Any reader not aware of the mythic stature of Old Rid would certainly get the message from these lines. The "First" that begins the passage alludes not so much to Old Rid's temporality – since he turns out to be younger than Owen Roblin and other historical figures portrayed in the book – as to his primacy in Purdy's imagination. The implication is that, in an important sense, history begins, for Purdy, with his grandfather.

Immediately after the transitional passage, *In Search of Owen Roblin* quotes slightly altered lines from the "Elegy" and tries to give more details to illustrate Old Rid's "misspent life":

> 250 slagheap pounds of ex-lumberjack
> barnbuilder and backwoods farmer
> all-night boozer and shanty wrestler
> prime example of a misspent life
> among ladies of the church sewing circle
> poker player and teller of tall tales
> to a boy – Listen he'd say Listen
> and when I listened everything happened
> again for the first time[.] (*IS* n.p.; BR 240)

The beginning of this passage combines lines from the third and fourth stanzas of the 1968 "Elegy" and may represent a stage in Purdy's rethinking of the ending of the poem; the reordering remains in the 1983 version. The details included hint at what is perhaps the most noteworthy aspect of the version of the "Elegy" that appears in *In Search of Owen Roblin*, namely that it adds surprisingly little to the portrait of Old Rid. Indeed, despite the licence offered by the form of the long poem, the 1974 version contains few new details about Purdy's grandfather, and these all fall within a narrow range of repeated motifs ("250 slagheap pounds ... a misspent life"). The relative lack of new information is evident again when Purdy imagines Old Rid's life as an eighteen-year-old lumberjack:

> six feet tall but only 200 pounds then
> axe balanced on his shoulder and stepping it out
> the long lifelong journey to anywhere
> having decided to live forever
> between these blue folded hills
> of the hawk's surveillance and sun's dominion
> at age 18 there he is[.] (*IS* n.p.; BR 241)

This passage adds little to the historical description of Old Rid. The lines contain a mix of imaginative reconstruction (what Old Rid might have looked like and thought about at eighteen) and possible projection (Purdy has no way of knowing what his eighteen-year-old grandfather was actually thinking, and may be projecting his own desire "to live forever" into the characterization).

The lack of new information is consistent with the treatment of Old Rid elsewhere in Purdy's work. Despite the fact that he looms so large in Purdy's imagination, Purdy's writings convey little about the actual life of his grandfather. This is the case even in Purdy's full-length autobiography, *Reaching for the Beaufort Sea*, which only quotes the three pages about Old Rid that appeared originally in the introduction to *Morning and It's Summer*. That introduction contains a couple of memorable vignettes about young Al and his grandfather, but even these remain, as Purdy puts it, "trivial moments in the 1920s ... gathered together at exactly the right time for memory to hold them" (MS 23). Major gaps in the portrait of Old Rid remain. The most obvious of these is that nowhere in Purdy's published work is there an account of how Old Rid actually became Purdy's grandfather – there is no account of his meeting Purdy's grandmother or of their life together, and, most glaringly of all, there is no account of Old Rid's relationship to his son, Purdy's father.

The lack of information extends to *A Splinter in the Heart*. Purdy's account of the origins of his novel makes it clear that the character of Portugee is a semi-biographical portrait of Old Rid (RBS 279). Even in the free space of fiction, however, Purdy can find little more to add about his grandfather than in the other texts. The portrait of Portugee repeats motifs – and even exact phrases – from earlier portraits of Old Rid. This is especially strange given that Patrick Cameron, the protagonist of *A Splinter in the Heart*, is sixteen years old, significantly older than Purdy was when he lost Old Rid, which extends the novelist's licence to invent scenes even further. And yet, beyond Patrick's short visit to Portugee on his deathbed, the most extended scene about the grandfather comes after his death, when Red McPherson, an old friend and fellow lumberjack, recounts how Portugee saved his life during a logjam (SH 156–7). Even this account, however, remains firmly within the range of repeated motifs; it also reads like any number of semi-romantic accounts of early Canadian lumberjacks, such as those of Joseph Montferrand, the legendary French-Canadian *bûcheron* of the Ottawa Valley (see Goyer and Hamelin).

The gaps can be explained in part by historical circumstance. Purdy's grandfather died when Purdy was a child. Purdy's first-hand knowledge, then, is limited to the bright but fragmentary memories of childhood. Just as importantly, Purdy's father died when Purdy was two years old, so he did not have access to an obvious source of stories about Old Rid (if Purdy's father had chosen to share them). The gap, however, is also indicative of the historical Old Rid's character. In different places, Purdy stresses how taciturn his grandfather generally was. In *Morning and It's Summer*, he writes that his grandfather "tolerated" him, and that Purdy "listened to his stories when he wanted to tell them, which wasn't very often" (*MS* 12). A similar portrait is found in "My Grandfather Talking – 30 Years Ago," which begins "Not now boy not now / some other time I'll tell ya," and ends with the grandfather confused and repeating himself: "whatever it was I was sayin / what I was talkin about / what I was thinkin of –?" (*BR* 90–1).

Interestingly, during the deathbed scene between Patrick and his grandfather in *A Splinter in the Heart*, the emphasis is on Portugee wanting to spend time with Patrick, while Patrick, in turn, looks for an excuse to get away (133–5). In other words, the emotional direction of the scene is reversed from other depictions of grandson and grandfather. Perhaps this reversal contains a bit of projection of Purdy's guilt about the death of his mother. In both *Reaching for the Beaufort Sea* and "On Being Human," Purdy confesses that he was typically anxious to leave his mother's deathbed, while she asked for a love that he could not return (*RBS* 173, *BR* 507–8).[2] The reversal intensifies Patrick's feelings of loss about Portugee. Patrick's decision to go home, despite Portugee's entreaties for him to remain, means that he misses his last chance to hear from his grandfather about his life. Perhaps Purdy's reversal of the emotional dynamic between grandson and grandfather helped him draw into sharper relief his own grief about Old Rid's death.

A similar reversal occurs in the line "Listen he'd say Listen" from *In Search of Owen Roblin* (compare with "Not now boy not now" in "My Grandfather Talking – 30 Years Ago," *BR* 90). This reversal implies emotional complexities similar to those in the novel, while underlining the book's larger argument about the importance of history. Viewed in the context of the paucity of detail about Old Rid, however, the imperative to learn history takes on another significance. Purdy suggests that his interest in Owen Roblin and other historical figures was a matter of accident. When he and Eurithe settled outside of Ameliasburgh, he writes, he "got interested in the place," since "what the hell else could I do" (*IS* n.p.; *BR* 245). Yet, as the second half of *In Search of Owen Roblin* unfolds, Purdy draws explicit parallels between Owen Roblin and Old Rid, O.R. and O.R.:

> Two characters in a forgotten melodrama
> conceived by an unknown author

> first my grandfather then Owen Roblin
> both parts minus stage directions (IS n.p.; BR 248)
> ...
>
> And now my mind zig-zags back and forth
> like the snake fences around Ameliasburg
> from Owen Roblin to my grandfather[.] (IS n.p.; BR 260)

And, in a key passage, Purdy reflects on how Owen Roblin and Old Rid occupy similar places in his imagination:

> Undoubtedly I made heroes of them
> men totally unlike myself
> and it never occurred to me
> that both were fallible
> human beings not entirely perfect
> not quite heroic not completely gods[.] (IS n.p.; BR 248)

The implication is that Owen Roblin is interesting not only on his own terms, but also as a way for Purdy to learn indirectly about Old Rid. Indeed, the text as a whole demonstrates that a key reason for studying history is that it allows us, by analogy, to learn more about our immediate ancestors. Purdy makes this explicit near the end of the text: "In search of Owen Roblin / I discovered a whole era / that was really a backward extension of myself" (IS n.p.; BR 270). Given Purdy's identification with his grandfather in the "Elegy," the "myself" in this passage could very well be read as "Old Rid."

The sixth version of "Elegy for a Grandfather" appeared in *Rooms for Rent in the Outer Planets*, the 1996 *Selected Poems*. What distinguishes this version is its new, extended, and somewhat bizarre ending – an ending that Purdy seemed to reject when he chose the fifth version for inclusion in *Beyond Remembering*. Why choose the fifth "Elegy" over the sixth as the definitive version?

The answer to this question begins, as I hinted earlier, with the fourth version of the "Elegy," which appeared in 1983 in *Morning and It's Summer*. The main difference between the 1968 and 1983 versions is the rewritten fourth stanza, which expands the eleven lines of 1968 into twenty-five lines. The stanza's new opening incorporates the lines from the third stanza that were moved in the 1974 version, and ends with yet another assertion of the reality of the grandfather's death:

> No, my grandfather was decidedly unbeautiful,
> 260 pounds of scarred slag,

> barnraiser and backwoods farmer:
> become an old man in a one-room apartment
> over a drygoods store,
> become anonymous as a dead animal
> whose chemicals may not be reconstituted. (MS 35)

The image of the "dead animal" has a touch of the uncanny about it, containing as it does a faint echo of the mice and "fox people" previously edited out of the 1956 version (ER 2). The new middle of the stanza replaces the surrealist image of the grandfather imagining the grandson into being from beyond the grave with a more realistic account of the grandson remembering the grandfather:

> There is little doubt that I am the sole
> repository of his remains: which consist of
> these flashing pictures in my mind,
> which I can't bequeath to anyone,
> which stop here: mustard, cayenne, ammonia,
> brimstone (trace only above his grave)
> – a dying soup-stained giant
> I will not let go of – not yet. (MS 35)

Both the 1968 and 1983 versions stress the uniqueness of the connection between grandson and grandfather, but the new lines ground this connection in an everyday reality consistent with other revisions of the poem. The new lines also emphasize the difficulty of sharing the personally known past with others – a continuation of the meditation on the subjective limits of historical research found in *In Search of Owen Roblin*. The list of strong-smelling substances evokes something of the grandfather's nature, but also subtly reinforces the difficulty of capturing the past: like the sense of smell itself, the list is evocative of character without offering a tangible historical memory. The "dying soup-stained giant" is perhaps such a memory, but it is also a repetition of earlier motifs ("died of sin and Quaker oats," WG 36), and it mainly works to reinforce the tensions in the poem between the godlike status of the grandfather and the fact of his death.

The connection between grandfather and grandson is given a last treatment in the new concluding lines:

> He scared hell [*sic*] out of me sometimes,
> but sometimes I caught myself, fascinated,
> overhearing him curse God in my arteries:

> even after death I would never dare
> admit to loving him, which he'd despise,
> and his ghost haunt the poem forever
> (which is an exaggeration of course,
> but he liked those) –[.] (MS 35)

These lines take on additional nuance when you understand their evolution from previous versions of the poem. The images of the grandfather "curs[ing] God in my arteries" and as a haunting ghost maintain something of the force of the supernatural portrayal of the grandfather in the 1968 and 1974 versions, but, in the last lines, Purdy admits that attributing such quasi-supernatural persistence to his grandfather is an exaggeration.

One apparently minor change in the new fourth stanza is actually telling. This is the revision of Old Rid's weight from "250 pounds" (WG 37) to "260 pounds" (MS 35). The revision suggests a continuation of Purdy's desire for greater realism: the roundness of "250 pounds" seems like an estimate, whereas "260 pounds" seems like it could be an actual measurement. At the same time, the choice of "260 pounds" as more realistic than, say, "240 pounds," is no accident: by further exaggerating the size of his grandfather, Purdy continues to mythologize him.

Only three small changes distinguish the definitive 1986 version of the "Elegy" from the version of 1983. Two of these are corrections of punctuation. In the first stanza, the colon in the line "after a bad century: a tough big-bellied Pharoah" is changed to a comma (CP 361). And a grammatical problem in the third stanza, in which a comma is followed by a capital letter – "he made people nervous, / And earth takes him" (MS 34) – is corrected by changing the comma to a colon and the capital *A* to a lower case *a* (CP 362). Neither of these seems of much import, although it is interesting to note that the grammatical problem is probably a leftover from Purdy's moving lines from the third stanza to the fourth in 1974. The change that has thematic significance is an alteration of the line "I will not let go of – not yet" (MS 35) to "I will never let go of – not yet" in the fourth stanza (CP 362). This change subtly encapsulates the tendencies characteristic of Purdy's mature work. The revision of "will not" to "will never" is a form of exaggeration: it adds emotion to the portrayal of Purdy's attachment to Old Rid, as in "I will *never* let [him] go!" (emphasis added). The exaggeration also adds drama to the qualification in the second half of the line. The line's first half now seems to arrive as a discrete thought, rather than as part of a larger thought represented by the whole line, and the correction seems to come now as a spontaneous response. It is as if Purdy first makes his exaggerated claim ("never!") and then, in the manner of "Trees at the Arctic Circle," realizes that he has "been stupid in a poem" (BR 104), and decides to offer a qualification ("well ... not yet").

The 1996 version of the "Elegy" (RR 124–6) contains a number of minor changes. In the first line, for example, Purdy reinserts the comma after "he died" that was present in 1956 but removed in 1968 and that is removed again in the final version of 2000 – a hint that he has reached the limit of useful revision. In the fourth stanza, "whose blood runs thin / in us" is changed to "whose blood runs thin / in mine," reinforcing the connection between grandfather and grandson, while the line "scared hell out of me" is changed to "scared hell outa me," the colloquial diction subtly reinforcing the connection between the voice that speaks the poem and the described voice of Old Rid. The line "I will never let go of – not yet" is cut entirely, despite its wonderful complexity, probably because it seemed redundant with the poem's new ending. Perhaps the most significant minor change is the insertion of "poker player and brawling lumberjack" after "barnraiser and backwoods farmer" early in the fourth stanza. These details about Old Rid first appeared, isolated from one another, in *In Search of Owen Roblin*. Inserting them here seems an attempt to flesh out Old Rid, but it just as clearly speaks to the limitations Purdy has encountered before: not only are the details repetitions from an earlier text, but they remain within the narrow range of terms with which Old Rid is consistently evoked.

The ending of the 1996 "Elegy" comes in the form of a new, thirty-seven-line-long fifth stanza. With this addition, the "Elegy" reaches eighty-six lines, quadruple the length of the original 1956 version, which had twenty-one lines. The stanza starts out as another self-correction in the style of "Trees at the Arctic Circle." The fourth stanza is cut off after "overhearing him curse God in my own arteries," and the fifth begins:

Which is a bit too romantic
– say again what he was:
parrot beak and watery blue
eyes that stared at you
like piss-holes in the snow[.] (RR 125)

"[P]arrot beak and watery blue / eyes" are details from the description of Old Rid in the introduction to *Morning and It's Summer* (MS 12). Like the "poker player" line above, they have the double quality of fleshing out Old Rid while also illustrating the dearth of new information about him. That Purdy describes what precedes these lines as "a bit too romantic" (RR 125) captures the way in which he has tried, in each new version of the "Elegy," to strike the right balance between evoking Old Rid as larger than life and grounding him in everyday reality – a hard balance to find. In 1983, "God in my own arteries" seemed an imaginary compensation for the loss of the supernatural imagery about Old Rid from 1968; now, in 1996, Purdy expresses doubt about allowing even this much mythologizing of his grandfather.

There is an irony in the self-correction that begins the 1996 ending, for much of what follows seems to propose a new, decidedly romantic, myth about Old Rid. After familiar assertions about Old Rid's larger-than-life character, the 1996 "Elegy" ends with the following speculation about his continuing presence in the world:

> I think it very probable
> there are other descendants
> besides myself
> but with different surnames
> than my own
> (knowing his propensities)
> maybe a few
> with that parrot beak
> watery blue eyes
> and not very loveable
> – on streets and rivers and mountains
> at meetings anywhere
> I will know them[.] (RR 126)

There is something moving about these lines. The words "not very loveable" resonate with a direct expression of love just before this passage: "yet I loved him / with no explanation for it" (126). This is the only place in Purdy's work where I can remember him directly stating that he loved his grandfather. The idea of other descendants also suggests a more diffused, shared heritage from Old Rid, and a temporary letting go of Purdy's claim to exclusive rights to his grandfather. This creates a hint of an end-of-life, almost Buddhist non-attachment to Old Rid. And yet, in the end, when the persona claims that he would "know" his fellow descendants anywhere, the poem devolves into a full-blown, blood-of-my-blood, kith-and-kin romanticism. For a moment the Purdy clan becomes a version of *clann Chalum Ruaidh* in Alistair MacLeod's *No Great Mischief* (1999), those red-haired cousins who, at a glance, have the ability to recognize one another, even in as unlikely a place as Calgary (30).

We can only speculate about why Purdy passed over this version of the "Elegy" and returned to the 1986 version for *Beyond Remembering*. At an early stage of this essay, I emailed Sam Solecki, the editor of *Beyond Remembering*, to ask if Purdy had given any reasons for the choice. He replied that he couldn't remember any. Even so, the choice seems like the correct one for various reasons. The most obvious reason is that the 1983/1986 ending seems so right. The final lines – "(which is an exaggeration of course, / but he liked those) –" (BR 437) – contain such a delicate balance between openness and a final assertion of key themes. The concluding dash feels right – a suspension in which, at the same time, the story goes on. Conversely, the 1996 ending seems to dissipate the energy of the poem. Even though the lines are short, the page-long fifth stanza hearkens back to the prolix style of Purdy's less successful poems from the 1970s, which tended to what D.G. Jones called "the seemingly interminable run-on sentence" (10). The lines themselves, sometimes only one or two words each, slow down the rhythm to the point where there is a distinctly anticlimactic trailing-off in the second half – until the final line rings out, all at once, with its rather forced sense of resolution.

There are a few last lessons I would draw from the changing versions of the "Elegy." One is the general observation that Purdy is a poet who revised his work constantly. This implies something about his character – perhaps a habit from the long apprenticeship – but also about poetry in the low-modernist mode in which speech-like rhythms predominate and in which there seems to be a direct expression of content. Low-modernist poems, like Purdy's, tend to present themselves as relatively artless. That "Elegy for a Grandfather" went through so many versions is a vivid reminder of how much art is involved in trying to create the impression of artlessness.

A second lesson has to do with how the six versions of the "Elegy" illustrate the delicate balance of elements that make up the best of Purdy's poems. His greatest poems contain trace elements from his poetic apprenticeship, even as they embrace new and sometimes very open forms. His great poems also contain a finely calibrated tension between his myth-making tendencies and his commitment to realism. This is the poet who, in the 1960s, wrote of the modernist emphasis on "archetypal myths" that it "seems rather a literary game to anyone who has to live in the world of now, go to work on a streetcar, say, and eat jam sandwiches for lunch" (SA 194); yet his larger-than-life portrayal of Old Rid hovers between realism and myth. Some of Purdy's most famous poems – "The Cariboo Horses," "Wilderness Gothic," and "The Country

North of Belleville" come to mind – have a similar productive tension between the mythic and the realistic.

Finally, as I worked my way through the six versions, I became aware of how much desire is involved in Purdy's seeking to know or honour Old Rid. Viewed as a sequence, "Elegy for a Grandfather" seems like a series of attempts, using different strategies, to bring back the near-mythic figure that Purdy's inner child will never let go of (at least, not yet). This makes the poem not so much an assertion of connection between grandson and grandfather as an expression of the *desire* for this connection. Version after version runs up against the limit of knowing that Purdy faces in trying to honour and name Old Rid. This limit is connected to his own circumstances but also speaks to the limit we all face in trying to honour and name our lost loved ones, since our attempts always run up against the selective nature of human memory and our impossible wish to bring lost ones back to life. Desire, then, and the limit of knowing, form the deep structure of the "imaginative engagement with local and national history" that Solecki sees in Purdy's "naming and honouring" of Old Rid (LCP 146).

NOTES

1 "The Tantramar Revisited" was published in *The Week* in 1883 and collected in Roberts's *In Divers Tones* in 1886.
2 From "On Being Human":
   – I wasn't feeling anything very much
   at the time and I guess it showed
   just thinking I'd have to travel
   those eighteen miles every day
   to visit her and grumbling to myself[.] (BR 507–8)

REFERENCES

Goyer, Gérard, and Jean Hamelin. "Montferrand, *dit* Favre, Joseph." In *Dictionary of Canadian Biography*. Vol. 9. University of Toronto/Université Laval, 2003–, http://www.biographi.ca/en/bio/montferrand_joseph_9E.html.

Jones, D.G. "Al Purdy's Contemporary Pastoral." *Canadian Poetry: Studies, Documents, Reviews*, no. 10 (Spring–Summer 1982): 32–43.

Lee, Dennis. "The Poetry of Al Purdy: An Afterword." In *The Collected Poems of Al Purdy*, edited by Russell Brown, 371–91. Toronto: McClelland & Stewart, 1986.

MacLeod, Alistair. *No Great Mischief*. Toronto: McClelland & Stewart, 1999.
Noyes, Alfred. "The Highwayman." In *Ballads and Poems*, by Alfred Noyes, 373–8. London: Blackwell and Sons, 1929.
Purdy, Al. *Beyond Remembering: The Collected Poems of Al Purdy*. Edited by Al Purdy and Sam Solecki. Madeira Park, BC: Harbour Publishing, 2000.
– *The Collected Poems of Al Purdy*. Edited by Russell Brown. Toronto: McClelland & Stewart, 1986.
– "Disconnections." *Essays on Canadian Writing*, no. 49 (Summer 1993): 180–221.
– *Emu, Remember!* Fredericton, NB: Fiddlehead Books, 1956.
– *In Search of Owen Roblin*. Toronto: McClelland & Stewart, 1974.
– *Morning and It's Summer: A Memoir*. Dunvegan, ON: Quadrant Editions, 1983.
– *Rooms for Rent in the Outer Planets: Selected Poems, 1962–1996*. Edited by Al Purdy and Sam Solecki. Madeira Park, BC: Harbour Publishing, 1996.
– *Starting from Ameliasburgh: The Collected Prose of Al Purdy*. Edited by Sam Solecki. Madeira Park, BC: Harbour Publishing, 1995.
– *Wild Grape Wine*. Toronto: McClelland & Stewart, 1968.
Solecki, Sam. *The Last Canadian Poet: An Essay on Al Purdy*. Toronto: University of Toronto Press, 1999.
Stacey, Robert David. "Purdy's Ruins: *In Search of Owen Roblin*, Literary Power, and the Poetics of the Picturesque." In *The Ivory Thought: Essays on Al Purdy*, edited by Gerald Lynch, Shoshannah Ganz, and Josephene T.M. Kealey, 103–18. Ottawa: University of Ottawa Press, 2008.
Thomas, Dylan. *Collected Poems, 1934–1952*. 1952. London: J.M. Dent, 1971.

10

"One of us":
Purdy, Elite Culture,
and the Visual Arts

Ernestine Lahey

A particular mythology surrounds the life and work of Al Purdy, according to which he was a rough-around-the-edges anti-establishment rebel who maintained a sneering attitude toward the ivory tower and elite culture. That he became one of Canada's most important twentieth-century English-language poets is treated within this narrative as something of a miracle. Mark Silverberg addresses this tendency in an article published in 2000, the year of Purdy's death; he notes that it is "a favourite critical gesture ... to construct Al Purdy as a native-speaking representative of the rugged, masculine, working-class Canadian" (233). For Silverberg, this "gesture" is problematic because it belies alternative approaches to Purdy's work: "[a]s we are encouraged to see Purdy as 'one of us', a representative Canadian big enough to fill a Mountie's uniform, we are also discouraged from seeing him in other ways" (228).

In the two decades since Silverberg's article appeared, there has been little further interrogation of the orthodox critical stance toward Purdy and his work.[1] If anything, the potency of the Purdy mythology has only increased since the poet's death. The emergence of a bona fide Purdy brand – one built up primarily through the efforts of friends and critics and on which Purdy himself had very little influence – has brought his poetry to a wider (and not so strictly elite) audience. At the same time, and perhaps partly as a result of the increasing democratization of his work, serious critical appraisal has become ever more marginalized, in some instances replaced entirely by the discursive trappings of nostalgia. In this chapter I attempt to provide redress by answering Silverberg's call to consider other ways in which we may view Purdy. My focus is on Purdy's relationship to and dialogue with elite culture and cultural practices, and, in particular, the visual arts. In what follows I prefer the term "elite culture" over "high culture." "High culture" refers to elite art forms, and thus subsumes much of the visual arts. However, I also discuss Purdy's stance toward academia – not "high culture," necessarily, but nevertheless an elite domain. I consider several lines of evidence which indicate that Purdy had an abiding interest in the visual arts, and I argue that Purdy's attitude to elite culture generally was not as straightforward as either he or his critics have proposed. I suggest that posthumous processes of "brand formation," together with Purdy's own tendency toward autobiographical posturing and revisionism, need to be considered together in accounting for his private and public enactments of class and culture.

"ONE OF US": PURDY AND THE COMMON-MAN MYTH

There exists among Purdy's critics a discursive habit of constructing Purdy as a rough-hewn, down-to-earth Canadian hero, a sort of poetic Everyman – plain-speaking, no-nonsense, and suspicious of the elite and elite culture. Manifestations of this reflex are not difficult to find; references to Purdy in which he is construed as the common man of Canadian letters are frequent, extending back to at least 1967, when Louis Dudek described him as "a Canadian aborigine, a natural primitive" (29). Three years later, George Bowering described Purdy's poems as akin to "a beer-parlour drunk's long rambling stories" (*Al Purdy* 100).[2] Since Purdy's death, this trend has gained momentum. A passage from the introductory essay in Linda Rogers's *Al Purdy: Essays on His Works* (2002) is representative of the tone of much recent commentary:

> Some people have it, what they call a jungle essence, not so much a peculiar odour (and Al did have that, his person a blend of passion and ink and, in the days before medical prohibition, a top note of beer) as a charismatic presence that changed the air in the room. I remember looking at him, not long before he died on Good Friday, his final antiestablishmentarian act, and thinking, He or They, Whoever, Whatever, threw the mold away when they made him. Al, our dear friend and stubborn adversary was at once himself and a poetic Paul Bunyan, the mythological Canadian of his generation. (Rogers 9)

Rogers's treatment contains all the elements of the classic mythology, in which Purdy is portrayed as an irksome (but lovable), hypermasculine, anti-intellectual mascot for Canada. Moreover, and exemplifying a second, more recent, trend in Purdy criticism, Rogers positions herself not only (or even primarily) as a critic of the poet's work, but also as his friend; it is a position which seems to justify an account that is at once effusive and unintentionally diminishing in its one-dimensionality.

Other contributions to the same volume, which includes both new and republished work, do little to counter Rogers's account. Dennis Lee writes in his essay of the "rough-hewn textures" of Purdy's poetry ("Poetry of Al Purdy," in Rogers, *Al Purdy*, 98–9).[3] Catherine Porter remarks that Purdy "approached [poetry] like he did bar brawls, directly, without blinking, never backing down" (155). She recounts her nervousness before first meeting the poet in a passage that reproduces several aspects of the common-man myth – failure, rebellion, and grit, culminating (despite all odds) in a miraculous ascension to poetic triumph. This myth is contrasted with Porter's narrative of her own experience as a privileged, educated, middle-class Canadian woman, thus rhetorically positioning Purdy in counterpoint to this experience:

> I was ... a sheltered, affluent, squeaky-clean twenty-something woman with too much education. And I was scared to death by my desire to write. Purdy was a 76-year-old high-school dropout who had rode [*sic*] the rails across the country during the Depression, taken up menial jobs at mattress factories to support his family (barely) ... and shown the courage to publish his own first volume of poetry himself in 1944. Since then, he had written more than thirty books of poetry and prose, won two Governor General's Awards and been honoured with the Order of Canada. (157)

Two other contributions to Rogers's volume are less anecdotal: Sam Solecki and Stan Dragland present careful analyses of Purdy's poetics, in which little (Dragland) or none (Solecki, "Al") of the "my pal Al" syndrome is evident. Rosemary Sullivan, in a piece reprised from a special issue of *Essays on Canadian Writing* (1993), is alone in her explicit acknowledgment of the craftedness of the Purdy persona, which she links to Purdy's tendencies toward self-invention and self-protection (66–8).

Rogers's volume is not unique in its replication of the common-man narrative. *The Ivory Thought: Essays on Al Purdy* (2008), the product of a 2006 symposium at the University of Ottawa, is a distinctly more scholarly volume, one which aims to provide a "balanced reassessment" of Purdy's legacy (Lynch, Ganz, and Kealey, "Introduction" 1). In this aim it largely succeeds. However, the common-man strain lives on in D.M.R. Bentley's concluding essay, in which Purdy is celebrated as "a true character," someone "with whom it was an uncomplicated pleasure to have a few beers," whose poems "convey a sense of ... his ribaldry, his unapologetic Canadianness, his hyper-, self-deprecating, and sometimes self-parodic masculinity, his bellowing, chugging, moving, and near-transcontinental larger-than-lifeness" (240). In a rhetorical move that appears to suggest a communion between the symposium participants and Purdy (and hence that frames the symposium as a site of homage rather than, or rather than foremost, one of debate), Bentley expresses regret that the other contributions to the volume do not reflect more of the "beery spirit" of the symposium itself, during which discussions often carried over from the conference room to the hotel bar (240).

Perhaps the best evidence of the continued fervency of the common-man myth in the wake of Purdy's death is *The Al Purdy A-Frame Anthology* (2009), a book produced to raise awareness and funds for the preservation of the poet's famous Roblin Lake home. The volume, which contains writing by Purdy, interspersed with reflections by his friends and contemporaries, is rife with elements of the orthodox Purdy mythology. Several authors echo Bentley's rhetoric of communion in their reminiscences about drinking with Purdy (see Galt, Helwig, McFadden, Reeves, Rosenblatt). Another expresses surprise that by the time he met Purdy, the poet had quit drinking (Heinricks). Lee's introductory essay describes "slam-bam six-pack Purdy" as "backslapping, argumentative, given to bumptious hijinks" ("Till" 16). Lee also notes that, with the completion of the A-frame house, Purdy and his wife were finally able to enjoy the comforts of a modern home, including electricity and indoor plumbing, but he is careful to add that "Al went on using the outhouse" (14). The outhouse is also the subject of a poem by Seymour Mayne (116), and figures again in an essay by Bowering in which Purdy appears as a rough-talking womanizer: "When [Bowering's wife] Angela in her short skirt climbed to look at the loft ... Al ... held the ladder and watched to make sure she didn't slip. When she went to the outhouse, he manfully flung the door open ... In our late-night discussion of poetics, Al said 'bullshit' twenty-one times and I said 'horseshit' eighteen times" ("Al" 76). Of course, the *Al Purdy A-Frame Anthology* is not a scholarly volume; it therefore stands to reason that the contributions should be more anecdotal than critical. My argument is not that accounts of Purdy's life by his friends should be judged by the same criteria as serious scholarship. Rather, I suggest only that it is problematic that such informal, anecdotal accounts dominate recent considerations of Purdy, far outnumbering scholarly treatments; and where the latter do exist (as in *The Ivory Thought*), they too may still be plagued by an insufficiently critical reliance on the common-man trope.

An important factor in the perpetuation of the standard narrative has been Purdy's success. He was already important enough during his lifetime to be able to work as a full-time writer. However, since his death he has come to be regarded not only as a significant Canadian poet, but also as a literary superstar (writ Canadian, of course), a "poetry celebrity" (Percy 190) worthy not just of readers but of *fans*. The activities of the Al Purdy A-frame Association – established in 2008 to preserve the Roblin Lake home – have been instrumental in cementing Purdy's celebrity status. An early initiative of the association was *The Al Purdy A-Frame Anthology*. A gala fundraiser in 2013 included performances by Canadian A-listers Gordon Pinsent, Margaret Atwood, and Gord Downie; their involvement in promoting the association's cause represents an inauguration of Purdy into an inner circle of Canadian celebrity.[4] Other A-frame Association activities have focused on the other end of celebrity, so to speak, namely Purdy's fans: the association runs an annual auction of Purdy paraphernalia (including photos of the poet and signed first editions), and the annual Purdy Picnic, which has been held at the A-frame since 2014, includes a visit to Purdy's grave. The work of the A-frame Association has also prompted outside initiatives in support of the cause. In 2014, for instance, Ontario brewery Barley Days launched a limited-edition Purdy-inspired beer – called "A Sensitive Man," after "At the Quinte Hotel" – with part of the proceeds going to the association.

All these activities have the hallmarks of a branding exercise, one in which Purdy is packaged, marketed, and sold (with the help of celebrity endorsements) in the form of souvenirs and fan "experiences." While the goals of the A-frame Association are undeniably noble, the unintentional outcome of such activities is the Disneyfication of Purdy, a process which inevitably smoothes over the inconsistencies and tensions in Purdy's life and work in favour of a simplified brand that is appealing to consumers. What appeals, in this case, is the myth of Purdy as "one of us." As Ken Babstock put it: "'He was literally a regular guy ... People who have read his poems fall in love with him for that reason – because he is not so up himself'" (qtd. in Barber).

Of course, it is not just the work of the A-frame Association that has contributed to the development of the Purdy brand, which is an outcome of a collective and emergent narrative built up out of many stories, told by multiple authors – including, most prominently, Purdy's publishers, readers, and critics (Holt 3). Other contributors to this emergent narrative include: filmmaker Brian D. Johnson, whose 2015 documentary *Al Purdy Was Here* featured many of the same celebrities who participated in A-frame Association fundraising activities; the City of Toronto and the several individual underwriters who enabled a statue of Purdy to be erected in Queen's Park in 2008; and the Bravo!FACT foundation and director Douglas Bensadoun with a short film dramatization of "At the Quinte Hotel" (featuring Gord Downie as the Purdy figure). Even the Prince Edward County tourism industry has been party to the simultaneous and interrelated processes of myth- and brand-formation by construing Purdy as an "authentic" piece of the county's history in the face of a regional trend toward gentrification (Reid). Through these and countless other converging stories, the myth of Purdy as common man – a myth to which Purdy himself contributed very little – has become entrenched in the Canadian cultural psyche. In the section that follows, I question the myth's relevance in light of one of the other ways in which we may choose to know Purdy.

PURDY, ELITE CULTURE, AND THE VISUAL ARTS

Underlying the common-man narrative is the tacit assumption that Purdy was suspicious of elites and elite cultural activities, including academia. One source for this assumption is Purdy's own tendency to decry anyone or anything he deemed to be inauthentic or "phoney," including academics and the "empty rhetoric" (RBS 219) of much scholarly discourse: "I mistrust almost entirely 'methods' and 'schools' of writing – those who act like 'I am the truth and the light,' the critic who knows best" (289). This bias is evident in comments Purdy made about the poet and scholar A.J.M. Smith, whom Purdy describes as "[s]o educated and cultured it fairly dripped from him, but not a phoney bone in his body" ("Disconnections" 195). A well-read autodidact, Purdy also bemoaned the ignorance of the students he taught at Simon Fraser University in 1970: "the lectures get me down. The kids know fuckall about CanLit, or just about any lit" (YA 155). Finally, in a now-famous first meeting with Atwood, Purdy allegedly insulted her by calling her an "academic." The story is recounted by Purdy in an essay in the 1993 special issue of *Essays on Canadian Writing*, where he contends that he never called Atwood an academic – because he "would never use such an insulting epithet" ("Disconnections" 197). In his autobiography, published in the same year, Purdy offers a slightly different account of the meeting: "Peggy A. received the mistaken idea that I was taunting her for being an academic. I deny this of course. I *referred* to the condition only" (RBS 231; emphasis original).

Here Purdy appears to exploit the polysemy of the word "condition" to undermine an otherwise straightforward denial of blame. *Condition* is roughly synonymous with both *state* (e.g., "the condition of the painting") and *precondition* or *prerequisite* (e.g., "on condition of anonymity"); in such uses, it has neutral connotations. However, *condition* also routinely co-occurs with terms relating to health problems ("underlying condition"), and as a result displays what corpus linguists call negative semantic prosody – even when *condition* is used with atypical collocates or alone, we should expect its negative connotations to be signalled for the listener or reader (Xiao and McEnery 107). Purdy's word choice here thus allows him to simultaneously suggest a neutral appraisal of academics, while obliquely alluding to academic life as an affliction. Not surprisingly, in a later reference to the incident, Atwood maintains that Purdy's comment was "an insult of course" (Johnson).

Purdy's outward low opinion of academia may have been a form of self-defence, an attempt to distract from feelings of inadequacy and insecurity about his own limited formal education (Fiamengo 169–70, Stevens 32). Whether Purdy did feel such insecurity is impossible to say. What is certain, however, is that if he expressed dismay at the phoniness and ignorance of academics and university students, he did so even as he sought to join their ranks. Unpublished letters in his papers at the University of Saskatchewan indicate that, in the 1960s, he took serious steps toward the pursuit of a university qualification, applying for a place as a student at York University. A July 1964 letter from the York University registrar's office acknowledges Purdy's application and requests further documentation (Draper). The collection also includes a letter of reference from *Tamarack Review* editor Robert Weaver, in which he has the following to say about Purdy's suitability for admittance: "I know nothing about Mr. Purdy's academic background, but I gather from a letter he has sent me that it would normally be less than adequate for your purposes. He is, however, one of the best poets writing in the country today" (Weaver).

There is no further correspondence to or from York University in the University of Saskatchewan collection. It is unclear whether Purdy followed up on the registrar's request, and if he did, whether his application was successful. Despite the import of this episode for what it reveals about his stance toward academia, Purdy's application to York is nowhere cited in Purdy scholarship. Neither his letter from York nor the letter from Weaver were included in Solecki's *Yours, Al: The Collected Letters of Al Purdy* (2004), and there are no further letters in that volume in which the application is explicitly mentioned, though a 1964 letter from Atwood contains an oblique reference which suggests that Purdy may have solicited her advice in the matter: "As for York U and you: I know little about it, but I expect that the university will get more out of you than you will out of it" (YA 86). Purdy's interest in York may have been purely strategic; perhaps he hoped a university degree would qualify him for a permanent teaching post, thus granting him a measure of job security. Nevertheless, the fact of his application undercuts his own anti-academic rhetoric and challenges the prevailing mythology. It is crucial that it be counted among the "materials for a biography of Al Purdy" (Solecki, "Materials") if an unbiased picture of his life is to emerge.

Another aspect of Purdy's biography that throws the common-man myth into question is his attitude toward and dialogue with the visual arts. Appreciation of the visual arts is generally regarded as a supremely elite practice, as John Berger notes: "The majority of the population do not visit art museums ... [They] take it as axiomatic that the museums are full of holy relics which refer to a mystery which excludes them" (24). As such, it might strike us as incongruous to find that Purdy's interest in the visual arts (and in painting in particular) was both earnest and enduring. His papers at the University of Saskatchewan contain numerous references in his earliest unpublished or uncollected poems to painting and painters.[5] These references are surprising in light of comments by Solecki, who contends that "[Purdy's] interest in the visual arts, Canadian or other, was minimal. Al was not a gallery-goer, and in conversation he rarely recognized the names of prominent contemporary painters."[6] The papers at the University of Saskatchewan, and indeed Purdy's later published poetry, tell a more nuanced story. If Purdy did not know much about "prominent contemporary painters," in his poems at least he presented himself as someone who was conversant with the works of the European masters.

The University of Saskatchewan collection includes seven leather-bound typescript volumes of Purdy's earliest unpublished poetry, dating from the late 1930s. Already in this very early poetry – widely acknowledged, including by Purdy himself, as the unsophisticated work of an immature writer – we see the poet playing with the theme of art and artists. In the earliest of these books ("The Road to Barbary," dated 21 March 1939), a poem called "The Artist's Dream" reads:

Oh Jeanie my Jeanie go back o'er the sea
The picture is painted of you
...
The artist is dreaming of Jeanie away
...
His brushes forgotten is losing his way.

Also in the University of Saskatchewan collection are hundreds of loose sheets of undated drafts and finished poems composed in the 1950s and 1960s. Among these are several in which painting features as a central organizing metaphor: "Artist's Magic," "Still-Life," "Mind-Painting," "She said herself into this poem" ("I feel somewhat like a bad painter / trying to cope with sunset"), and "After Yeats' Lapis Lazuli" ("My engraving, woodcut, medieval tapestry or water colour / doesn't sit on the mantel piece"). Others make reference to particular European painters or particular periods in European art history, such as "What about Gauguin in Tahiti?," "Spanish Hilltop" ("Here, on top of a hill, is El Greco"), "The Dutch Masters," "Looney with Sunlight" ("Looney with sunlight, van Gogh stood and stared"), and "In Bed" (which mentions both Van Gogh and Eugène Delacroix).

Van Gogh held a particular fascination for Purdy. Several of Purdy's poems contain allusions to his paintings – the unpublished poems "Looney with Sunlight" and "In Bed," both mentioned above, but also the published poems "The Country of the Young," from *North of Summer: Poems from Baffin Island* (1967), "I Think of John Clare," from *The Woman on the Shore* (1990), and "To Paris Never Again," from the volume of the same name (1997). The cover of *Rooms for Rent in the Outer Planets* (1996) is a reproduction of Van Gogh's *Café Terrace at Night* (1888). Purdy's library at Ameliasburgh included a book on Van Gogh that features colour plates and a biographical essay by American art historian Meyer Shapiro (Solecki, "Ameliasburg"). His Sidney, BC, library contained a catalogue for a 1960 exhibition of Van Gogh paintings and drawings at the Montreal Museum of Fine Arts, suggesting that he may have seen this exhibition (Solecki, "Sidney"). Finally, photographs taken by Solecki of Purdy's Sidney home show Van Gogh prints on the bedroom wall. Though the prints are mostly out of frame, one is almost certainly *Vase with Fifteen Sunflowers*; the other could be *Wheat Fields with Cypresses* (Solecki, "Unpublished"). Van Gogh was largely self-taught, and developed his signature style only late in his career. It may have been that Van Gogh appealed to Purdy because he saw these (or other) parallels with his own life and artistic development.

Two poems in the Saskatchewan collection – "Here's Kane" and "Paul Kane" – focus on nineteenth-century Irish-Canadian painter Paul Kane. "Paul Kane" challenges the common-man myth by showcasing Purdy's understanding of the trajectory of twentieth-century Canadian art and art criticism, the nation-building function of art in Canada, and the importance of the idea of the North in this context:

> If one should ask, "What is Canadian art?"
> Then lead him to the north, the solemn land,
> Where Thomson left his brush beside a northern lake ...
> And take that stranger gently by the hand:
> Here's Morrice with his half-Parisian style,
> And Emily Carr whose totems drink the rain;
> Then lead your skeptic through the painted past
> To where the Indians wait, and say, "Here's Kane."

Purdy's treatment here of the central, interrelated Canadian cultural themes of identity, geography, and representation show him grappling with many of the same issues that have troubled and fascinated Canadian intellectual elites. The indexical final words – "Here's Kane" – become the title of the second poem on Kane, in which Purdy again shows his familiarity with Canadian painters and their works, referring to J.E.H. MacDonald's *The Solemn Land*, as well as to Homer Watson ("Here's Watson, called / the Canadian Constable") and Cornelius Krieghoff ("And Krieghoff, called the Canadian Breughel"). Ekphrastic description of works by these artists furthermore suggests that Purdy may have seen their canvases first-hand. He writes of the "[l]ead coloured lakes" in *The Solemn Land*, and of Watson's work he writes: "so close to earth / his paintings brought a blade of grass to life." The suggestion of a first-hand viewing is clearest in his lines on Kane:

> The light inside a building's much too dull
> For Kane's "Encampment" hanging on the wall;
> It takes the sun – the golden sun, to bring
> His work to life; museum shadows fall
> On buffalo lodges, savage copper faces,
> Obviously posed and patently unreal.

There are several Kane paintings with "encampment" in the title – *Indian Encampment on Lake Huron*; *Indian Encampment on Big Bay at Owen Sound*; *Encampment, Winnipeg River*; *Native American Encampment* – as well as sketches and engravings: *Encampment with Conical Shaped Lodges*, *Encampment amongst the Islands of Lake Huron*. It is not clear which of these (if any) Purdy refers to in this poem, as there does not appear to be any picture by Kane titled simply *Encampment*. "Here's Kane" goes on: "The critics had a field day with Kane's 'Encampment.'" This reference, together with the mention of obviously posed Indigenous subjects, suggests that Purdy may in fact have been conflating two Kane paintings: *Big Snake, Chief of the Blackfoot Indians, Recounting His War Exploits to Five Subordinate Chiefs* and *Assiniboine Hunting Buffalo*.[7] The first of these depicts a group of Indigenous warriors. The second has been remarked upon for its portrayal of a breed of horses unknown in the Canadian West at the time of its painting (Davin 616). Both Kane's critics and the posed Indigenous subjects come up again in "Paul Kane":

> He painted Indian chiefs. He posed them neatly
> With pseudo-Arabic horses – that was when
> He made a big mistake, because the critics
> Said Arab mounts were not imported then[.]

Donald W. Buchanan's *Canadian Painters: From Paul Kane to the Group of Seven* was among the books Purdy had in his library at his Sidney home (Solecki, "Sidney"). It includes discussion of all the artists mentioned in "Paul Kane" and "Here's Kane," save Emily Carr. Given the apparent conflation of themes in Purdy's poems on Kane, it may be that Purdy relied on this book (and perhaps other sources) as the inspiration for his poems, rather than any actual first-hand experience with a Kane canvas.

Allusions to painting are prevalent in Purdy's early unpublished and uncollected work, and are perhaps symptomatic of his early reliance, for both his poetic subject matter and his style, on a romantic model of poetry as "high art." However, his later poetry attests to his continued fascination with painters and painting. Some of his best-known poems feature allusions to painting and painters: "Wilderness Gothic," from *Wild Grape Wine* ("That picture is incomplete, part left out / that might alter the whole Dürer landscape," WG 51; BR 158); "The Country of the Young," which alludes to work by A.Y. Jackson, as well as Gauguin, Van Gogh, and Pieter Bruegel the Elder (NS 79; BR 126); and "Poem for One of the Annettes," from *Poems for All the Annettes* (1962) ("big unpainted Rubens breasts," PA 7; BR 35), for instance.[8] And there are several artists who feature repeatedly in Purdy's work: Van Gogh, as in "The Names the Names," from *To Paris Never Again*; Bruegel (in addition to "The Country of the Young," "Notes on Painting," from *The Cariboo Horses*; "The Son of Someone Loved–," from *Piling Blood*; and "Bruegel's *Icarus*," from *To Paris Never Again*); and Katsushika Hokusai ("Hokusai at Roblin Lake," from *Poems for All the Annettes*; "Japanese Painter," from *Wild Grape Wine*; and "Old Man Mad about Painting," from *Sex and Death*). Purdy's abiding interest in painting, and in the stylistic motif of the painter, informs his poetry, from its first stirrings in unpublished works until his last mature volume.

A draft of "Poem with Vase with Mountain Landscape" (later published in *Poems for All the Annettes*) in the University of Saskatchewan collection is interesting for what it reveals about Purdy's developing poetics. By the time he wrote it, the strict syllabic parallelism and rhyming of his earliest work had already been replaced with a freer verse form. His use of formal Latinate terminology ("avoirdupois," PA 32) prefigures this tendency in later poems, such as "Trees at the Arctic Circle" ("*Salix Cordifolia*," NS 29; BR 102) or "The Beach at Varadero" ("*latifundia*," WG 22; BR 137).[9] Purdy's interest in Greek mythology, also prominent in much of his later work (and especially *North of Summer*), is likewise in evidence here:

Poem with Vase with Mountain Landscape

Its lines were reasons
for astronaut Daedalus:
the vase
(76 ounces of fired clay
with mathematics included)
revoked its own weight,
but held a mountain's avoirdupois
with the belted slenderness of a girl
in the last pause
before she's a woman ...

The poem's title mimics the archetypical vocabulary and syntax of still-life painting titles (e.g., Van Gogh's *Vase with Fifteen Sunflowers*), inviting the reader to reconsider the arbitrariness of the textual symbol. In the published version of this poem (PA 32), this effect is strengthened through the adjustment of the poem's layout. The poem's lines are no longer uniformly justified left, as they are in the draft version; this variable justification contributes to the sense of the text as a visual, as well as a linguistic, medium. This concretization strategy is one Purdy would use again, more explicitly, in poems such as "Metrics," where the words "we raise it into an east wind" are configured in a tent-shape (NS 37; BR 105), and in "Archaeology of Snow," where the poem's layout visually represents the lovemaking of the poem's subjects and the imprint of the female figure's buttocks in the snow (PA 15–18; BR 37–41).

"The Sculptors," written during Purdy's travels in the Canadian Arctic in 1965 and collected in *North of Summer*, focuses on the work of traditional Inuit carvers. His encounters with Inuit art may also have been the inspiration for a review of the book *Sculpture of the Eskimos*, by George Swinton – Purdy erroneously refers to the book as *Eskimo Sculpture* – which is among his papers at the University of Saskatchewan. The review is interesting not only because it shows Purdy in the role of art critic, but – and perhaps ironically in light of this last point – because it also suggests his feelings of inadequacy about his lack of knowledge of Inuit art. His uncertainty about his suitability to appraise the book is suggested in the first sentence, in which he turns to the work of another writer – scholar and poet Louis Dudek – for an opening: "Here's a quote from a Louis Dudek piece … that seems relevant to my own ignorance on the subject of Eskimo sculpture." Elsewhere, however, Purdy's remarks on sculpture have been more assured. In a letter to long-time correspondent Margaret Laurence, he compares Inuit and African sculpture to "white" sculpture, noting that the former are "much more typical of those cultures than white sculpture is of white culture, especially since the physical medium of soapstone and ivory is more limited than material available to white sculptors" (Purdy and Laurence 44). While these comments are problematic for other reasons – Purdy sets up a crude (some might say racist) dichotomy between "white" and non-white sculptural traditions – his remarks indicate that he had (or at least felt he had) sufficient knowledge of stylistic conventions in different sculptural traditions to enable him to make the comparisons he offers here.

North of Summer contains colour reproductions of eight oil sketches of the Arctic by Group of Seven painter A.Y. Jackson. Purdy's opinion of Jackson's work, and of the *North of Summer* sketches specifically, is difficult to ascertain. Letters from Purdy suggest that he did not care for Jackson's aesthetic and felt the sketches in *North of Summer* were a poor match for his poems. It is perhaps for this reason (in addition to the more obvious fact that it was unusual for authors to have much say in the design of their book covers) that some have assumed that the decision to include Jackson's work in *North of Summer* was one in which Purdy had little involvement (MacLaren 123; van der Marel 42). In a letter to George Woodcock, Purdy writes: "They don't fit, not the way I feel or talk" (Purdy and Woodcock 19). He is even more scathing in a letter to Laurence: "I think they're terrible, and Jackson is a study in retarded development … [Jackson's] paintings look like geriatric vomit done from habit. One step above *Autumn Woods* if you ever saw that abortion on suburban walls" (YA 129).[10] It has been suggested – no doubt on the basis of such remarks – that Jack McClelland, of McClelland & Stewart, was primarily responsible for the decision to include Jackson's sketches in a book that consequently "panders" to a southern Canadian vision of the Arctic (MacLaren 120, 123). I.S. MacLaren suggests that readers must see past those aspects of the book's production and marketing for which McClelland was responsible if they are to access the alternative vision of the North offered by Purdy (123).

It is true that Purdy initially had different plans for the volume. Published letters show that he had originally asked an Inuit artist to make some drawings to accompany his Arctic poems (YA 113). Unpublished letters suggest that he was also considering another publisher – Alan Bevan – and another artist, in the event that McClelland & Stewart declined the project (Purdy, letter to Kilvert). In fact, Barbara Kilvert may have been the driving force behind the eventual decision to include Jackson in the *North of Summer* project. Kilvert, a public-relations officer for the Hudson's Bay Company during the 1960s, assisted Purdy with practical arrangements ahead of his trip – advising him regarding the purchase of winter clothing from the HBC's Merchandise Depot, for instance – and was also responsible for including "The Country of the Young" in a 1967 special issue of the HBC magazine, *The Beaver*, featuring the same Jackson reproductions that appear in *North of Summer*.[11] In a letter dated 23 November 1965, Jack McClelland writes to Purdy: "Yes I did talk to Barbara Kilvert and I think it is an extremely interesting idea." While it is unclear from this short note what the idea is, further letters from Kilvert to Purdy suggest that it may have concerned the inclusion of the Jackson sketches. On 14 December 1966, Kilvert writes to Purdy: "I haven't heard anything more from McClelland but have written to Jackson and I enclose a copy." On 12 January 1967, she again writes: "MARVELLOUS about the book ... I got a letter from A.Y. yesterday which said: 'Fine and dandy, go ahead with my permission for reproduction rights.'" Another letter (3 February 1967) confirms: "I saw Jack McClelland again ... and our plans are going ahead in regard to the Jackson project."

There is further reason to question the veracity of Purdy's negative comments regarding Jackson's work, and by extension the claim that Purdy was not involved in the decision to include Jackson's sketches in the book. In a letter to his wife, Eurithe, composed during his stay in the Arctic (15 July 1965), Purdy writes:

> Intend to work on this "Arctic Diary" piece for MacLean's [*sic*], and it's fortuitous that A.Y. Jackson is at Pang [Pangnirtung, Baffin Island], which will give me more to write about – ... Jesus – tho, wouldn't it be wonderful if I could get some A.Y. Jackson pieces, pictures I mean – to illustrate both article and book. He probably has a high opinion of his own value. Still, even a frontispiece by old A.Y. might make the thing sell out. What are poems compared to the Group of Seven? Whee! Zowie! Etc.

Purdy's comments on Jackson's work following the publication of *North of Summer* cannot easily be accounted for in light of his initial enthusiasm, but it is clear that Purdy *had* an opinion, as well as an awareness of the significance of Jackson's oeuvre.[12] His remarks before and after the publication of *North of Summer* may be hard to reconcile, but it would be wrong to dismiss either as an uninformed response. Here as elsewhere we see a version of Purdy that does not sit comfortably with the common-man narrative and its implicit rejection of elite culture. Furthermore, his stated distaste for the work of one of the darlings of twentieth-century Canadian high culture suggests a measure of self-assurance that likewise seems out of place within this narrative.

Purdy was an avid book collector. His interest in the visual arts was reflected in the books in his personal libraries at his Ameliasburgh and Sidney homes, catalogued after his death by Solecki. Several volumes on art, including the biography of Van Gogh mentioned above, are included in the Ameliasburgh catalogue (Solecki, "Ameliasburg"). The Sidney catalogue includes more than two dozen books on art, from surveys of Western art to books on particular mediums and schools. Canadian art and art institutions are represented by a Royal Ontario Museum catalogue, several books on the Group of Seven and Tom Thomson, two catalogues of the McMichael Collection, and copies of the magazine *Canadian Art* (Solecki, "Sidney"). These inventories are incomplete. Several shelves of books from the Sidney library had already been sold or discarded by the time Solecki prepared his catalogue in 2006 (email from Solecki, 1 November 2016). A selection sold to a private collector has likely never been catalogued (email from Solecki, 11 January 2017). Another selection of approximately three thousand books was sold to the Laidlaw Library of University College, University of Toronto. These books have been catalogued, and while most of them deal with Canadian history and literature, there are also a few books on art, including an autobiography of Robert McMichael (founding curator of the McMichael Collection), a biography of Tom Thomson, and a biographical dictionary of Canadian creative and performing artists.

It may be true that Purdy was not a gallery-goer, as Solecki notes. However, this does not preclude an interest in art, and Purdy's Ameliasburgh and Sidney libraries indicate the breadth of his appreciation of both international and Canadian art and artists. As for his familiarity with contemporary artists – "in conversation he rarely recognized the names of prominent contemporary painters" – books on Québécois painter Jean-Paul Lemieux, Italian painter Giuseppe Zigaina, and American painter Andrew Wyeth in the Ameliasburgh and Sidney catalogues suggest that he may have been more knowledgeable about contemporary art than is suggested by Solecki's comments. Purdy was also personally acquainted with a number of contemporary figures in the Canadian art world, including Marian Scott, whom he met in Montreal in the early 1960s. The wife of poet F.R. Scott, Marian Scott was an important Canadian modern artist. In his 1993 autobiography, Purdy writes of her and of another artist, the unrelated Louise Scott: "And we met some painters. Marian Scott, Frank's wife, was a very good artist. Louise Scott, no relation, whose work I thought impressive. A sort of bohemian art colony in Montreal, gradually becoming surer of its own abilities, or at least pretending to be sure" (RBS 155). Correspondence at the University of Saskatchewan also shows that Purdy was acquainted with poet and artist Roy Kiyooka (1926–94). While the friendship may have had more to do with Kiyooka's reputation as a poet, an undated letter from Kiyooka appears to be a response to a question from Purdy about Kiyooka's work as an artist. It begins: "Dear Al: the last painting I did was 5' × 9' it took me approx four months to complete."

In 1983 Purdy wrote Solecki a letter which neatly encapsulates the contradictions in his stance toward the visual arts, and toward elite culture more generally: "I hate the idea of 'painterly' writing. I was once commissioned to do a review of Joyce Weiland for *Arts Canada*. I thought she was terrible and all the reviews about her shit. They turned down the review when I said so. It's like wine-talk, this painterly stuff, pretension without body" (YA 369). Purdy was unapologetic in his criticism of those artists whose work he disliked, and his outspokenness may have rankled some within the arts establishment in Canada (the *Arts Canada* editors, for instance). However, the evidence belies a view of Purdy as either uninterested or uninitiated in the visual arts. Purdy's poetry shows a continued fascination with the motif of the painter. His library demonstrates a broad interest in the visual and creative arts, across various modes and art-historical moments. The very fact of his having accepted the offer to review Weiland's work suggests his confidence in his abilities in this regard. If Purdy was sometimes disparaging of intellectuals and other cultural elites, this may have had less to do with his interest in elite cultural practices per se, and more to do with what he perceived as the deliberate obtuseness of much arts-and-culture scholarship and criticism. His comments on the pretension of art-critical discourse echo his remarks on the "empty rhetoric" of academics and literary critics, suggesting that the common thread in his stance toward both was his intolerance of linguistic registers that distract from what is truly important in both literature and art – the work itself.

Like any myth, the common-man myth is grounded in a number of truths. Purdy's writing style – in both his poems and his prose – is characterized by its reliance on vernacular diction and the manipulation of typographical and orthographical norms to mimic phonological features of spoken discourse (e.g., he frequently used the forms "hafta" and "migawd"). His poetic subject matter was often commonplace, and sometimes base (e.g., "When I Sat Down to Play the Piano," from *North of Summer*). The facts of his life also lend themselves to mythology. Purdy was largely self-educated. He worked countless menial jobs before his success as a writer meant that he could live from his writing alone. He drank. These and other aspects of his writing and life constitute the objective materials from which the prevailing view of him has been derived. Purdy himself was complicit in assembling these materials in such a way as to allow the common-man myth to flourish. Stan Dragland notes, for instance, that Purdy frequently began readings with "Home-Made Beer" and "At the Quinte Hotel" (18). However, Purdy also openly acknowledged and contested the common-man narrative. In a letter to Dennis Lee, he writes: "I certainly reject that 'common man' bit – come on, Dennis! Really ... I make no claim to be extraordinary, an intellectual or what have you, but whatever sensibilities I have are not at all similar to those you find in a pub" (YA 202). Eurithe Purdy, too, has resisted this view of her late husband. In reflections published in the *Al Purdy A-Frame Anthology*, she confesses her dislike of one of Purdy's best-known poems (and the one which arguably contributes most forcefully to the common-man myth), "At the Quinte Hotel," citing its macho tone as "off-putting" (52). She notes that, while Purdy has been branded with this hypermasculine identity, "he was much more than that" (52). It is a corrective to the picture of Purdy that she has offered elsewhere. In *Al Purdy Was Here*, she remarks: "[t]here was a lot of a poetic persona, yes. At home he was very quiet. Unless he was boozing it up with pals" (Johnson).

The speaker of Purdy's "The Invisible Man" is a still-life model in an art class taught by Group of Seven painter Arthur Lismer:

> And then this Group of Seven guy
> who ran the place came round
> and looked at everyone's work
> in which I was abstracted from me
> and nodded approvingly at some of it
> and didn't notice me up there[.] (NSM 97)

Like the version of Purdy dramatized here, the real Al Purdy has been displaced by our representations of him, each of which has been built up out of the same stock of truths. The Purdy of "The Invisible Man" is, like the real Purdy, the focus of a communal gaze which constructs him in such a way as to render him invisible to the very authorities whose work it is to regard him – here metonymically represented by Lismer. Efforts to memorialize Purdy, while undertaken with the noblest of intentions, have led critics and scholars to cling to an oversimplified, ready-made narrative in which the complexities of his life and work dovetail into an attractive and easily digestible brand. Purdy may at times have helped perpetuate the common-man narrative that has effaced the force of other perspectives on his work, but its consolidation as critical orthodoxy in the years since his death is the responsibility of other authors. The irony that so much of this perpetuation comes from elite scholarly corners seems to be lost on those responsible. As if in some final posthumous trickery, Purdy seems to have ensured that the joke's on us.[13]

NOTES

1 For exceptions to this rule, see Fiamengo, Solway.
2 See Fiamengo 162–3 for a partial summary of similar critical gestures.
3 Lee's essay was originally published in a slightly different form as the afterword to *The Collected Poems of Al Purdy* (1986); see Lee, "The Poetry of Al Purdy: An Afterword."
4 For an extended discussion of the A-frame Association and Purdy's celebrity status, see Pratt.
5 Many of these allusions are identified by Solecki (LCP 223–7).
6 Email to the author, 16 October 2009.
7 *Big Snake* ... is alternately referred to as *Blackfoot Chief and Subordinates* (see Lord 95).
8 In *North of Summer*, the painter's name is spelled "Breughel" and the title "Hunters in the Snow" appears in quotation marks (79); in *Beyond Remembering*, the text gives "Bruegel" and the title in italics (126).
9 In *Wild Grape Wine*, the Cuban name in the title is spelled "Veradero" (22–3).
10 Purdy is probably referring here to the painting *Autumn Woods* (1925), by Group of Seven member Frank Carmichael.
11 See letters from Kilvert to Purdy, 3 February 1966, Purdy Papers (Saskatchewan), Box 21.IX.B; and from McClelland to Purdy, 7 April 1966, Purdy Papers, Box 21.IX.F. For details of Kilvert's work with Purdy and other poets, see Ross and York.
12 For further discussion of Purdy's attitude to Jackson's work, and his involvement in the publication of *North of Summer*, see Lahey 93–4.

13 Thank you to Sam Solecki for permission to quote from personal correspondence, and for his generosity in sharing unpublished materials (photographs of Purdy's homes and catalogues of Purdy's books). Thanks also to Hans Bloemsma for his comments on a draft of this chapter.

ARCHIVAL SOURCES

A.W. Purdy Papers, Morton Manuscript Collection MSS 4, University of Saskatchewan Library.
    V. Draper, letter to Al Purdy, July 1964, Box 23, IX.J.
    Barbara Kilvert, letter to Al Purdy, 14 December 1966, Box 21, IX.B.
    Barbara Kilvert, letter to Al Purdy, 12 January 1967, Box 21, IX.B.
    Barbara Kilvert, letter to Al Purdy, 3 February 1967, Box 21, IX.B.
    Roy Kiyooka, letter to Al Purdy, n.d., Box 22, IX.H.39.
    Jack McClelland, letter to Al Purdy, 23 November 1965, Box 21, IX.F.
    Al Purdy, letter to Eurithe Purdy, 15 July 1965, Box 23, IX.I.1.
    Robert Weaver, letter to V. Draper, Box 23, IX.J.
    Poems by Al Purdy:
        "After Yeats' Lapis Lazuli," Box 1, I.A.1.
        "The Artist's Dream," Box 3, I.B.1.
        "Artist's Magic," Box 1, I.A.1
        "In Bed," Box 3, I.A.14.
        "The Dutch Masters," Box 1, I.A.1.
        "Here's Kane," Box 1, I.A.1.
        "Looney with Sunlight," Box 3, I.A.14.
        "Mind-Painting," Box 1, I.A.1.
        "Paul Kane," Box 1, I.A.1.
        "Poem with Vase with Mountain Landscape," Box 1, I.A.1.
        "She said herself into this poem," Box 1, I.A.4.
        "Spanish Hilltop," Box 1, I.A.3.
        "Still-Life," Box 1, I.A.1
        "What about Gauguin in Tahiti?," Box 1, I.A.1.
    Review of *Sculpture of the Eskimos*, Box 8, H.7.
Letter from Al Purdy to Barbara Kilvert. "Dec 31" [no year]. Hudson's Bay Company Archives. HBC Executive Assistant for Public Relations files. Barbara Kilvert Correspondence 1957–1966. RG2/68/9. Archives of Manitoba, Winnipeg.

REFERENCES

Barber, John. "Why Canada's A-List Wants to Save Al Purdy's A-Frame." *Globe and Mail*, 5 February 2013, https://www.theglobeandmail.com/arts/books-and-media/why-canadas-a-list-wants-to-save-al-purdys-a-frame/article8278881/.

Bensadoun, Douglas, dir. *At the Quinte Hotel*. Bravo!FACT, 2002.
Bentley, D.M.R. "Conclusion, Retrospective, and Prospective." In Lynch, Ganz, and Kealey, *Ivory Thought*, 239–46.
Berger, John. *Ways of Seeing*. London: BBC and Penguin Books, 1972.
Bowering, George. "The Al Frame." In Vermeersch, *Al Purdy*, 75–7.
– *Al Purdy*. Toronto: Copp Clark, 1970.
Buchanan, Donald W., ed. *Canadian Painters: From Paul Kane to the Group of Seven*. Oxford: Phaidon, 1945.
Davin, Nicholas Flood. *The Irishman in Canada*. Shannon: Irish University Press, 1968.
Dragland, Stan. "Al Purdy's Poetry: Openings." In Rogers, *Al Purdy*, 15–57.
Dudek, Louis. "Some Luxury Books on Life in the Rugged North." *Montreal Gazette*, 23 September 1967: 29.
Fiamengo, Janice. "'Kind of ludicrous or kind of beautiful I guess': Al Purdy's Rhetoric of Failure." In Lynch, Ganz, and Kealey, *Ivory Thought*, 159–71.
Galt, George. "Al Purdy at Home." In Vermeersch, *Al Purdy*, 55–7.
Heinricks, Geoff. "From *A Fool and Forty Acres*." In Vermeersch, *Al Purdy*, 66–72.
Helwig, David. "Al Purdy at Home." In Vermeersch, *Al Purdy*, 131–5.
Holt, D.B. *How Brands Become Icons: The Principles of Cultural Branding*. Boston: Harvard Business School Press, 2004.
Johnson, Brian D., dir. *Al Purdy Was Here*. Purdy Pictures, 2015.
Kane, Paul. *Assiniboine Hunting Buffalo*. c. 1850–56. Oil on canvas. National Gallery of Canada, Ottawa.
– *Big Snake, Chief of the Blackfoot Indians, Recounting His War Exploits to Five Subordinate Chiefs*. c. 1850–56. Oil on canvas. National Gallery of Canada, Ottawa.
– *Encampment, Winnipeg River*. 1846. Oil on paper. Stark Museum of Art, Orange, TX.
– *Encampment amongst the Islands of Lake Huron*. Woodcut engraving. In *Wanderings of an Artist among the Indians of North America*, by P. Kane, 7. London: Longman, 1859.
– *Encampment with Conical Shaped Lodges and Canoe*. 1845. Graphite on paper. Royal Ontario Museum, Toronto.
– *Indian Encampment on Big Bay at Owen Sound*. 1845. Oil on paper. Stark Museum of Art, Orange, TX.
– *Indian Encampment on Lake Huron*. 1845. Oil on canvas. Art Gallery of Ontario, Toronto.
– *Native American Encampment*. 1845. Oil on canvas. Granger Collection, New York.
Lahey, Ernestine. "Blended Discourses: Reading the Multimodal North in Al Purdy's *North of Summer*." In *Contemporary Canadian Literature: European Approaches*, edited by D. Zetu, 68–99. Iasi, Romania: Al. I. Cuza University Press, 2012.

Lee, Dennis. "The Poetry of Al Purdy." In Rogers, *Al Purdy*, 69–107.
– "The Poetry of Al Purdy: An Afterword." In *The Collected Poems of Al Purdy*, edited by Russell Brown, 371–91. Toronto: McClelland & Stewart, 1986.
– "Till the House Was Real." In Vermeersch, *Al Purdy*, 11–17.
Lord, Barry. *The History of Painting in Canada: Toward a People's Art*. Toronto: NC Press, 1974.
Lynch, Gerald, Shoshannah Ganz, and Josephene T.M. Kealey. Introduction to Lynch, Ganz, and Kealey, *Ivory Thought*, 1–8.
–, eds. *The Ivory Thought: Essays on Al Purdy*. Ottawa: University of Ottawa Press, 2008.
MacLaren, I.S. "Arctic Al: Purdy's Humanist Vision of the North." In Lynch, Ganz, and Kealey, *Ivory Thought*, 119–36.
Mayne, Seymour. "Al's Outhouse." In Vermeersch, *Al Purdy*, 116.
McFadden, David W. "From *A Trip around Lake Ontario*." In Vermeersch, *Al Purdy*, 117–22.
Percy, Owen. "Re: Focusing (on) Celebrity: Canada's Major Poetry Prizes." In *Celebrity Cultures in Canada*, edited by Katja Lee and Lorraine York, 185–99. Waterloo, ON: Wilfrid Laurier University Press, 2016.
Porter, Catherine. "The Declining Days of Al Purdy." In Rogers, *Al Purdy*, 155–63.
Pratt, Brooke. "Preserving 'the echoing rooms of yesterday': Al Purdy's A-Frame and the Place of Writers' Houses in Canada." In *Canadian Literature and Cultural Memory*, edited by Cynthia Sugars and Eleanor Ty, 84–99. Don Mills, ON: Oxford University Press, 2014.
Purdy, Al. *Beyond Remembering: The Collected Poems of Al Purdy*. Edited by Al Purdy and Sam Solecki. Madeira Park, BC: Harbour Publishing, 2000.
– *The Cariboo Horses*. Toronto: McClelland & Stewart, 1965.
– "Disconnections." *Essays on Canadian Writing*, no. 49 (Summer 1993): 180–221.
– *Naked with Summer in Your Mouth*. Toronto: McClelland & Stewart, 1994.
– *North of Summer: Poems from Baffin Island*. Toronto: McClelland & Stewart, 1967.
– *Piling Blood*. Toronto: McClelland & Stewart, 1984.
– *Poems for All the Annettes*. Toronto: Contact Press, 1962.
– *Reaching for the Beaufort Sea: An Autobiography*. Edited by Alex Widen. Madeira Park, BC: Harbour Publishing, 1993.
– *Rooms for Rent in the Outer Planets: Selected Poems, 1962–1996*. Edited by Al Purdy and Sam Solecki. Madeira Park, BC: Harbour Publishing, 1996.
– *Sex and Death*. Toronto: McClelland & Stewart, 1973.
– *Wild Grape Wine*. Toronto: McClelland & Stewart, 1968.
– *Yours, Al: The Collected Letters of Al Purdy*. Edited by Sam Solecki. Madeira Park, BC: Harbour Publishing, 2004.

Purdy, Al, and Margaret Laurence. *Margaret Laurence–Al Purdy: A Friendship in Letters: Selected Correspondence*. Edited by John Lennox. Toronto: McClelland & Stewart, 1993.
Purdy, Al, and George Woodcock. *The Purdy–Woodcock Letters: Selected Correspondence, 1964–1984*. Edited by George Galt. Toronto: ECW Press, 1988.
Purdy, Eurithe. "If Those Walls Could Talk: A Reminiscence by Eurithe Purdy." In Vermeersch, *Al Purdy*, 39–53.
Reeves, John. "Al Purdy, Photographed November 1965." In Vermeersch, *Al Purdy*, 63.
Reid, Scott. "Late Poet Al Purdy's Home a Retreat for Writers Once Again." *Ottawa Citizen*, 31 October 2014, https://ottawacitizen.com/news/national/late-poet-al-purdys-home-a-retreat-for-writers-once-again.
Rogers, Linda, ed. *Al Purdy: Essays on His Works*. Toronto: Guernica Editions, 2002.
– "Introduction: Reaching for the Beaufort Sea." In Rogers, *Al Purdy*, 9–14.
Rosenblatt, Joe. "Big Al: The Bardic Oenophile and Bacchus, circa 1970." In Vermeersch, *Al Purdy*, 58–60.
Ross, Michael, and Lorraine York. "Imperial Commerce and the Canadian Muse: The Hudson's Bay Company's Poetic Advertising Campaign of 1966–1972." *Canadian Literature*, no. 220 (Spring 2014): 37–53.
Silverberg, Mark. "The Can(adi)onization of Al Purdy." *Essays on Canadian Writing*, no. 70 (Spring 2000): 226–51.
Solecki, Sam. "Al Purdy among the Poets." In Rogers, *Al Purdy*, 108–27.
– "Ameliasburg, ON, Catalogue." Undated, unpublished document.
– *The Last Canadian Poet: An Essay on Al Purdy*. Toronto: University of Toronto Press, 1999.
– "Materials for a Biography of Al Purdy." In Lynch, Ganz, and Kealey, *Ivory Thought*, 13–30.
– "Sidney, B.C., Catalogue." Undated, unpublished document.
– Unpublished photographs of Al Purdy's Ameliasburgh and Sidney homes.
Solway, David. "Standard Average Canadian, or the Influence of Al Purdy." *Canadian Notes and Queries*, no. 59 (Spring–Summer 2001): 18–20.
Stevens, Peter. "The Road to the Cariboo Horses." *Essays on Canadian Writing*, no. 49 (Summer 1993): 32–41.
Sullivan, Rosemary. "Purdy's Dark Cowboy." In Rogers, *Al Purdy*, 61–8.
van der Marel, L. Camille. "Unsettling *North of Summer*: Anxieties of Ownership in the Politics and Poetics of the Canadian North." *ARIEL: A Review of International English Literature* 44, no. 4 (October 2013): 13–47.
Vermeersch, Paul, ed. *The Al Purdy A-Frame Anthology*. Madeira Park, BC: Harbour Publishing, 2009.
Xiao, Richard, and Tony McEnery. "Collocation, Semantic Prosody, and Near Synonymy: A Cross-Linguistic Perspective." *Applied Linguistics* 27, no. 1 (March 2006): 103–29.

"Concerning Ms. Atwood":
Purdy, Margaret Atwood,
and the *Malahat Review*

Natalie Boldt

In January 1977, the forty-first issue of the *Malahat Review* was devoted to an up-and-coming Canadian literary celebrity: Margaret Atwood. *Malahat* 41, which Linda Hutcheon later dubbed "Margaret's *Malahat*," emerged on the heels of Atwood's third novel, *Lady Oracle* (1976) – ten years after she received the Governor General's Award for her first book of poems, *The Circle Game* (1966), but still years prior to such huge popular successes as *The Handmaid's Tale* (1985), *Cat's Eye* (1988), and *Alias Grace* (1996).[1] Created in the spirit of what guest editor Linda Sandler calls a "tenth anniversary tribute" ("Preface" 5), "Margaret's *Malahat*" is a portrait of Atwood at the beginning of her rise to international renown. The issue is notable not only for the variety of contributions, ranging from scholarly analyses to poetic homages, but also for the number of well-known Canadian writers who were willing, or who felt compelled, to comment on and celebrate the success of one of their own. Thanks in large part to Sandler's editorial persistence, the table of contents is a Who's Who of Canadian authors and critics – among them three Georges (Bowering, Jonas, and Woodcock), Susan Musgrave, and Gwendolyn MacEwen.

    Malahat 41 also included the familiar voice of Al Purdy, who contributed a poem, "Deprivations" (from *Sundance at Dusk*, 1976), and an anecdotal essay recounting his tumultuous first meeting with Atwood several years earlier. Purdy's contributions are not, on the surface, especially notable. The poem's style, tone, and theme are familiar from other poems, such as "Trees at the Arctic Circle" and "Wilderness Gothic," and how "Deprivations" relates to Atwood (if at all) is not obvious. The second contribution is, likewise, easily taken at face value – as the kind of humorous, but nevertheless fondly nostalgic, statement expected in a laudatory volume of this kind. It may then come as a surprise that

Purdy was initially reluctant to contribute to Margaret's *Malahat*, writing in a series of letters to Sandler that he did not "particularly like what [he thought was] happening to her [Atwood], and what she seem[ed] to be becoming" (2 February 1975), and later insisting that he had "no particular wish to write about her" (5 August 1975). Though Purdy relented, his hesitation is perplexing, particularly given the genuinely affectionate tone of the essay he ultimately submitted and, for that matter, the lifelong friendship he enjoyed with "Peggy," as he and other friends called her.

Clearly there was more to Purdy's unwillingness than personal dislike or professional jealousy. Likewise, there is more to his *Malahat* contributions than a preliminary or cursory reading suggests. This chapter is thus an attempt to contextualize Purdy's stated aversion, and his essay, in terms of both his relationship to a fellow artist – his friend Margaret Atwood – and his attitudes toward literary celebrity during a culturally complex period in Canada's literary history – namely, the 1970s.

PURDY AND MARGARET'S *MALAHAT*: A POLEMIC ON LITERARY CELEBRITY

Little can be said about Margaret's *Malahat* without reference to the now fifty-year-long critical fascination with Atwood's literary celebrity. Perhaps because the extent of her celebrity was largely unheard of in Canada at the time, or perhaps because the notion of a *literary* celebrity still seemed like a contradiction in terms, *Malahat* 41 gives the impression of being an "Introduction to Literary Fame in Canada." Sandler's tongue-in-cheek preface is a testament to the issue's ambivalence, for, in a volume that comments extensively on the often dangerous anomalies of fame and myth-making, she paints a portrait of Atwood that is ironically mythical. Having just crowned Atwood the "presiding genius of Canadian letters," Sandler declares that "[n]othing quite like Atwood has ever happened to Canada before":

> eleven books (poetry, fiction, criticism), cross-country readings and public lectures, a political stand and a mythical aura, have made her the thinking person's alternative to that other symbolic Queen who lives in England ...
>
> Her followers, like the English Queen's, consist of a mass of loyalists and a self-conscious academic minority which is inclined to ask itself: Does this woman truly represent me? Is she capable of resolving our historic identity crisis? And what is she doing about the rate of inflation? (5–6)

Though Sandler's comments were clearly made in partial jest, her questions (apart from the one about inflation) are seriously addressed throughout the issue. Indeed, Sandler herself poses similar questions to Atwood in the following interview: "How do you see the relation of your art to popular art?" (10); could that art be "an agent of change?" (23); and, more personally, "Has it made any difference to you, getting the kind of recognition you have?" (9).

Elsewhere in the issue, the questions asked and answered range from "Who is Atwood?" to "Why is Atwood famous?" to, more broadly, "What does it mean to be famous in Canada?" Whether obliquely through poems, or directly in essays, the seeming contradiction or paradox of literary fame is treated as extensively as the author herself. Readers are given Atwood's own perspective (in her interview with Sandler and in the form of printed pages from her notebook), the outside perspective of scholars and critics, and the middle-ground perspective of friends and colleagues like Purdy. The result, in short, is a more nuanced compendium of opinions than Sandler's introduction indicates.

Robert Fulford's "The Images of Atwood" stands out as a critical counterpoint to the contributions of friends, close colleagues, and fellow artists. It is, for this reason, one of the more illuminating essays in the issue – for while the impulse of friends, peers, or fans might be to demonize the media for transforming Atwood into, as she put it, "a Thing" (Fulford 97), Fulford's essay addresses the author's complicity in the construction of celebrity. At the same time, it celebrates Atwood's concomitant resilience and business savvy. Though Atwood maintains, even in her interview with Sandler (see "Interview" 8), that her public image has been generated for her by the media – "a creation ... of commentators, editors, critics, common gossips" (Fulford 96) – that is not, Fulford insists, "how the media work" (97). Rather, "[t]heir creation of mythology of a public personality begins with a series of cues from inside the myth itself ... the raw materials of hagiography" (97). In Atwood's case, these "raw materials" are notoriously illusive and changeable. According to Fulford:

> One year she assails Mordecai Richler for satirizing Canadian nationalism; the next year she's hard at work on a novel that performs the same office in a more immediate and more penetrating way. One year she is writing tough and resentful poems about the relations between men and women; a few years later there are photographs of her with her newborn child in the newsmagazines. She writes a feminist novel and then denies she's influenced by feminism. (96)

But since "[o]urs is a tissue-paper culture, in which both art and personality are as disposable as Kleenex" (97), this kind of "Protean" (98) flexibility, Fulford concludes, makes Atwood "the perfect literary media star for this period" (97).[2]

In addition, Fulford reflects on Atwood's resilience to the strange state of affairs that is Canadian literary celebrity. "The Canadian media," he contends, "operate much of the time in a vacuum":

> Canada has American-style vehicles for stars (magazines, weekend supplements, TV interview shows) but few stars to fill them. Undaunted, the media reach eagerly for every demi-star or near-star who appears on the horizon. The result is that in Canada it is possible to become the focus of a great deal of media attention – to be endlessly interviewed, profiled, criticized – without actually becoming what would in another country be called successful. It is possible here to be both famous and poor, to be an actor with his face on the cover of *Weekend* and yet be unable to get parts. (97)

Here again, he argues, lies the value of Atwood's protean nature, which has manoeuvred her beyond the impoverished state of Canadian celebrity and allowed her to become an author simultaneously popular and critically acclaimed – an internationally recognized national hero.

Of course, Fulford's opinion is only one among many. In addition to being a highly gendered account of Atwood's celebrity, it is also a perspective skewed in favour of the media.[3] Juxtaposed with his contribution is Purdy's inevitably more affectionate, but hardly straightforward, tribute to Atwood's successes. Purdy's essay, "An Unburnished One-Tenth of One Per Cent of an Event," recalls his "somewhat ambivalent first meeting" (61) with Atwood in the summer of 1963 – an "event" that involved a few slurs against scholarship and a great deal of beer-swilling (cf. RBS 230–1). Even readers already familiar with the anecdote may appreciate the sarcastic but self-deprecating way in which Purdy recounts his early impressions of "Peggy" (he claims that he has never called her by any other name) ("Unburnished" 61). In the context of the *Malahat*, however, the essay is perhaps more notable for Purdy's contribution to the issue's ongoing, if unintended, dialogue about celebrity, for his essay is a direct counterpoint to Fulford's. Indeed, if Fulford's contribution is weighted toward the media, Purdy's is dead-set against anything or anyone – media or critical personality – who would make claims upon a celebrity's "image." Before mentioning Atwood, Purdy takes aim at John Glassco for attempting something of the kind in a recent article:

> In *Time* magazine a couple of years ago, John Glassco (who should know better) called Irving Layton a professional wild man, Margaret Atwood a professional virgin and myself a professional hick – meaning that was how other people thought of us and of course we arranged it deliberately.
>
> Bullshit, Mr. Glassco! Are you a professional pornographer after writing *The English Governess*? I would hate to think so. Because no one knows one-tenth of one per cent of any other person: the human facets are multitudinous as sea-sands and just as different under any but a self-serving microscope. (61)

Only after these qualifications does Purdy proceed to his anecdote. Even then, he wonders in closing what he is now guilty of contributing to the growing body of Atwood lore. In an effort to countermand whatever negative or one-dimensional impression he has left, he offers the following, apparently without irony or sarcasm: "I'll finish by saying that Peggy Atwood is someone I admire and like as a writer, who happens also to be a warm and alive human being" (64). For Purdy, Atwood's image was "far off from reality" (63) – distorted, his introduction hints, by the "turbulent death-stricken years of the 1970s" (61). Neither inconsequential nor an out-and-out hero, Purdy's "Peggy" is human and imperfect: "She reacts to insult and denigration like a human being ... speaks her own mind in interviews," and then "lives her own life after them" (64). She is, in short, a complex, inconsistent, and multi-dimensional writer, much like himself.

Whether or not Fulford's or Purdy's assessments of either Atwood or celebrity in general are entirely accurate, they suggest the extent to which a writer's success was increasingly tied to visibility and the capacity to weather changes in popular and critical opinion. Where Fulford arguably falls short is in representing the view from the "other side" – the inner conflict that results from having one's private self irretrievably altered by years of performance and (mis)perception. Purdy's assessment, on the other hand, while it reflects his affection for "Peggy" and his respect for her talent, is coloured by his own struggles to achieve recognition – for his style and his vision of a national literature – during a period when it seemed to him increasingly difficult to do so.

More extensive and sophisticated studies of literary fame in Canada have appeared since the 1970s, chief among them Lorraine York's *Literary Celebrity in Canada* (2007) and Joel Deshaye's *The Metaphor of Celebrity: Canadian Poetry and the Public, 1955–1980* (2013). Given the benefit of over thirty years' hindsight, these analyses are admittedly more nuanced in their accounts of celebrity than those in *Malahat* 41, though their conclusions are surprisingly similar to those of the earlier commentators. Like Fulford and Purdy, York and Deshaye address the role of the media in celebrity performance, arguing, again like Fulford, that celebrity operates as a co-constitutional project. York, for example, subscribes to film and television critic John Ellis's definition of a celebrity as "a performer in a particular medium whose figure enters into subsidiary forms of circulation, and then feeds back into future performances" (qtd. in York 12).[4] York argues that in the case of *literary* celebrity, this performance often registers as ironic, given that writing, "[t]he very activity that has given rise to the writer's well-knownness," typically occurs in private (12). Likewise, public promotion – a necessity in the modern publishing world – "take[s] [the] author away from what he or she would no doubt prefer and need to be doing at that moment: writing, alone" (13). Those deemed "serious" writers may, furthermore, feel conflicted about the commercialization of their private selves and public art – a conflict that, while not exclusive to Canadian writers, registered frequently among modern and early postmodern authors in Canada, many of whom were socialists or proletariat "peoples' poets" (as in the differing examples of Margaret Laurence and Milton Acorn). Though this particular conflict appears in various guises, it recurs most often in conjunction with the high-versus-popular culture debates that rage perennially in various literary circles and that crop up in conversations about Atwood's star-status, especially in relation to her role as author of speculative fiction.

Deshaye likewise emphasizes the feedback loop between celebrity performance and the media, with the added emphasis that a literary celebrity's texts are a central – and potentially detrimental – part of this cycle. Unlike film stars, who may or may not be related in any way to the roles they perform on screen, the literary star is fused to his or her persona as established in the literary works themselves. Because the reading public cannot always tell where the author's persona begins and ends, the author's texts and public appearances and performances are taken up, in Fulford's words, as the "raw materials of hagiography" (97). Public interest in an author's private life, is, as Deshaye notes, "both an opportunity for publicity and a multifaceted risk" (5), since the persona, no matter how true to life, is heavily weighted in the creation of the celebrity "image." The loss of identity and agency that registers frequently among literary celebrities is thus, in some sense, more acute, because one of the author's most versatile techniques, metaphor, has become implicated in the perceived obligation to the media. Though, as Deshaye maintains, this "obligation is not actually total," it feels totalizing because the "metaphor [of celebrity] is totalizing" (202).

For this reason, celebrity and the amorphous "public" and/or "media" register as overwhelmingly threatening in the poetry of the authors in Deshaye's study.

Moreover, Deshaye and York are quick to point out that, even at the height of the mid- to late-twentieth-century publishing boom, literary celebrity would have been treated with suspicion by those who achieved it for the reasons that Fulford gives in his essay – that it was possible in Canada to be famous and poor, critically acclaimed and unpopular, or monetarily successful and critically unrecognized. That Atwood managed to be both popular and critically acclaimed was unusual, as Sandler's preface to the *Malahat* makes amply clear. Indeed, Deshaye concludes that, despite heightened interest in poetry in the 1960s, there were only three poets in Canada with a credible claim to national celebrity: Irving Layton, Leonard Cohen, and Atwood, none of whom achieved celebrity on the basis of their poetry alone. Layton was renowned because of the controversy he created (47), while Atwood gained recognition (and capital) by making the jump to fiction (as well as criticism, with *Survival* in 1972) (53), and Cohen by becoming a musician (54). In the cases of Atwood and Cohen, timely transitions meant that the authors weathered the aforementioned shifts in publishers' and public interest when appreciation for poetry, and a certain version of Canadian nationalism, began to fade.

That the 1970s were a period of change for Canadian literature, and for Purdy more personally, is attested to by much of the poet's correspondence from the time, which features multiple reflections on the notions of persona, perception (both critical and public), and media influence. Purdy's exchanges with Sandler number among them and establish a context for his *Malahat* contributions.

Early in 1975, Sandler and Purdy were in conversation about the possibility of an interview – Sandler was on staff at the *Financial Post*, but was also a freelance writer and broadcaster with an interest in Canadian authors.[5] On 2 February 1975, Purdy responded to her request for an official exchange and to comments she had presumably made regarding Atwood's poetry.[6] Though he agreed almost immediately to the interview, he spent much of the letter describing his hatred of stereotyping and his frustration with the rote nature of interviews, and tempering Sandler's notions about his poetic voice. This excerpt provides a representative glimpse of the original letter and includes Purdy's assessment of Atwood in full:

> No, I don't think of myself as plain-voiced. I think of myself
> as using more or less everyday speech jargon ... I don't regard

> myself as Farmer John in the back pasture, which is what "plain-voiced" would indicate. Nor, as Glassco mentioned in *Time*, as the professional hick. Those are interpretations without evidence, at least not enough for the premise that results ... Re Atwood, she seems to me a very powerful and flawed poet. But then, I think all poets are flawed, since they can't be all things to all people. As well, I don't particularly like what I think is happening to her, and what she seems to be becoming. (2 February 1975)

The letter seems to function as a preliminary warning that, should their interview proceed, Purdy would not respond well to formulaic questions. His appraisal of Atwood likewise indicates that he had begun to see her as a kind of limit-case for the media-generated dissolution of identity that he was determined to avoid.

Despite these earlier assessments of Atwood, Sandler nevertheless broached the idea of a special issue of the *Malahat Review* later that year, and kept encouraging Purdy to contribute to it. In a letter dated 5 August 1975, Purdy expressed his unwillingness to do so (the text in italics appears in red in the original):

> You seem to be bringing all the pressure on me you possibly can, to write a piece on Atwood. Especially with that bit at the end of your note: "I hope when I edit a special issue on Al Purdy, Atwood will contribute." Now that's a form of blackmail, don't you think? I doubt that you ever do an issue on Al Purdy, and I don't care greatly one way or the other, whether you do or not. Because apparently you don't read my mind very well.
>
> Let me try to read it for you about Atwood. I like Peggy, respect her, think her probably the most important writer in the country today. That last for other reasons than writing. I don't necessarily think she's the best writer, since there are several very good writers in Canada, but probably the most important. *But I have no particular wish to write about her. If she knew about your request and thought it a good idea that I should, then I'd definitely go along. But I doubt that Peggy would either want me to or not want me to. And you're welcome to show her this letter.*[7]

Two weeks later, Purdy again communicated his frustration over the ways in which writers, and poets in particular, are pigeonholed, their works expected to be consistent in form, mood, and content. He suggested that his failure to find a consistent voice might prove his critical downfall:

> I doubt readers will revere [me] or do so now. I expect to be paid little attention in future, a perhaps slightly unusual figure who will nevertheless be thought not worth very much attention …
>
> Critics seem to demand that you "find a voice" and that alone militates against individuality, demands that the writer be recognizable as himself. Well, "himself" is many people, himself is musical morbid depressed happy bright and all the adjectives. Why should that seem unusual? It isn't in a person himself, but seems to be in a writer. And critics are largely responsible for this inhibition of poets, in which the traits are more noticeable than in fiction writers. (20 August 1975)

Though neither Atwood nor the *Malahat* is mentioned in this letter, the connection to Purdy's future essay is easily perceived: the mediated persona you see is "an unburnished one-tenth of one per cent" of the complex and dynamic poet-self you don't. In this instance, however, it is not Atwood's mediated persona with which Purdy has taken issue, but instead his own.

Here the epistolary trail disappears until January of the following year. By that time, Purdy had agreed to contribute to the *Malahat*, but was struggling to write something. On 1 January 1976, he communicated to Sandler that his mind was "quite blank" regarding Atwood. "Would like to write a poem about her," he stated in his letter, "but here again nothing comes." Obviously something did "come" eventually, for when Margaret's *Malahat* was published one year later, it included Purdy's essay, as well as "Deprivations."

Purdy's letters to Sandler are illuminating, not least because parts of the exchange reappear almost word for word in his finished essay. His stubborn disavowal of a "consistent voice" may appear strange given that Purdy remains known for what could reasonably be described as his "plain-voicedness." Dennis Lee offers a somewhat more expansive, but nonetheless similar, description of Purdy's characteristic style in his analysis of *The Cariboo Horses* (1965): "There is now a wonderful sure-footedness in the rangy, loping gait which had become his signature – with its ability to open out into vast perspectives of space and time, then narrow down to a single moment or image. It was with this volume that he reached a wide critical and popular audience" (76–7). It seems odd that Purdy would resist Sandler's suggestions that his colloquial style was recognizable and that he was critically relevant when, as Lee suggests, this "signature" had gained him "a wide … audience." Was Purdy being falsely modest, or did he really put so little stock in critical opinion? Was he justified in doing so? Was Lee mistaken?[8] Or was Purdy simply uninterested in public or popular recognition? These questions do not invite simple answers, though they are all addressed, in some form, in a letter that Purdy sent to Susan Musgrave in 1977, only a few months after Margaret's *Malahat* had gone to press:

> May I brag a little modestly? There's an academy of Can. writers. Some sixty thousand people voted for three best poets, novelists etc. Voting figures weren't released publicly, but my intense ego made me ask. I came in 7,000 votes ahead of Atwood. Then I go to Coles and see eighteen thousand of her books there and none of mine. But novelist [Farley] Mowat (who doesn't write novels) was ahead of M. Laurence. And that ruins my ego completely. If voters don't know the difference between Laurence and Mowat, how the hell would they know a poet from Rod McKuen? Which leads me to: what shit it all is! (YA 278)

Purdy wanted recognition, and unlike many artists, he was fortunate enough to receive it. But he was also concerned that his recognition was meaningless; in this case he was convinced, it seems, that acknowledgment from his peers was diluted by the tastes of other readers.

Purdy's frustrations also seem to be tied to what Fulford recognized as the anomalous nature of stardom in Canada – including the fact that it was possible to receive media attention "without ... becoming what would in another country be called successful" (97) – with the slight change in emphasis that, for Purdy, it seemed possible to be called successful, even canonical, one year, and to be rendered ostensibly passé the next. Though in Purdy's case this was not entirely true – he published *four* collections in 1977, the year of Margaret's *Malahat* – his fears were not unfounded. The 1970s, 1980s, and 1990s saw a succession of paradigm shifts that affected poets' reputations, as modernist concerns about a common humanity and a singular Canadian nationalism gave way to postmodernist, postcolonial, and feminist articulations of difference. In *The Last Canadian Poet: An Essay on Al Purdy* (1999), Sam Solecki describes this shift rather more polemically, characterizing the critical concerns of the 1990s: "*in* [were] contemporary literature, feminism and feminist poetry, postmodernism, language poetry, colonial and postcolonial theory, and various so-called theoretical approaches; *out* [were] the poetry and fiction of the first generation of Canadian modernists, especially those whose work [did] not lend itself to these approaches" (ix; emphasis original). But even in the 1970s, with the increased influence of the media and the erosion of boundaries between high and popular culture, Purdy clearly felt that there was a corresponding decline in critical accountability. Neither did there appear to him to be a path to success that did not involve losing control of one's image.

Implicated in both Purdy's letter to Musgrave and Solecki's assessment is another significant area of inquiry – namely, audience. For whom was Purdy writing? Or, perhaps more importantly, who was reading Purdy and in what context? Was his audience popular or literary? Was it predominantly local, or did he have national appeal? Even in retrospect, the nuances of these matters – and the value-laden terms on which they rely – prohibit definitive conclusions. Faced with a similar dilemma vis-à-vis readership in *Arrival: The Story of CanLit* (2017), Nick Mount admits that, despite the measurable increase in *potential* readers throughout the 1960s – due, in large part, to postwar immigration and a generation of baby boomers come of age – statistics that accurately record what, how, and how much people read are elusive. Whereas "[p]ublishers leave accounts," and authors "leave us their books" and other ephemera, "most readers," Mount writes, "leave nothing behind, no record of their existence other than a page turned down, maybe a name on a bookplate, a note in a margin, a digital footprint in a device bound for the nuisance grounds" (79). National bestseller lists that today give an imperfect sense of who is buying (and potentially reading) books did not appear in Canada between 1962 and 1970 (Mount 79–80) – the peak of Purdy's popularity and the period which Deshaye deems the "era of celebrity in Canadian poetry" (6).

And indeed, even had they existed, bestseller lists could never adequately account for the unusual conditions that gave rise to the artistic frenzy of the 1960s – a period when the possibility of government funding made publication more feasible for artists of all sorts, regardless of the market. During this period of unprecedented cultural production, writers now considered more or less canonical served as one another's editors, reviewers, and, in many cases, readers – not only because, as Atwood intimates, there was no one else to do the work (*Burgess* 35–6), but also because, as Mount notes, in the eyes of most authors, "the most important readers are other writers" (89) – those, in short, who can appreciate literary nuance, the difficulty of the creative process, and the tradition that one writes within or reacts against. Purdy's letter to Musgrave suggests that his audience was particularly engaged, composed as it was of a comparatively small network of poets, artists, academics, and public intellectuals, all of whom were invested in what Atwood describes as a quest to fill the "relative cultural emptiness" the postwar generation had inherited (*Burgess* 35).[9]

At the same time, Purdy was a familiar voice on CBC Radio during an era when radio was, as Deshaye notes, "much more central to the day-to-day experience of the media than it is now" (45). Purdy appeared frequently on the program *Anthology* and contributed to the network, among other things, a number of radio plays.[10] He was also, at one point, involved in a Hudson's Bay Company advertising campaign that ran in a number of prestigious periodicals between 1966 and 1972.[11] Given the potentially expansive audience made possible through these different media, whom did Purdy count among his audience?

The difficulty of this question lies at least partly in the inherently amorphous nature of "the public," a term we use frequently, but define almost never. How does one become part of a reading public? How much need one read to gain membership? What degree of participation in a public constitutes fandom? Writing in answer to some of these questions in *Publics and Counterpublics* (2002), Michael Warner defines a public in part as a body that has been "self-organized" (67), by which he means that it is brought together "by something other than the state" (68). Warner differentiates between a public in the Lockean sense of "polis" and one in the Kantian sense of a civil, discursively organized society. Following from Kant, he also distinguishes "publics" as being "space[s] of discourse organized by nothing other than discourse itself" (67). In this sense, publics are both notional (implicitly or explicitly theorized by an author or orator) and empirical (able to be measured in some way). To further impress the notional nature of publics, Warner points out that the conception of "a public" must precede its existence, since in order for a public to come into being, it must be addressed by a discourse that presumes its a priori existence:

> Public discourse says not only "Let a public exist" but "Let it have this character, speak this way, see the world in this way." It then goes in search of confirmation that such a public exists, with greater or lesser success – success being further attempts to cite, circulate, and realize the world understanding it articulates. Run it up the flagpole and see who salutes. Put on a show and see who shows up. (114)

This paradoxically notional and empirical existence is also what makes publics so difficult to assess, especially given that, according to Warner, a public may be "constituted through mere attention" (87). Thus while quality or accuracy of engagement is certainly a factor in the way a public figure might gauge his or her success, it need not be a factor in the constitution of a public per se. Here Warner uses the example of a sleeping audience member at a public meeting or cultural performance; he argues that conscious or unconscious, the sleeper nonetheless constitutes part of a public (88). Truly public venues or media like radio and television are also poor indicators of engagement insofar as they are media to which people might generally subscribe or, in the case of magazines and newspapers, purchase for reasons unrelated to their commentary on or inclusion of a particular figure. Indeed, as Deshaye suggests, these venues – great though their reach may be – "are not commodities that can give their buyers a sense of ownership or star-specific prestige" (51). Nor, I would add, are they venues that give stars themselves an accurate sense of their reception. They provide only a "general sense of prestige" (51) and one that, it would seem from Purdy's letter, may be easily diminished by concrete numbers or a browse through the neighbourhood Coles (or, today, Indigo).

The reception of poetry in this period is even more difficult to measure than the reception of novels or non-fiction. As Mount and Deshaye both attest, we know from the journalistic record that poetry enjoyed a window of popularity; we can even pinpoint, in some cases, the number of people who attended readings and ascertain their reactions from archived reviews. What we cannot be sure of is the number of people who bought (or read) whole collections of poetry, read a single poem in the *Globe and Mail*, or heard Purdy on an episode of *Anthology* on the CBC. Both the performative nature of poetry and its potentially piecemeal consumption complicate a purely numerical (sales-related) measure of "success." Atwood's timely shift to novels (like Cohen's shift to music) explains, in part, the spike in success she saw during the mid-to-late 1970s. More importantly, at least with respect to celebrity, it also made that success more calculable.

Whether frustration with "Atwood Inc." weighed in Purdy's initial reluctance to contribute to Margaret's *Malahat* is impossible to say for sure. I would suggest, though, that his contributions have more to say about his personal experience with literary celebrity than they do about his relationship to, or opinion of, Atwood. As his experience was ambiguous, it is perhaps unsurprising that he chose to highlight an uncomplicated and pre-fame "Peggy" in his essay and to link his personal anecdote to a polemic on stereotyping. Indeed, if Purdy was feeling deprived of self, as his essay suggests, then perhaps his unexpected contributions to the *Malahat* represented his rebellion against typecasting in a post-Centennial period of waning poetic celebrity.

CONCERNING MS ATWOOD

Even contextualized in this manner, Purdy's essay reveals relatively little about his professional or personal opinion of Atwood's work. "An Unburnished One-Tenth of One Per Cent of an Event" is a carefully edited expression of the opinions that appeared in less adulterated form in his letters to Sandler. For a more nuanced assessment of Atwood, we must look to Purdy's published and epistolary reviews of her novels and collections of poetry, and, in one notable instance, to his poetry.

Readers acquainted with either Purdy or Atwood are likely familiar with his poem "Concerning Ms. Atwood" (BR 496–7) – a satirical commentary on her celebrity. Published in a limited, two-poem volume in 1990, reprinted in the *Globe and Mail* (1 October 1994), and included in *Naked with Summer in Your Mouth* (1994), the poem depicts Atwood's "meeting Premier Peterson," christening a "super icebreaker," "accepting the Nobel Prize," and, when earthly honours have been exhausted, jetting into space, where she is introduced to God and "the First Cause." Both entities are, of course, familiar with Ms Atwood. She, on the other hand, must write God's "name down promptly / in her little notebook to prevent / forgetfulness." The poem ends with the author "being interviewed by the neutered blessed seraphim" – there is apparently no realm in which Atwood is not known and loved.

The poem is an apt example of the teasing but affectionate stance toward Atwood that Purdy demonstrated in "An Unburnished One-Tenth of One Per Cent." It is, moreover, a fitting example of his engagement with the "Peggy"/Atwood dialectic. Are Purdy's poetic jests made in good faith? Who exactly is the butt of this particular joke? Atwood? The media who perpetuate the Atwood myth, or the reader/fan who consumes and therefore feeds it? An envious Purdy? Anticipating such questions, Purdy included a note on the poem in *Naked with Summer in Your Mouth*, insisting that the subject matter was not, in fact, "Ms. Atwood," but rather "fame and celebrity" (NSM 128). "Ms. Atwood," he declares, "read an earlier version, viewed it calmly, and allowed it to stand" (128). Indeed, the epistolary evidence suggests that Purdy was right. In a 1995 letter to Purdy, Atwood maintained a sense of humour around Purdy's public (and private) jabs:

> Thank you for the beautiful handprinted poems – though I dunno – is the one about me a compliment? Let's just say I'm glad I don't have pigtails, because if I did, you'd get them into that inkwell in no time flat ...
>
> But if you get very, *very* bad, I will utter the following curse: May Elspeth Cameron Write Your Biography (every flaw revealed ...)
>
> So *look out*, eh? (15 January 1995)

As Atwood suggests in her letter, the tongue-in-cheek tone of Purdy's references recalls the dynamics of a harmless classroom flirtation; though his regard for her was certainly more fraternal than anything else, one wonders, were Atwood to have red hair instead of black, pigtails instead of a curly halo, whether Purdy might have called her "Carrots."

Purdy was not always so ambiguous in his assessments, however, noting in letters to both friends and colleagues that Atwood was an undeniably formidable talent in Canadian letters. In 1976, for example, he declared to John Newlove that Atwood was "[t]he only really good woman poet I know" (7 January 1976, YA 260), and he later wrote to Jack McClelland that "[a]t the present time [Atwood is] the only writer on the horizon ... capable of surpassing anything written previously in Canada" (23 June 1980, YA 327). He was also sure to include Atwood in his anthology of Canadian poetry, *Fifteen Winds: A Selection of Modern Canadian Poems* (1969). Atwood was one of only four women in the collection – a mark of esteem, to be sure, however concerning this statistic might be in other ways.[12]

Purdy's reviews of early works like *The Animals in That Country* (1968) and *The Journals of Susanna Moodie* (1970) also mark his appreciation for Atwood's skill as a writer, though they are not without their critical aspects.[13] The former collection is, he admits, "pretty black" ("Poet" 94) – "[t]he writer seems besieged from without by her own inner perceptions" (94) – but Atwood is, nevertheless, to be commended for her profoundly simple treatment of complex themes in what are ultimately "tremendous, soul-stirring, awesomely analytical, [and] penetrating" poems (96). His review of *Journals* was only slightly less effusive, but still positive. In this instance, Purdy struggled with Atwood's poetic persona, wondering at length just how much of the author's "sub-basic" qualities were lost in her act of historical ventriloquism" ("Atwood's" 81). He also objected to the collection's lack of humour ("other than satire") and the corresponding lack of joie de vivre one sees in truly "magnificent" lyrics (82). In both cases, however, Purdy was careful to distinguish his own personal opinions about tone, style, and content from what he considered the successful gestalt of Atwood's work. Atwood/Moodie was, he concluded, a convincing figure: "I believe," he declares midway through the review, "(Hallelujah!)" (83). As to Atwood's chilly tone, his objections were chiefly subjective – related, he explains, to gender, upbringing, and outlook (82) – and should not detract from the "clarity of intellect" that Atwood demonstrated (84).

In many respects, these early reviews are representative of Purdy's overall opinion of the work that Atwood published throughout the 1970s – both its strengths and its weaknesses, as he understood them. Atwood regularly numbers among those poets, and later novelists, that Purdy considers the best in Canada, but his admiration is frequently qualified with complaints that her poetic/authorial persona is "cold" or "inhuman." His assessment of *Power Politics* (1971), for example, though not public, was a similar conglomeration of professional admiration and aesthetic objections to Atwood's glacial tendencies. Reacting to the book in a letter to Margaret Laurence, he wrote:

> migawd, it's good! Also monotonous if read right thru. Same tone, same woman, same feelings mostly. But jesus, does she get it across! But I must admit that she strikes me as inhuman in some way, tho I like her personally much. The woman bit is carried too far in her, just as the man bit is in others ... We're all fallible whatever the gender. Maybe your bit about being forlorn and bereaved because a woman writer etc. is true. Neither man nor woman ought to have to somehow compete on the same ego trip as writing. (2 November 1971; YA 187)

Purdy's half-hearted concession to Laurence that Atwood might have political motivations for adopting her characteristically sardonic persona suggests, somewhat to the contrary, that the plight of the "poetess"[14] never truly registered with the aesthetically "masculine" poet.[15]

Instead, for Purdy, this persona and its corresponding emphasis on "the woman bit," though initially effective, was quickly becoming monotonous. It was, moreover, leaving Atwood vulnerable to pigeonholing by critics and the media. Reflecting, over a decade later, on Atwood's international appeal in a letter to Stan Dragland, Purdy declared that, while Atwood seemed to "travel well," he was still "put ... off" by the "glacial" "coldness" of her persona:

> I don't like a world in which everything is so fuckin cold, nor really believe in it. And since Miss Peggy herself does not impress as a cold person – only a cerebral one – it occurs to me that her writing may be method writing, method in order to be published and popular? But then, all writing is method writing, even if a personal method. (25 February 1982; YA 346)[16]

Purdy's suggestion that Atwood "travel[s] well" obliquely refers to her international appeal, which, by the 1980s, was indisputable. Given the critical sea change of the 1970s and after, was he finally beginning to begrudge Atwood her popularity? Do his comments betray the bias that "popular" literature cannot be "good" literature? Again, in retrospect, Purdy's comments – both to Dragland and as they appeared more ambiguously in the *Malahat Review* – can be traced back to a literary landscape that the writers shared, but experienced quite differently. What had registered as glacial and monochromatic with Purdy had resonated with an up-and-coming generation of feminists who found in Atwood a spokeswoman, and with a host of others who may or may not have been drawn to any number of her protean images: Circe, Medusa, or National Prophet.[17] By 1986, Purdy's heyday had ended, and while he would continue to publish prolifically, his experience with a certain form of "literary celebrity" was effectively over. In a letter to George Bowering written in December 1985, Purdy seemed notably conflicted about the relative worth of either his or Atwood's contributions to Canadian literature:

> The older generation – [Irving] Layton, [Earle] Birney, and that's really all there are unless you include me as well – has really passed from the scene. And that leaves you and [Michael] Ondaatje, as well as Atwood. But I can't regard Atwood the same way or as relevant in the same way. She seems to me a sport of the media as much as a good writer, which last of course she is too. But she is a writer more than being a poet, if you get me. Somebody invented her, and it wasn't her.
>
> Anyway, the chief reason for hoping and maybe perhaps believing that we – you and I and whoever – are good is to feel ... that we haven't wasted our lives. That we have contributed something to this country and the world ... And to feel that way we need some praise occasionally from someone we respect, to heal the open ego-wound that never heals ... For myself, and I expect you'd agree, I couldn't see spending my life in any other way than I have[.] (11 December 1985; YA 416)

Here again, however, it seems appropriate to reiterate that Purdy's aversion to Atwood as media icon never seems to diminish his respect for "Peggy," his friend and colleague. As these excerpts indicate, he was always careful to distinguish between the two. If Purdy at one point envied Atwood's success or critical relevance, that reaction is contextualized by the breadth and depth of their relationship as it appears throughout their correspondence. If "Atwood the icon" was suspect, "Peggy" was the brilliant mind, touchy academic, loyal editor, in at least once instance medical advisor, and steadfast friend. And eventually, even the distinction between Atwood and "Peggy" seemed unnecessary to Purdy. Writing to Atwood in 1996, he continued their ongoing riff about the possibility of her winning the Nobel Prize, but his tone was uncharacteristically earnest: "I hope much you get the Nobel ... Both for your own reward and satisfaction, and for the country itself. We need heroes (you'll never be a heroine – they're in old movies), for more reasons than to counter US bullshit" (4 December 1996; YA 522). Far less ambiguous or satirical here than in the slightly earlier "Concerning Ms. Atwood," Purdy seemed ultimately to concede that the Atwood/"Peggy" construct had done the country more good than harm.

Much like Purdy's essay, this chapter is a fraction of what could be said about the two authors' mutual influence over forty years. Perhaps because critical precedence has been given to his affiliation with another famous Margaret – Laurence – or because Atwood has long been considered overexposed in terms of scholarship, comparatively little attention has been paid to the Atwood-Purdy dynamic. Though their friendship was relatively public, there has been, to my knowledge, no in-depth study of their mutual literary influence, nor has there been a sustained look at their personal relationship – another irony of fame, perhaps, and a shame given what is an informative and entertaining body of personal and professional engagement extending from the late 1960s to Purdy's death in 2000. Though a number of their letters have been published in *Yours, Al: The Collected Letters of Al Purdy* (2004), there is a trove of unpublished archival correspondence that has yet to be collated or analyzed. And although Purdy's commentary on Atwood is fascinating, Atwood's commentary on Purdy is likewise worth exploring, particularly in light of the fact that Atwood was involved in editing Anansi's reprint of Purdy's *Poems for All the Annettes* in 1973. Their exchanges during this period are an interesting mixture of personal and professional concerns, and no doubt reveal much about the power dynamics and tensions between writers of different generations, schools, and – to be sure – genders. If nothing else, the candour of Purdy's correspondence speaks to the multiplicity that, he insisted, was his only constant.

NOTES

1 See Hutcheon.
2 Fulford's analysis is a highly gendered account of Atwood's allure: she appeals to a flighty and inattentive public because she, as a woman, is likewise flighty and inconsistent. The suggestion that motherhood and feminism are mutually exclusive is equally problematic. Fulford equates a critique of patriarchy with a uniform critique of all men. In his efforts to highlight Atwood's "protean flexibility," he also vastly oversimplifies her

relationship to the term and movement of feminism as it appeared in the 1960s and early 1970s. On this subject see Atwood's "On Being a 'Woman Writer': Paradoxes and Dilemmas" (*Second* 190–204).

3 Fulford's contribution may be skewed in other respects as well. Fulford has gone on record saying that Percy Marrow, the "disreputable" and "disloyal" journalist nicknamed "Vedge" in Atwood's short story "Uncles" (from *Wilderness Tips*, 1989), is a version of himself. Though Atwood has not confirmed the connection, Fulford's perception of a parallel is suggestive. See Cooke 19–20.

4 In a more detailed analysis of Atwood's celebrity, *Margaret Atwood and the Labour of Literary Celebrity*, York likewise emphasizes the role that others have played in the construction of what we might call "Atwood Inc." Like Jack Stillinger in his influential *Multiple Authorship and the Myth of Solitary Genius* (1991), York deconstructs the myth of the solitary celebrity, shedding light on the multitude of people who labour to produce the "star text" that is a celebrated author (8, 15).

5 See Sandler's bibliographical entry in the University of Calgary's Special Collections online archive: https://searcharchives.ucalgary.ca/index.php/linda-sandler-fonds.

6 Only Purdy's side of this exchange has been preserved in the Robin Skelton fonds in the University of Victoria Libraries' Special Collections.

7 Sandler again broached the idea of a special issue on Purdy in a subsequent letter. Purdy was adamant that she not proceed, writing "I'd prefer you did not do a Purdy-ish. ish. [*sic*]. I don't want to react to you in any way because you're doing that. So don't, please" (15 September 1975).

8 Though "mistaken" is almost certainly the wrong word here, given that it oversimplifies both Lee's analysis and Purdy's impact on the national poetry scene, it is worth noting that Lee was at least aware that, in casting Purdy as the heart and soul of Canadian poetry, he was causing the poet some discomfort. In the 1988 film *Al Purdy: "A Sensitive Man,"* Lee is recorded saying, "[Purdy] has given voice to so many of the things that are central in our life ... To me, Purdy is the first Canadian writer who has stood as articulator of the conscious [*sic*] of his people. And that sounds so pompous and pretentious and Purdy would throw a beer bottle at me just to hear me say that out loud because it goes against every way he's prepared to think about himself." It is impossible to say how expansive the "public" that Lee envisions was, though the heartfelt nature of the tribute and Purdy's role as artistic mentor to a number of Canadian authors might suggest that this "public" was predominantly literary. In an aside on this documentary, Deshaye suggests that Purdy's "performance" in the film speaks to his lack of interest in celebrity. "The NFB film," Deshaye writes, "shows that [Purdy]

indulged in clowning for the cameras only at a distance": "notwithstanding his determination to publish a lot of poetry, he never aspired to fame through celebrity as Layton, Cohen, Ondaatje, and MacEwen seemed to do" (53). Deshaye also cites a passage from Purdy's autobiography, in which he eschews the "kind of immortality" to which figures like Layton aspired (RBS 281; qtd. in Deshaye 53). Though Deshaye may be right in suggesting that the Purdy of the 1990s "did not feel affected by celebrity" (53), I am not convinced such perceptions can be applied retroactively to Purdy in the 1970s, when his feelings about success and celebrity – and what those terms meant – seem conflicted at best.

9 The careers of both Purdy and Atwood support Mount's assertion. Atwood, for example, in addition to her polemical work of criticism, *Survival: A Thematic Guide to Canadian Literature* (1972), which brought a number of her contemporaries into conversation with one another, edited the revised and expanded edition of Purdy's *Poems for All the Annettes* for Anansi in 1973. Following "the boom," she also compiled and edited *The New Oxford Book of Canadian Verse in English* for Oxford University Press (1982), followed by two compilations of short stories with Robert Weaver, again for Oxford University Press, in 1986 and 1995, respectively. Purdy likewise compiled and edited several collections of Canadian poetry, including *Fifteen Winds* (mentioned above), *Storm Warning: The New Canadian Poets* (1971), and *Storm Warning 2* (1976), as well as individual collections by Milton Acorn (*I've Tasted My Blood: Poems, 1958 to 1968*, 1969; *Dig Up My Heart: Selected Poems, 1952–83*, 1983) and Andrew Suknaski (*Wood Mountain Poems*, 1976).

10 Deshaye records Purdy appearing on the CBC ninety-four times between 1955 and 1980, as compared to Layton's 138 appearances, Atwood's 135, and Cohen's 118 (45).

11 During this period, two of Purdy's poems ("Arctic Rhododendrons" and "Whoever You Are") were acquired by The Bay in an effort to modernize the company's image. Notably, "Arctic Rhododendrons" was among the first of the poems purchased for the campaign by Barbara Kilvert, the executive assistant of public relations for HBC at the time. The list of poets involved included Atwood, Earle Birney, Louis Dudek, MacEwen, Alden Nowlan, and others (see Ross and York).

12 The other poets included were Pat Lowther, Annette Murray (whose poem was written with her husband, Jim), and Anne Szumigalski. Purdy included only one poem from each, but three poems from Atwood: "Dreams of the Animals," "At the Tourist Centre in Boston," and "Backdrop Addresses Cowboy."

13 Both reviews appeared first in *Canadian Literature* (issues 39 and 47, respectively) and are collected in Purdy, SA 236–8, 238–44. The following references in this chapter are to the original reviews.

14 In *The Burgess Shale: The Canadian Writing Landscape of the 1960s* (2017), Atwood remarks that "in 1970, I used to be called a poetess ... which ... used to mean an inconsequential poet, inconsequential because female" (3).

15 In her account of Atwood's early years, Rosemary Sullivan reminds readers that, even in Bohemia, the early part of the "liberal" sixties was hardly liberating for everyone all at once. Sexual politics, though acknowledged privately among female artists, was not discussed openly, since "the language to understand it had not yet been explored" (106). Women in the arts might be muses, mistresses, or groupies, but they were rarely deemed authors in their own right. Neither did they have a diverse list of artistic role models. Perhaps this was why, having read Atwood's self-published collection *Double Persephone* (1961), fellow poet MacEwen declared:

> With the onslaught of Persephone, both of them, I at last struck that very subtle and rather vicious vein of authenticity under the sometimes innocent skeleton caging it ... [I] like it very much is what I mean ... [P]ossibly the female poet has to emphasize the anti-primrose and candyfloss business more than the male ... hair ribbons and all that – can be hampering, I think. To achieve that clean-cut, uncomprising slant on things is an achievement. (Qtd. in Sullivan 111)

Like Phyllis Webb, another poet with a famously chilly aesthetic, Atwood and MacEwen were attempting to "see," or perhaps more accurately *speak*, "into the dark" of a social and literary milieu that lacked the language and resources to assist them. If what Purdy called "the woman bit" appeared over-articulated, it was for good reason. If the voice Atwood found was joyless, it was certainly resonant (see Purdy, "Atwood's" 82–3).

16 What Purdy somewhat uncharitably reduces here to a grab at popular appeal, but identifies perhaps more accurately as a "method," was no doubt part of a rhetorical strategy that began in the 1960s and involved navigating, on paper and in person, a literary scene dominated by such hypermasculine figures as Acorn, Layton, Cohen, and, of course, Purdy himself.

17 Sandler, in her interview with Atwood in the *Malahat*, suggests that Atwood has been portrayed variously as both "prophet" and a Circe figure. In her response, Atwood claims not to have heard about the comparison, but notes that Alan Pearson, in a review of *You Are Happy* (1974), likened her to Medusa (see Pearson). In this instance, however, Atwood claims that the comparison had more to do with her hair than her writing (Atwood, "Interview" 8).

ARCHIVAL SOURCES

Al Purdy Fonds. 5093.1 Queen's University Archives.
 Letter from Margaret Atwood to Purdy, 15 January 1995, Box 1, Folder 2.
Robin Skelton Fonds. 1999-045. University of Victoria Libraries Special Collections and University Archives.
 Letter from Purdy to Linda Sandler, 2 February 1975, Box 1, Folder 29.
 Letter from Purdy to Sandler, 5 August 1975, Box 1, Folder 29.
 Letter from Purdy to Sandler, 20 August 1975, Box 1, Folder 29.
 Letter from Purdy to Sandler, 15 September 1975, Box 1, Folder 29.
 Letter from Purdy to Sandler, 1 January 1976, Box 1, Folder 29.

REFERENCES

Atwood, Margaret. *The Burgess Shale: The Canadian Writing Landscape of the 1960s*. Edmonton: University of Alberta Press/Canadian Literature Centre, 2017.
– "Interview with Margaret Atwood." Interview by Linda Sandler. *Malahat Review*, no. 41 (January 1977): 7–27.
– *Second Words: Selected Critical Prose*. Toronto: House of Anansi Press, 1982.
Cooke, Nathalie. "Lions, Tigers, and Pussycats: Margaret Atwood (Auto-)Biographically." In *Margaret Atwood: Works and Impact*, edited by Reingard M. Nischik, 15–27. Toronto: House of Anansi Press, 2002.
Deshaye, Joel. *The Metaphor of Celebrity: Canadian Poetry and the Public, 1955–1980*. Toronto: University of Toronto Press, 2013.
Fulford, Robert. "The Images of Atwood." *Malahat Review*, no. 41 (January 1977): 95–8.
Hutcheon, Linda. "Margaret's *Malahat*." *Canadian Poetry: Studies, Documents, Reviews*, no. 5 (Fall–Winter 1979): 132–5.
Lee, Dennis. "The Poetry of Al Purdy." In *Al Purdy: Essays on His Works*, edited by Linda Rogers, 69–107. Toronto: Guernica Editions, 2002.
Mount, Nick. *Arrival: The Story of CanLit*. Toronto: House of Anansi Press, 2017.
Pearson, Alan. "A Skeletal Novella in Plain Diction: A Bestiary under Iron Grey Skies." Review of *You Are Happy*, by Margaret Atwood. *Globe and Mail*, 28 September 1974: 33.
Purdy, Al. "Atwood's Moodie." Review of *The Journals of Susanna Moodie*, by Margaret Atwood. *Canadian Literature*, no. 47 (Winter 1971): 80–4.
– *Beyond Remembering: The Collected Poems of Al Purdy*. Edited by Al Purdy and Sam Solecki. Madeira Park, BC: Harbour Publishing, 2000.

– "Deprivations." *Malahat Review*, no. 41 (January 1977): 100–1.
– "Poet Besieged." Review of *The Animals in That Country*, by Margaret Atwood. *Canadian Literature*, no. 39 (Winter 1969): 94–6.
– *Reaching for the Beaufort Sea: An Autobiography*. Edited by Alex Widen. Madeira Park, BC: Harbour Publishing, 1993.
– *Starting from Ameliasburgh: The Collected Prose of Al Purdy*. Edited by Sam Solecki. Madeira Park, BC: Harbour Publishing, 1995.
– "An Unburnished One-Tenth of One Per Cent of an Event." *Malahat Review*, no. 41 (January 1977): 61–4.
– *Yours, Al: The Collected Letters of Al Purdy*. Edited by Sam Solecki. Madeira Park, BC: Harbour Publishing, 2004.
Ross, Michael, and Lorraine York. "Imperial Commerce and the Canadian Muse: The Hudson's Bay Company's Poetic Advertising Campaign of 1966–1972." *Canadian Literature*, no. 220 (Spring 2014): 37–53.
Sandler, Linda. "Preface." *Malahat Review*, no. 41 (January 1977): 5–6.
Solecki, Sam. *The Last Canadian Poet: An Essay on Al Purdy*. Toronto: University of Toronto Press, 1999.
Sullivan, Rosemary. *The Red Shoes: Margaret Atwood Starting Out*. Toronto: HarperCollins, 1988.
Warner, Michael. *Publics and Counterpublics*. New York: Zone Books, 2002.
Winkler, Donald, dir. *Al Purdy: "A Sensitive Man."* 1988. Montreal: National Film Board of Canada, 2006. DVD.
York, Lorraine. *Literary Celebrity in Canada*. Toronto: University of Toronto Press, 2007.
– *Margaret Atwood and the Labour of Literary Celebrity*. Toronto: University of Toronto Press, 2013.

12

Purdy's Poetics: Intuitive Formalism in *A Splinter in the Heart*

Carl Watts

In his introduction to *The New Canon: An Anthology of Canadian Poetry* (2005), Carmine Starnino suggests that the slack free-verse poetics he sees as defining contemporary Canadian poetry – "the plain, the soft-spoken, the flatly prosy, the paraphrasingly simple, the accessibly Canadian" – is, at least he hopes, "in its last throes" (26). Elsewhere, he still more pithily describes "our current literary dispensation" as one in which free verse "continues its ascendancy with the emphasis on 'free' rather than on 'verse'" ("Introduction to *David Solway*" 10). The mission statement in his *Anthology*, meanwhile, describes the free-verse status quo as having come under attack since the 1980s by both experimental poets and those who are demonized as "capital-F formalists" or, worse, formalists "prefixed with 'neo' to convey the drasticness of their suspected conservatism" (27). Starnino approaches the latter group in a strange way, first claiming that, at least in its caricatured form, "no such formalism exists – if it ever did" (27–8). Then he launches into his description of the dynamic but "very loosely confederated group of poets" whose "detestation of the prose-domesticated mainstream" (28) inspires the works in his *Anthology*. Starnino is at pains both to speak for and to transcend formalist challenges to free verse, using his well-honed skills as an opinionated critic explicitly to position himself and his "new canon" as a rebellion against all that is bland in Canadian poetry. Yet, as I will suggest in this chapter, the poet Starnino erects as the figurehead of that blandness – Al Purdy – may, upon closer inspection, share much with Starnino, in poetic theory, if not practice.

Starnino has associated Purdy, the "last Canadian poet" (as Sam Solecki's polarizing study has it; see Solecki, LCP), with this prosaic mainstream, at times seemingly agitating for open insurrection against the celebrated poet's legacy.¹ Given Starnino's statement that Purdy's "earnestness" is indicative of Canadian critics' tendency to rank poets "not because of the sophistication of their style but because of the cultural themes carried by their content" (*Lover's* 68), Solecki's somewhat audacious proclamation of Purdy's quintessential Canadianness is all the ammunition Starnino needs to assert that Canada's free-verse aesthetic has been "neatly folded into our catechism on nationalism" ("Introduction to *New Canon*" 26). Indeed, Starnino's bluntest dismissal of Purdy may be his statement that high praise for the poet is "Canadian self-adulation at its most delusional" and an indication that "'world-class' means nothing for us. The word is a special prize handed out by Canadianists – a placebo, a publicity-kit term, an illusion-enabler, a gift of our group loyalty. Mordecai Richler nailed it years ago when he mocked the locally fêted as being 'world-famous in Canada'" ("Interview" 11–12).²

I want to make the case that, despite the vigour of such criticism and the enthusiasm with which he decries – rightly, in my view – the predictability of much recent mainstream Canadian poetry, the formalist philosophy of poetry propounded by Starnino, an influential and controversial poet and editor born more than fifty years after Purdy, and the implicitly formalist philosophy of poetry held by Purdy himself, are not quite as distinct as Starnino's provocations may suggest. (Starnino's own poetic practice more obviously reflects this philosophy than does Purdy's free verse, and, as I will discuss, Purdy articulates this poetics in a vastly different way than does Starnino.) I will do so by exploring a glaring blank spot in Purdy scholarship: his only novel, *A Splinter in the Heart* (1990). I want to make the perhaps unlikely argument that the novel, despite its critical neglect, can be read as a late-career *Bildungsroman*, or novel of poetic development, which provides the description of poetic philosophy that is largely absent from Purdy's critical writing proper.³ That is, Purdy's statement of poetics is to be found not in his free-verse poetic practice, nor in his scattered, often rambling pieces of non-fiction, but in his little-studied novel. My primary argument is that *A Splinter in the Heart* dramatizes the distinctions between sound, literal meaning, and overall or implied meaning that lie at the centre of Starnino's conception of formalism. Unlike Starnino, however, Purdy's novel grasps these distinctions holistically – by revealing them in phenomena as diverse and quotidian as bodily sensation, human encounters with non-human animals, and distinctions between a speaker's explicit and implicit meanings – and thus puts forth a broadly formalist poetic philosophy that is inescapably intuitive, as opposed to rigorously explained or programmatic.

I also want to expand this argument to account for, first, the novelty of *A Splinter in the Heart* in Purdy's body of work, and, second, the implications of Starnino's use of Purdy as Canada's quintessential free-versifier. As I will suggest, Purdy's trying his hand at a novel distances him from his role as unofficial poet laureate, enabling him to explain his poetics without undermining the intuitive nature of his formalism. The very fact that his poetics is woven into the prose of his only novel underscores the intuitive quality of this philosophy. The somewhat paradoxical result of this strategy is that it at once exposes a greater rigour in Purdy's poetics and yet justifies the formal laxity of which he has sometimes been accused, indicating that notions of Purdy's quintessential Canadianness may rely as much on his casual expression of a broad poetic formalism as on the supposedly formally unadorned content of his poems. Considering Purdy's poetics in this way – as an underlying, multiply manifesting poetic philosophy, as opposed to an easily identifiable set of poetic techniques – in turn suggests that Starnino's criticisms say less about Purdy the actual poet and more about Purdy as Solecki reads him: that is, as a figurehead, standing in this case not for Canadian identity but for a poetic practice existing in isolation, or else in the form of other writers' iterations of his poetic attitude or imitations of his style.

Solecki sees that style as having evolved to incorporate both traditional and modernist forms, a process that works in tandem with the expansion of Purdy's regional points of reference from his beginnings in Ontario into a "synecdoche for the national and universal"; the result is what Solecki calls, borrowing from Helen Vendler, a "compelling aesthetic signature" (LCP 12). This merging of local content and larger literary context both accounts for and effaces the lack of identifiable formal elements that Starnino decries. Regarding Purdy's free-verse "signature" as intertwined with the nationalist zeitgeist and themes of the 1960s and 1970s has certainly inspired a long tradition of Canadian free verse that focuses on content more than form. Yet while any large body of this kind of writing, which Charles Bernstein has since the early 1980s dismissed as the product of "official verse culture" (246), will produce some mediocre material, Purdy was nevertheless distinctive in laying the groundwork for this fusion of nationalist content with a loose free-verse aesthetic. Because of this fusion, and also because he was one of Canada's most prolific poets, Purdy's legacy, especially as it is described by Starnino and other critics, has come to refer not only to his own work, but also to decades of free-verse treatments of Canadian experience.

Purdy is indeed far from formally experimental, but he is consistent; his form, as unspectacular as it may be when read in isolation from his subject matter, nevertheless exists in symbiosis with the persona that emerged from this confluence of content, context, and stylistic regularity. The lack of formalist rigour detectable in Purdy, and in many of the later admirers Starnino has taken to task in opinionated book reviews, needs to be read as an element of the work of an extraordinarily prolific writer, from whose hundreds of poems any generalizations about style must be extracted.[4] Given this broader relationship between context, commentary, and poetry, whatever formalism is at play in Purdy's work needs to be read not in the form of representative examples from specific poems, but rather as the cumulative effect of his years of versification on the topics that make him seminal in twentieth-century Canadian poetry. A lack of tightly coiled, quotable examples does not necessarily mean that Purdy's understanding of poetry had no room for formal nuance. A closer look at *A Splinter in the Heart*, as well as scattered critical contributions from throughout Purdy's career, indicates that his corpus combines a general understanding of formal distinctions among poets with a consistent understanding of poetry as essentially intuitive, and not in need of explication or systematization.[5]

Starnino, on the other hand, is no stranger to formalist manifestos. Yet even this difference from Purdy reveals a commonality. Despite Starnino's critical acumen and the consistency of his editorial statements, his explanations of appealing formalist poetics frequently prize vague qualities such as "pounded-on spontaneity" and "aggressive musicality" ("Introduction to *New Canon*" 22).[6] Such descriptions suggest that Starnino supports a poetics defined less by the metre or closed forms of previous North American formalisms than by a strict separation of sonic qualities from literal meaning and, via the subtle interplay of these two elements on the level of the individual line, an overall intellectual and aesthetic effect. Still, this explanation must be extrapolated from Starnino's many spirited, yet ultimately subjective and somewhat imprecise, articulations of this formalism. A clear picture can only be constructed from the cumulative effect of his series of manifestos; his indirection is in some ways similar to Purdy's oblique, novelistic attention to poetic form.

In *The New Canon*, Starnino turns to specific poems by writers such as Anita Lahey, Ken Babstock, and Adam Sol; the passages are not instances of individual formal techniques so much as concentrated examples of Starnino's preferred relationship between sound and sense. The poems he quotes showcase sonic complexity, precise imagery, and brief vignettes of identifiable metre. Take, for instance, the compacted consonance and monosyllables that are rendered especially choppy by an abundance of bilabials in lines taken from Babstock's "Tractor": "The small hinged cap atop a burping exhaust pipe / flapped in slow panic like the mother killdeer who'd taken a clip" (qtd. in Starnino, "Introduction to *New Canon*" 22). These condensed representations of an indirectly articulated formalism render Starnino's poetics as painstakingly crafted, but also as natural, comprehensible, and unequivocally appealing – and, by extension, part of an intuitive understanding of what constitutes accomplished verse.

Starnino is also a long-time supporter of David Solway, whose polemical essay against Purdy's poetics, "Standard Average Canadian," makes the case that, despite the significance of his poems' content, Purdy's delivery is "mere narrative or reportage, the structure muddled and amorphous, the tone laid on with a trowel, lumberingly mock-plaintive and corny" (88).[7] Both Solway and Starnino support a poetics in which the intuitive and the well-crafted are one and the same. It is no surprise that Solway's critique employs a litany of subjective, hard-to-pin-down adjectives, many of which, including "alert, robust, patterned and mettlesome," as well as his requirement that good writing avoid "lexical sag" (90), connote strength or efficiency; such descriptors are at home with Starnino's "aggressive musicality." Despite the quarrelsome nature of these disagreements, the acerbity of their delivery itself indicates a shared commitment among Solway, Starnino, and Purdy to a non-systematic arrangement of sonic, syntactical, and semantic elements.

Marjorie Perloff, as far back as 1991, criticized a poetics that combined ostensibly formalist rigour with a relatively simple attention to distinct elements of form and content. In *Radical Artifice: Writing Poetry in the Age of Media*, she takes aim at two groups: first, the American New Formalist poetry of the 1980s (3–4), as described by Frederick Feirstein and Frederick Turner, and whose practitioners include Dana Gioia, Tom Disch, and (arguably given the range of her interests and formal techniques) Molly Peacock; and, second, the less rigid "Deep Image" writing of poets such as Robert Bly, Galway Kinnell, and James Wright, which Perloff characterizes as "perfect" yet "oddly unambitious" (21).[8] The latter – in which, according to Perloff, images are "presented directly in a series of simple declarative present-tense sentences" and enhanced by the poem's corresponding "sound features" (21) – exhibit a tight form-content relationship that is similar to Starnino's fixation on the simultaneous separateness and connectedness of sound and sense. What Starnino adds to the Deep Imagism that Perloff defines (and dismisses) is attitude – the conviction that a similar, vaguely formalist poetics, when honed further and aligned with the experiences of the Canadian writer, is not only serious and authentic, but also brave and bold for opposing the avant-garde poets Starnino regards as having found success in "peddling their antagonistic, unnuanced theory of innovation" ("Introduction to *New Canon*" 28).

Perloff's ideas are relevant in a contemporary Canadian context because of what she regards as the ideological shortcomings that are part of a purported lack of formal ambition. In Wright's "From a Bus Window in Central Ohio, Just before a Thunder Shower," from *The Branch Will Not Break* (1963), she finds – in its use of "slow trochaic rhythm, stressed diphthongs, and ... alliteration and assonance" to replicate the situation described in its title – a "minimalism" that signifies an unwillingness to probe the relationship between nature and culture behind the poem's picture of country life (21). The poem's misplaced nostalgia matches its well-wrought yet predictable intertwining of sound and sense. Poetry of this kind ceases to be innovative, according to Perloff, becoming instead a mere craft with agreed-upon rules and thus more or less objective standards of excellence. Such standards are in many ways at the centre of contemporary debates about Canadian poetry, with claims to universality (or even national commonality, such as Solecki's) coming under scrutiny for failing to accommodate, or even undermining, diversity.

Indeed, Starnino and others have been criticized for casting narrow conceptions of formalism as universal poetic standards. Sina Queyras has stated that Starnino's project of "outing the frauds" has, not coincidentally, been supported by a series of "white, middle-classish males, cut from similar aesthetic cloth" (12).[9] Regardless of the extent to which the identities of such writers animate or limit their poetics, *The New Canon* does discuss an intuitive formalist aesthetic in a way that edges into universalizing ideas of skill and quality. Perhaps the most explicit Canadian formalist equation of poetics and quality is Jason Guriel's statement, in a review of Eric Ormsby's *Time's Covenant: Selected Poems* (2007), that "a poem's primary responsibility is to be excellent" (32). In a sense, Starnino's and Guriel's arguments are new salvos in the perennial debate over innovative versus conservative styles (and the politics of form generally), here charged with the ideas of American Formalism and the politics of present-day Canadian poetry publishing and teaching. Not only is Starnino seemingly nostalgic for specific ideas of community and family, as in his celebration of gendered domestic labour in the poem "What My Mother's Hands Smell Like," which describes the speaker's mother's having "scoured / the mucked pan and scrubbed the smeared plates, / after she's flushed the glasses free of wine-stains / and wiped the grease speckling the top of the oven" (*Credo* 33), but his delineation of universal poetic standards is also, to Queyras and other feminist poets and critics, ideologically suspect. Starnino's statement that form is an apolitical, "vacant" entity that "stays forever open to multifold meanings" ("Introduction to *New Canon*" 32) assumes that all writers will use similar means to express ostensibly universal experiences and perspectives. Understood only in terms of aesthetics or the poet's commitment to technique, Starnino's emphasis on craft is quite reasonable, and not as original or threatening as some of the rhetoric from either side suggests. Yet its valorizing of combinations of intuition and rigour has, in colliding with other debates about demographic representation and the place of progressive values in literary culture, been deemed either contentious and conservative (according to his detractors) or, to Starnino and his supporters, radical and courageous.

The irony is that Purdy, the supposed epitome of dull free verse, seized on the same combination of intuition and consistent poetic practice (if not rigour) without attracting much controversy. It is perhaps to be expected, then, that some of Purdy's writing both engages with a vaguely formalist poetics and disavows it as an unnecessary dissection of omnipresent linguistic and aural characteristics. What is less expected is that he made this statement of poetics indirectly, in a novel that could, reasonably if uncharitably, be described as a haphazard fictionalization of previously published autobiographical material. It is fitting that, while Starnino casts the combination of the intuitive and the well-crafted as an indication of literary value, and thus deserving of spirited explanation and endorsement, *A Splinter in the Heart* construes this dynamic as occurring naturally, in its narrative and dialogue and, by extension, in a poet's verse and everyday idiom. Purdy's use of the novel to dwell on poetry is not merely a curiosity; instead, his shambolic version of the *Bildungsroman* – in some ways a *Künstlerroman*, or novel of artistic development, given the allusion to Canadian literature with which it concludes – adds an element of authorial distance from his topic. Purdy emphasizes the intuitive quality of his poetics by suggesting that the poet himself ought not to articulate directly the intuited relationship between sound and sense.

That Purdy's prose has an indirect, yet multi-faceted, relationship with his poetics should not come as a surprise. His autobiography, *Reaching for the Beaufort Sea* (1993), uses his poetry – both excerpts and poems republished in their entirety, sometimes with small variations – to reinforce key moments in his narrative. For instance, when Purdy introduces "the town idiot," Joe Barr – who also appears in a fictionalized form in *A Splinter in the Heart* – the brief prose description ends with a simple, open-ended statement about Joe's condition: "Of course he knew there was something wrong with him, but never found out why the world was such a cruel place" (RBS 29). The statement is followed immediately by an excerpt from the poem "Joe Barr," from *Wild Grape Wine* (1968):

> I could have learned from Joe myself
> but I never did
> not even when gangs of children
> followed him down the street
> chanting "aw-aw-aw" in mockery
> children have for idiots[.] (RBS 29–30; cf. WG 65, BR 178)

The poem provides a different take on Joe, unpacking the experience of a figure in whom Purdy the autobiographer takes comparatively little interest. Whether pausing briefly to consider something, as is the case here, or adding to a prose description – such as when "Transient," a poem from *The Cariboo Horses* (1965) about riding the rails, fills out his open-ended description of "the rail music that has pounded and throbbed into a long silence" (RBS 79) – Purdy uses poems in his autobiography to complement the content of his prose.

Purdy does not use poetry in this way in *A Splinter in the Heart*. W.J. Keith notes (171–2) that reworked lines from "Joe Barr" appear in the novel, and he finds passages that similarly build on poems such as "Pre-School" (from *Sundance at Dusk*, 1976), "Elegy for a Grandfather" (from *Wild Grape Wine* and other volumes), and "My Grandfather Talking – 30 Years Ago" (from *The Cariboo Horses*). Yet while Purdy does draw on previous publications to enhance or anchor his narrative, they are never set off as visibly identifiable poems; they are fully integrated with what Keith calls the novel's "straightforward, third-person narrative," which "communicates the story clearly enough but does little else" (168). Keith concludes that Purdy's prose style lacks evidence of the long and complex development of his poetics, and that his attempt at a "unification" of his poetry and prose fails, because he is "unable to create a form that could contain the variety of tone and attitude that he is capable of producing in short pieces" (175). Still, Keith's statement that those familiar with Purdy's works will, upon reading the novel, "experience a series of shocks of recognition and a recurrent sense of déjà vu" (165) indicates an important difference between the role of poetry in the novel and the role of poetry in his other autobiographical writings. Indeed, the absence of whole poems from the novel is far from an absence of Purdy's poetics. Russell Brown criticizes *Reaching for the Beaufort Sea* for merely providing a prose version of the content of Purdy's poems, and thus resembling "one of those self-absorbed speakers who keeps telling the same story over and over again" (221). The repackaging enterprise that is Purdy's novel, however, makes more sophisticated use of previously published material, drawing on the author's autobiographical writing or collapsing specific poetic techniques into its prose. Brown concludes that "[m]ost events important enough to warrant inclusion in *Reaching for the Beaufort Sea* have already had poems made out of them," and that "some may be included here only *because* Purdy knows that he has made good poems about them" (221; emphasis original). But in *A Splinter in the Heart*, Purdy's invocation of poetry instead explores the fundamentals of form and poetic voice in the abstract without being bogged down by the documentary (or lazy) practice of including whole examples of Purdy the poet plying his trade.

A Splinter in the Heart takes place in Trenton, Ontario, toward the end of the First World War; it resembles Hugh MacLennan's treatment of the Halifax Explosion in *Barometer Rising* (1941) in that it is built around the historical event of the 1918 fire at the British Chemical Company's Trenton works. The novel tells the story of Patrick Cameron, a character who is distinct from Purdy, despite biographical similarities. Considering the matters of recycling Keith discusses, it is difficult not to read Cameron as a version of Purdy; still, Patrick's fictionality creates an additional degree of separation between Purdy the poet or critic and the free-indirect discourse of the novel, allowing Patrick to sketch out a broad poetics in a way Purdy himself tended not to do.

Purdy's commentary on his own poetry and the techniques of other writers fits with a broadly formalist poetics based on knowledge of the distinctions between form, content, and overall meaning, as well as a dynamic of intuition and authorial consistency. Unlike the abstract picture created in *A Splinter in the Heart*, however, Purdy's critical contributions are based on a typically cavalier collapsing of any conscious poetic commitment into his everyday persona. He certainly meets the free-verse standard of regarding authentic speech as central to a viable poetics; in a review essay on several of Leonard Cohen's books, Purdy addresses Cohen's own description of the "sounds" that appear in *Flowers for Hitler* (1964): "By sounds I take it he means his idioms, tone, and contemporary speech rhythms" ("Leonard" 14; SA 202). Often, however, Purdy provides a more nuanced understanding of form. In his introduction to *The Poems of Al Purdy* (1976), he refers to his early self acquiring "the monotonous Carman iambic habit which took twenty years to kick" (6). Describing the influence that Dylan Thomas, T.S. Eliot, and Irving Layton came to have on him, he writes, "the style of crap I was writing began to change. I used off-rhyme and assonance in poems. I used multisyllabic words whose meanings I kept forgetting after I wrote the poems. I used line breaks about that time. I used home brew" (7). That Purdy mentions line breaks as one of the newer items in his repertoire so shortly after dismissing his early "iambic habit" suggests that he viewed the individual line both as a unit of semantic meaning and as a compartment for formal embellishment such as "off-rhyme and assonance," both indispensable devices in any attentive lyric poetry.

Other scattered comments emphasize Purdy's understanding of any such poetics as necessarily intuitive. Reviewing Raymond Souster's *New Wave Canada* (1966), he criticizes Black Mountain College "methods" as "corrupted in narcissistic love of technique itself"; he states that the strongest poems in Souster's anthology are those that keep from being "overwhelmed by technique-mystique" (44; SA 348). The irony here – aside from the fact that his dismissal of explicating one's technique appears in a piece of critical writing – is that Purdy's criticism of systematic explanation, while directed at a foundational Canadian example of the self-consciously experimentalist writing that Starnino frequently criticizes, could just as easily be applied to Starnino's own delineations of appropriately sophisticated technique.

In *A Splinter in the Heart*, however, Purdy avoids the trap of direct explication by approaching the matter of poetics indirectly, using a few closely related themes and motifs to demonstrate the omnipresence of meaning and aural effect as discrete elements, as well as to inscribe this distinction as central to communication (and even to interspecies interactions). Early on, the novel foreshadows Patrick's repeated negotiation of the two with its reference to the influence of a formal effect (repetition) on meaning. Ketcheson, stating his desire to leave Trenton because of the hazardous activities of the chemical industry, repeats the phrase "[j]ust a hunch" in a way that, by invoking his greater knowledge of a potential explosion and thus expanding Purdy's representation of language use into the realm of the novel's plot, historical concerns, and non-linguistic themes, transforms "words into ciphers" (SH 7). This early reference to the separation of verbal meaning, formal effects, and a larger thematic and aesthetic significance anticipates and includes a cleaving of form and meaning of the sort that Starnino later describes. *A Splinter in the Heart* repeatedly expands on these distinctions; in so doing, it enacts a formalist poetics in the sense of both putting this poetics into practice and acting it out via the everyday utterances of Purdy's characters.

At moments of distress, fear, or uncertainty, Patrick takes refuge in disentangling the interaction of verbal meaning from the (frequently non-rational) connotations of the phonemes in question. Venturing into the chemical works, he describes "[a] roar of laughter" that "poured out of the workmen, rebounding from narrow walls and sounding like 'ah-ah-ah.' It was eerie, this place – and so was Pumper" (*SH* 73). The reliance on onomatopoeia that is inspired by the factory setting is a foil to the failure of language in the scene, the sinister "ah-ah-ah" echoing both the mocking "aw-aw-aw" in "Joe Barr" and Patrick's non-verbal, intuitive understanding of the situation. Pumper, whose name complements the aural and atmospheric effects Patrick remarks, introduces himself by saying, "Name's Jim Pumper. 'Pumper this and Pumper that,' my wife says"; looking puzzled, he continues, "I don't know what she means. But come along now" (71). Shortly afterwards, when considering his surroundings and reception, Patrick thinks, "he couldn't remember telling the man his name was Patrick, or saying anything about himself at all" (73). Another, more directly threatening, encounter occurs when Mr Merker "frog-marched him to the entrance, with a final tweak of the ear," uttering, "If I catch you" (94). The novel's free-indirect discourse draws attention to Merker's saying this phrase "in measured tones, repeating it for emphasis," but then narrows its focus to Patrick, who observes that "the word's isolation made it even more terrible – 'Again!'" (94). The consistency with which such interior monologues further isolate the effects of sound from sense suggests that Purdy's ideas about language are well attuned to the simultaneous distinctness and complementarity of content and formal effect.

Patrick's testing of the boundaries separating sound, sense, and meaning, along with his penchant for daydreaming, resonates with Laurie Ricou's study of childhood language in *Everyday Magic: Child Languages in Canadian Literature*. Ricou draws on studies by linguists Breyne Arlene Moskowitz and Eve V. Clark to find a process in language acquisition in which "a child first uses a word to designate a specific object, but almost immediately generalizes the word to refer to many other objects" (6). Ricou designates such slippage, and the productive language use that results from it, as "exactly the sort of transformation that makes poetry possible," even though a child would likely not be aware of the poetic potential of, for instance, "[s]eeing a cake, or the letter 'O,' as the moon" (7). Episodes such as Patrick's interactions with Joe Barr do not depict his recapturing of this non-syntactical enlargement of words' specific meanings as much as they do his consideration of the process, which emphasizes the precise distinctions between semantic content, verbal meaning, and sound that structure adult language and that must be consciously crossed or disregarded by the poetically minded. Purdy's many treatments in *A Splinter in the Heart* of childhood and adolescent explorations of the boundaries separating the components of oral communication – the scenes with Joe, Patrick's confused initiation into the worlds of work and sexuality, and, as will be discussed shortly, his non-rational or intuitive engagement with communicating animals – resemble Ricou's conception of child language as being central to poetry, thus casting poetic practice as intuitive, despite what could be regarded as its inherent artifice.

Such separations of sound from meaning also often involve non-human animals, whose utterances the novel renders as, and then compares with, human speech. One instance of animal-based onomatopoeia occurs when Patrick observes a robin that "said something nearby" (SH 48). The order of events in these episodes is relevant; often, they begin with Patrick's perception (and the narrative's transcription) of abstract, holistically or imprecisely comprehended sound itself, and then continue with Patrick's thinking through his own conception of such sounds as onomatopoeia (that is, their reproduction in language), and, finally, his reflection on the potential wordplay yielded by such consideration. The robin episode continues with Patrick's "slow[ing], turning his head toward the sound. The bird said two things, and sometimes three things. You had to listen hard to select the robin's voice from a continual slight hum in his ears, remove it from sound of sluffing feet on the gravel road" (48). This heightened attention leads Patrick to a realization in which "the sound came to him, the triumph sound, an *ee* sound, with an *ur* on the end of it. He tried to say the same thing with his own tongue. 'Eerily, eerily,' he said, then raised his voice louder and said it again. But it was a human voice, and the robins flew away. 'Eerily,' he said, trying to coax them back" (49). The unsettling qualities of this particular combination of animal sound, onomatopoeia, and symbolism are also atavistic in their recreation of childhood experiences of fear and belief in the supernatural, connecting Patrick's interaction with the crows to the confusion he experiences in the coming-of-age vignette in the chemical works.

The fascination with the sounds of animals is also linked explicitly to questions about the nuances of perception and independent thought. When Patrick spends three days in bed convalescing, the family dog, Gyp, is allowed inside the house. After expressing disappointment with the books he is reading, Patrick observes that, as far as adults were concerned, "[t]here was a public world and all these private ones, but you caught a glimpse inside the private worlds only rarely" (SH 82). He then wonders whether Gyp also "possessed this lighted place in his head, where pictures were forming and fading." He calls to the dog and receives another onomatopoeic response – "*ur-r-r*" – and asks what the sound means. In the scene that follows, Patrick himself participates in this mutual understanding, which requires neither precise verbal confirmation nor insight into the formation of such utterances: "prolonged scrutiny and urgent words had gotten Gyp excited. He leaped onto the bed, lifted his muzzle, and howled. An ear-breaking sound so close to Patrick's head; the sound of puzzlement and dog frustration." Patrick "howled, too, but with laughter" (83), briefly indulging in non-verbal association before his mother cuts the episode short.

Several descriptions build on this dynamic by placing the sonic qualities of commonplace statements in the context of physical habits, experiences, and needs. Exercise and physical activity frequently forge this bond, such as when Patrick trains as a runner, "lengthen[ing] his stride over the footbridge, then var[ying] it so the drumming sound pleased his ears" (*SH* 47). At one point, an exhausted Patrick considers the aural effects of the word "hallucinate" as he ponders the convergence of bodily and conversational fatigue: "That was a nice word. Patrick felt a slight dizziness from talking, but savoured the word: I hallucinate, you hallucinate, we hallucinate" (80). Elsewhere, sonic qualities are described with culinary imagery that rounds out a picture of unspoken domestic trauma, such as when a childless couple, Ian and Emma McMaster, refer to their horses "as if they were the children they never had": "'But Een,' his wife said, pronouncing his name like food and adding salt. 'But Een –'" (21). Such situations create an environment in which the separate components of language, along with their centrality to everyday, arguably universal, human experience, are constantly foregrounded.

The novel's references to animals and the body also set meaning apart from verbal information. While the above examples do so by emphasizing the connotative meaning of aural qualities, at other points overall or implicit meaning is represented as non-verbal by foregrounding the materiality of verbal signifiers. At one point, an insult is marked as effective for its penetration of Patrick's cognitive processes and, subsequently, his body: "He was afraid ... But then, Billy Coons's 'I dare you!' had soaked into his mind. The loathsome, unendurable thought of being a coward, making his hands tremble in sun heat, turning his leg muscles to wood" (*SH* 87). In an almost surrealist passage, the physical finality of death is foregrounded by the atrophying of thought itself. Patrick considers his recently deceased grandfather as "a 'body', a 'corpse'"; after thinking about the inevitability of corporeal decay, he realizes that "[w]hatever the dead man had been thinking about before death was still imprinted on his brain, a message no undertaker could read or brain surgeon decipher" (137). The blunt factuality of death here stands apart from verbal meaning to such an extent that it recalls the ciphers of Ketcheson's earlier implication, foreclosing these layers of meaning, as well as impeding Patrick's very enunciation of the news of his grandfather's death: "At the police station, a fat man with several chins was on duty at the desk. Patrick said to him, 'My grandfather—' The last word stuck in his throat, somewhere between death and life" (137).

Significantly, however, Purdy spends less time using death to represent this dynamic than he does the quotidian details of Patrick's coming of age. A similar separation of speech from underlying meaning occurs when Patrick talks to a romantic interest, Jean: "He hadn't warned himself he was going to speak, he just blurted it out. And held his breath. The die was cast, Caesar was about to cross the Rubicon into Gaul" (*SH* 97). As if to underscore the coming bifurcation of what is said (small talk) and what is intended (pursuit of a deeper relationship with Jean), Patrick's monologue includes a Purdyism: "or whatever that damned river's name was" (97). Shortly after Patrick decides that more indirect verbalizing is necessary – "If he didn't say some very ordinary things about the weather, about school, about the war, about anything … their little dialogue would die" (97–8) – the pair begins talking about a failure of communication rather than any notable or defined topic:

> "And you know," he said.
> "Know what?"
> Then Patrick's mind went blank. He couldn't think of anything to say.
> "My name is Patrick," he finally said, and knew she must know that already. "I live across the river. I run for exercise, I run because it's something to do –"
> He stopped, foolishly aware that he was burbling, then went on determinedly. "I wanted to talk to you …"
> "I can see that," she smiled.
> "And I'm talking, but it isn't getting me anywhere." (98)

This separation of intent from excessive verbalizing – and the latter's masking, yet working in service of, the former – mirrors a broadly defined formalism's dependence on the way sonic qualities (here a repetition that is as incantatory as it is comically phatic) alternately enhance or contrast (and thus call into question) a word, phrase, or line's semantic content. This dynamic is present in the novel generally, in that the prose that makes up Purdy's *Bildungsroman* allows him to narrate the finer mechanics of his poetry.

The encounter with Jean is a positive example of Patrick's identifying the interstices of sound, verbal meaning, and intent. Interactions that are comparatively uninflected by romantic or bodily instinct, however, reveal a distracting, duplicitous quality inherent in ostensibly direct verbal meaning. When Patrick lies about having lived up to a dare to jump off a bridge a year before, thus rescuing Billy Coons from having to meet a more dangerous challenge, he is "surprised at his own duplicity": "the power of words to manipulate other people was interesting. Also dangerous" (*SH* 88). Yet, in positive interactions, sound (as opposed to verbal signification) evades such sophistry and enhances central meaning, often by emphasizing intuition. Key in establishing this connection is Joe, who plays an important role in the novel's adaptations of poetic material. Joe introduces a basic form of communication that exists outside of, yet reifies, the separation of sound and meaning. Bodily imagery appears again when Patrick is confronted with shouting boys and their victim, "idiot Joe," whose appearance elaborates on the paralinguistic onomatopoeia of the poem "Joe Barr." At first, Patrick compares Joe's speech to the "speech" of crows: "'Aw,' Joe said. Then, 'Aw, aw, aw!' like a human crow" (124). Then he considers Joe's utterance to be meaningful in human terms: "'Aw,' Patrick replied. And tentatively, 'Aw?'"; "It seemed to mean something. There was kindness in Joe's face. Here was communication, here was a friend?" (124).

After pulling Joe aside and finding refuge from his pursuers, Patrick, who had previously compared Joe to the crows, makes a more sympathetic consideration that encompasses both subjects. After saying "Crazy Joe" and noticing Joe's "face darke[n]," Patrick determines that "it was all right. Joe knew he didn't mean it. Joe knew. It was a knowledge that made Patrick feel good, lifted his spirits" (*SH* 125). After this triumph of kindness and common experience, Patrick again meditates on the sonic qualities of the encounter, separating vowels and consonants and deciding, perhaps because of their common understanding, that vowels – Joe's preferred phoneme – are more meaningful: "His face had a strange expression, as if he wanted to speak but couldn't. His lips moved, his chin trembled. It seemed that he could make hoarse vowel sounds – *a, e, i, o, u* – but couldn't handle consonants. And Patrick would have sworn that Joe felt the same as himself about the blue sky. He pointed up at the ceiling of the earth, and said, 'Blue – blue, blue, blue!'" (126). Empathy and communication connect Patrick and Joe, but Patrick and Purdy are quick to fold this experience into a cleaving of verbal utterance from intent and action.

Purdy's emphasis on intuition serves more than a narrative purpose; it complements the novel's narrativizing of a mistrust of pedagogy. This process foregrounds Purdy's distancing of himself – the poet with a vested interest in matters of speech and aural effect – from the poetic import of the novel's exploration of the interstices of components of verbal and written communication. Paradoxically, it is the book's lengthy denials of systematic explications of intuition that get closest to conveying the apparent views of Purdy the poet. His use of animal communication, association of sound value with the body, and depictions of thought as tangible or visible, such as when Patrick imagines someone "looking inside his head and squinting at something shameful there" (*SH* 43–4), resemble Starnino's portrayal of a natural formalism while also effectively marking such language use as a quotidian phenomenon instead of a rigorous poetics. The novel form especially facilitates a certain artificiality in this sense, in that an author's transformation of childhood memories into adult language is inevitably an act of reconstruction; nevertheless, even this kind of reading reveals a spontaneity of sorts. Patrick's early statement about words being ciphers quickly retreats into a prosaic, reasoned-out description of this statement, its pleonastic artificiality underscoring the futility of expounding upon the "formalist" elements of everyday speech: "'Just a hunch,' he repeated, turning the words into ciphers that meant something different from what they said" (7). The reconstruction of non-verbal perception as something more universally comprehensible occurs here via the arrangement of phatic exchanges and conventional verbal constructions. The process itself involves a retreat into accepted, socially recognizable, and therefore "natural," communicative devices.

Rejections of pedagogy and erudition become increasingly visible in the novel, especially in lengthier episodes that fuse its ability to describe experiences precisely with the indirect descriptions of linguistic matters that are relevant to its author's poetics. Early on, Patrick notes wearily that "Mr. McIver taught Latin, a dead language that was chanted in church and made animal names sound like Roman citizens" (*SH* 14). The ridiculousness of such a profession is expressed in a way that recalls the novel's other negotiations of the bodily, the spoken, and the intended: "When Mr. McIver said something to him in Latin, he stiffened and came instantly alert, not wanting to admit he hadn't been paying attention" (14). Purdy's working-class identity emerges here – in suitably ironized form – to bring the novel's rejection of formal instruction full circle: "'I never did understand why they teach Latin,' Jack Corson said. 'It hasn't been spoken by ordinary working people for hundreds of years. I read that somewhere'" (86).

Purdy's use of the novel to explore matters of form and intuition is not without precedent; some of his poems also hint at a rejection of systematic explication and the pedagogical. "At Roblin Lake" does so, like the novel, with recourse to images of animal sound and communication; despite its appearance thirty years before *A Splinter in the Heart*, it too mocks the language of higher learning. The poem begins by describing the "batrachian nightingales" of a fervid, interconnected animal world, "[e]ach with a frog in his throat, / rehearsing the old springtime pap / about the glories of copulation" (PA68 24; BR 30). It is suspicious even of anthropomorphic categorization:

> The pike and bass are admirably silent
> about such things, and keep their
> erotic moments *a mensa et thoro*
> in cold water. After which I suppose
> comes the non-judicial separation.
> Which makes them somewhat misogynists? (PA68 24; BR 30)[10]

It then runs through several lines of what Purdy construes as philosophical jargon – "bogged / down in dialectics and original / sin of discursiveness" (PA68 25; BR 31) – and concludes by returning to a holistic view of animal sound, sense, and sensation, the speaker holding a captured frog "like an emerald breathing" and expressing wonder at "the beginnings of understanding, / the remoteness of alien love–[.]" "At Roblin Lake" performs the same investigation of form as *A Splinter in the Heart*, only in reverse; the poem's simple language alludes to the complex interaction of sound and implied meaning, but, in limning this duality, it mocks language that seeks to articulate this relationship systematically.

By extension, the novel's rejection of the pedagogical in favour of the instinctive also manifests itself in its simultaneous reverence for and rejection of its most obvious literary antecedent, *Barometer Rising*.[11] The novel's superficial resemblance to that book in plot and thematic structure is folded into Purdy's treatments of language, communication, and, implicitly, poetic philosophy. The irruption of history and industrialization is characterized as "[t]he old fear, whose focus was British Chemical … fear that invaded the blood, joining systole and diastole, racing outward and inward with the pumping of the heart" (SH 193). Such images fuse even a seemingly singular historical catastrophe with the quotidian, visceral experiences of the bodily; the plant's explosion is described as "one syllable long, drawn out to become a short explosive sentence. The sound of a fat man eating soup with a large spoon, spilling half of it, and going *ur-r-p*. Pants ripping. Somebody farting in the big room of the world" (217). For all the goofiness of the later Purdy's jokes and self-effacements, the low humour here indicts Canadian literature's occasional pretentiousness, whether it occurs in Halifax Harbour or later, in the romanticism of manifestos that attempt to systematize omnipresent relations between form and content, intuition and rigour, and history and personal experience. The above passage ends, after all, by stating that "[t]he ear made its own adjustments and parallels, in order that the brain might rationalize and comfort itself" (217).

Ultimately, *A Splinter in the Heart* can be read as both a product of and a reflection on the easy routine in which Purdy eventually found himself – releasing new and repackaged poetry collections, producing prosaic reflections on his life and work, repeating already-published anecdotes, and effortlessly fusing his authorial persona with the style that, thanks to the increasing volume of reviews, scholarly articles, and dissertations throughout the late 1980s, would come to be regarded as a quintessentially Canadian poetics. Reminiscing, cracking bad jokes, and reinforcing (though occasionally complicating) his thoughtful tough-guy image, the Purdy of these passages achieves a fusion of consideration, comfort, consistency, and perhaps stasis. But this routine includes within it the whole of Purdy's writing practice, including a more directly visible iteration of the formalist imagination that animated his poems in spirit, if not always so palpably in practice. Aside from his few treatments of his early development beyond the constraints of Carman, Purdy the elder statesman seemed no more interested in directly examining the darker corners of his writing process than he was in engaging the parts of his personal life that could not easily be attributed to the affable rascal of his autobiography. Faced with the freedom of the novel, however, and writing with the comfort of an established reputation, Purdy seems to have justified, or at least in some small way engaged, what some have described as his poetic shortcomings, folding them into an oeuvre and persona that reliably, if only slightly, resist complete consistency or exhaustive explanation. For this reason, Starnino's attacks, while valuable for holding to account the prosaic free verse of Canadian poetry after Purdy, are directed at a poetic practice viewed in isolation or in the person of Purdy's imitators. It is a revolt that, like Solecki's case for Purdy's legacy, renders the poet as an unnecessarily polarizing figure.

NOTES

1 Solecki's *The Last Canadian Poet* (1999) is a touchstone in Purdy scholarship. Still, even early reviews pointed out its shortcomings; Jonathan Kertzer, for instance, identified its failure to engage contemporary theories that undermine the nation, describing Solecki's portrait as "a projection of [Purdy's] writing as it takes shape through the joint efforts of Purdy the author and Solecki the reader" (119).
2 Regardless of the merits of particular poets, few would claim that twentieth-century Canadian poetry has contributed many paradigm-changing figures to the world of anglophone poetry. Christian Bök and Darren Wershler-Henry are regarded as having been instrumental (along with the American Kenneth Goldsmith and others) in creating conceptual writing (see Goldsmith), continuing a minor Canadian experimental genealogy that stretches from the work of bpNichol through that of Anne Carson. The unabashed avant-gardism of such figures, however, further underscores the relative obscurity of Canadian free-verse practitioners – or "mainstream" poets generally – south of the border and elsewhere.
3 This chapter uses the term "poetics" in two senses: to mean an underlying philosophy of poetry and a set of stylistic techniques resulting in identifiable characteristics in a body of work. I have tried to make this distinction clear throughout; still, Don Byrd's definition of poetics as "the study of how a man must behave when his words are out of control" (37), from his study of Charles Olson (whose work is a precursor to *Tish*, as well as the locally anchored voice of Purdy), captures Purdy's steady laxity, as well as his blurring of the distinction between the two senses.
4 Starnino has published negative reviews of influential figures such as Margaret Atwood and Don McKay, admonishing them for a lack of formal adventurousness. A review of Atwood's *The Door* (2007), for instance, concludes that "[o]ne of the oddities of our free-verse precepts is that we are willing to consider bad prose good poetry" ("Knock" 39). He has also dismissed less celebrated poets, such as Susan Musgrave, whom he mocks for her tendency to "forfeit the technical possibilities of the art" ("Sea-Witch" 58).
5 Given Purdy's attention to place, instinct, and foreign poetic influences, it is no surprise that George Bowering, a founder of *Tish* (a movement that addressed these same concerns), has commented on his arbitration of disputes between experimentalists and the plain-spoken Purdy. In stating, "[a]ll my adult life I have explained or defended one side to the other" (63 n1), Bowering recognizes Purdy's (however limited) transcendence of the divide between free-verse poets and those who are more preoccupied with form.

6 In a review of David Solway's *Chess Pieces* (1999), Starnino explicitly describes the indefinability of the truly poetic element, listing Solway as one of the few Canadian poets who "forc[e] us to come to terms with the quiddity of poetry: that mysterious ingredient, at once opulent and ineffable, which binds sound, rhythm, and vocabulary into a happy convergence" ("Power" 18).
7 In his introduction to a collection of essays on Solway, Starnino distinguishes Solway's poetics from Purdy's, describing Solway's reaction to an "unwelcome" letter of praise Purdy sent him in 1972 ("Introduction to *David Solway*" 12). Starnino's enthusiasm for Solway, and my own references to him, are concerned only with the author's poetics and his critiques of Purdy's free verse. Starnino's endorsements largely predate Solway's recent anti-feminist positions, and, by quoting Starnino's affirmations, I seek neither to link Solway's poetic and political attitudes nor to validate them.
8 Peacock founded the *Best Canadian Poetry in English* series, the 2012 edition of which was edited by Starnino.
9 Queyras counts Jason Guriel, Zachariah Wells, James Pollock, and Michael Lista among this group (12). All have made arguments similar to Starnino's.
10 "[T]horo" appears as "*toro*" in *Beyond Remembering* (30).
11 In a 1992 letter to Alistair MacLeod, Purdy acknowledged, in response to MacLeod's recent tribute to MacLennan, that he had some positive personal experiences with MacLennan and that *Barometer Rising* "made an impression on me" (YA 480). In a letter from 1971, however, Purdy agreed with George Woodcock about MacLennan's limitations, writing that "as their own time passes," the "conventional naturalists will probably fade" (YA 173).

REFERENCES

Bernstein, Charles. "The Academy in Peril: William Carlos Williams Meets the MLA." In *Content's Dream: Essays, 1975–1984*, by Charles Bernstein, 244–51. Los Angeles: Sun and Moon, 1986.

Bowering, George. "Purdy among the Tombs." In *The Ivory Thought: Essays on Al Purdy*, edited by Gerald Lynch, Shoshannah Ganz, and Josephene T.M. Kealey, 63–70. Ottawa: University of Ottawa Press, 2008.

Brown, Russell. Review of *Reaching for the Beaufort Sea: An Autobiography*, by Al Purdy, edited by Alex Widen. *University of Toronto Quarterly* 64, no. 1 (Winter 1995): 221–4.

Byrd, Don. *Charles Olson's* Maximus. Urbana: University of Illinois Press, 1980.

Goldsmith, Kenneth. "Conceptual Writing: A Worldview." *Harriet: A Poetry Blog*, 30 April 2012. Poetry Foundation, https://www.poetryfoundation.org/harriet/2012/04/conceptual-writing-a-worldview/.

Guriel, Jason. *The Pigheaded Soul: Essays and Reviews on Poetry and Culture.* Erin, ON: The Porcupine's Quill, 2013.

Keith, W.J. "Purdy's Novel: The Recycling and Fictionalizing of Memory." *Essays on Canadian Writing*, no. 49 (Summer 1993): 163–76.

Kertzer, Jonathan. "Voice of the Nation." Review of *The Last Canadian Poet*, by Sam Solecki. *Canadian Poetry: Studies, Documents, Reviews*, no. 47 (Fall–Winter 2000): 116–21.

Perloff, Marjorie. *Radical Artifice: Writing Poetry in the Age of Media.* Chicago: University of Chicago Press, 1991.

Purdy, Al. "Autobiographical Introduction." In *The Poems of Al Purdy*, by Al Purdy, 6–8. Toronto: McClelland & Stewart, 1976.

– *Beyond Remembering: The Collected Poems of Al Purdy.* Edited by Al Purdy and Sam Solecki. Madeira Park, BC: Harbour Publishing, 2000.

– "Leonard Cohen: A Personal Look." *Canadian Literature*, no. 23 (Winter 1965): 7–16.

– *Poems for All the Annettes.* 2nd ed. Toronto: House of Anansi Press, 1968.

– *Reaching for the Beaufort Sea: An Autobiography.* Edited by Alex Widen. Madeira Park, BC: Harbour Publishing, 1993.

– Review of *New Wave Canada*, edited by Raymond Souster. *Quarry* 16, no. 3 (March 1967): 42–5.

– *A Splinter in the Heart: A Novel.* Toronto: McClelland & Stewart, 1990.

– *Starting from Ameliasburgh: The Collected Prose of Al Purdy.* Edited by Sam Solecki. Madeira Park, BC: Harbour Publishing, 1995.

– *Yours, Al: The Collected Letters of Al Purdy.* Edited by Sam Solecki. Madeira Park, BC: Harbour Publishing, 2004.

Queyras, Sina. "Trajectory and Trace: An Interview with Sina Queyras." Interview by Tanis MacDonald. *Contemporary Verse 2* 37, no. 3 (Winter 2015): 9–21.

Ricou, Laurie. *Everyday Magic: Child Languages in Canadian Literature.* Vancouver: University of British Columbia Press, 1987.

Solecki, Sam. *The Last Canadian Poet: An Essay on Al Purdy.* Toronto: University of Toronto Press, 1999.

Solway, David. *Director's Cut.* Erin, ON: The Porcupine's Quill, 2003.

Starnino, Carmine. *Credo.* Montreal and Kingston: McGill-Queen's University Press, 2000.

– "An Interview with Carmine Starnino." Interview by Tim Bowling. *Contemporary Verse 2* 36, no. 2 (Fall 2013): 7–19.

– Introduction to *David Solway: Essays on His Works*, edited by Carmine Starnino, 7–15. Toronto: Guernica Editions, 2001.

– Introduction to *The New Canon: An Anthology of Canadian Poetry*, edited by Carmine Starnino, 15–36. Montreal: Signal Editions, 2005.

– "Knock, Knock: Is the Real Atwood Still There?" Review of *The Door*, by Margaret Atwood. *Arc*, no. 59 (Winter 2008): 33–41.

– *A Lover's Quarrel: Essays and Reviews*. Erin, ON: The Porcupine's Quill, 2004.
– "The Power of the Pawn." Review of *Chess Pieces*, by David Solway. *Books in Canada* 28, no. 8–9 (Winter 2000): 17–19.
– "The Sea-Witch's (Sham)anistic Glamour." Review of *What the Small Day Cannot Hold*, by Susan Musgrave. *Arc*, no. 47 (Winter 2001): 58–62.

APPENDIX

Purdy's Self-Repetitions

LIST 1: "ILLUSION"

- bright illusions of extraordinary freedom ("In the Wilderness," CH 37)
- Or else that's another illusion ("Fidel Castro in Revolutionary Square," CH 73; BR 87)
- some / of the more easily kept illusions ("The Country North of Belleville," CH 75; BR 79)
- how illusions seem to end ("Wine-Maker's Song," CH 97)
- and destroy the illusion of paradise by mistake ("The North West Passage," NS 21; BR 98)
- my illusion / of upness ("South," NS 60)
- drink to all our illusions ("South," NS 62)

LIST 2: "IMMORTAL," "IMMORTALITY"

- senile but certified immortal ("Gilgamesh and Friend," CSL 23; BR 30)
- I'll say this about Alex'[s] immortality ("Old Alex," CH 57; BR 70)
- his immortal quote ("Canadian," WG 16)
- The immortal gods have condemned you ("Beaudoin," WG 97)
- inside an immortal hour glass ("Antenna," Sun. 58; BR 287)[1]
- my immortal soul ("Funeral," PB 17; BR 309)
- in that sense immortal ("A Handle for Nothingness," WS 20)
- that was his immortality ("Oh God Oh Charlottetown," NSM 57)
- an immortal goddess still lives ("Aphrodite at Her Bath," TP 83)

- And that is a curious form of what might be called immortality ("Home Country," *TP* 125)
- all of us, the shape-changers, the transitory immortals ("Home Country," *TP* 127)

LIST 3: "PERMANENCE," "PERMANENT"

- As permanent as my shadow body is ("Visitors," *CSL* 20)
- as permanent as any in / Maisonneuve's cynical metropolis ("Poem for One of the Annettes," *PA* 8; *BR* 36)
- a noisy masquerade / of permanence ("Malcolm Lowry," *CH* 10)
- "Song of the Impermanent Husband" (*CH* 27; *BR* 61)
- no irritating / questions re love and permanence ("Song of the Impermanent Husband," *CH* 28; *BR* 63)
- let the stupidity remain permanent ("Trees at the Arctic Circle," *NS* 30; *BR* 104)
- the land of permanent ice cream ("When I Sat Down to Play the Piano," *NS* 45; *BR* 113)
- to make the painting permanent ("The Horseman of Agawa," *SD* 14; *BR* 209)
- menacing and permanent ("Mantis," *SB* 82; *BR* 351)
- permanence is flux ("Mantis," *SB* 82; *BR* 351)
- the thought / of permanence ("The Strangers," *PB* 100; *BR* 405)
- this permanent moment ("Moses at Darwin Station," *PB* 40; *BR* 336)
- my small passion for permanence ("An Arrogance," *WS* 66; *BR* 468)
- trivial enough to have some permanence ("For Margaret," *WS* 70; *BR* 470)

The cognate term *permafrost* occurs in "Eskimo Graveyard" (*NS* 27; *BR* 101) and (famously) in "Trees at the Arctic Circle" (*NS* 30; *BR* 103).

LIST 4: "SHADOW," "SHADOWED," "SHADOWY"

- like light / Or shadow ("Where the Moment Is," *CSL* 8; *BR* 28)
- In the big world-room his shadow ("For Oedi-Puss," *CSL* 13)
- As permanent as my shadow body is ("Visitors," *CSL* 20)
- And can dispose themselves like shadows ("Passport," *CSL* 21)
- The mountains' intersecting shadows ("Kispiox Indian Village," *BB* 11)
- two horizontal plates of shadow ("Kispiox Indian Village," *BB* 11)

- The faucet is cool green shadowed spring ("Mind Process re a Faucet," PA 22; BR 49)
- sun shadowed gnomons ("Jade Stag," PA 31)
- apartments / in spilled shadows ("Eli Mandel's Sunday Morning Castle," PA 42)
- the criss-cross / rivers of shadows ("Remains of an Indian Village," PA 57; BR 53)
- snapping and biting / at shadows ("The Madwoman on the Train," CH 14; BR 67)
- the long foreshortened shadow of a poet all in one place ("Portrait," CH 29)
- the roads are shadowy with swaying nooses ("In the Wilderness," CH 38)
- soft outlines and / shadowy differences ("The Country North of Belleville," CH 75; BR 80)
- like dogs looking for shadows ("'A Very Light Sort of Blue Faded from Washing,'" CH 77)
- leaving the other half shadowed ("Observer," CH 89)
- sun stream shuttle threading thru / curtain shadows ("Late Rising at Roblin Lake," CH 101; BR 88)
- shadowy figures ("Innuit," NS 32)
- shadows aren't shadows but proxy things ("Metrics," NS 38; BR 106)
- the shadowy kennels ("When I Sat Down to Play the Piano," NS 45; BR 113)
- islands of shadow ("The Beach at Varadero," WG 23; BR 137)
- a collection of shadows ("After the Miscarriage," WG 29)
- with the shadow beside me ("Horses," WS 4; BR 449)
- *our shadows long in the long grass* ("Vertical versus Horizontal," WS 9)
- sweet shadow in the bedroom ("Seven Ways of Looking at Something Else," WS 12)
- those who perceived beyond shadow ("A God in the Earth," WS 47)
- shadows pretend to be shadows ("The Woman on the Shore," WS 81; BR 472)
- I noticed someone moving in the shadows ("In the Desert," NSM 29; BR 485)

LIST 5: "BEING ALIVE"

- being alive for instance ("Wilf McKenzie," SD 47; BR 225)
- being alive is a luxury ("Atomic Museum," SD 123)

- surprised at being alive ("Birds and Beasts," PB 39; BR 374)
- ["]the marvel of being alive in the flesh["] ("Death of DHL," PB 95; BR 391)
- the old melancholy / of being alive ("Doug Kaye," PB 139)
- I loved being alive ("Fragments," NSM 125; BR 520)
- the puzzle of being alive ("'Happiness,'" TP 66)
- horror of being / alive ("The Stone Bird," SB 105; TP 115; BR 573)
- a double reward for being alive ("For Curt Lang," BR 587)

NOTE

1 In *Beyond Remembering*, the line breaks after "hour" (287).

Contributors

DOUG BEARDSLEY taught at the University of Victoria from 1981 to 2006. The author of many books of poetry, including *Swimming with Turtles* (2014) and *Rain Music* (2013), he collaborated with Al Purdy on *No One Else Is Lawrence!* (1998) and *The Man Who Outlived Himself* (2000).

NATALIE BOLDT is a doctoral candidate in the Department of English at the University of Victoria and co-editor of *Christian Humanism and Moral Formation in "A World Come of Age": An Interdisciplinary Look at the Works of Dietrich Bonhoeffer and Marilynne Robinson* (2016).

NICHOLAS BRADLEY is an associate professor in the Department of English at the University of Victoria. He is the editor of *We Go Far Back in Time: The Letters of Earle Birney and Al Purdy, 1947–1987* (2014), and the author of numerous studies of Canadian literature, as well as a volume of poetry, *Rain Shadow* (2018).

MISAO DEAN is a professor in the Department of English at the University of Victoria. She has published extensively on early Canadian women writers, on the literature of wilderness travel, and on animals and hunting in early Canadian writing. Her most recent book is *Inheriting a Canoe Paddle: The Canoe in Discourses of English-Canadian Nationalism* (2013).

JAMIE DOPP is an associate professor in the Department of English at the University of Victoria. He is the co-editor of *Writing the Body in Motion: A Critical Anthology on Canadian Sport Literature* (2018) and *Now Is the Winter: Thinking about Hockey* (2009), as well as the author of many reviews and essays on aspects of Canadian literature.

ERNESTINE LAHEY is an associate professor in linguistics and stylistics at University College Roosevelt, the Netherlands, and the co-editor of *World Building: Discourse in the Mind* (2016). She is a former member of the executive board of the Association for Canadian Studies in the Netherlands.

ELI MACLAREN teaches Canadian literature at McGill University. He is the author of *Dominion and Agency: Copyright and the Structuring of the Canadian Book Trade, 1867–1918* (2011) and *Little Resilience: The Ryerson Poetry Chap-Books* (2020).

SHANE NEILSON completed his PhD in the Department of English and Cultural Studies at McMaster University in 2018, where he won the Governor General's Gold Medal. He is a poet, physician, essayist, and editor. His recent publications include *New Brunswick* (2019), a volume of poems, and *Constructive Negativity: Prize Culture, Evaluation, and Dis/ability* (2019), a book of criticism.

IAN RAE is an associate professor and coordinator of the Canadian Studies Program at King's University College at Western University. His publications include *From Cohen to Carson: The Poet's Novel in Canada* (2008).

LINDA ROGERS is a poet (*Homing: New and Selected Poems*, 2012) and novelist (*The Empress Letters*, 2007), as well as the editor of *Al Purdy: Essays on His Works* (2002). She is a former Poet Laureate of the City of Victoria.

CARL WATTS teaches at Huazhong University of Science and Technology. His articles, book reviews, and poems have appeared in various Canadian and American journals. He has also published two poetry chapbooks, *Reissue* (2016) and *Originals* (2020), as well as a short monograph, *Oblique Identity: Form and Whiteness in Recent Canadian Poetry* (2019).

J.A. WEINGARTEN is a professor of Language and Liberal Studies at Fanshawe College. He is the author of more than two dozen articles, interviews, and reviews that have appeared in magazines and journals across Canada, as well as the author of *Sharing the Past: The Reinvention of History in Canadian Poetry since 1960* (2019), published by the University of Toronto Press. He is co-founder of *The Bull Calf: Reviews of Fiction, Poetry, and Literary Criticism*.

Index

Figures indicated by page numbers in italics

Abel, Jordan, 162–3, 165n34; *Injun*, 162; *The Place of Scraps*, 162, 165n36
academia, 223–5
Acorn, Milton, 13, 179, 245; *Dig Up My Heart*, 259n9; *I've Tasted My Blood*, 259n9; "Live with Me on Earth under the Invisible Daylight Moon," 68
A-frame: Beardsley on, 46–7; preservation of, 65, 72–3, 179, 222; Purdy Picnic at, 222; Purdy's evolution in, 49; reminiscences about, 221; role in Canadian poetry, 77, 179; "Visiting Poet" (Johnston) on, 182–3
Ahmed, Sara, 120–1; *The Cultural Politics of Emotion*, 120
Akhmatova, Anna, 6
Alcheringa (journal), 160
Allard, Donna, 77
alliteration, 189, 198–9, 205

The Al Purdy A-Frame Anthology (Vermeersch), 221, 222, 234
Al Purdy A-frame Association, 72, 222
Al Purdy: "A Sensitive Man" (documentary), 258n8
Al Purdy Was Here (documentary), 180, 222, 234
Ameliasburgh (ON), 209. *See also* A-frame
appropriation, cultural, 157–8, 161, 165n34
Arctic, 108–9, 123n4. *See also* Inuit; *North of Summer* (Purdy)
argillite carving, 152, 153–4, 161–2
Arts Canada, 233
"At the Quinte Hotel" (Purdy): beer named after, 222; comparison to other poems, 97, 107, 142, 186, 201–2; as entry point to Purdy's poetry, 52; Eurithe Purdy on, 90; film dramatization, 191, 223; mentions, 9, 23, 129; in readings, 234; romantic and modern duality, 80–1; self-description in, 4; variants of, 191–2

Atwood, Margaret: A-frame and, 73, 179; at Al Purdy A-frame Association gala fundraiser, 222; in "Archilochus in the Demotic" (Purdy), 22; bouquet sent to Purdy's hospital room, 60, 61; on Canada, 138; Canada Council fellowship, 12; "Canada's Whitman" trope and, 99n3; Canadian literature and, 9, 10–11, 250, 259n9; CBC appearances, 259n10; colonialism and, 121–2; in *Fifteen Winds* (Purdy), 254, 259n12; Fulford on, 242–3, 257n2; George Elliott Clarke and, 127; Hudson's Bay Company and, 259n11; importance of, 88; "method writing," 255, 260n16; "most important writer" trope and, 84; picture on Purdy's bulletin board, 47; on "poetess" label, 260n14; "protean images" of, 243, 256, 260n17; on Purdy, 37n44, 79; on Purdy and York University, 224–5; Purdy on, 240, 243–4, 252–7; Purdy's influence on, 89–91, 98n2; Purdy's insult of, 223–4; reprint of *Poems for All the Annettes* (Purdy) and, 257, 259n9; scholarship possibilities, 257; shift to novels, 252; student interest in, 4; woman's voice of, 255, 260n15; York on, 258n4; works: *Alias Grace*, 240; *The Animals in That Country*, 254; *Cat's Eye*, 240; *The Circle Game*, 240; *The Door*, 281n4; *Double Persephone*, 260n15; "Fruition," 13; *The Handmaid's Tale*, 240; *The Journals of Susanna Moodie*, 90, 91, 254; *Lady Oracle*, 240; *Power Politics*, 255; *Surfacing*, 107, 121–2; *Survival*, 8, 89, 246, 259n9; "Uncles," 258n3. See also *Malahat Review* 41 (Margaret's Malahat)

Auden, W.H., 22; "In Memory of W.B. Yeats," 34n32; "In Praise of Limestone," 36n41

audience, 250–2, 259n9

Babstock, Ken, 222, 266; "Tractor," 266–7
Bailey, Alfred, 161
Barbeau, Marius: Abel's adaptation from, 162; Canada Council and, 12; correspondence with Purdy, 150–1; "Marius Barbeau: 1883–1969" (Purdy), 159–60, 165n30, 165n36; problems with, 157; Purdy's adaptation from, 149, 152, 153–5; works: *Haida Carvers in Argillite*, 153; *Haida Myths Illustrated in Argillite Carvings*, 153, 154, 157; *The Indian Speaks* (with Melvin), 155; *Totem Poles*, 162
Barley Days (brewery), 222
Barnett, Homer G.: *The Coast Salish of British Columbia*, 158–9
Bauman, Richard, 136
Beardsley, Doug, 34n31, 46–7, 48–9, 59
The Beaver (magazine), 119, 231
beer, Purdy-inspired, 222
"being alive," 15–16, 22
Bensadoun, Douglas, 191, 223
Bentley, D.M.R., 63, 65, 127, 175, 191, 220–1
Beowulf, 50
Berger, John, 225
Bernstein, Charles, 265
Best Canadian Poetry in English series, 282n8
bestseller lists, 250
Bevan, Alan, 231

Beynon, William, 157, 164nn26–7
Beyond Forgetting (White and Skagen), 5, 30n6
Beyond Remembering (Purdy), 19–24; Beardsley on, 46; connections within, 21; death and existence themes, 20–1, 22–4; editing of, 30n5; historical and literary-historical obsessions, 20, 21–2; motive and omissions, 19–20, 173, 174, 175; place themes, 21; poems collected in, 32n20; prolificness reflected in, 14, 19, 147; title, 15; poems: "At the Quinte Hotel," 192; "Elegy for a Grandfather," 197, 206, 210, 215; "House Guest," 183, 185; "The Runners," 135–6
Birney, Earle: A-frame and, 179; biography of, 24; Canada Council funding for, 12; in *Canadian Forum*, 13; "CanLit" term and, 31n11; celebrity status over, 256; Hudson's Bay Company and, 259n11; importance of, 88; influence on Purdy, 16, 17, 199; modernized traditional elements in poetry, 200; "most important writer" trope and, 84; Ryerson publications, 190; works: "Beyond the Meadhall," 156; "David," 33n30, 200; "Five Poor Men Speak Up c. 1931," 13; *Ice Cod Bell or Stone*, 11; "Mappemounde," 156; "Pacific Door," 158; "She Is," 68; "Wind-Chimes in a Ruin," 13
Bissell, Claude, 24
Black Mountain College, 272
Blais, Marie-Claire: *La belle bête*, 11
Blaser, Robin, 25
Blodgett, E.D., 29n2
Blok, Alexander, 22
Bly, Robert, 267

Bök, Christian, 281n2
Bolster, Stephanie, 29n2
Bowering, George: A-frame reminiscence, 221; biography of, 25; in *Canadian Forum*, 13; *Malahat Review* 41 contribution, 240; on nationalist literary circles, 139; Pollock on, 25; on Purdy as writer, 8, 64, 77, 127, 219, 281n5; on Purdy's interest in Barbeau and Indigenous peoples, 149, 158; works: *Al Purdy*, 64, 82, 127, 147, 149; "Inside the Tulip," 67
Brand, Dionne, 29n2
Bravo!FACT foundation, 112
Briesmaster, Allan: *And Left a Place to Stand On*, 77
Bringhurst, Robert, 52, 65, 127; *The Raven Steals the Light* (with Reid), 164n29, 165n32; *A Story as Sharp as a Knife*, 161
Brooke, Rupert, 4
Brown, E.K., 79, 81
Brown, Russell, 28, 270–1; *The Collected Poems of Al Purdy*, 49, 173–4
Bruegel, Pieter, the Elder, 228
Buchanan, Donald W.: *Canadian Painters*, 228
Buckley, Joan, 175
Budde, Robert, 83, 87, 90, 127, 142; *The More Easily Kept Illusions*, 77–8, 88, 93
Bukowski, Charles, 72
Byrd, Don, 281n3

Callaghan, Morley, 11, 32n17; "Letter to Morley Callaghan" (Purdy), 50
Cameron, Elspeth, 253; *Earle Birney*, 24
Campbell, Maria, 88, 101n14; *Halfbreed*, 87, 95, 100n13

Campbell, Sandra, 190
Campbell, William Wilfred, 3
Canada: cultural pride, 78–9; identity issues, 78, 82–4, 129, 139–40, 141–3, 143n5; Purdy as "quintessential Canadian poet," 5–6, 63–5, 77, 78–82, 127
Canada Council: Canada Council Medal, 12; fellowships and funding, 12, 149; Governor General's Literary Awards, 12, 29n2, 63, 174, 220; nationalism and Canadian arts and literature, 9, 79; Purdy's affiliation with, 24
Canada Reads competition, 180
Canadian Broadcasting Corporation (CBC), 24, 147, 250–1, 252, 259n10
Canadian Forum (journal), 12–13, 20
Canadian literary studies, 9, 31n15, 78. *See also* canonization
Canadian literature: "Canada's Whitman" trope, 79, 81–2, 99n3; comparison to Indigenous art and poetry, 139; development of, 9, 10–11; early poets, 3–4, 30n3; modernist writing, 32n17; "most important writer" trope, 84; nationalism and, 9–10; term, origins and use, 31n11, 101n14
Canadian Literature (journal), 11
canonization: authors' self-portrayals and, 96–7; "Canada's Whitman" trope, 79, 81–2, 99n3; Canadian identity and, 82–4; Fowler on, 100n12; Lecker on, 84–5, 100n11; "most important writer" trope, 84; need for new approach, 88–9, 98; oversimplifications, 78, 88; positional scholarship and, 97–8; private canons, 85–7; Purdy as "quintessential Canadian poet," 5–6, 63–5, 77, 78–82, 127; self-criticism and, 87

Carman, Bliss, 49, 57, 174, 175, 271; "Spring Song," 57–8
Carr, Emily, 227, 228; *Klee Wyck*, 122, 123n11
Carrier, Roch, 12
Carson, Anne, 131, 281n2
celebrities. *See* literary celebrities
Chapnick, Adam, 96
Chatterton, Thomas, 16
Chesterton, G.K., 16, 17, 164n23, 174; "Lepanto," 33n28, 156
children: childhood language, 273–4; Purdy and, 61
Chinese Immigration Act (1885), 83, 100n9, 121
Christianity, 45, 52. *See also* transcendence and spirituality
Clark, Eve V., 273
Clarke, Austin, 24
Clarke, George Elliott, 127–8
Clarke Irwin (publisher), 10
Clements, Marie: *The Edward Curtis Project*, 165n36
Clutesi, George, 12
Cogswell, Fred, 13
Cohen, Leonard: biography of, 24; Bowering on, 127; Canadian literature development and, 9, 11; CBC appearances, 259n10; celebrity status, 246; death, 7; love poems, 68; "most important writer" trope and, 84; shift to music, 252; works: *Flowers for Hitler*, 271; *Let Us Compare Mythologies*, 11; *The Spice-Box of Earth*, 11
Coleman, Daniel, 86, 98n1
Coleman, Patrick: *Equivocal City*, 32n17

Coleridge, Samuel Taylor, 46, 51
Coles, Don, 29n2, 31n9, 47
The Collected Poems of Al Purdy (Purdy): revisionist practice in, 173, 191; works written after, 29n2; poems: "The Country North of Belleville," 191; "The Darkness," 49; "Elegy for a Grandfather," 192, 206; "House Guest," 183, 185; "The Madwoman on the Train" ("Sestina on a Train"), 32n18; "The Runners," 143n1; "Shopping at Loblaws," 23, 24
Colombo, John Robert, 13; *The Mackenzie Poems*, 154
colonialism, 121–2, 141. *See also* shame
conceptual writing, 28n2
Contact Press, 191
Cook, Ramsay, 13
Creighton, Donald, 24
Crozier, Lorna, 29n2
cultural appropriation, 157–8, 161, 165n34

Davey, Frank, 64–5, 66, 67, 112, 127
Davis, Laura K.: *Margaret Laurence and Jack McClelland, Letters* (with Morra), 31n16
Day, David, 61
Deep Image poetry, 267
de la Mare, Walter, 49
depressive position, 113, 123n9
Deshaye, Joel, 250, 252, 258n8, 259n10; *The Metaphor of Celebrity*, 244–5, 245–6
DiAngelo, Robin, 124n12
Dickey, James, 51; *Buckdancer's Choice*, 51
Dickinson, Peter: *Here Is Queer*, 140

Disch, Tom, 267
Djwa, Sandra, 175–6; *Journey with No Maps*, 24–5
Donne, John, 16, 17, 48, 52; "The Canonization," 13
Dorothy Livesay Poetry Prize, 162
Douglas, Elizabeth: "The Mechanics of Being Alive," 30n7
Dowling, Sarah, 165n34
Downie, Gord, 191, 222, 223
Dowson, Ernest, 16
Doyle, Mike, 14, 179–80, 193
Dragland, Stan, 15, 49, 138, 220, 234
Dudek, Louis, 7, 50, 190, 219, 230, 259n11
Dumont, Marilyn: "Letter to Sir John A. Macdonald," 95–6

Edenshaw, Charles, 151, 152
elegies, 200
"Elegy for a Grandfather" (Purdy), 197–216; about, 28, 197; 1956 version, 197–200, 213; 1968 version, 200–6, 210–11; 1974 version, 207–8; 1983 version, 206, 210–12, 214; 1986 version, 206, 212–13, 215; 1996 version, 210, 213–15; alliteration, 198–9, 205; balance between mythic and realistic, 215; in *Beyond Remembering*, 197, 206, 210, 215; childlike perspective in, 205–6; connection between grandfather and grandson, 204–5, 211–13, 214, 216; form, 197–200, 201, 203–4, 205; lack of new information about grandfather, 207–9, 211; mythologizing grandfather, 212, 213–14; new stanzas, 202–5; persona, 201–2, 205–6; publications and variants,

192, 197, 215; Purdy's reputation and, 191; rhyme, 198, 199; in *In Search of Owen Roblin*, 192, 206–7, 209–10, 213; and *A Splinter in the Heart*, 270
Eliade, Mircea: *Cosmos and History*, 49, 50
Eliot, T.S., 22–3, 52, 99n3, 174, 271; "Burnt Norton," 33n23; "The Hollow Men," 23
elite culture, 218–19. *See also* visual arts
Ellis, John, 245
emotions, 106. *See also* shame
Empson, William, 200
The Epic of Gilgamesh, 48, 49
Erick the Red's Saga, 122, 129, 143n1. *See also* "The Runners" (Purdy)
Esolen, Anthony, 51
Essays on Canadian Writing (journal), 140, 220, 223
ethnography, 148, 153. *See also* "Yehl the Raven and Other Creation Myths of the Haida" (Purdy)
ethnopoetics, 160
Everson, William, 47, 52

Fee, Margery, 94, 164n27
Feirstein, Frederick, 267
Ferry, David: *Gilgamesh*, 34n31
Fiamengo, Janice, 110
Fifteen Winds (Purdy), 254, 259n9, 259n12
Finch, Robert: *Acis in Oxford*, 12
Findley, Timothy, 47
flexible influence, 89–92
formalism: critiques of Starnino's position, 268–9; Perloff on, 267–8; Purdy and, 264, 265–6, 271–2, 279, 280; Solway on, 267; and *A Splinter in the Heart* (Purdy), 266, 272–8, 279–80; Starnino on, 266–7

Fowler, Alastair: *Kinds of Literature*, 100n12
francophone rights, 83, 99n8
Frank, Adam: "Shame in the Cybernetic Fold" (with Sedgwick), 123n2
Fraser, Hermia Harris: *The Arrowmaker's Daughter and Other Haida Chants*, 161; *Songs of the Western Islands*, 161
free verse, 175, 201, 263, 265, 281n2
Friedman, Susan Stanford, 89, 92
frogs, 181–2
Front de Libération du Québec, 97
Frost, Robert, 22, 36n39
Frye, Northrop, 12, 13, 24, 130, 132, 133, 137, 139–40; *Anatomy of Criticism*, 133; *Literary History of Canada*, 130, 139–40
Fulford, Robert, 13, 242–3, 244, 246, 249, 258n3; "The Images of Atwood," 242–3, 257n2

Galt, George, 221
Ganz, Shoshannah: *The Ivory Thought* (with Lynch and Kealey), 5, 64, 142, 220–1
Gauguin, Paul, 228
Geddes, Gary: *15 Canadian Poets x 3*, 129
Gibson, Shirley, 90
Gilmour, David, 85, 87
Gioia, Dana, 267
Glassco, John, 243–4, 247
Globe and Mail, 64, 127, 143n3, 147, 252, 253
Goldsmith, Kenneth, 281n2
Gooder, Haydie, 121
Governor General's Literary Awards, 12, 29n2, 63, 174, 220
Grant, George, 24
Greek mythology, 20, 34n34, 229

Greetham, David, 175
Grierson, David, 59
Griffin Poetry Prize, 162
Guriel, Jason, 268, 282n9
Gustafson, Betty, 68
Gustafson, Ralph, 13, 22, 68, 165n31

Haida mythology, 164n29. *See also* "Yehl the Raven and Other Creation Myths of the Haida" (Purdy)
Halfe, Louise Bernice, 87–8
Hall, Nat, 77
Harbour Publishing, 46, 149, 150
Harris, Lawren, 12
Hasan-Rokem, Galit: *Untying the Knot* (with Shulman), 132, 134–5
Heaney, Seamus, 6, 31n9
Heath, Tim, 32n19, 181
Heighton, Steven, 149, 179
Heinricks, Geoff, 221
Helwig, David, 221
Hemingway, Ernest, 22, 36n39
high culture, 218–19. *See also* visual arts
Hill, Colin: *Modern Realism in English-Canadian Fiction*, 32n17
Hilles, Robert, 29n2
Hillger, Annick: *Not Needing All the Words*, 140
Hillmer, Norman, 96
Hine, Daryl, 13
Hokusai (Katsushika Hokusai), 228
Homer, 22, 50
Hope, Laurence, 16
Hopkins, Gerald Manley, 12, 32n19, 52
Horace, 18, 34n31, 50
Hornby, John, 108–9
"House Guest" (Purdy), 177–90; about, 28, 177; first version, 185–6, 189; importance in Purdy's corpus, 179–80; layout variations, 184–5, 187–9; other Canadian poetry and, 181–3; Purdy's poetic evolution and, 186, 189–90; quarrelling and binary pattern, 180–1; self-reflexive questioning in, 96; text, 177–9; wording and punctuation changes, 183–4, 194n1
House of Anansi Press, 184, 257
Housman, A.E., 16, 17, 19, 49
Houston, John, 109, 123n5
Hoy, Helen, 101n17; *How Should I Read These?* 92
Hudson's Bay Company, 147, 163n4, 231, 251, 259n11
Hunt, George, 164n27
Hutcheon, Linda, 240; *Other Solitudes* (with Richmond), 31n14
Hymes, Dell, 160

identity, Canadian, 78, 82–4, 129, 139–40, 141–3, 143n5
incest, in myths, 135–6
Indian Act, 100n10
Indian Chiefs of Alberta, 99n7
Indigenous peoples: appropriation, 157–8, 161, 165n34; art and poetry, comparison to Canadian literature, 139; Canadian identity and exclusion of, 83, 100n10; contemporary Indigenous writers, 165n36; "Letter to Sir John A. Macdonald" (Dumont), 95–6; literary engagement with, 161–3, 165n31; Métis, endurance of, 96, 101n18; Purdy and, 93–5, 115–16, 118–19, 158–9; residential schools, 83, 99n6, 115, 123n11. *See also* Inuit; "Yehl the Raven and Other Creation Myths of the Haida" (Purdy)

influence, flexible, 89–92
Innis, Harold, 24
interviews, 246–7
intuition, 51, 269, 277–9
Inuit: art, 229–30; diet and traditional lifeways, 109, 123n5
irony, 128
Irvine, Dean, 35n36, 173–4, 175, 176; *Editing as Cultural Practice in Canada* (with Kamboureli), 31n16
"The Ivory Thought" (symposium), 46
The Ivory Thought (Lynch, Ganz, and Kealey), 5, 64, 142, 220–1

Jackson, A.Y., 5, 12, 228, 230–2
Jacobs, Jane M., 121
Jeffers, Robinson, 16, 17, 19, 21
Jews, 83, 100n10
Johnson, Brian D.: *Al Purdy Was Here* (documentary), 180, 222, 234
Johnson, E. Pauline, 4
Johnston, Gordon: "Visiting Poet," 182–3
Jonas, George, 240
Jones, D.G., 7, 14, 29, 33n30, 37n46, 215; *The Sun Is Axeman*, 13–14
Jung, Carl: "On the Relation of Analytical Psychology to Poetry," 50

Kamboureli, Smaro: *Editing as Cultural Practice in Canada* (with Irvine), 31n16; *Making a Difference*, 85
Kane, Paul, 226–8
Katsushika Hokusai, 228
Kazin, Alfred: *New York Jew*, 36n39
Kealey, Josephene T.M.: *The Ivory Thought* (with Lynch and Ganz), 5, 64, 142, 220–1
Keeshig-Tobias, Lenore, 101n14

Keith, W.J., 9, 270, 271
Kelly, M.T.: *Out of the Whirlwind*, 123n4
Kelly, Peggy, 86, 100n12
Kertzer, Jonathan, 28n1
Kierkegaard, Søren, 128
Kilvert, Barbara, 231, 259n11
Kinnell, Galway, 267
Kipling, Rudyard, 47, 49; *Just So Stories*, 155
Kiyooka, Roy, 233
Klein, A.M., 49
Klein, Melanie, 113, 123n9
Kolodny, Annette, 28
Krieghoff, Cornelius, 227
Kroetsch, Robert, 7, 9, 99n5, 142
Kruk, Laurie, 84

Ladoo, Harold, 24
Lahey, Anita, 266
Lamming, George, 12
Lampman, Archibald: "The Frogs," 181–2
landscape and place, 21, 59, 141
Lane, M. Travis, 134
Lane, Patrick, 7, 99n3, 179
language: childhood language, 273–4; francophone rights, 83, 99n8
L'Anse aux Meadows, 28, 142
Larkin, Philip, 11
Laurence, Margaret, 9, 31n16, 47, 60, 91–2, 245, 249, 257; *The Diviners*, 91–2
Lawrence, D.H., 15–16, 22, 23, 33n26, 47, 48, 50–1, 52; *Apocalypse*, 15–16, 33n26; "Being Alive," 15; "Fish," 53, 54n6; *Lady Chatterley's Lover*, 10
Lawson, Henry, 4
Layton, Irving: in *Canadian Forum*, 13; CBC appearances, 259n10;

celebrity status, 11, 246, 256; influence on Purdy, 12, 16, 17, 50, 191, 271; modernized traditional elements in poetry, 200; on standard for judging poets, 46; works: "Divinity," 68; "Keine Lazarovitch 1870–1959," 200; *Love Where the Nights Are Long*, 70; "Sacrament by the Water," 200; "Whatever Else Poetry Is Freedom," 200

League of Canadian Poets, 59, 66, 127

Lecker, Robert, 64, 82, 84–5, 86, 100n11; *Keepers of the Code*, 64, 100n11

Lee, Dennis: on A-frame, 73, 221; and *Being Alive* (Purdy), 183; on *The Cariboo Horses* (Purdy), 248; on "The Darkness" (Purdy), 49; on intuition, 51; on *North of Summer* (Purdy), 106, 110; on Purdy as Canada's poet, 65, 77, 81, 258n8; on Purdy's persona, 201; on Purdy's style, 49, 220, 248; on "The Runners" (Purdy), 138; transcendence and, 52, 54; works: "Poetry and Unknowing," 51; *Riffs*, 51

Lemieux, Jean-Paul, 232

Lévi-Strauss, Claude, 136

Lewis, C.S., 52

Lilburn, Tim, 52

Lischke, Ute: *The Long Journey of a Forgotten People* (with McNab), 101n18

Lismer, Arthur, 234, 235

Lista, Michael, 282n9

literary celebrities: audiences and publics, 250–2; changing literary trends and, 249, 255–6; Deshaye on, 244–5, 245–6; Fulford on, 242–3; *Malahat Review* 41 on, 241–4, 246; Purdy and, 243–4, 248–50, 258n8; York on, 244–5, 246, 258n4

Livesay, Dorothy, 25, 190

love: Purdy's dislike of, 59, 69–70, 71–2; in Purdy's poetry, 61

love poems, 67–72; expectations for, 67; *Love in a Burning Building* (Purdy), 70–1; "Necropsy of Love" (Purdy), 71–2; parodic nature of, 67–8; pessimism in, 69

Lowell, Robert, 48, 52; "The Quaker Graveyard in Nantucket," 156

Lowes, John Livingston: *The Road to Xanadu*, 48

Lowry, Malcolm, 12, 179; *Hear Us O Lord from Heaven Thy Dwelling Place*, 12

Lowther, Pat, 259n12

Lynch, Gerald: *The Ivory Thought* (with Ganz and Kealey), 5, 64, 142, 220–1

McCall, Sophie, 162, 165n36

McCarthy, Dermot, 85

McClelland, Jack, 31n16, 70, 120, 230–1

McClelland & Stewart, 10, 147

McConnell, William, 13

McCrae, John: "In Flanders Fields," 3

MacDonald, J.E.H.: *The Solemn Land*, 227

MacEwen, Gwendolyn, 13, 240, 259n11, 260n15; "House of the Whale," 161–2; *Noman*, 161

McFadden, David W., 7, 221

McGill, Robert: *War Is Here*, 140

McGill Group, 190

McGill University, 83

McKay, Don, 29n2, 52, 281n4

McKinnon, Barry, 98n2

McKuen, Rod, 249
MacLaren, I.S., 113, 119–20, 176, 230–1
Maclean's (magazine), 147, 231
MacLeish, Archibald, 22, 36n39, 47
MacLennan, Hugh, 10–11, 32n17, 282n11; *Barometer Rising*, 271, 279–80, 282n11; *Two Solitudes*, 31n14; *The Watch That Ends the Night*, 11
MacLeod, Alistair, 282n11; *No Great Mischief*, 214
McLeod, Neal: *Cree Narrative Memory*, 165n36
McLuhan, Marshall, 24
McMichael, Robert, 232
Macmillan (publisher), 10
McNab, David T.: *The Long Journey of a Forgotten People* (with Lischke), 101n18
Macpherson, Jay, 7
Mair, Charles, 3
Malahat Review: proposed Purdy special issue, 247, 258n7
Malahat Review 41 (Margaret's Malahat): about, 29, 240–1; Fulford's contribution, 242–3, 257n2; on literary celebrity, 241–4, 246, 260n17; Purdy's contribution, 240, 243–4, 252–3; Purdy's reluctance to contribute, 241, 247–8
Mandel, Eli, 13–14, 16, 33n24, 141; *Poets of Contemporary Canada*, 141
Mandelstam, Osip, 6
Marriott, Anne, 13
Marshall, Tom, 106
Masefield, John, 49
Mathews, Robin, 13
Maud, Ralph, 157
Mayakovsky, Vladimir, 22
Mayne, Seymour, 221

melancholia, 121
Melvin, Grace: *The Indian Speaks* (with Barbeau), 155
Menzies, Charles R., 157
Métis, 93–6, 101n18. *See also* Indigenous peoples
Milbank, John, 51
Miłosz, Czesław, 6, 31n9, 47
misogyny. *See* sexism and misogyny
Mitchell, W.O.: *The Vanishing Point*, 107
modernism: balance with romanticism and myth, 79–81, 215; in Canadian literature, 32n17; modernized traditional elements, 199–200
Mohanty, Chandra, 92
Montferrand, Joseph, 208
Montreal, 50, 191, 233
Morra, Linda M.: *Learn, Teach, Challenge* (with Reder), 100n13, 101n17; *Margaret Laurence and Jack McClelland, Letters* (with Davis), 31n16; *Unarrested Archives*, 31n16
Morse, Garry Thomas: *Discovery Passages*, 165n36
Morton, W.L., 13
Moses, Daniel David, 101n14
Moskowitz, Breyne Arlene, 273
Moss, Laura: *Is Canada Postcolonial?* 100n13
Mount, Nick: *Arrival*, 250, 252, 259n9
Mowat, Farley, 249
Munro, Alice, 9
Murray, Annette, 259n12
muses, 56–62; Canadian landscape, 58–9; cancer diagnosis and, 59–60; children and, 61; Eurithe Purdy and, 58, 60, 62; poetry as, 57–8, 61–2; Purdy's grandfather,

204; Purdy's mother, 56–7, 62; women and, 60–1

Musgrave, Susan, 65, 180, 240, 281n4

Nadel, Ira: *Various Positions*, 24
Narayan, Uma, 92
National Film Board, 24, 147
nationalism, 8–10, 30n8, 78–9, 119–20. *See also* canonization; identity, Canadian; *North of Summer* (Purdy); "The Runners" (Purdy)
National Museum of Canada, 153
Neruda, Pablo, 35n38
New Canadian Library, 183
The New Canon (Starnino), 263–4, 266–7, 268, 269
New Formalism, 267
Newlove, John, 25, 98n2, 99n3; *Grave Sirs*, 11; "The Pride," 161
Nichol, bp, 281n2
Nichols, Miriam: *A Literary Biography of Robin Blaser*, 25
non-narrative poetic forms, 134
North of Summer (Purdy): about, 27–8, 106; bodily shame and, 107–10; comparisons within to other travellers, 116–17; critiques of, 110, 112; encounter with own pretensions, 117; existential philosophy and, 141; inability to communicate with hosts, 117–18; on Indigenous peoples, 118–19, 120–1, 123n10; Jackson artwork in, 5, 230–2; melancholia and, 121; nationalism and, 5, 8–9, 30n8, 119–20; public shaming and, 120–1; reparative reading and, 122; self-judgment and embarrassment, 110–12; shame and, 106–7, 113, 122; tourist gaze, 112, 114–16, 118–19, 123n7; as travel narrative, 113–14; white fragility in, 122

Nowlan, Alden, 13, 14, 259n11; "For Claudine Because I Love Her," 68; *The Things Which Are*, 13–14
Noyes, Alfred, 49; "The Highwayman," 198
Nussbaum, Martha, 106, 107, 109, 122

Oberon Press, 149
October Crisis, 97
Official Languages Act (1969), 99n8
Ondaatje, Michael, 9, 140, 179, 256
onomatopoeia, 273, 274–5, 277
Ontario: "Where Am I?" commercials, 143n5
Otto, Rudolph, 49
Ovid, 22, 50
Owen, Wilfred, 4
Oxford University Press, 10

Pacey, Desmond, 13
Page, P.K., 7, 24–5, 84, 88
Pagis, Dan: "Toward a Theory of the Literary Riddle," 131, 137
Palmer, Bryan: *Canada's 1960s*, 100n13
Parkhurst, Jim, 179
Parmenides, 156
Pasternak, Boris, 22
Peace, Barbara Colebrook, 52
Peacock, Molly, 267, 282n8
Pearson, Alan, 191–2, 260n17
Perloff, Marjorie, 165n34, 267–8; *Radical Artifice*, 267
persona, 201–2, 205, 220, 234, 245
Pickthall, Marjorie, 3
Pierce, Lorne, 183, 190
Pindar, 22
Pinsent, Gordon, 222
place and landscape, 21, 59, 141

Poems for All the Annettes (Purdy):
in *Beyond Remembering*, 20;
context for, 11–12; Mandel on,
13–14; poems collected in, 32n20;
reprint by House of Anansi, 257,
259n9; role in career, 8, 191;
Stevens on, 31n12; variations
between editions, 173; poems:
"Archaeology of Snow," 14–15,
17–18, 33n25, 33nn29–30, 229;
"At Evergreen Cemetery," 193;
"House Guest," 183, 185

poetics, use of term, 281n3. *See also* formalism; *A Splinter in the Heart* (Purdy)

Pogostin, Victor: "Moths in the Iron Curtain," 68

Pollock, James, 25, 282n9

Porter, Catherine, 220

positional scholarship, 92–8;
canonization and, 97–8; overview,
92–3; Purdy's approach to
Indigenous peoples and, 93–6;
Purdy's self-portrayals and, 96–7

Pound, Ezra, 13, 22, 36n39, 99n3, 174

Pratt, Brooke: "'Preserving the echoing rooms of yesterday,'" 72–3

Pratt, E.J., 12, 49, 84, 121, 175–6, 189; *The Titanic*, 34n32

Prism (literary magazine), 11

public promotion, by authors, 245

publics, 251–2

Purdy, Al: approach to, 4–5, 6–7,
26–9; against academia, 223–5;
appeal of, 4; archives of, 31n16,
148, 150, 163n7, 225; assessment
challenges, 19; Atwood and,
89–91, 98n2, 223–4, 240, 243–4,
252–7; audiences and public
engagement, 147, 163n2,
250–1, 259n9; balance between
romanticism and modern, 79–81,
215–16; birth, 29n1; cancer
diagnosis and death, 29n1, 56,
59–60, 64; celebrity status and
brand development, 222–3;
children and, 61; common-man
myth, 218, 219–21, 223, 225,
233–5; cosmopolitanism, 97;
critical assessments of, 5, 13–14,
25, 30n4, 30n7; development
as poet, 8, 11–13, 186, 189–91;
Eurithe Purdy and, 58, 60, 62,
69; flexible influence and, 89–92,
98n2; formalism and style,
51, 265–6, 269, 271–2; future
areas for research, 24–5, 31n9;
historical and literary-historical
obsessions, 20, 21–2, 34n34, 98n2;
Indigenous peoples and, 93–5,
115–16, 118–19, 158–9; influences
on, 6, 16–17, 31n10, 32n19, 33n26,
45, 49–51, 174, 191, 199, 271–2;
on interviews, 246–7; later works,
29n2; love, dislike of, 59, 69–70,
71–2; nationalism of, 8–9, 30n8;
need to reassess, 66–7, 77–8, 88–9,
98, 127–8, 142, 218; obsessive
and allusive qualities, 17–19,
36n42; persona, 201–2, 205, 220,
234; positional scholarship and,
92–8; as "quintessential Canadian
poet," 5–6, 63–5, 77, 78–82, 127;
recognition concerns, 248–50,
255–6, 258n8; recurring images
and phrases, 14–16, 22, 33n30;
revisionist practice and disavowal
of early work, 163n1, 173–4,
191–2, 200, 215; Starnino on,
263–4, 265; textual scholarship
and, 173–7, 191, 192–3;
transcendence and spirituality,
45–6, 52–4, 180–1; as Voice of the

Land, 59, 66, 127; writing process and theory, 47–9; York University and, 224–5. *See also* muses; sexism and misogyny; visual arts; *specific works*
- anthologies: *Fifteen Winds*, 254, 259n9, 259n12; *Storm Warning*, 259n9; *Storm Warning 2*, 31n16, 259n9
- poems: "After the Rats," 12, 32n20; "After Yeats' Lapis Lazuli," 226; "Alive or Not," 60; "Archaeology of Snow," 14–15, 17–18, 33n25, 33nn29–30, 229; "Archilochus in the Demotic," 22; "Arctic Diary," 231; "Arctic Places" ("Ballad of the Arctic"), 176; "Arctic Rhododendrons," 59, 106, 163n4, 259n11; "Arctic River," 15, 113; "The Artist's Dreams," 225; "Artist's Magic," 226; "Aspects," 110; "At Evergreen Cemetery," 20, 21, 22, 193; "At Mycenae," 34n34; "At Roblin Lake," 21, 56–7, 62, 279, 282n10; "At the Movies," 111, 112, 115; "The Battlefield at Batoche," 80, 93–5; "The Beach at Varadero," 229, 235n9; "Bear-Mother," 151; "Bestiary," 33n30, 53; "Biography," 12, 13, 32n20, 34n34; "Birds and Beasts," 33n26; "Birdwatching at the Equator," 52; "Bruegel's *Icarus*," 34n34, 228; "Bullfrogs," 181; "Canadian," 6; "Canso," 33n30, 34n34; "Capitalistic Attitudes," 22; "The Cariboo Horses," 66, 88, 93, 129, 159, 215–16; "Chac Mool at Chichen Itza," 22–3, 36n41; "Collecting the Square Root of Minus One," 12, 32n20; "Complaint Lodged with L.C.B.O. by a Citizen in Upper Rumbelow," 37n51; "Concerning Ms. Atwood," 253, 257; "Country Living," 35n38; "The Country North of Belleville," 8, 22, 46, 80, 98, 129, 186, 191, 215–16; "The Country of the Young," 106, 113, 226, 228, 231; "Critique," 12, 13, 32n20; "The Crucifix across the Mountains," 22; "The Darkness," 46, 47, 49, 53–4; "The Dead Poet," 46, 53, 56, 138; "Dead Seal," 109–10; "Death of DHL," 16, 23, 33n27, 36n40; "Deprivations," 240, 248; "D.H. Lawrence at Lake Chapala," 53, 54n5; "Dominion Day," 6; "Driftwood Logs," 12, 32n20; "The Dutch Masters," 226; "Dzelarhons," 151; "Eli Mandel's Sunday Morning Castle," 33n24; "Epilogue," 151–2, 155–6; "Evergreen Cemetery," 20, 21, 34n32, 57; "For Curt Lang," 15, 18, 164n17, 288; "For Eurithe," 23; "For Norma in Lieu of an Orgasm," 12, 13, 18–19, 32n20; "From the Chin P'ing Mei," 12, 13, 20, 32nn20–1; "A Ghost in the House of Commons," 6; "Girl," 112, 113, 118–19, 120; "Glacier Spell," 37n43; "Gondwanaland," 36n41; "Grosse Isle," 22; "Haida Genesis," 151, 155; "A Handful of Earth," 36n41, 147, 163n3; "Hazelton, B.C.," 159; "Here's Kane," 226, 227–8; "Her Gates Both East and West," 53, 62; "Herodotus of Halicarnassus," 34n34; "Hokusai at Roblin Lake," 34n33, 228; "Home-Made Beer," 52, 67–8, 96, 234; "Home Thoughts," 46; "The Horseman

of Agawa," 17, 80, 94, 147, 163n3; "House Party–1000 BC," 34n34; "How Yehl Brought Water to the People," 151, 155; "How Yehl Gave the People Salmon," 151, 155, 156; "How Yehl Stole the Sun and Moon," 151, 154; "Hunter, New Style," 112, 118; "I Am Definitely on the Side of Life I Said to Pausanias," 34n34; "In Bed," 226; "In Mexico," 23, 37n43; "In Mid-Atlantic," 32n19; "Innuit," 115, 118, 119, 120; "Inside the Old Mill," 80; "In the Desert," 23; "In the Wilderness," 34n34; "The Invisible Man," 234–5; "Invocation," 32n19; "I Think of John Clare," 226; "Jade Stag," 34n33; "Japanese Painter," 228; "Joe Barr," 91, 270, 273, 277; "John Diefenbaker," 6; "Joint Account," 94; "Kikastan Communications," 118; "Kispiox Indian Village," 159; "Lament for the Dorsets," 6, 33n30, 34n33, 94, 129, 136; "The Last Picture in the World," 34n32; "Late Rising at Roblin Lake," 11; "Lawrence to Laurence," 36n42; "Letters of Marque," 32n19; "Letter to Morley Callaghan," 50; "Liberal Leadership Convention," 6; "The Listeners," 34n32; "Listening," 33n30; "Listening to Myself," 4; "Looney with Sunlight," 226; "Lu Yu," 34n33; "The Machines," 12, 13, 32n20, 164n17; "Mackenzie King's Ruins," 6; "The Madwoman on the Train" ("Sestina on a Train"), 11, 32n18; "Mantis," 53; "Man without a Country," 61–2; "Marius Barbeau: 1883–1969," 159–60, 165n30, 165n36; "Married Man's Song," 60–1; "Menelaus and Helen," 34n34, 36n41; "Metrics," 113, 114, 117, 229; "Mind-Painting," 226; "Moonspell," 53; "My '48 Pontiac," 21; "My Grandfather's Country," 24, 197; "My Grandfather Talking – 30 Years Ago," 12, 32n20, 197, 209, 270; "The Names the Names," 228; "Nanasimgat," 151, 156; "Neanderthal," 37n45; "Near Tofino, Vancouver Island," 36n41; "Necropsy of Love," 15, 59, 71–2; "News Reports at Ameliasburg," 37n43; "The North West Passage," 6, 8–9, 31n13, 113, 115, 116–17; "Notes on Painting," 228; "Odysseus in Kikastan," 117; "Old Man Mad about Painting," 228; "Olympic Room," 12, 13, 32n20; "On Being Human," 22, 57, 69, 98, 209, 216n2; "On Being Romantic," 68; "On My Workroom Wall," 31n9, 36n42; "On Robert Frost," 22, 36n39; "On the Death of F.R. Scott," 53, 54n5; "On the Decipherment of 'Linear B,'" 20, 21, 34n34, 35n35; "Orchestra," 46; "O Recruiting Sergeants!" 33n28; "Over the Hills in the Rain, My Dear," 129; "Over the Pacific," 6; "Paul Kane," 226–7, 228; "The Peaceable Kingdom," 96–7, 101n19; "Piling Blood," 25–6, 37n49; "Place of Fire," 36n41; "Pneumonia," 23; "Poem for One of the Annettes," 12, 32n20, 228, 235n8; "Poem with Vase with Mountain Landscape," 229; "Pound," 22; "Pre-School," 270; "Procne into Robin," 22; "Procne into Swallow," 22; "Prologue," 151, 152; "Rain Poem?" 12, 13, 32n20; "R.C.M.P. Post," 93; "Realism 2," 31n9; "Remains of an Indian Village," 21, 22, 35n37, 37n43, 94, 192; "Roblin's Mills [II]," 80, 91; "Salmon-Eater," 151; "Say the Names," 7, 27, 58, 60; "Scholarly Disagreements," 34n34; "The Sculptors," 114, 229; "She said herself into this poem," 226; "Shoeshine Boys on the Avenida Juarez," 15, 156–7; "Shopping at Loblaws," 23–4, 37n44; "Side Effect," 70–1; "Song of the Impermanent Husband," 4, 58–9, 66, 67, 70, 90; "The Son of Someone Loved–," 34n34, 228; "South," 115; "Spanish Hilltop," 226; "Spring Song," 21, 23, 35n36, 192; "St. Francis in Ameliasburg," 34n34; "Still-Life," 226; "Still Life in a Tent," 111–12, 186; "The Stone Bird," 32n19; "Strong-Man," 151, 156; "The Tarahumara Women," 37n50; "Tent Rings," 33n30; "In the Snow," 54; "Thunderbird," 151; "To Paris Never Again," 226; "Towns," 164n17; "Track Meet at Pangnirtung," 115–16, 123n11; "Transient," 191, 270; "Transvestite," 53, 54n5; "Trees at the Arctic Circle," 110–11, 141, 165n30, 213, 229, 240; "The Turning Point," 113, 116; "Uncle John on Côte des Neiges" ("Uncle Fred on Côte des Neiges"), 37n51; "Untitled," 46, 53, 54n5; "Waiting for an Old Woman to Die," 12, 13, 32n20; "A Walk on Wellington Street," 6; "Washday," 118; "What about Gauguin in Tahiti?" 226; "What Can't Be Said," 115, 117–18; "What It Was–," 15; "When I Sat Down to Play the Piano," 107–8, 109, 110, 123n3, 234; "Where the Moment Is," 58; "Whoever You Are," 163n4, 259n11; "The Widower," 12, 13, 32n20; "Wilderness Gothic," 47, 215, 228, 240; "William Lyon Mackenzie," 6; "The Winemaker's Beat-Étude," 129; "Winter Walking," 33n23, 34n32; "The Woodworm of Masset," 151; "Yeats," 22. See also "At the Quinte Hotel" (Purdy); "Elegy for a Grandfather" (Purdy); "House Guest" (Purdy); "The Runners" (Purdy)

- poetry collections: *Being Alive*, 15, 183, 184; *The Blur in Between*, 31n12, 32n20, 34n34, 49, 164n7; *The Cariboo Horses*, 8, 31n12, 91, 158, 191, 248; *The Collected Poems of Al Purdy* (audio cassette), 129; *The Crafte So Longe to Lerne*, 11, 12, 32n20, 186, 193; *Emu, Remember!* 11, 197, 200; *The Enchanted Echo*, 8, 49, 129, 175; *Hiroshima Poems*, 67; *Love in a Burning Building*, 32, 70–1; *Naked with Summer in Your Mouth*, 21–2, 253; *To Paris Never Again*, 29n2, 32n19, 34n34, 46, 159, 226; *Piling Blood*, 33n26, 34n34, 37n50, 228; *The Poems of Al Purdy*, 183, 184, 271; *Pressed on Sand*, 14, 183, 185; "The Road to Barbary" (unpublished), 225; *In Search of Owen Roblin*, 80, 147, 192, 197, 206–7, 209–10, 211, 213; *Selected Poems*, 64, 129, 183,

184; *Sex and Death*, 19, 34n34, 101n19, 147, 228; *The Stone Bird*, 33n26, 33n30, 53; *The Woman on the Shore*, 29n2, 34n34, 226. See also *Beyond Remembering* (Purdy); *The Collected Poems of Al Purdy* (Purdy); *North of Summer* (Purdy); *Poems for All the Annettes* (Purdy); *Rooms for Rent in the Outer Planets* (Purdy); *Wild Grape Wine* (Purdy); "Yehl the Raven and Other Creation Myths of the Haida" (Purdy)
- prose: "Arctic Poems and Prose," 109, 115, 119; *Cougar Hunter*, 150; *Morning and It's Summer*, 197, 205–6, 208, 209, 210, 213; *Reaching for the Beaufort Sea*, 15, 69, 150, 197, 208, 209, 269–71; *Starting from Ameliasburgh*, 15, 30n5; "An Unburnished One-Tenth of One Per Cent of an Event," 243–4, 252–3; *Yours, Al*, 30n5, 149, 224, 257. See also *A Splinter in the Heart* (Purdy)

Purdy, Brian (son), 61
Purdy, Eleanor (mother), 20, 22, 45, 56–7, 209
Purdy, Euriithe (wife): A-frame and, 179; Al and, 69; on "At the Quinte Hotel" (Purdy), 90; burial plans, 62; on common-man myth, 234; invitation to Beardsley to A-frame, 46; as muse, 58, 60; picture on Al's bulletin board, 47; on Purdy's spirituality, 45–6; son, 61, 69–70; Soviet Union trip, 68; Voice of the Land title and, 59; "Yehl the Raven and Other Creation Myths of the Haida" (Purdy) and, 150, 151
Purdy, Jim (son), 61, 69–70
Purdy, Ridley Neville (grandfather), 197. See also "Elegy for a Grandfather" (Purdy)
Pushkin, Alexander, 22

Quebec, 97
Queen's Park (Toronto), 61, 127, 223
Queyras, Sina, 268, 282n9

racism, 66, 78, 88, 93–5, 119, 120–2
Reaney, James: "The Canadian Poet's Predicament," 139, 140, 142; *Twelve Letters to a Small Town*, 13–14
recognition. See literary celebrities
Reder, Deanna, 87; *Learn, Teach, Challenge* (with Morra), 100n13, 101n17
Red Paper, 99n7
Reeves, John, 221
Reid, Bill: *The Raven Steals the Light* (with Bringhurst), 164n29, 165n32
reparative reading, 122
residential schools, 83, 99n6, 115, 123n11
Rexroth, Kenneth, 52
rhyme, 189, 198, 199
Richler, Mordecai, 242, 264; *The Apprenticeship of Duddy Kravitz*, 11; *The Incomparable Atuk*, 8; *Solomon Gursky Was Here*, 123n4, 164n29
Richmond, Marion: *Other Solitudes* (with Hutcheon), 31n14
Ricou, Laurie, 89; *Everyday Magic*, 273–4
riddles, 130, 131–3, 134–5, 136, 137
Rilke, Rainer Maria, 6, 31n14, 52
Rimbaud, Arthur, 16
Roberts, Charles G.D., 3–4, 189, 190; "The Tantramar Revisited," 190, 198, 216n1

Rogers, Linda, 142; *Al Purdy: Essays on His Works*, 30n4, 219–20
romanticism, 46, 79–81
Rooms for Rent in the Outer Planets (Purdy): cover, 226; Neilson's experience with, 63; title, 15; variants in, 192; poems: "Elegy for a Grandfather," 210, 213–15; "House Guest," 180, 183, 185; "Spring Song," 35n36, 192
Rosenberg, Isaac, 4
Rosenblatt, Joe, 221
Ross, Malcolm, 183
Rothenberg, Jerome, 160
Roy, Gabrielle, 47
Rumpelstiltskin, 137
rune, 130–1, 140
"The Runners" (Purdy), 126–43; about, 28, 122–3; Canadian identity and, 129, 141–3; confrontation with "nothing," 141; incest suggested in, 135–6; interplay of riddle and rune, 131–4, 140; mood, 137–8; neck riddle, 129–38; open-ended conclusion, 134–5, 140, 142; power reversals and gender roles, 136–7; riddling method in, 130; rune and, 130–1; status within Purdy's corpus, 127–9; variants of, 143n1
Ryerson Poetry Chap-Books, 183, 190
Ryerson Press, 10, 161

Saklikar, Renée Sarojini: *Children of Air India*, 100n13
Sandler, Linda, 240, 241–2, 246–7, 248, 253, 258n7, 260n17
Scofield, Gregory, 87; *Thunder through My Veins*, 100n13
Scott, Duncan Campbell: "The Half-Breed Girl," 120; "The Onondaga Madonna," 120
Scott, F.R. (Frank), 10, 23; "All the Spikes but the Last," 121
Scott, Louise, 233
Scott, Marian, 233
Scott, Peter Dale, 13
Sedgwick, Eve Kosofsky, 113, 122, 123n9; "Shame in the Cybernetic Fold" (with Frank), 123n2
self-criticism, 87
sentimentality, 59, 68
Service, Robert, 4, 176
Seton, Ernest Thompson, 108
sex, 19, 62, 71–2
sexism and misogyny: A-frame preservation and, 72–3; in love poems, 63, 67–72; in personal relationships, 90, 91–2; and Purdy's reputation as Canada's poet, 65–7, 78, 88
Shakespeare, William: Sonnet 24, 17
shame: Arctic and bodily shame, 107–10, 123n4; from colonialism and racism, 121–2; encounter with own pretensions, 117; inability to communicate with hosts, 117–18; melancholia and, 121; nature of, 107; in *North of Summer* (Purdy), 106–7, 113, 122; primitive shame, 122; public shaming, 120–1; self-judgment and embarrassment, 110–12; tourist gaze and, 114–16, 118–19
Shapiro, Karl, 22
Shelley, Percy Bysshe, 156
Shulman, David: *Untying the Knot* (with Hasan-Rokem), 132, 134–5
Silverberg, Mark, 66, 67, 82–3, 142, 218
Simon Fraser University, 223
Simonides, 22

Sitwell, Edith, 16
Skagen, Emma: *Beyond Forgetting* (with White), 5, 30n6
Smith, A.J.M., 161, 223
Snyder, Gary, 47
Sol, Adam, 266
Solecki, Sam: on 1990s shift in literature, 249; contribution in *Al Purdy* (Rogers), 220; on free verse, 175, 201; on influences on Purdy, 32n19, 33n26, 33n28, 199; inventories of Purdy's personal libraries, 232; Kertzer on, 281n1; Kroetsch on, 99n5, 142; *The Last Canadian Poet*, 5, 20, 26, 64, 82, 99n5, 127, 142, 147, 281n1; on nationalism, 9–10; on omitted poems, 20; on Purdy as Canada's poet, 6, 77, 106, 127; on Purdy's development, 12, 174, 175, 265; on Purdy's grandfather, 197; on Purdy's poetic soul, 141; scholarship on Purdy, 30n5; on visual arts, 225; Ware on, 37n47; on Purdy's poetry: "Archilochus in the Demotic," 22; "Country Living," 35n38; "The Country North of Belleville," 191; "Death of DHL," 36n40; "Elegy for a Grandfather," 215, 216; "Eli Mandel's Sunday Morning Castle," 33n24; "From the Chin P'ing Mei," 32n21; "The Last Picture in the World," 34n32; *North of Summer*, 112; "On Robert Frost," 36n39; "On the Decipherment of 'Linear B,'" 35n35; "O Recruiting Sergeants!" 33n28; *Piling Blood*, 33n28; "Piling Blood," 37n49; *In Search of Owen Roblin*, 206; "Spring Song," 35n36; *The Stone Bird*, 33n28; "Trees at the Arctic Circle," 111; "Yehl the Raven and Other Creation Myths of the Haida," 149–50, 151

Solway, David, 127, 282n7; *Chess Pieces*, 282n6; "Standard Average Canadian," 267

Souster, Raymond, 190; *New Wave Canada*, 272

Soviet Union, 68

Spettigue, Douglas O., 150

spirituality and transcendence, 45–6, 51–4, 180–1

A Splinter in the Heart (Purdy): about, 29, 264–5; animal-based onomatopoeia, 274–5; as *Bildungsroman*, 264, 269; childhood language and, 273–4; comparison to *Barometer Rising* (MacLennan), 279–80; distinction between speech and meaning, 275–7; intuition, 277–9; poetics of, 266, 269, 270, 271, 280; Purdy's grandfather in, 197, 208, 209; sonic qualities of commonplace statements, 275; synopsis, 271

Spragge, Shirley, 150

Stacey, Robert, 134, 199

Stanley, George, 95–6

Stanley, Timothy, 83–4

Starnino, Carmine: on avant-garde and free-verse poets, 263, 267–8; *Best Canadian Poetry in English* series and, 282n8; critiques of, 268–9, 280; on formalism, 266–7; negative reviews by, 281n4; on poetry, 282n6; on Purdy, 263–4, 265; on Solway, 282nn6–7; works: *The New Canon*, 263–4, 266–7, 268, 269; "What My Mother's Hands Smell Like," 268

Stevens, Peter, 11, 14, 31n10, 31n12

Storm Warning (Purdy), 259n9

Storm Warning 2 (Purdy), 31n16, 259n9
Sugars, Cynthia: *Home-Work*, 100n13
Suknaski, Andrew, 98n2, 99n3; *Wood Mountain Poems*, 259n9
Sullivan, Rosemary, 220, 260n15
Sutherland, Fraser, 180–1
Swinburne, Algernon Charles, 16
Swinton, George: *Sculpture of the Eskimos*, 230
Szumigalski, Anne, 29n2, 259n12

Taylor, Charles: "A Place for Transcendence?" 51–2
Tedlock, Dennis, 160
textual scholarship, 173–7; challenges of, 176; for correcting errors, 194n2; *vs.* dismissal of early writing, 174; nature of, 175; Purdy's revisionist practice and, 173–4; purpose and need for, 173, 175–6, 176–7, 191, 192–3. *See also* "Elegy for a Grandfather" (Purdy); "House Guest" (Purdy)
Thammavongsa, Souvankham: *Found*, 100n13
Thien, Madeleine: *Simple Recipes*, 100n13
Thomas, Clara: *Our Nature–Our Voices*, 64
Thomas, Dylan, 16, 17, 19, 174, 198, 271; "Fern Hill," 198
Thomas, Edward, 4
Thompson, Lawrance, 36n39
Tish (poetry journal), 11, 14, 281n3, 281n5
Tomkins, Silvan, 106, 107, 108, 123n2
Toronto: Queen's Park statue of Purdy, 61, 127, 222–3
tourist gaze, 112, 114–16, 118–19, 123n7
Town, Harold, 70

Traill, Catharine Parr, 91
Trakl, Georg, 4
transcendence and spirituality, 45–6, 51–4, 180–1
Trehearne, Brian, 32n17
Trower, Peter, 7
Trudeau, Pierre, 5–6, 83, 97, 99n7
Turner, Frederick, 267
Turner, W.J., 174

University of Ottawa: "The Ivory Thought" symposium, 46, 220
University of Toronto, 83
Uppal, Priscila, 37n50
Urry, John, 112, 114, 123n7

Van Gogh, Vincent, 226, 228, 229, 232; *Café Terrace at Night*, 63, 226
Van Rys, John, 113–14, 123n10; "Alfred in Baffin Land," 115
Vendler, Helen, 265
Vermeersch, Paul: *The Al Purdy A-Frame Anthology*, 221, 222, 234
Virgil, 50
visual arts: about, 28–9, 218–19; art books in Purdy's personal libraries, 226, 232–3; Canadian art, 226–8; common-man myth and, 225; Inuit art, 229–30; *North of Summer* artwork, 5, 230–2; personal acquaintance with artists, 233; in Purdy's early work, 225–6; in Purdy's later work, 228–9; Purdy's stance towards, 233; Van Gogh, 226
Voice of the Land (title), 59, 66, 127, 128
Voznesensky, Andrei, 6, 22

Waddington, Miriam, 12
Wagoner, David: *Who Shall Be the Sun?* 161

Walcott, Derek, 6, 31n9
Wallace, Bronwen, 60
Waller, Edmund, 16
Ware, Tracy, 37n47
Warner, Michael: *Publics and Counterpublics*, 251
war poetry, 3, 4, 67
Watson, Homer, 227
Watson, John, 190
Watson, Sheila: *The Double Hook*, 11
Weaver, Robert, 224, 259n9
Webb, Phyllis, 260n15; *The Sea Is Also a Garden*, 11
Weiland, Joyce, 233
Weir, Lorraine, 84, 87
Wells, Zachariah, 282n9
Welsh, Christine: "Women in the Shadows," 101n18
Wershler-Henry, Darren, 281n2
White, Howard, 46; *Beyond Forgetting* (with Skagen), 5, 30n6
white fragility, 122, 124n12
White Paper (*Statement of the Government of Canada on Indian Policy*, 1969), 83, 99n7
Whitman, Walt, 6, 48, 79, 81, 99n3
Widen, Alex, 150, 151, 164n29
Wigod, Rebecca: *He Speaks Volumes*, 25
Wild Grape Wine (Purdy): Laurence on, 31n16; nationalism and, 5–6; title, 129; poems: "The Beach at Varadero," 235n9; "Elegy for a Grandfather," 200–6, 270; "Spring Song," 35n36. *See also* "The Runners" (Purdy)
Wilkinson, Anne, 13
Wilkinson, Peter, 52–3
Williams, William Carlos, 22, 99n3
Wilson, Ethel, 12
Wilson, Jean: "The Sense of Place and History in the Poetry of A.W. Purdy," 30n7
Wilson, Milton, 13
Winger, Rob: "The People's Poet," 65
women. *See* muses; sexism and misogyny
Woodcock, George, 13, 64, 149, 163n6, 240, 282n11
Wordsworth, William, 46, 79
Wright, James, 267; "From a Bus Window in Central Ohio, Just before a Thunder Shower," 268
Wyatt, Thomas, 24
Wyeth, Andrew, 232

Yeats, W.B., 16, 17, 22, 23, 138, 174, 189; "Sailing to Byzantium," 190; "Symbolism in Painting," 138
"Yehl the Raven and Other Creation Myths of the Haida" (Purdy), 148–63; about, 28, 148–9; background and versions, 149–51; comparison to other writers, 160–3, 164n29; contemporary edition, possibility of, 164n28; contents, 151; derived from Barbeau's ethnography, 153–5; ethnopoetics and, 160; Indigenous culture and, 151–2, 153, 157–8, 159; inward focus, 160; other borrowings and influences, 155–7; Purdy's intentions for, 152; Yehl, other contexts for name, 164n18
Yevtushenko, Yevgeny, 6
York, Lorraine, 112; *Literary Celebrity in Canada*, 244–5, 246; *Margaret Atwood and the Labour of Literary Celebrity*, 258n4
York, Thomas: *Snowman*, 123n4
York University, 224–5

Zigaina, Giuseppe, 232
Zwicky, Jan, 29n2